LEAN, AGILE & SIX SIGMA INFORMATION TECHNOLOGY MANAGEMENT

NEW STRATAGEMS TO ACHIEVE PERFECTION

Peter K. Ghavami
325 Ninth Ave., Seattle, WA 98104
pghavami@u.washington.edu, fax: (206)744-3581

Copyright © 2008 Peter K. Ghavami, Seattle, WA. All rights reserved. This publication is protected by copyright, and permission must be obtained from the copyright holder prior to any prohibited reproduction, storage in a retrieval system, or transmission in any form or by any means, electronic, mechanical, photocopying, recording or likewise. For information regarding permissions, write to:

Peter K. Ghavami
325 Ninth Ave
Seattle, WA 98104.

The author and publisher have taken care in preparations of this book, but make no expressed or implied warranty of any kind and assume no responsibility for errors or omissions. No liability is assumed for the incidental or consequential damages in connection with or arising out of the use of the information or designs contained herein.

Keywords: 1. Chief Information Officers, 2. Information Technology, quality, strategy, management, Lean, Agile, Six Sigma

Cover Design by Mihaela Susan

Acknowledgement 5
Summary 7
Chapter 1. Why Lean, Agile & Six Sigma IT? 21
Chapter 2. What's Lean IT Leadership? 35
Chapter 3. The Twelve Axioms of Lean, Agile and Six Sigma IT Management 49
Chapter 4. Eliminate Waste: First Steps to Recovery 61
Chapter 5. Create Exceptional Value 83
Chapter 6. Lean & Agile IT Framework 99
Chapter 7. Reduce Complexity 121
Chapter 8. Design for Quality 133
Chapter 9. Compress Time: Applying Agile Principles 163
Chapter 10. Build IT Factory 177
Chapter 11. Introduction to Six Sigma 191
Chapter 12. Continuous Testing & Measurements 213
Chapter 13. Continuous Risk Management 221
Chapter 14. Value People 237
Chapter 15. Continuous Learning 245
Chapter 16. Service Excellence 251
Chapter 17. Six Sigma IT and ITIL 263
Chapter 18. Decide for the Long Haul 275
Chapter 19. Build Intelligent Organizations 287
Chapter 20. New Stratagems for a New Era 313
Appendix A – IT Laws 316
Appendix B – Process and Project Templates 319
Appendix C – Sample Scrum Project Plan 329
Appendix C – Sample Scrum Project Plan 330
Appendix D - Quality Indicators & Confidence 333

"We are here to make another world."
W. Edwards Deming

Acknowledgement

In one of the Star Wars episodes, a Jedi master once declared, "Your focus determines your reality."[1] What was true a long time ago in a galaxy far, far away holds true here and now. Once again, we find ourselves in a new turbulent world where rules and odds have changed. It's time again to focus on the fundamentals... on the customer and on managing information systems in a new way, and to make a major difference in the outcomes. I began writing this book in 2006 with the intent to write a handbook for my staff, to provoke thinking and renewed focus on quality. As the handbook grew thicker, my colleagues suggested that I publish it so that IT managers and executives alike, could take the journey of applying Lean, Agile and Six Sigma management principles to their information technology practices.

This book would not have been possible without the support and opportunity extended to me by colleagues and family. It all started as a collection of essays, articles and research grant proposals. Over the years that I consulted and managed various technical organizations, I collected the best practices and management strategies that brought success to my teams. Some of my prior research on software development process and simulation was applicable and provided additional sources of material. Soon, I came to realize that my staff and colleagues could benefit from a reference manual on how to apply Lean, Agile and Six Sigma principles to their IT work. As a consequence, the book was born.

I'm indebted to many professionals at Microsoft Corporation, Boeing Company, and Amazon.com for their review and invaluable comments. I wish to thank Dr. Dundar Kocaoglu, Department Chair of Engineering and Technology Management Program and Dr. Wayne Wakeland, Professor, Systems Science Graduate Program at Portland State University for their guidance and patience during my graduate work in the 1990's. Some of the book material was directly influenced by the research that I conducted under their direction.

I'm grateful to Georgetown University library system for making their research databases available to me. This book was completed only because of my family's support, much encouragement from my father, and much support and patience from my wife Massi who despite my long hours at work, accepted the time and focus that I spent at home working on the manuscript.

I wish to thank my daughter Kamilla, and support staff Brian Taylor and Amanda Potter for reading an early draft of this text and for their comments. My gratitude goes to Steve Long at Boeing Company, and Irinel Susan at Microsoft for providing great input on the early drafts. Among reviewers, Dr. Donald Dotty

---

[1] From the movie "Star Wars", Lucasfilm Ltd., SanFrancisco, CA.

professor of LEAP program and Dr. Michel Mestre at Northwest University MBA Graduate program made outstanding recommendations to improve the book.

Finally, I owe much gratitude to my employer for their support and the opportunity to apply many of the principles presented in this book. In particular I wish to thank Cynthia Hecker and Dr. Norm Beauchamp, who as in Deming's quote are always making a better world, for their continued support and guidance through my work in the last five years.

Peter K. Ghavami
November 2008

"A good opera conductor produces a play and not just a sound."
Peter Drucker

Summary

Lean changes everything. If you have picked up this book, something about change has attracted you to this topic. Perhaps your IT organization is fatigued by endless projects that are failing or languish unfinished. Perhaps your IT department gives you excuses when you expect service. Or you get lip service when you expect results. Perhaps you expect a lot more benefits from information technology than you're getting. Or you're tired of giving into IT organization's demands for more funding and staffing, while having little to show in return?

This book is written as a management handbook for *You*, the indispensible information technology leader: the corporate executive, the CIO, the CTO, or the business unit manager in pursuit of IT excellence. If you are looking to achieve extraordinary results on a skeletal budget, this book is for you. The concept of Lean Management is not a fad. It has been around and practiced for at least 2 decades with great results.

Lean Thinking became popular in the late 80's as the US manufacturing industry began to learn and adopt Japanese styles of management: total quality management, Kaizen and Lean production systems. The notion of Lean has come to vogue again recently because its principles are so applicable in today's business. Yet topics presented in this book go beyond Lean management. They combine Lean, Agile and Six Sigma IT techniques to connect the dots of quality journey towards perfection. Lean IT is frugal IT. Frugal in the sense those failures are turned into success. Rework and waste are eliminated. And the entire life cycle cost is minimized, not just the upfront cost of acquiring new technologies. Lean IT is about making sound decisions in every aspect of IT, whether strategic or tactical. Lean IT converts technology into value. It advocates considering long term effects of short term decisions.

When information technology has reached a state of perfection, technology is transformed into product; product is turned into services, and services deliver exceptional value to the customer. Given the financial and economic crises that has plagued so many industries and companies, it's not a shocker that CFOs will continue to slash IT budgets as they consider cutting costs everywhere.

A recent article in Business Week quoted Harvard Business Online in October, 2008 pointing to the coming trend of IT cost cutting: "IT spending is particularly vulnerable to the cold calculus of a CFO because it's difficult to provide that IT investments provide business value and that ongoing, keep the lights on, costs are well managed."[2] The challenges facing CIOs are now even more colossal and complex as IT managers attempt to reshape their image as a cost center and instead justify their role as a value center. To maximize value, we must reduce costs and increase benefits. A basic explanation of the drivers for *Cost* and *Benefit* are covered later in the book. In the following chapters, I'll show in depth principles, which govern the

---

[2] "Where Leaders Get Their Edge", Harvard Business. Also, "Painless IT Cost Cutting", by Susan Cramm, Harvard Business Online, October 7, 2008.

relationship between *Cost, Benefit* and *Value*. An article published in a 2001 issue of the Current Issues in Economics and Finance Journal, claims that not only is there improved productivity in the industries which intensively use IT, but analysis of a wide range of industries supports the role of IT as "a driving force behind the U.S. productivity revival". While quality and process improvements are not technology topics, Information Technology has been recognized as a critical enabler of new business and management processes. Despite that however, in some sectors there is still under-investment in Information Technologies. Return on investment and value are intertwined as we shall see in the coming chapters. This manuscript describes the guiding principles of Lean, Agile and Six Sigma Information Technology Management. It's for those who seek perfection from their IT organization. The principles offered in this document expand on the pioneering work done by James P. Womack and others[3] in Lean and Toyota Production System. Kaizen or pursuit of continuous improvement is not just a method but a management system by itself.

To illustrate, I offer examples, scenarios, and success stories as a result of Lean thinking, Agile and Six Sigma IT adoption. While the examples come from manufacturing, banking and healthcare industries, these principles can be universally applied to any IT organization in any industry.

The goal of this manuscript is to compile & document Lean, Agile and Six Sigma IT practices into a single document for reference by IT executives and as a training tool for IT managers. On one hand, IT is an enabler of Lean and Kaizen. On the other, it can benefit from Lean itself. Ergo, this book has a two fold purpose: 1) to describe how Lean, Agile and Six Sigma principles can be applied to Information Technology management, and 2) To provide a set of structured methodologies for IT managers so they can sustain and even lead the company's Lean and process improvement initiatives. This book is a collection of management tools and stratagems to achieve perfection and extraordinary results. IT Stratagems presented here provide management with advice, methods and practices to achieve greatness in Information Technology.

Studies show that IT organizations who employ Lean, Agile and Six Sigma methods are on all measures of quality, delivery time, customer satisfaction, strategic achievement and return on investment (ROI) at least four to nine times more productive and effective than the traditional IT organizations. The return on investment (ROI) for these firms follows the coveted J-curve, prominent with its rapid rise. (The J-curve is a tool used to plot the returns generated from an investment against time.) As shown in Figure 1, the returns for these firms occur earlier in time and rise faster. In contrast, the traditional IT organizations could only achieve a linear and moderate return on investment[4]. Because traditional IT management practices deliver results later in time, they carry a higher cost basis and thus later break-even point. The difference in project costs is illustrated by the shaded area below the Time axis.

A telling example is how K-Mart upgraded its systems including automating point of sale scanners at its stores. Through these technology investments over the

---

[3] "Lean Thinking: Past & Future", James P. Womack, Lean Management Summit, Aachen, Germany, Nov 12, 2004. Also, see Lean Enterprise Institute and www.Lean.org

[4] The next case study is based on "CIO 100 – Innovation For Growth", The CIO Magazine, Cxo Media Inc. 2006

course of five years, K-Mart was able to double its inventory turn-over. While this improvement is respectable, it paled in comparison to what Wal-Mart had achieved in the same period. By 2007, Wal-Mart's inventory turnover was three times better that K-Mart. Was something wrong with K-Mart's automation projects? No, only that Wal-Mart had completed the same information system upgrades two years earlier, and thus was able to reap the results faster.

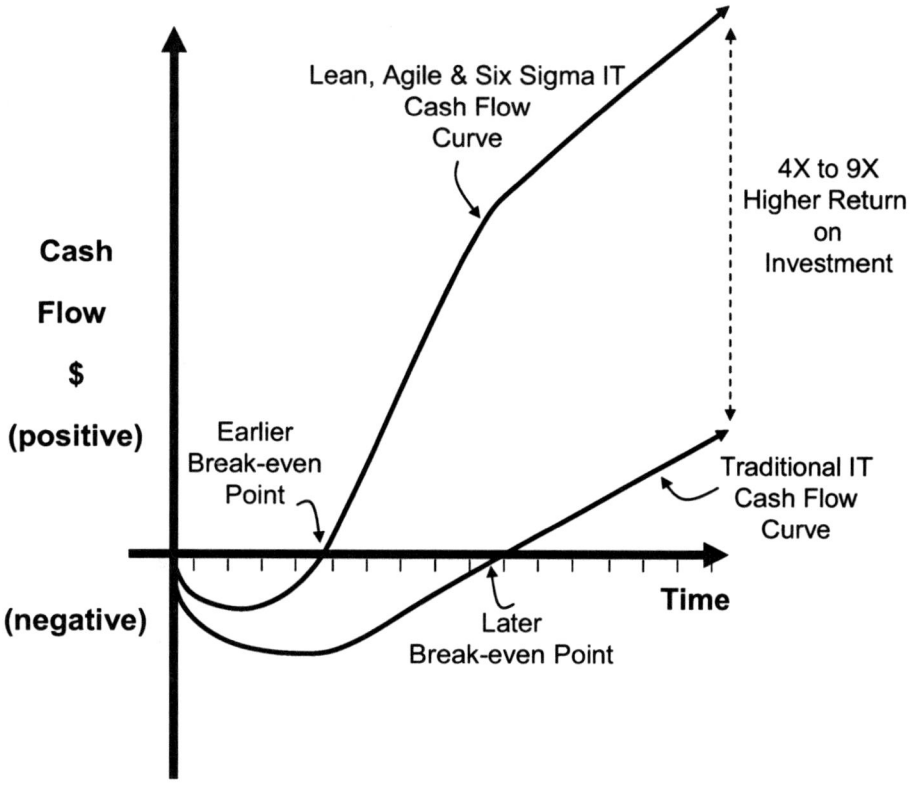

Fig 1 – The J-curve: Return on Investment Comparison Between Two IT Management Practices: Traditional IT Versus Lean, Agile and Six Sigma IT Management

Success Stories: Cases of Lean and Agile IT

Take for example, H&R Block, a $3.8 billion financial services company that has reaped the benefits of Agile & Lean implementations. When the company decided to build new offices in 552 Wal-Mart stores, it had to overcome many IT issues ranging from communications to transaction processing capability and database capacity. A team of internal IT staff became a virtual team of consultants available to project managers. The implementation of 552 new offices was successfully completed within the 17-day timeline. When Michael Goff, President of T. Rowe Price…

> ... Investment Technologies wanted a new product for managing investment rollovers, he challenged the IT organization to think Lean and Agile. Rather than building a system from scratch, the technology group formed a skunk-works team to reuse and re-factor existing components from other systems in production. The team was able to complete the product in 30 days. Getty Images in Seattle, Washington offers image and media content to its customers. The company has developed an Application Service Provider (ASP) model for customer websites in which IT manages components of the content delivery. The new system has contributed to 41 percent revenue growth in one year.

The Principal Laws of IT

Over the years observations about IT have formed opinions and insight in form of general theories, axioms and laws of information technology. When I was working on my doctoral thesis, I began compiling a list of laws, paradigms, pearls of wisdom, and axioms about IT and software development. A summary of those laws are included in the final chapter. It helps now and then to reflect on these laws knowing that when a new law surfaces it makes the old ones obsolete. But these laws, although at times less applicable than others, form our understanding and a framework of reasoning and thinking about IT. Overall, IT decisions are affected, situated and suffused by these laws whether we like them or not. They may not be as exact as the laws of physics and sometimes they contradict each other, but those are acceptable reflections of peculiarities, non-linearity and complexity of our IT universe.

Let's take a moment to define strategy, stratagem, maxim and laws of IT. Strategies are concepts. Stratagems are means of execution. According to Henry Mintzberg, in his 1994 book, "The Rise and Fall of Strategic Planning", strategy can epitomize four common notions[5]. A strategy can be a plan, a position, a pattern and a perspective. Stratagems are the progeny of strategies. Stratagems are a series of differential decisions turned into action. I use the term differential decision because they are intended to cause intentional change and to reduce distance between our current situation and the ideal position we wish to reach.

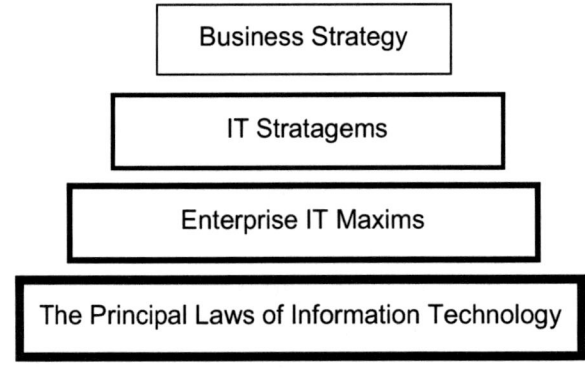

Fig 2 – Layered Domains of IT Laws, Maxims, Stratagems and Strategy

---

[5] "The Rise and Fall of Strategic Planning", Henry Mintzberg, 1994, Basic Books

Stratagems enable leaders to turn over an untenable position into a successful situation. For example, stratagems might include plans for new technology introductions, avoiding project failures, controlling costs, navigating through unexpected obstacles and competing objectives. This book offers stratagems that explain how you can achieve more with fewer resources. You'll find how on a small budget you can deliver as much productivity, - if not more - than most traditional large IT organizations. There are also maxims to consider. Maxims determine how the business and IT realities and challenges are to be understood. While the laws of IT are universally applicable across the industry, maxims are unique to each firm. They form the fundamental culture and attitude of employees towards their work. Maxims are established and often embodied by upper management. They are the tacit and endogenous group mindset, guiding the values, mores and acceptable employee behaviors in each firm. The difference between strategy and maxims is that maxims are principles about *now*, shared by all members of the enterprise; strategies are concepts about the *future*. In his book, "Strategy Paradox", Michael Raynor suggests that the same commitments to a strategy that lead to a firm's success can be also responsible for the firm's failure[6]. His position only strengthens my point about the importance of stratagems, and in particular the need for using Lean and Agile methods as stratagems to increase the odds of success. In today's dynamic business climate, we need more than the right IT strategies to succeed.

We need perfect planning, execution, the right people and the right foresight. We need IT stratagems and maxims. IT management stratagems are tactics to lead and win in the pursuit of perfection. Maxims are the guiding principles that shape the desired culture and attitudes. The laws of IT are general observations and philosophies about various disciplines and approaches in information technology. They are the collective understanding of how information systems, development efforts, quality and project outcomes are interconnected and affect one another. Throughout the book, I offer stratagems for information systems and technology management. The goal of the tools, methods and concepts described here is to deliver the most value at the lowest cost to your organization. Although examples in this book often reference situations in healthcare, finance or manufacturing industries, the techniques universally apply to almost any IT organization.

Any realistic discussion of Lean management of IT, is likely to progress towards Agile methods and Six Sigma. Lean management is a management approach for streamlining operations and production systems while creating value for the customer. Agile management and specifically Agile development methods grew out of the software development community to produce "real software" quickly, instead of loads of plans, schedules, and documents.

> **Stratagem:** Look into how you can turn a weakness or vulnerability into strength using information technology. When solving a problem or overcoming a challenge, choose a solution that not only overcomes the challenge, but also delivers an overwhelming advantage or a strategic asset to your organization.

---

[6] "Strategy Paradox: Why Committing to Success Leads to Failure (and What to Do About It)", Michael E. Raynor, Currency Books, 2007

Agile is more of a philosophy than an approach, and has been applied successfully to software development projects. Agile methods assume that initial specifications are not final but subject to iterative refinement. In fact practitioners of Agile encourage iterative modifications of specification by the customer to identify features. Agile imposes strict quality guidelines and check points for quality control. It also calls for having professionals or subject matter experts perform the key jobs efficiently. Six Sigma strives to bring near perfection quality, thereby eliminating costly rework and product recalls. Six Sigma offers powerful problem solving and design methods for manufacturability, maintainability, testability and error prevention. These goals are in synergy with Lean and Agile methods. While Lean focuses on improving process flow, Six Sigma focuses on reducing process variation. Agile simply focuses on flexibility in process which delivers the best chance of success for a given project. Pundits suggest that an IT organization should begin its journey towards perfection, starting by implementing Lean methods. Then we should advance to Agile and finally implement Six Sigma methods.

Stratagem Defined

The Oxford Dictionary defines "stratagem" (pronounced 'strattejem') as a plan or scheme intended to outwit an opponent. The origin of the word comes from Greek term strategama, from "strategein" to mean 'be a general' or maneuver. It's akin to "stratos" meaning army + "agein" to lead. Accounts of leading companies that outperform the rest in valuations are filled with stratagems. The founders of companies like Google, Netflix, eBay and Amazon.com did not begin their plans with elaborate strategies to be shelved among MBA case studies on strategic planning. They were more convinced in their abilities and products and less certain about strategy. As their companies grew, facing new obstacles, their management devised stratagems to solve issues and maneuver through business challenges. Often they turned an obstacle into an advantage, emerging out of such challenges stronger and better. For these pioneers, strategy mattered less. The stratagems they devised to overcome daily obstacles were key to survival and eventually led to their success.

Toyota and Honda Motors did not set out with the strategy to dominate the auto industry. Toyota wanted to build better cars. Honda simply sought to build harmony through cars that were amicable to people's driving habits. Over the years, Toyota had to solve a myriad of logistic and process issues. Whenever it solved a problem, Toyota gained another stratagem to its repertoire of knowledge and how to improve quality. Many of these stratagems are now referred to as the Toyota Production System and are being taught to other automobile manufacturers around the world. The net result of accumulated stratagems is that Toyota is the number one automobile company in the world.

Lean IT is about adopting the right virtues and mindset that produce the most value for the customer. It's a results-driven approach to managing IT. Studies of IT projects have shown that *Quality* and *Time* are both direct determinants of *Cost*.

Generally, success comes from establishing a *high-quality, high-velocity* and *high-precision* work culture.

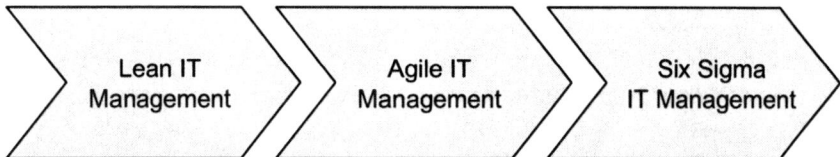

Fig 3 - The IT Journey of Process and Quality Improvement to Achieve Perfection

To mobilize an IT team to produce high-quality, high-velocity and high-precision work, I've advocated that Quality and Time must be viewed and managed as separate vectors of IT management. For example, among the recognized 100 most Agile companies, Alcoa with revenues of over $21 billion has implemented its business systems based on the Toyota Production System to focus on efficiency and continuous improvement to ensure Lean business practices. Dow Chemical Co. implemented a five hundred interactive video conferencing rooms to reduce travel costs by $143 million per year. It has successfully handled more than 40 acquisitions and joint ventures worldwide in less than 3 years using structured Lean and Agile methodology and best practices.

The *drivers of Quality* are: documentation, requirements analysis, specification, and design. The emphasis here is to promote the importance of architecture, detailed design (both high-level and low-level design) before jumping into implementation. On the other hand, the stratagems for reducing *"Time"* dictate qualities that shorten duration of each task and overall project duration. Here, I use "Time-Compression" to represent reducing turnaround time on an entire project schedule, or duration of a specific task or assignment. Time-compression techniques can universally apply to any task in the enterprise. It may seem counter intuitive, but experience suggests that the *drivers of Time-compression* are: quality inspections, design reviews, stage-gating projects, and ample testing before releasing an IT solution. The steps we take to improve quality invariably reduce project schedules as well. Adding to these stratagems we should emphasize a few more principles, such as: *Reusability*, focus on re-using existing solutions and re-factoring existing applications; *De-coupling*, identifying and removing or disentangling interdependencies; *Risk mitigation*, identifying risks early and having a risk-response plan, either backup or alternate plans.

Emphasis on design results in high-quality products. Emphasis on continuous testing results in time-compression. These principles are suggested by studies and experience that reducing rework and delays will consequently reduce cost. Both "quality" and "time-compression" are stratagems achievable by applying specific Lean, Agile and Six Sigma processes described in this book. To amplify the IT Benefits, we must emphasize the virtues of *customer-tailored services* and *total customer satisfaction*. Both are leverage points for maximizing IT value to the organization. Consider a small team of 10 IT individuals managed by Lean management principles: The Lean IT team can support more than a dozen mission critical applications concurrently; serve over five hundred users on 24x7 basis; release at least one major application into production every month; and enjoy a high customer satisfaction rate. In contrast, a much larger IT group in another organization managed as a traditional IS shop fails to meet customer expectations; falls short on delivering its projects on time or within acceptable quality almost 50% of the time. Sounds familiar? Both of these organizations actually do exist. Which of these two organizations will be yours? The decision is mostly up to you. Fortunately, to remedy their issues, the larger IT group has started to adopt Lean methods and has experienced considerable improvements in customer satisfaction and deliverables. At another large enterprise, Lean IT principles have brought the IT staff and the users community closer together and has fused IT deep into business workflows.

As example, consider a $12 billion leader in financial industry who has emerged stronger than ever from the financial crisis of 2008. This financial organization implemented a new claims management dashboard that gives business managers real-time claims information. To maximize business agility, its data model consolidated information across several business units. The company reports that its fixed IT costs were lowered by 20 percent in one year by applying Lean and Agile methods. Another example is illustrated by Con-Way Transportation Services a $2.2 billion company with 18,000 employees. The IT department applied Agile methods; it re-used business software components to support launch of a new business unit. The re-factored application used web based, real time alerts that led to an on-time rate of more than 98% and guaranteed delivery of service. When considering project management stratagems, Agile approaches like Rapid Application Development and SCRUM processes to accelerate projects, are recommended.

A few years ago, when I was the director of engineering at a large broadband company, I began to appreciate the benefits of Lean principles because of the results we were able to achieve. At the time, the company had announced six new product lines with much fanfare to the market. But the engineering department could not deliver any of the products dependably. When I arrived at the company, the stockholders were angry and anxious to see the much anticipated products finally get released. But, as I discovered there were many problems, in particular with the development process and lack of standards.

Basically, the products had so many defects that at the final testing stages, they were crashing all over. The company was virtually void of standard system architectures, methods and processes for new product introduction. The executives had heard their own marketing hype so often that they falsely believed the products were real. At best, the company had a collection of technologies fastened together more like a prototype, not robust enough for commercial use. The products demonstrated well in a sales meeting, but could not be shipped to customers. Essentially we had good demo-ware but no real commercial solution.

My predecessor had accumulated tremendous technical debt for the company by shipping incomplete and low quality products. I began to segment the products into their basic technology components and fixed each component separately, but in parallel. My focus was on the applications that delivered the most revenues and were closest to be completed.

After many root cause analysis sessions, the key product components became stable and the entire product could be tested in what we called the FITS Lab. FITS stood for Final Integration and Testing Systems. Using Kano's method, which is explained in the following chapters, I identified the key customer requirements. We limited the first release to those key customer requirements. Along the way, as we devised new processes, namely our development standards and stratagems, I asked the project managers to document them. At the end, the collection of these documents served as the standard processes for future product development projects. We had not only developed new products but also had built the foundation of a Lean and Agile development organization. I outsourced one of the products to a third party company who happened to be a technology partner. On another product, there was no need to invent everything in house. I purchased the rights to a technology package from a third party company which cut the overall development time and cost in half.

In a few months revenues were pouring in and new features were being added in quick, incremental cycles. To keep costs low, you have all considered outsourcing at one time or another.

Lean thinking is a proponent of *smart-sourcing*. Smart-sourcing advocates such stratagems as: persuade vendors to do as much as possible au gratis on your projects; outsource non-critical tasks but not activities which are strategic or a core competency; outsource only to those companies who can do it better at a lower cost. Such stratagems need to be complemented with a heavy dose of Six Sigma and Kaizen. Kaizen is a Japanese term consisting of "Kai" meaning school and "Zen" meaning wisdom. Kaizen has been cornerstone of continuous improvement. The chapters that follow describe how Lean and Six Sigma methodologies can be harnessed to bring high-quality, high-precision and high-velocity results to an IT productions system.

The savings can be enormous. It is reported that Six Sigma Black belts[7] save companies approximately $230,000 per projects. General Electric, one of the early adopters of Six Sigma has estimated benefits on the order of $10 billion during the first five years of implementation. Almost every Kaizen event and process improvement initiative has an IT component in it. And as the impact of such initiatives get bigger, the share of IT role grows proportionately larger. Six Sigma IT management strives to bring "engineering" disciplines to information technology management. I emphasize the importance of design for Six Sigma for several reasons. Here is one: It is reported that design directly influences more than 70% of the product life cycle cost.

One industry benchmarking survey reports companies that reach high product development effectiveness as a result of Six Sigma implementation, enjoy 3 times the average earnings of all companies in that industry. The emphasis on Six Sigma design must be a strategic intent for overall cost reduction and value based management. The common theme in this book is essentially new IT management stratagems to achieve perfection. Across the business landscape, whether in public or private sector, there is a deficit of effective IT management. Failures in all echelons of government and private industry are reflected in management's inability to plan, organize, direct, execute and control IT initiatives to meet objectives as expected. There are

---

[7] Six Sigma Black belts are individuals who are experts in Six Sigma methods and devote their entire time to implementing Six Sigma programs in a firm. They are certified and work under the direction of Master Black Belts, individuals with proven Six Sigma success.

exceptions, but few. One result of this internal management failure is over reliance on vendors, technology hype and outsourcing.

Outsourcing might solve some immediate problems, but does not help bolster the organization's process capability, problem solving maturity, ingenuity and competitiveness in the long run. Given that information technology is in the realm of technical innovation, continuous ingenuity is just as important as continuous improvement. Agile methods prescribe techniques for delivering continuous innovations and ingenuity to the enterprise.

Today, globalization of economy seems to have settled at least for the time being on simple division of work across the globe. We have optimized production of materials and intellectual property on a regional basis: America invents and Japan improves it; China manufactures and India supports it. But this division of work does not funnel vital feedback, either direct or indirect from customer to the developer, which are essential to continuous improvement. Unless information systems are designed to enable value creation across all functional and regional boundaries, immediate gains from such divisions of work will be short lived.

Finally, a few words about Lean IT organizational models: Organizations powered by cohesive information systems collectively operate in unison and exhibit intelligent behavior. Such firms are likely to adapt and thrive more successfully than those which are fragmented over internal islands of information. The intelligent organizations are enabled and patterned by intelligent IT designs and vice versa. In such firms, information technologies and organizations are so morphed that it's difficult to distinguish one from the other.

Lean & Agile IT Success Stories

Consider how agility was instrumental to the quick the merger of Palm and Handspring, where both firms were able to operate as a single entity in just a few days. PalmOne, was the result of the merger between Palm and Handspring.

When the merger was complete the company had merged 740 people, and was generating revenues of over $872 million. On the first day of the merger, the company had already combined ERP, finance, supply and HR applications and combined communication systems, so it could operate as one company. Manpower is a supplier of temporary professional staffing. The company has revenues in excess of $12 billion and employs about 25,000 employees. Management asked for a web-based ordering system to allow customers handle online pricing and ordering. The IT department championed an online system and was able to build a pricing wizard module in one month.

The application generated $3 million in new revenues. Lifespan in Providence, Rhode Island is a $1.1 billion healthcare institution. The company implemented a computerized physician order entry (CPOE) enabled by wireless network to improve patient care and safety. Shortly after, the IT department completed ....

> ... a new contract management application which resulted in $17 million improvement in payments for the institution. Delphi Corporation, a leader in automotive part manufacturing, embarked on a web-based information system strategy to improve sales.
>
> The IT group developed an internal web portal which allowed auto parts suppliers to access and order through Delphi's web application. Data mining was accessible by a PDA. Usage increased from 10 percent to 100 percent once the application was released.

A Brief History of Quality Movement

Much of the continuous improvement principles stem from the work by Edward Deming. Deming helped Japanese manufacturing improve their quality by applying his 14 principles. Deming's concept of quality is based on the Plan-Do-Check-Act quality wheel. The Plan phase of the continuous improvement process begins with defining the objectives and understanding the problem at hand. It defines what changes are to be implemented.

The Do phase is concerned with how the plan will be implemented, and with the execution of the plan. The Check phase emphasizes metrics, measurements and reporting after the changes have been implemented. The goal of check phase is to determine whether the desired improvements are being realized. The Act phase of continuous improvement provides guidelines for additional changes and finer modifications to sustain the quality improvement. The following diagram illustrates the major segments of Deming's quality wheel, and how the contents of this book are organized. This cycle appears in other forms including Hoshin Kanri. I'll explain this concept in the upcoming chapters, but briefly described, Hoshin planning is a methodology for long range planning. Hoshin cycle tracks Deming's quality wheel and has been one of Toyota's well kept secrets to success.

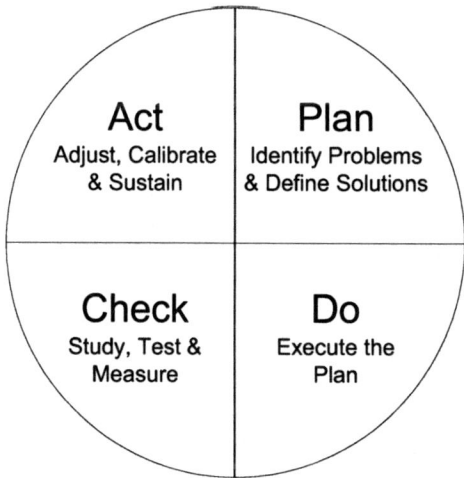

Fig. 4 – Deming's Quality Wheel

The history of Lean and quality movement dates back to early 1900's. A brief history can be viewed according to this chronology:

- **1914:** Henry Ford launches automobile assembly line manufacturing with standard parts. First moving assembly line for automobile production is invented.

- **1924:** Walter A, Shewhart develops Statistical Process Control (SPC) at Bell Laboratories. Later, collaborates with Edward Deming on operational aspects of statistical quality control.

- **1926:** Sakichi Toyoda, Japanese industrialist and inventor builds standard, automatic Loom manufacturing from interchangeable parts. His key invention is an automatic power loom that automatically stops itself when a problem occurs.

- **1937:** Sakichi Toyoda sells automatic Loom patents to start automobile manufacturing with his son Kiichiro Toyoda. He develops the concept of "5 Whys" to find the source of the problem.

- **1941:** Ford applies assembly line manufacturing techniques to assembling war planes during WWII. His plant can produce one B-42 bomber every hour around the clock.

- **1945:** Taiichi Ohno invents "just in time" manufacturing and "autonomation". In collaboration with Kiichiro Yoyoda and Sakichi Toyoda, develops a set of management philosophy and practices to eliminate waste an inconsistency, the precursor to Lean manufacturing. Toyota Production System is born.

- **1946:** Ichiro Ishikawa organizes JUSE, Japanese Union of Scientists and Engineers to promote quality and revive Japanese industries.

- **1949:** Dr. Edward Deming is invited by JUSE to give lectures on Statistical Quality Control in Japan. Lectures are received with great enthusiasm.

- **1951:** Inspired by Dr. Deming's lectures, JUSE establishes the Deming Prize. A recognition award to individuals who have made significant contribution to quality control and to firms who have achieved significant quality.

- **1954:** Joseph Juran, management consultant and quality guru is invited by JUSE to Japan. Juran gives lectures on quality management, continuous improvement, quality circles and quality as business strategy. Pareto principle is rediscovered.

- **1955:** Shigeo Shingo, Japanese industrial engineer develops Non-stock production, and zero inspection manufacturing. He conceives the "mistake-proofing" concept in product development and manufacturing. The concept of Single Minute Exchange of Dies is developed that allows rapid change over of process to manufacture a new product, thereby reducing production lot sizes.

- **1965:** Komatsu applies Hoshin Kanri principles to link planning to corporate strategy, vision and goals.

- **1980:** Shingo's book on Toyota Production System is translated into English.

- **1984:** Eliyahu Goldratt, an Israeli physicist introduces the Theory of Constraints, applying scientific methods to resolve organizational constraints (or bottlenecks) in manufacturing and operational processes.

- **1986:** Masaaki Imai, leading quality management consultant authors his book on Kaizen and continuous improvement. In the same year he establishes the Kaizen institute to teach and promote Kaizen concepts and tools to companies.

- **1989:** Toyota launches Lexus, a luxury line of automobiles. Within ten years, Lexus becomes the highest selling luxury car in the U.S. Its factory is known to have the fewest defects of any manufacturing plant in the world. Lexus's slogan is *The Pursuit of Perfection*.

- **1990:** Lean Production is coined by James Womack, Daniel Jones and Daniel Roos in their book: "The Machine that Changed the World". James Womack continues to promote Lean thinking and establishes the Lean Enterprise Institute to promote and educate the world about Lean thinking.

- **Today:** Lean methods are commonly used in manufacturing, operations, supply chain and product development. In Japan the number of registered quality circles is more than 400,000. Several national and international prestigious awards for quality including the Juran Quality Medal, Deming's Prize, President's Quality Award and Malcolm Baldridge Award are given each year to qualifying corporations with most notable quality improvement.

How to Read This Book

This book is organized around 21 chapters that can be read independently. Each chapter represents a principle of Lean, Agile and Six Sigma Information Technology around Deming's quality wheel. As shown in Figure 5, first we will describe value, value streams and how IT can be the value engine of your corporation. In later chapters, we will evaluate Lean architectural frameworks. Chapters 6 to 11 cover Lean IT methods, Six Sigma IT, design for quality and standards.

Risk management, testing and measurement topics are covered in chapters 12-13. If you are interested in cultivating better customer relationships and satisfaction, you'll be interested in Chapter 14 to 16. In Chapter 19, we will review techniques and organizational models that culminate to an intelligent organization. The diagram below shows Deming's wheel and how the book is organized around the main four phases of Deming Cycle.

My hope is that this book will give you new perspectives and better prepare you for information technology management challenges. I don't expect that you'll agree with every stratagem in this book. In fact some topics may seem controversial. But, this is how I see the IT management problems and the solutions that fit them.

Fig 5 – Book organization

My goal is to spark Lean thinking, Agile planning and Six Sigma engineering in the readers mind. Just as conducting a chamber orchestra is drastically different from writing music, the success of your IT organization will depend on how well you execute and conduct the people in the organization.

It's said that when Brahms was asked to conduct a Beethoven symphony, Brahms said, "I would not conduct what Beethoven wanted me to conduct. I would conduct what I wanted Beethoven to write." I hope this text provides the notes and cues that help you achieve a perfect performance.

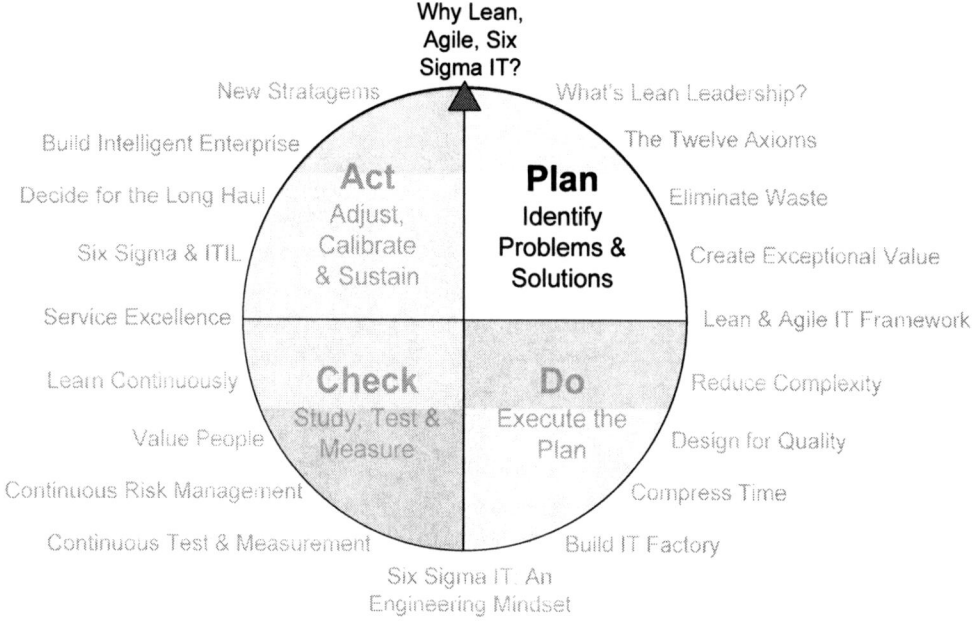

"Be ahead of the times through endless creativity, inquisitiveness and pursuit of improvement."

One of the Five Toyota Precepts

Chapter 1. Why Lean, Agile & Six Sigma IT?

Lean Information Technology Management is about delivering the most value at the lowest cost. Just like beauty, "value" is in the eyes of the beholder, i.e. the customer is the final arbiter of "value". Value is defined by the customer, as perceived by the customer. Depending on an IT customer's preferences, the IT value proposition might range from an operational task like delivering a service, or perhaps as simple as answering a technical question to high impact deliverables such as a strategic application. We have finally arrived at a time when nearly every conceivable IT problem has been solved by either prior research, off the shelf tools, software, consultants, or by one company or another[8]. Yet, over 60% of IT projects still fail to deliver solutions on time, within budget or meet users' expectations[9]. Specialized IT disciplines like medical Informatics[10] are no exception.

Neither are the IT organizations in other industries, ranging from service companies to dot-coms to manufacturing, to financial institutions. Becoming Lean is epitomized by IT managers controlling cost drivers while enhancing benefits

---

[8] "Enterprise Service Oriented Architectures", James McGovern, Oliver Sims, et al., Springer Publishing, 2006
[9] "A Rash of IT Failures – Healthcare IT", by Scott Berinato, CIO Magazine, June 15, 2003 issue.
[10] American Medical Informatics Association (AMIA) defines Medical Informatics as "A discipline that has to do with all aspects of understanding and promoting the effective organization, analysis, management, and use of information in health care".

systemically. Containing costs could entail eliminating waste, rework, poor execution or as direct as avoiding wrong technology decisions. Perfection in this context can be defined as an IT organization delivering value to its customers at zero cost. Is it possible? The answer is contained in this book.

I'm often asked why IT failures occur so frequently and how failures can be avoided. Most project failures are caused by internal and inherently false sets of management assumptions, rules and maxims, or lack of maxims. Clearly the approach and assumptions that IT executives endow to frame the problems and arrive at decisions make a big difference in the results they achieve. I believe that a Lean approach creates the framework for inherently good IT decisions and a common compass for the IT organization to follow.

Why Lean IT?

There are several industry-wide indicators that demonstrate why we need Lean IT management. A summary of salient points from hundreds of surveys conducted over the last 5 years and a collection of industry wide issues that CIOs face are listed as follows:

- High failure rates of IT projects: More than 60% of IT projects still miss their target on schedule, cost and quality.

- Long waits for solutions: IT customers are often dissatisfied with long delays associated with release of new applications.

- Return On Investment: Customers are generally not satisfied with return on their IT investments.

- RISK: IT projects still carry huge risks due to technology, rising complexity and changing business & clinical requirements.

- Backlog: Growing backlog of IT projects & unfinished work is a concern.

- Data Overload: Business and clinical data volume are growing rapidly, but finding relevant, useful and timely information still a challenge.

- Islands of Information: Many disparate, disjointed applications form islands of information as they do not integrate or exchange data as expected

- Growing Technical Debt: Legacy problems and technical debt are accumulating fast as many IT problems go unresolved.

- Solutions Gap: Bridging the gap between what vendors' products promise and what actually can be practically delivered requires tremendous IT effort.

In today's turbulent business environment, business and IT challenges alike are increasingly growing faster than our intellectual capacity and ingenuity solve them using the old methods. Our approach to solving these issues requires a fresh new look. To be effective, IT managers must respond to these challenges differently than they have done before. As IT leaders we must tackle the new and mounting challenges with new ideas, methods and frame of thinking. Over the last 2 decades, a flurry of articles and consulting practices have flourished around the notion of Lean Management, Kaizen, Lean Enterprise and production techniques developed by Toyota Corp[11]. Only a modest amount of that knowledge has made headway into the financial segment or medical practice, and even less into Information Technology Management. This in itself represents an opportunity for more experimentation and research. To compare and contrast the trio of Lean, Agile and Six Sigma, some of the characteristics of each approach are listed on Table 1.1.

Lean IT	Agile IT	Six Sigma IT
Improves process flow	Adapts process to situation	Reduces process variability
Creates pull system of flow	Builds flexibility into the flow	Measures and controls flow
Define customer expectations and meet them	Gets customer involved in requirements definition	Anticipates customer requirements & expectations
Focus on value add vs. non-value add	Prioritize what is important and critical to be done "NOW"	Relies on data-driven, evidence-based decisions
Provides tools for analyzing flows and delays	Focus on appropriate breakdown of development and assign the right people to the right task	Limits variations that hinder our ability to deliver predictably and reliably
Quantify and eliminate complexity	Reduces complexity by modular approach and component reuse	Offers tools for effective problem solving
Focus on maximizing process velocity	Adapts processes to meet the development objective	Eliminates defects as defined by the customer
Learns from your mistakes and problem solving	Learns from other people's mistakes	Learns by asking the right questions

Table 1.1 – Comparison of Lean, Agile and Six Sigma IT Principles

Case Study: **IT Projects Doomed from the Start**

During the 1980's and the 1990's, a wave of IT projects at the state level failed. The Oregon Department of Motor Vehicles (DMV) started on a $2M project to overhaul its information systems in the early 1990's. After several delays and repeated postponement of the production date, the project sponsors finally decided to release a partially completed system into production, four years later than planned. One week

---

[11] "The Toyota Way, 14 Management Principles from the World's greatest manufacturer", Jeffrey K. Liker, McGraw-Hill, 2004

before the go-live date, the project sponsor announced that only a fraction of the entire project would be released and that to complete the rest of the project another $12M was necessary. The tax payers were outraged. The key question was how could a $2M project end up four years late and still need $12M to complete?

Only five years earlier, the California DMV had embarked on a similar project with the same failed results. California and Oregon DMV were not alone. Many of the state DMV projects had the same ill fated ending during those two decades. "What prevented one DMV IT organization from learning the lessons of the other DMV projects?", you might ask. All across the U.S., many DMV IT projects were failing one after another. What's striking is the functional similarity between the DMV workflows across the country. For example, there are a few common, basic business functions that are carried out at any DMV; such as registering vehicles, changing address or obtaining a drivers license. And yet, no CIO made an attempt to learn from these project failures or, better yet, to attempt to re-use an existing implementation from another state.

Each DMV project essentially reinvented the wheel; built the same solution from scratch and at very high costs. I was asked to provide an analysis and independent audit of one of those failed IT projects as a consultant. State legislators were adamant to find the root cause of failure. There were several root causes. But the most fundamental root cause which affected the project negatively was the lack of IT staff's technical knowledge and familiarity with the new technology being implemented. The IT staff was excellent at maintaining their existing application, an antiquated and outdated system. But that had kept the IT staff from learning the newer technologies and application development environments. The causal diagram of this root cause analysis –which I'll cover in the following chapters- revealed a much deeper and troubling problem. Because this particular DMV department was unwilling to pay higher compensation for its IT positions, it could not competitively recruit new IT talent. Essentially when it came to hiring top IT talent, it could not compete with other employers.

The project needed staff with specific skills and talent which could not be recruited. The department's penny pinching hiring practices cost the tax payers millions of dollars. While this is just one example, it demonstrates how root cause analysis and causal methods (or influence diagramming) can help with taking the correct long term decision. As you might have discovered already, many IT projects are doomed to fail before they start. In another, less fortunate project in California, a firm embarked on a $50M project to build a new electronic medical record system. The project deadline was extended several times.

Eventually, when it was released into production, the system had severe performance and functionality problems. The project cost over $100M and caused millions of dollars more in operational expense because users simply could not use the application in their clinics.

The CIO blamed everyone; the application vendor, the executive sponsors and consultants except himself. Clearly, this project was destined to fail because it lacked certain fundamentals. These fundamentals are collectively supported by Lean, Agile and Six Sigma IT management principles.

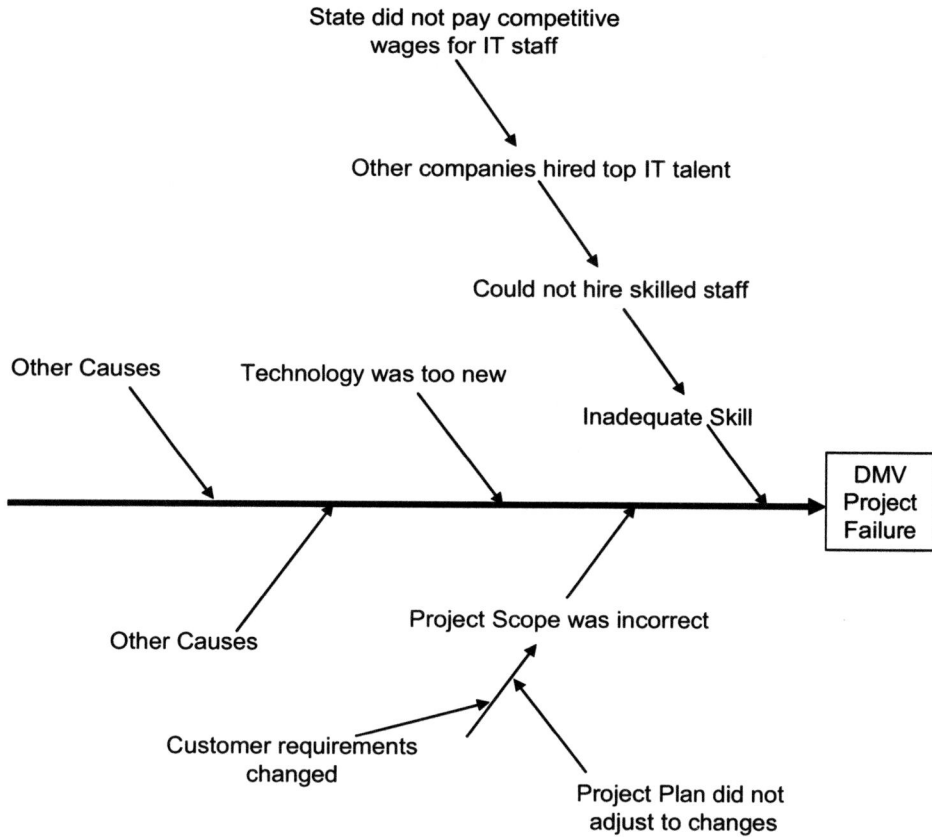

Fig 1.1 – Partial Root Cause Analysis of DMV Project Failures

IT project failures have been a recognized problem since computer systems were invented. A KPMG study in 1988 found that 35% of their largest clients had a runaway project and in 1991 the percentage had increased to 60%[12]. Learning from IT project failures is an expensive way to gain experience. Failures can be dramatically reduced by applying Lean IT principles. In this case, the CIO was aware of similar failed projects with the same vendor, but did not attempt to find out why; nor put the appropriate risk mitigation plans in place. In contrast IT departments that apply Lean, Agile and Six Sigma principles accomplish great business and technical feats.

Rigid Models in a Dynamic World

In 1986, Watts Humphreys then an IBM fellow published his seminal book entitled Managing the Software Process. In it, Humphreys disclosed findings from research project funded by the US Department of Defense Software Engineering Institute (SEI) conducted at Carnegie Mellon University. Regarded as the father of software quality, Humphreys observed five distinct levels of process maturity in

---

[12] "Recognizing Runaway IS Projects When They Occur: The Bank consortium Case", Joan Ellen Cheney Mann, in Annals of Cases in Information Technology, Editor Mehdi Khosrow-pour, Idea Group Publishing, Information Science Publishing, Volume 4-2002

software development companies. He called it the Capability Maturity Model (CMM). Since then the model evolved to become Capability Maturity Model Integration (CMMI) and was applied to other technology arenas including IT and even to testing organizations.

The initial five levels of CMM were surrogate indicators of quality and each meant a level of capability. **The five levels were**:

Level 1: Ad hoc. Processes in this level are not defined. They are not documented and not repeatable. The activities are often reactive leading to unstable and chaotic environments.

Level 2: Repeatable. Basic processes are recognized and documented. Management tracks and encourages processes. The processes are repeatable.

Level 3: Defined. Processes are defined, standardized and used consistently. Management supports improving processes over time.

Level 4: Managed. Processes have metrics and methods of control. The measurements are reviewed periodically and adjustments to processes are made as necessary.

Level 5: Optimized. The organization makes continuous efforts to improve process performance through incremental and innovative technical changes and improvements.

While CMM was instrumental to show a cause-effect relationship between process maturity and quality, it was nonetheless a descriptive, rigid model. As a descriptive model it could explain the results that we achieved. But it had little prescriptive value as it could not suggest what we should change to achieve the intended results. Moreover, reaching higher levels did not guarantee or lay a path to success. The interim steps, the stratagems to reach the finish line were missing. In 1997, CMMI replaced CMM and delivered additional process guidelines. CMMI is based on 16 core process areas that guide development, service and acquisitions. Overall, CMMI is a great tool for appraisal of situations, but rarely adequate for IT problem-solving or finding appropriate stratagems to solve complex IT challenges.

There are perhaps two major weaknesses that CMMI cannot overcome in a dynamic world. The model is inherently rigid and cannot morph and adapt to the dynamic and ever changing world of technology and information systems. The rapid pace of change does not allow lengthy appraisals. And, while it's defined for software engineering practices, its ability to cover the diverse, multi-disciplinary and complex IT endeavors is limited. We need Lean and Agile stratagems to take us through the journey to perfection. Let's visit the twelve axioms of Lean, Agile and Six Sigma IT management[13].

---

[13] The case study is based on "100 Most Agile Companies Honored. Which Companies Lead in Agility?", Edward Prewitt, The CIO Magazine, August 2004

Cases of Lean & Agile Success

The Information technology landscape is filled with Lean and Agile success stories1. Take for example, the Allstate Insurance Co. with 40,000 employees and revenues more than $32 billion. The company wanted customized websites for its agents but on a single architecture. Using Agile and Lean approach, the IT department developed customizable website architecture to server more than 110,000 agents. It also launched the Auto Express application which allows handling of fender-benders with no injuries or liability issues quickly online. These implementations have given Allstate an edge over competition and reduced its operating costs drastically.

SecureWorks an Atlanta based company, used open source software to develop a Customer Relations Management (CRM) application at a very low cost. The in-house programmers and implementation team worked closely to implement the application within 2 months, 120 days ahead of schedule. At Land's End, the IT staff supported fast, radical shift in business model after the company was acquired by Sears. A new business intelligence software was implemented quickly to prevent sales loss due to inadequate inventory. ABF Freight Systems, a leading transportation company applied Rapid Application Development (RAD) process to deploy an online application for customers and Business to Business (B2B) partners. The new application provided shipment tracking, rate quotations, reports, dynamic routing of in-transit shipments, a wireless tracking solution and XML data interchange. ABF Freight System is a leading e-commerce company and regarded as one of 100 most Agile companies.

Lean and Agile success are not limited to manufacturing or service sector. Schneider National of Green Bay, Wisconsin took a customer-developed, load sharing website and re-purposed the application as a new IT tool. The company saved a huge amount by refactoring an existing application. The company has over 21,000 employees with revenues in excess of $2.9 billion. The IT project management office has been successful by implementing IT infrastructure solutions based on Agile software development process.

Rapid delivery of results at low costs, low risks and short timeframe are characteristics of Lean and Agile IT management. Chico's Retail Services of Fort Myers, Florida replaced and upgraded its entire IT infrastructure and mission-critical applications in 18 months, while launching over 139 new retail stores at the same time frame. The massive IT project included communications, global sourcing, merchandize planning, pattern making, distribution, logistics, financial systems and e-commerce.

The 12 Axioms of Lean, Agile and Six Sigma IT Management

Because Information technology is complex and multi-faceted no single rule applies to managing IT at all times. But, as managers we are interested in fundamental principles or axioms of management that give us the guidelines to manage from.

It would be great if we could distill all lessons, experience and knowledge about managing IT into a simple set of rules. The essence of this book is a summary of all those things which can be written in twelve irrefutable axioms of Lean, Agile and Six Sigma IT management. They are:

1. **Eliminate Waste:** Identify sources of waste and eliminate them. Perform Kaizen events to remove non value adding tasks.

2. **Deliver exceptional value:** Identify customers' value drivers and focus on delivering value beyond customers' expectation.

3. **Reduce Complexity:** Manage risk by reducing complexity & interdependencies. Apply 5S methods to reduce IT complexity

4. **Design for Quality:** Develop processes for every IT task. Establish a high expectation for quality. Perform high-level and low-level designs followed by design reviews to ensure quality

5. **Compress Time:** Apply Lean and Agile methods to deliver IT solutions faster by reducing Cycle Time.

6. **Build IT Factory:** Practice continuous innovation. Create consistent processes and component-based development to deliver solutions at regular intervals.

7. **Continuously Test & Measure:** Develop a culture of testing, gathering facts and measurement data about processes, applications and services.

8. **Continuously Manage Risk:** Continuously identify risks and mitigate them. Prepare risk response plans in advance.

9. **Value People:** Respect your people. Keep them accountable and trust them with the responsibility to make decisions.

10. **Learn Continuously:** Implement IT projects with intent to create new knowledge and apply it to other projects. Learn from your customers about their business and listen to the voice of the customer.

11. **Decide for the Long Haul:** Maintain a long time horizon for IT decisions. Defer decisions to the latest time possible until more facts are available.

12. **Build Intelligent Organizations:** Create intellectual bonding by providing real time, collaborative and relevant information to employees. Strive to make decisions that optimize across the entire organization and workflows.

Continuous Improvement and Continuous Innovation

Kaizen is about continuous improvement. But Information Technology management needs continuous innovation to excel. Innovation is a key ingredient of day-to-day information technology work. Innovation and improvement are not conflicting goals, rather they reinforce one another. For example, Agile methods call for continuous delivery of solutions and development. This is a goal congruent with continuous innovation. Small, incremental steps towards process improvement and innovation bring the ideal interlock of IT and business change in small improvement cycles. This is the Lean and Agile approach. In contrast, intentional quantum leaps are made possible by taking more drastic steps of improvement and ingenuity. While this approach is possible, it carries higher risks that might bring unsatisfactory and unmanageable consequences. These two approaches are illustrated in Figure 1.2.

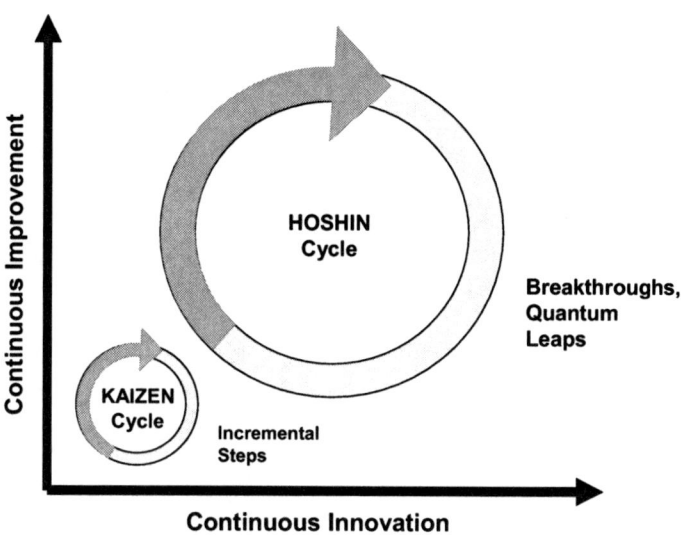

Fig 1.2 – Continuous Innovation & Continuous Improvement on a PDCA cycle

The cycles as shown on the next diagram represent the thinking process along both dimensions. Sparked by an idea to improve a process, the cycle begins along the innovation (or ingenuity) axis. It then turns to the continuous improvement axis when it considers how to improve a process or quality. Potential IT solutions powered by creative ideas turns another revolution. Each spin revolves along ingenuity to continuous improvement, and repeats in cycles. The similarity between these cycles and Deming's Quality Wheel are deliberate. As the wheel turns faster, your firm achieves higher returns on investment. We can think of these cycles as wheels that generate intellectual productivity. Information systems are great multipliers of intellectual productivity as they help automate and orchestrate workflows consistently through an organization. From the traditional productivity perspective, during the industrial age, productivity was measured by efficiency of machine output. In the present information age, the intellectual productivity of people is a key measure of productivity. That is the combination of innovation and process improvement. For example, when Intelsat, a leader in satellite bandwidth services saw a major shift in its business from flat-rate and treaty-based satellite communications to market-driven, for-profit telecommunications services, it had to respond to this change rapidly. The company executives began a business intelligence initiative to identify new opportunities, new product and services. The company had already invested in certain network capacity. It had to better understand utilization and patterns of use by its customers. This innovative idea utilized data mining of a new database. The result was a complete win for the company. The new application system identified $150 million in saleable network capacity that became available by changing its product packaging. By improving the product and offering additional services, the company improved its processes and as a result improved free cash flow by 15 percent. Continuous Improvement, as shown in the next diagram is the role of Lean, Six Sigma and Kaizen. Continuous innovation is in the province of Agile methods.

> **Stratagem:** As an executive, your posture on process and quality will set the attitude for the rest of the organization. To reach perfection, you must respect processes and demonstrate a passion for quality. Treat "process" as sacred, and "quality" to be revered.

For example, consider the case of AT&T, Inc (Formerly SBC Communications, the largest US telecommunications company headquartered in Dallas, Texas. Faced with a large portfolio of application development projects waiting in the queue for resources, the IT leadership sorted its application project queue into two groups: the high priority, high impact unique applications and the lower priority, lower-risk projects. The IT leadership was able to shift more than $60 million in project budgets to higher priority projects (an example of Lean and continuous improvement). The remaining 316 low risk projects went through a Rapid Application Development (RAD) and repeatable IT solutions process (an example of continuous innovation). The results were stunning. The high priority projects received the resource and attention that they deserved. The low priority projects were also completed using repeatable IT processes. The company realized a 49 percent increase in IT staff productivity. Continuous innovation brings value and longevity to the corporation. In a recent survey of the 100 most innovative companies, the common theme was that these companies applied technology to solve internal problems ranging from logistics and security to forecasting. Wal-Mart uses data mining and other technologies to forecast what customers will buy and when, how much and at what price. Pfizer developed a smart card solution to enable digital signatures to eliminate paper. Removing paper out of the process made transactions to be booked faster and thus for improved cash flows[14].

In a recent survey of 100 most agile companies, the CIOs indicated that they spend almost 40 percent of their IT budget on new projects and almost 60 percent on operations and maintenance. When asked what works, the majority believed that creating cross-functional innovation teams and close relationship with customers are ingredients for success. Seventy percent of the CIOs in these most innovative organizations agreed that urgency of business needs is the driving factor for new IT initiatives, followed by 57 percent of new initiative decisions were made based on cost-benefit analysis. Building web services and business intelligence are still the top applications of concern in the most innovative IT organizations. The systems view of Lean implementations can reveal a great deal about efficiency of your business. Each cycle consumes financial or human resources as input and produces results as output.

---

[14] "CIO 100 – Innovation For Growth ", The CIO Magazine, Cxo Media Inc., 2006

When we consider a Lean project as a system of inputs and outputs, we can measure its effectiveness as a ratio of outputs on inputs. Inputs can be capital investment or operational expense or human resources invested in the organization. Outputs can be financial return, cost reduction or reduction in inventory levels. Whether you are contemplating an incremental or quantum leap Lean initiative, you can benchmark the outcome against status quo or other possible initiatives.

Lean thinking cannot go far without touching on organizational dynamics. After all, many Lean organizations, Toyota Motor Corporation being an excellent example, reached a high point of organizational maturity, where small teams excelled in high precision execution and problem solving. Despite many issues or obstacles that arise in any enterprise on a daily basis, these mature organizations solve their problems on the spot, and much more effectively than their rival companies who look to the boardroom for a solution. Lean organizations exhibit intelligent behavior in many forms because they allow decision making at the lowest level of organization.

As a result, Lean organizations are better at adapting to change, responding to challenges, proactive planning, and learning (see Chapters 15-19). Developing an intelligent organization where individuals make appropriate decisions at the right time and the right place in their work is the sign of achieving perfection in Information Technology. Hiring intelligent individuals is one thing. But creating the intellectual harmony and cohesiveness so the organization behaves as one living intelligent organism without internal rifts and counterproductive frictions, is nirvana. As we apply Lean methods and improve quality, our sensory awareness towards quality and process grows. You'll expect the right decisions to be made at the right time and the right place based on facts and data. Your staff develops streamlined processes that are universally adopted with high degree of regard for quality. You'll begin to notice and get bothered by indecisions, bureaucratic setbacks, rework, delays, and lost opportunities because you will have mastered the Lean decision making process.

From the perspective of a Lean manager, it will be hard not to miss the comical aspect of the traditional organizations as you observe the dysfunctional results and spot their ad-hoc approach to everything, smoke-stack divisions that work against one another, lack of clarity of purpose, mass confusion and sense of helplessness that employees feel. On the one hand these seem laughable mishaps for traditional organizations. On the other hand, they are painful reminders of how firms miss on opportunities to improve. Examples of failed IT projects, from local government institutions, to the FBI, CIA and other non-profit and for-profit organizations are a sign that we can no longer afford treading on the same traditional approaches to IT management. In her book, "The Company of the Future", Frances Cairncross lists ten key attributes of good management for the new economy[15]: manage knowledge, make decisions, focus on customers, manage talent, manage collaboration, build the right structures, manage communications, set standards, foster openness and develop leadership. She places high emphasis on managing knowledge and decision making. But all ten attributes are highly enabled by information systems in her vision for the company of the future. Asking the right questions is a Six-Sigma practice. It is also the basis for *second order thinking*. Second order thinking, which I'll explain in detail in the following chapters, is a mindset for finding the underlying causes and conditions that

---

[15] "The Company of the Future", Frances Cairncross, Profile Books / Harvard Business Press, 2002

lead to effects or outcomes. Second order thinking asks why and how certain root causes come to exist in the first place.

Lean & Agile IT Business Framework

The IT Business Framework encompasses both business analysis and process re-design to enable the specific Lean and Agile objectives of the IT organization and the entire enterprise. It also includes other business aspects of Information Technology management such as vendor management, contract management, procurement practices, technology management and knowledge transfer. These topics deserve some coverage, but our focus in this book will primarily be on business analysis and process re-design for Lean management.

For a focus on Quality Management to be successful, information management must be linked to organization's business quality objectives and strategies. **The IT management must be able to answer the following questions:**

1. What are the organization's highest priorities?
2. Which value streams are the strategic intent of the organization?
3. What business consequences have resulted from weak or ineffective focus on quality management functions?
4. What is the root cause of the problems?
5. What action is being taken to correct each cause? What can IT provide to correct the cause?
6. How can IT support a quality focus for the organization's process improvement objectives?

There are several areas where IT can help Lean business analysis, quality circles and Total Quality Management initiatives. Among those areas, IT can be a great tool to:

1. Create single-flow processes. Eliminate batch processes
2. Eliminate paperwork, faxes and scanning
3. Eliminate redundant steps in processes
4. Eliminate waste and re-work
5. Provide quality alerts and measurements in real time

IT managers should partner with the organization's Lean business specialists to provide metrics and measurements to workers and management that are needed to improve quality and reducing waste. To be successful, it is important for Lean IT managers to understand business process design and re-engineering, and translate desired changes into IT system specification, functions and features.

The Lean IT business framework attempts to define the root causes in the current state and the solutions required to create a future Lean state. The current state describes what we have vs. future state describes what we want to create. The Lean business framework should also identify how the gap can be bridged between current and future state.

Six Sigma IT Business Framework

Companies who have mastered Lean and Agile IT are experimenting with Six Sigma methods. We are interested in applying Six Sigma when high-precision execution is required and no deviations from the corporate strategy are tolerated. One of the Six Sigma tools available to us is the Hoshin Kanri. Hoshin Kanri has helped many companies including HP and Toyota to align their IT initiatives and activities with the corporate strategies.

Hoshin Kanri

For Six Sigma IT managers, *Hoshin Kanri* is a valuable tool that provides focus and direction to their staff. By some accounts, Hoshin is based on the Chinese words, "Ho" - meaning direction and "Shin" - meaning needle. It stands for way of setting direction. By other accounts, Hoshin in Japanese means shining of purpose. Kanri means control or management. Hoshin Kanri was first used by Komatsu in 1965, but has been applied extensively by Global2000 companies including Hewellett-Packard, Toyota and Bank of America. It provides the means for Strategy deployment and planning.Some Lean experts attribute some of Toyota's success to implementing Hoshin Kanri. The purpose of Hoshin Kanri is to formulate clear corporate objectives and goals, spreading those objectives throughout the organization and linking action plans to achieve those objectives. At the core of Hoshin Kanri is Plan-Do-Check-Act (PDCA) sequence that provides management with focus and plans to move from vision to execution in just a few cycles. IT managers can use Hoshin Kanri to focus their staff on plans that link and support the corporate strategy. There are a few steps to implementing Hoshin Kanri as described below:

1. Define organization's vision.
2. Identify critical business issues that need to be addressed.
3. Translate vision into tangible and measurable objectives. Establish lower level business objectives to address those issues.
4. Perform cross functional planning to identify and align short term lower-level objectives with long term vision.
5. Define sub-goals or tactics that support each strategy.
6. Establish metrics and indicators for measuring performance. Periodically check against plan.
7. Establish business fundamental measures.

Steps 1-3 are handled by top management while the rest of the organization implements steps 4-7. A key attribute of Hoshin Kanri is a review table that lists a number of tactical plans for each strategy, the strategy owner, the timeframe, the performance metrics, the targets for each strategy and actual results at the time of the review. The Hoshin Kanri reviews must be conducted at least once a year, which completes a PDCA cycle. The results of the review translate into new plans for the next cycle. This methodology is the most comprehensive and practical approach that I've seen where all elements of strategy stratagems and maxims can be defined and modified on a long time horizon.

Summary

So, why we need to pay attention to Lean, Agile and Six Sigma methods in IT management? There are a variety of reasons because we don't want IT to be viewed as the cliché cost center. Instead, we want to enable change that brings tremendous stakeholder (customers, employees and share holders) value, and increase in profitability and quality. For some it's a pure improvement in IT management, the ability to reach perfection in IT. To summarize what practitioners of these principles can look forward to, we can number a list of reasons:

1. Drastically improve quality of IT services, products and processes
2. Dramatic improvement in quality and profitability
3. Rapid and sustainable alignment of IT direction with corporate strategy
4. Dramatic improvement in stakeholder satisfaction (customers, employees and share holders)
5. Significant and tangible value increase for stakeholders (customers, employees, and share holders)

"Quality planning consists of developing the products and processes required to meet customer's needs."

Joseph M. Juran

Chapter 2: What's Lean IT Leadership?

Just as the CIOs are concerned with the overall effectiveness of IT, they must be also concerned with their effectiveness as individual C-executives. There are three attributes that make a CIO effective. First, the CIO must be able to convey trust and win the trust of the executive leadership. Credibility is fundamental to winning trust. Credibility is enhanced when the CIO delivers on what was promised. Without trust, the CIO has lost the most important foundation for effectiveness and may never recover. Second, the CIO must possess and demonstrate that he or she brings personal value as a leader to the organization. CIOs must instill the notion that they add significant value as a member of the executive team. Third, The CIOs must lead with a heart of serving for IT to deliver genuine value to the entire organization. Their most notable and palpable value add is delivering service to their peers. Credibility comes from delivering results that your enterprise leadership cares about. It requires building strong personal relations with executive customers. It means anticipating, planning and delivering a consistent and predictable stream of information technology solutions to the enterprise.

Leading with Vision, Maxims and Stratagems

Key abilities of the successful CIOs that separate them from the rest are being results-driven, combined with delivering on vision, communication and relationship building. Promoting a common theme around Lean, Agile and Six Sigma IT can set a powerful and clear vision for achieving success for the CIO and for the IT organization.

These common themes also form the basis for the IT maxims –the commonly held beliefs in the IT organization. Applying Lean, Agile and Six Sigma principles as a common management theme can the new vision. This is of particular importance when we consider the role of the CIO towards building trust, leadership and added value in the CEO-CIO relationship equation.

A study conducted by Gartner group in 2004, surveyed more than 950 CIOs about challenges they face and how they make their enterprise succeed. Results of this survey are chronicled in a book by Marianne Broadbent and Ellen S. Kitzis called "The New CIO Leader". The authors note that critical to success of the CIO are two points. First, they must lead not manage. Second, they must know their enterprise and its business as thoroughly if not better than their executive colleagues.

One of the key roles of the CIO, one that actually cultivates better relations with C-executives, is to educate the C-executives about IT. The CEO-CIO relationship, according to research by Gartner Group, can exist in four different levels: adversarial, transactional, aspiring and trusted ally. When the CIO is not delivering on the executive team's expectations, the relationship tends to be adversarial. When the CIO is delivering services and on the business strategy, the relationship with CEO is transactional. This is the most common level. In the aspiring level, the CIO has delivered on all expectations, but also strives to be pro-active and engage the CEO and other officers in business issues and operations. Finally, when a CEO trusts the CIO as an ally, the CIO and CEO collaborate together on the co-creation and formulation of strategy.

Similarly, the CFO may view IT as merely a cost-center, and thus strive to minimize IT investments to the lowest expense without considering the impact on IT deliverables. Alternatively, the CFO can become CIO's best ally by recognizing the enterprise-wide role of IT and the benefits that new information system projects can bring. Since Agile and Lean IT principles are drivers for higher value while minimizing cost, they empower the CIO to deliver results that matter, and consequently improve the CIO-CEO and CIO-CFO relationships.

Enter the Lean CIO: powered by Lean, Agile and Six Sigma methods, the IT leadership can devise strategic IT vision and execute them with high precision, high velocity, and high quality. How do we craft a vision for IT? We can chart our Lean IT vision by considering five fundamental factors:

1. What is the basic economic model of the enterprise?
2. What is the strategic intent of the firm?
3. What are the strategic plans of the firm and its individual business units?
4. What are the underlying customer-facing workflows and what are the back-end and internal workflows?
5. How information systems can improve, even revolutionize the enterprise?

A hint that experts offer is that to look for patterns in answers to these questions. All five elements can be translated into sets of IT objectives, specific actionable decisions and specific IT projects. The answers to fourth and fifth factors can point to the underlying value streams for the organization using Lean methods. IT objectives can then be prioritized using Agile methods. Finally, each deliverable can be designed and precisely executed using Design for Six Sigma methods. The common threads in these factors can serve as the basis for a Lean IT vision.

In their book the "New CIO Leader"[16], Marianne Broadbent and Ellen Kitzis point out ten new priorities for the effective CIO leadership. The ten points are:

1. CIOs must lead, not just manage. They must have a personal vision and a point of view about how information and IT can make the organization more effective.

2. Understand the fundamentals of the business, including the industry, trends, competitive forces and key decisions that affect the business

3. Create a vision for how IT will build your organization's success. As CIO you must apply your knowledge of the business with vision on how to better IT-enable your enterprise.

4. Identify and communicate expectations for an IT-enabled enterprise. This is accomplished by identifying business needs, strategies and working with your colleagues to articulate the IT guidelines. The authors call the IT guidelines, maxims.

5. Create clear and appropriate accountability and governance. Successful governance leads to improved credibility and trust.

6. Enable business strategy using IT by melding business and IT strategy together.

7. Build a new, leaner IT organization by focusing the IT staff on three primary stratagems: boost process maturity, focus on service excellence and improve product quality.

8. Build and promote high performing teams in your IS organization. Recruit and retain staff with skills that match the complexity and demands of your business and to build needed competencies.

9. Recognize risks associated with projects and technology decisions. Maintain flexibility and backup plans as options for alternate decisions. Manage IT risks by minimizing regret.

10. Communicate the value of IS in business-relevant language. Describe how IT is adding value and increasing share holder value.

IT vision, strategy, maxims and stratagems vary depending on a firm's status. From the IT leadership perspective, an organization will find itself in three possible states: The enterprise may be struggling and fighting for it's survival; or it is maintaining its competitive position; or is breaking away from its competitors as its' growth is taking off in a surge of business revenues. In the struggling enterprise, IT is affected by cutting costs, cancelling projects and going through layoffs. In the maintaining enterprise, the business mirrors the economy and IT leadership is cautious

---

[16] "The New CIO Leader, Setting the Agenda and Delivering Results", Marianne Broadbent, Ellen S. Kitzis. Gartner, Inc., 2005, Harvard Business School Publishing.

about major projects, but does invest in smaller projects. For the surging business, IT is a major place for investment and time is of essence for delivering solutions. Sometimes a surge occurs as a result of mergers and acquisitions, while at other times one IT organization absorbs the other. In such situations, the organization with stronger processes, standards and skilled labor is likely to emerge as the winning model of IT organization. In all cases, the Lean IT leader is flexible and adaptable by choosing a different set of maxims and stratagems. But attributes of high-velocity, high-quality, high-precision, quality, service, design and process improvement remain as universal IT management themes. In all three states of business, Lean and Agile methods are invaluable although their application varies. In all cases, the goal of IT leadership is to deliver maximum value at the lowest cost.

Struggling enterprises apply Lean methods to eliminate waste and reduce costs. They might outsource portions of their services to outside agencies, or narrow the list of projects down to the most essentials. The maintaining enterprises, may segment large projects into smaller, more manageable chunks and apply Agile methods to complete them. The surging enterprises, may decide to out-source major projects with the goal of minimizing delivery time and increasing their market share. They might acquire other smaller businesses to improve their market positioning. Mergers and acquisitions pose interesting IT challenges of their own. Flexibility that Agile methods deliver will be an asset in these situations.

Don't get me wrong. Strategy is important, and the Lean leader is resolute in his or her commitment to the firm's vision, mission and strategy. However, it's through continuous problem solving and series of formulating stratagems that the Lean leader wins against the odds. The Lean IT leader is not afraid of tackling complex, tough IT problems. Lean IT leaders are measured by their effectiveness in the enterprise. The effective CIOs have mastered two domains of leadership:

1. They manage the demands of their customers. This is the demand-side of the IT leadership, the customer requests, expectations and objectives.

2. They also manage the internal IT resources, known as the supply-side of leadership, which delivers services. This involves managing the internal affairs and operations of the IT organization.

One of the challenges facing the CIOs is managing the IT organization in a structured way. IT organizations that rely on ad-hoc processes tend to have chaotic and unpredictable performances. A research study done at Ford Motor Corporation revealed that 80% of its management time was spent on firefighting. The study also showed that 50% of problems fixed were recurring again. Since problem solving was ad-hoc, decisions were made based on inadequate or inaccurate data and analytical tools. The result of constant firefighting severely affected the company's profit margins. Management was rewarding the best firefighters. It attacked the symptoms not the root causes. These findings eventually led to Ford Motor's 8D program and later to a Six Sigma initiative. The other challenge is the escalating complexity of IT. Competing priorities, conflicting roadmaps, new technology introductions, regulations, and changing customer demands add to the complexity of IT decisions. Recently several CIOs were interviewed about IT complexity. One described IT complexity as "leading to brittleness and high costs". Another CIO proposed that "When you reduce complexity, you increase your ability to implement new solutions."

To reduce complexity, Lean CIOs have discovered some new stratagems to be more effective:

1. Make process central to technology management; in particular devise processes that deliver high-velocity, high-quality and high precision work.
2. Define business strategy and business architecture in terms of IT architectural language. Define IT architecture that maps to business architecture.
3. Increase governance of technology infrastructure and relationship between IT and business. IT's processes must be based on architecture and architecture must be driven by key business processes. To manage complexity, architecture must be flexible to enable and anticipate change.

> **Success Stories of Lean & Agile Executive Vision**
>
> Staples, an office supply retail chain with 60,000 employees and revenues over $13 billion had a vision to implement a system that allows its managers link up to third-party vendors quickly without Information System Department's involvement. The IT group delivered a single gateway to third-party vendors' systems. Next, the company looked to improving financial efficiency. It implemented a fraud detection engine rapidly which reduced charge backs by more than 100%. When Marriott International executives decided to streamline their property management and room reservation systems, they turned to IT for help. The company embarked on a project to upgrade its reservation system to guarantee the best available room rate regardless of booking channel. A corporate CRM system was developed to integrate with each hotel's property management system while ensuring personalized service to its clients.
>
> Management at ProCard, headquartered in Golden, Colorado needed a new web-based flagship product to re-establish the company's presence on the web. They decided on a rapid development process and skunk work projects. Within five months the company had completed its web-based flagship product, while building a web services credit card processing system in less than six months.

IT Architecture as Business Architecture

Reliance on process and governance are good places to start. But as we shall read later, Lean principles can help reduce both IT complexity and cost. For example, Dow Chemical has a complex IT environment as it covers multiple business entities, business subsets and divisions. Dow Chemical uses a structured enterprise architecture and a service-oriented architecture to manage the subsets and changing relationships among those subsets within the overall architecture. Dow Chemical has successfully implemented an alignment of IT with its businesses through standardization of architecture and process. Strong governance on IT infrastructure and linkage to business objectives brings clarity to execution. Governance also forces establishing internal standards and performance metrics. Increasing links between IT and business implies that CIOs make joint decisions with their business counterparts being involved in the decision process. To achieve great results, we all recognize that IT must deliver on its promise in a visible and palpable way, benefiting the end customer. Let's look at some examples from Healthcare and Finance industries. Since user satisfaction with IT can directly impact delivery of quality patient care, being service-oriented is perhaps one of the easiest and lowest-cost approaches for IT to deliver tangible benefits that translate into value. In finance, the ability to service customers requires high availability of systems and detailed information services tailored to individual customers. These examples underscore the importance of service on the demand side of information technology as a benefit highly valued by IT customers. Lean IT leaders emphasize building service oriented mindset in both IT architectures and IT staff's attitude towards their work. I believe that using Lean methods and having a service oriented IT -whether it's architectural or just plain daily support, reinforce each other in a positive way.

IT architecture must map directly to the business architecture. In many successful companies, the IT architecture is the business strategy. Lean IT leaders participate in formulating business architectures for their firms. Business literature is filled with success stories where changing information structure rather than capital investments in physical plant have paid off the most by raising both the top-line and the bottom-line. In their book, "Value Acceleration: The Secrets to Building Unbeatable Competitive Advantage", authors Mitchell Gooze' and Ralph Mroz argue that competitive advantage goes to those firms who implement new management processes based on new technologies before their competition[17]. Firms that have implemented Lean production systems have a leading advantage over those who are just starting to consider its implementation.

Six Sigma has been applied to problem solving since its development in 1980's. These concepts are highly applicable to IT processes, services and application development. In a paper that evaluated *business process redesign* (BPR) cases, authors Rajiv Kohli and Ellen Hoadley note that IT executives typically focus on process improvements that increase productivity, customer value or profitability[18]. However, the executive perceptions of success were more favorable when all three goals were combined for process redesign. Continuous innovation and continuous improvement are the two benefits of Lean, Agile and Six Sigma IT. After an interview with several European CIOs, Andrew Ward, a journalist with Manufacturing Computer Solutions magazine reports that creating Agile information systems is a better investment than creating Agile inventory levels[19]. The CIOs conceded that "Customers are becoming more demanding and more unpredictable. And, with global over-capacity, manufacturers have to compete more on their ability to supply what customers want when they want it. That requires 'agility' - at least if there's a high degree of unpredictability and a lot of product variants ..." In his article, "Information

---

[17] "Value Acceleration, The Secrets to Building an Unbeatable Competitive Advantage", Mitchell Gooze and Ralph Mroz, by Elevate Publishing, 2007
[18] "Towards Developing a Framework for Measuring Operational Impact of IT-Enabled BPR: Case Studies of Three Firms, Rijiv Kohli and Ellen Hoadley, The DATA BASE for Advanced in Information Systems, Winter 2006 (Vol. 37, No. 1)
[19] "Information Instead of Inventory Going Agile", Andrew Ward, Manufacturing Computer Solutions, April, 2004

instead of inventory going Agile", he cites examples where using ERP applications, integrated forecasting tools and vendor managed inventory applications provided better information sharing between multiple suppliers and customers, thus reducing the need for carrying high inventory levels. For example, Dow Chemical was able to avoid building an expensive warehouse by implementing an agile material management system.

At Motorola, the CIO envisions IT architecture to accommodate and anticipate business goals by using business process management (BPM) principles and an enterprise reference architecture to define a common plan for business and IT. The enterprise reference architecture is a broad set of blueprints that shows the business, operations and systems layers. Success is built into these firms in the shape of information technology processes and process quality excellence. In a nutshell, information system process and quality should be the two uncompromisable organizational virtues. Neglecting IT governance, process and standards can bring costly consequences. Many of the failed IT projects are replete with such stories. The firms that have applied Lean IT leadership have tremendous success stories to tell. Those that created the business architecture before the IT architecture have aligned business and IT perpetually.

Case Study: Business Architecture Before IT Architecture

Texas Instruments, Inc, is a global semiconductor company and the world leader in manufacturing digital signal processing (DSP) and analog semiconductor components. Through 1980's the company's core operations such as material management, purchasing, inventory, logistics, sales, finance and accounting were carried on disjointed mainframe based applications. The company has over 30,000 customers worldwide. Its customer and manufacturing operations span 25 countries. In 1999, the company began an enterprise wide restructuring to revamp its operational information systems through a four-year, $250 million project. It started with business process re-engineering and then issued an RFP to select the right application for single Enterprise Resource Planning (ERP). After careful analysis and site visits, the company selected SAP, partly due to SAP's ability to handle very large volume database transactions. It also chose i2 system for advanced planning and optimization. The company released an early prototype in 1999 based on an open system platform. In phase two, the company released the SAP Procurement and Material Management module followed by the Financial Management and Reporting module. In the middle of 1999, TI completed the i2 Technologies software release. Finally, TI completed the remaining financials, new fields sales and distribution modules. It included a web-client package to be used with SAP and a next generation distributor-reseller management system.

The system is used by 10,000 TI employees to handle over 45,000 semiconductor devices and 120,000 orders per month. More than 3,000 external customers, resellers and distributors use the web client software. In total, over 70% of the business transactions with IT are done via the web or electronic data interchange (EDI). Among the factors in TI's success...

... were initial business and IT architectural decisions. As far as business architecture, TI decided that English will be the sole language for the application regardless of country of operation. It also decided to maintain a single global inventory of parts, regardless of which warehouse had a particular part. It instituted standard business operations for orders, order processing, supply chain management and standard information systems globally. The company's goal was to move toward supplier-managed inventory and customer-managed orders. Over the years, TI's business had shifted from commodity semiconductor manufacturing to customized, build to order products. This shift dramatically had increased the number of parts and complexity of resource planning, manufacturing, delivery and managing sales channels. The web client became a standard application for resellers and customers. TI's management are extensive users of metrics and fact-based decision making process. Strategic goals are translated into tactical and operational quantifiable objectives. Key metrics are developed and used as a fact-based management approach that help management keep clarity in their direction and decisions.

The metrics include standard operational and organizational measurements, such as Time, Cost, Flexibility and Quality. Since TI's manufacturing equipment is quite capital intensive, its management decided to measure level of use, Utilization as a key metric. TI's massive reengineering effort for the whole organization intended to set standard processes globally. The success of this effort was due in part to setting a single inventory globally and a single instance of MRP system. Unlike some firms who have implemented multiple MRP instances, TI management insisted on one standard, common MRP system. It was anticipated that the restructuring would bring 3%-5% improvement in output which amounts to cost savings of several hundred million dollars. Among standardized business architecture changes, TI decided on an 18-character, globally accepted part number. This decision required huge IS and business effort because changes had to be made to databases and programs, in addition to notifying customers of this change. Also, the company standardized on the authorization amounts for purchases. The number of levels of approvals on a purchase order was reduced to four (some countries had fifteen levels).

The New Economics of IT

The Lean and Agile thinking bring a new set of economics to IT. Lean IT leaders identify the sources of value and cost. The fundamentals are simple. *Return on Investment* (ROI) increases as new systems and applications are released to production. ROI decreases when waste rework and unfinished projects accumulate. Work in progress, rework and any unfinished project forms the IT *Inventory*. The positive driver of profitability is *Throughput*, namely how quickly we release solutions into production. A negative driver of profitability is *Operating Expense*, namely the cost of maintenance, application support, operational costs and repairs. Investments consist of the initial capital investments (known as the initial liability) and the deferred investments (known as the deferred liability). Initial capital investments are used for upfront acquisition costs of technology and solutions. Deferred liability is about expenses which are deferred (for the time being) but are inevitable. Some of our poor decision making can lead to deferred expenses, namely technical debt which must be eventually resolved in the future and sometimes at very high costs.

Just as an example, let's assume that the cost of acquiring a new system, the upfront system purchase cost is $15 million. This is the initial *Liability*. Also assume that the Throughput, or cash generated from this project is $85 million per year. And, the operating expense annually is $20 million. The project takes 2 years to complete, so the total operating expense for the project is twice that amount, or $40 million. During implementation, the IT group decides to postpone implementing a redundant database which would offer the optimal business continuity. The cost of implementing a redundant database is $3 million. This is the deferred cost or future Liability.

The next diagram describes the major drivers of ROI with Information Technology perspective[20]. Let's start with defining *Net Profit* and ROI. Assuming a constant rate of investment, we can calculate:

Net Profit = Throughput − Operating Expense

Investment = Initial Liability + Future Liability

Initial Liability = Upfront Capital Expenses

Future Liability = Deferred Technical Debt

$$\text{Return on Investment} = \frac{\text{Net Profit}}{\text{Investment}}$$

Using the example above, we can compute the Net profit as follows:

Net Profit = $85M - $40M = $45M

Investment = 15M + $3M = $18M

Return on Investment = $45M/$18M = 250%

Of course, we're simplifying the calculation outright by not showing the net present value of money here, but in the next chapters, we will review a financial model that analyzes return on investment per project in more detail. The point from this calculation is that if the company was able to complete the project in half that time by using Agile and Lean methods, then its Net Profit would be $65 million and Return on Investment would be 361%! Lean thinking advocated keeping no inventories. Similarly

---

[20] Agile Management for Software Engineering, Applying the Theory of Constraints for Business Results. David J. Anderson, Prentice Hall, 2004

the goal of faster throughput is to minimize the unfinished and lingering IT projects. In fact a company did something very close to that. Consider Group Health Cooperative located in Seattle, Washington. This managed health organization employs about 9,500 staff with revenues of $1.9 billion. The company has implemented several Lean programs for the last 2 years. It began a workflow redesign program that allows physicians see 20 percent more patients daily. The IT department upgraded its member website to include patient information and secure messaging with doctors, thus increasing revenues and return on its IT investment. Since the company was able to cut the development time from two years to one year, in effect it cut its IT operating cost and inventory in half. This concept is illustrated in the next two diagrams. First a definition for IT Liability, Throughput and operational components are given below.

Throughput Rate of cash generated from IT solutions & deliverables released into production	
Investment (Initial Liability) Upfront cost of purchasing, acquisition of technology or products to satisfy a client-valued function or idea	**Inventory** Sum of money vested in partially developed solutions, unfinished projects, work in progress, fixes pending final test and release, and incomplete projects
Investment (Future Liability) Technical debt: all deferred expenses associated with release of technology, products, or projects which need to be fixed or completed in the future	**Operating Expense** Cash to pay for implementation of solutions and applications. Plus the cash for repairs, upkeep & maintenance of existing applications, & infrastructure

Fig 2.1 – The Elements of New IT Economics

To summarize, IT management must focus its attention on managing five things to make greater profits and better ROI:

Increase Throughput: This is the rate of cash that a firm can generate from IT solutions. To increase throughput (namely cash from receivables) is to accelerate the rate at which IT delivers solutions to business ideas. Increasing Throughput is proportional to the rate of completing IT deliverables. Deliverables are simply projects that include new applications, new infrastructure, tools, upgrades, application or system integrations or feature enhancements in response to client demand.

Decrease Operating Expense: This is the cash spent on maintaining the existing systems, support and service for users (internal clients) and the sum of money required to build new IT solutions based on client ideas or work requests.

Decrease Inventory: This is the volume of unfinished projects, work in progress, solutions that require rework and fixes pending final test. One approach to decreasing inventory is to outsource certain portions of IT projects or to apply Lean and Agile methods to complete the unfinished projects quickly.

Decrease Investment (Initial Liability): This is the sum of money spent for acquisition of new technology or applications, typically the upfront cost of acquiring new solutions and implementing them. Investment includes the upfront cost of implementation from idea inception to final release and acceptance of solutions.

Decrease Investment (Future Liability): These are the deferred investments and expenses that will be required in the future by the organization, namely the *technical debt*. The expenses are deferred because the client has agreed to receive such client valued functionality in the future or because IT cannot deliver such solutions in a short time horizon. Certain IT projects that get postponed should be regarded as future liability. Certain poorly conceived decisions or architectures result in technical liability, which need to be addressed in the future. To properly account for Future Liability, we apply the present value of such investments. But, in many cases this technical debt is hidden from the C-executives and unfortunately can be a substantial liability.

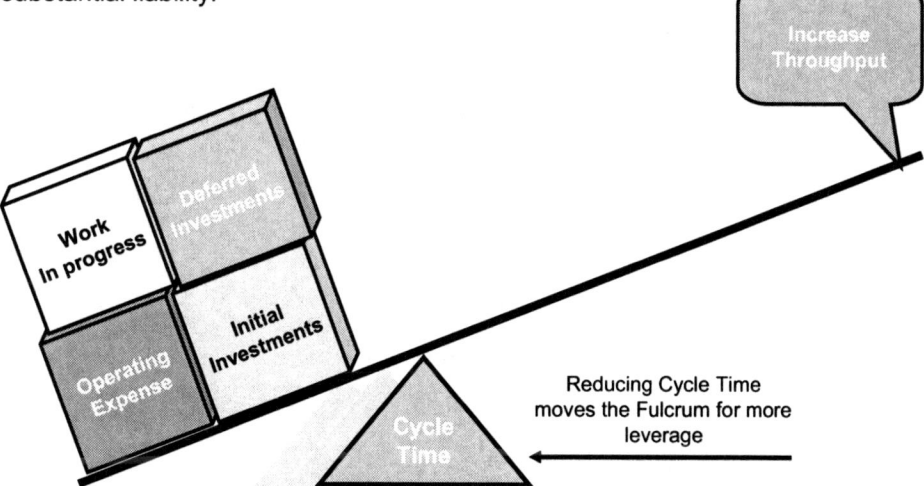

Fig. 2.2 – How Reducing Cycle Time Increases Leverage for Return on IT

This diagram illustrates the power of decreasing cycle time by showing an IT lever lifting the capital (both initial and deferred investments), inventory (work in progress and unfinished projects) and operating expense. Cycle time is the frequency in which IT delivers solutions to the firm. As we accelerate the frequency of deliverables, the cycle time decreases, thereby the fulcrum of leverage moves to give the IT management more leverage in form of return on IT investment. The Lean IT leader's goal should be managing this lever (by increasing throughput) in order to raise return on investment for the firm.

Linking Business Stratagems and IT Stratagems

IT stratagems must come from business strategies. IT Stratagems explain why as well as what. The main purpose of IT stratagems is to communicate the implications of business strategy in the context of information systems. To illustrate this by examples, consider the following table. In each row a business stratagem is listed along with its corresponding IT stratagems. If an IT activity is going against the stratagems, it's easy to correct it, because at any given time, we can link the IT stratagems to business stratagems.

> **Stratagem:** Define and craft the firm's business architecture first before building the IT architecture.

Business Stratagem	IT Stratagem
- Maximize synergy between all business functions in the enterprise	- Develop enterprise-wide standards and processes for implementation and services
- Provide services to clients from any service point	- Deliver information and access to applications for users from anywhere and anytime
- Be able to detect and respond quickly to shifts in market and change services accordingly	- Maintain component-based and service-oriented architectures that can be implemented in parallel and integrated quickly - Agile developers must be combined in company's product development teams. - Maintain a rapid product evaluation process for evaluating off-the-shelf products.
- Maximize economies of scale through shared and synchronized quarterly objectives	- Enable quarterly objectives by delivering shared infrastructure and consistent best practices across multiple divisions. - Remove barriers to sharing information and customer support across the enterprise.

Table 2.1 – Example of Linking Business Stratagems and IT Stratagems

Business strategies and stratagems must be developed first. They must be normalized and communicated across the enterprise before we embark on formulating the IT stratagems. IT stratagems can be developed in leadership workshops or at retreats consisting of select business managers representing a functional cross section of the business and IT managers. IT architects, directors of development and infrastructure should attend such workshops.

The workshop begins with review of business strategies and understanding the business intent of those strategies. The outcome of this phase is a blue print for business architecture. Often in every organization, there is an executive who is the de facto business architect. This executive might have the title of CEO, COO, CFO or VP of marketing, but they have clear vision of what the business strategies are and how they will be realized. The business architect must be present in the IT stratagem workshops. The business architecture discussions include answering questions about how integrated or autonomous each business divisions are. It considers all business models used by each division, and how the firm delivers value to its customers. The business architecture would articulate the interdependencies between different aspects of the business. It would describe how internal functions support one another to deliver value to the customer.

Ultimately, the discussions surrounding business architecture carry to IT architecture as they define the requirements for IT infrastructure, whether each function requires shared "thin" or "thick" services, and what should be the critical and mission-critical critical information system capabilities. The astute IT managers can sense the formulation of IT stratagems evolve as they consider the business architect discussions.

In the next phase of stratagem workshop, the group develops maxims and rules that enable each business stratagem. They also consider barriers to implementing each business stratagem and how information systems can overcome those barriers. The next chapter presents twelve axioms that can be used as management model by Lean IT leadership to govern and lead the IT organization.

GQM: Goal-Question-Metric as a Lean Governance Tool

GQM is an important problem solving and design tool. GQM was originally developed by Basili's group at the University of Maryland as the disciplined approach to define and collect metrics. Later it was adopted as part of Software Engineering Institute (SEI) Capability Maturity Model Integration (CMMI). This 10 step process is used to identify business goals, questions related to those goals and measurements that help answer them and how those measurements can be collected. The result of applying this approach to an IT problem is the specification of a system targeting a particular set of issues or requirements. The resulting model has three levels:

1. **Conceptual Level (Goal):** The goal defines the ideal, future state services, features, workflows and products
2. **Operational Level (Question):** A set of questions that define how the goal can be achieved and which features and functions are critical to achieving the goal.
3. **Quantitative Level (Metric):** A set of measurements associated with each question that indicate and track our progress towards achieving the goal.

GQM is a hierarchical model. Each level is connected to lower levels by links. A modified GQM model can map to a balanced score card model[21]. If you are able to assign a priority to Goals, Questions and Metrics at each level, you can create a balanced score card. The weight associated with each link determines the importance or degree of influence that a parameter has on it predecessor. GQM is a critical tool for Lean, Agile and Six Sigma IT governance. Using GQM, IT governance can be accomplished with clarity and enforcing priorities easier to manage.

For example, Figure 2.3 shows how an IT governance committee was able to simplify the enterprise vision (Goals), translate those goals into IT initiatives (Questions) and measure IT performance (Metrics).

---

[21] Balanced Score Card is a Six Sigma tool described in Chapter 19.

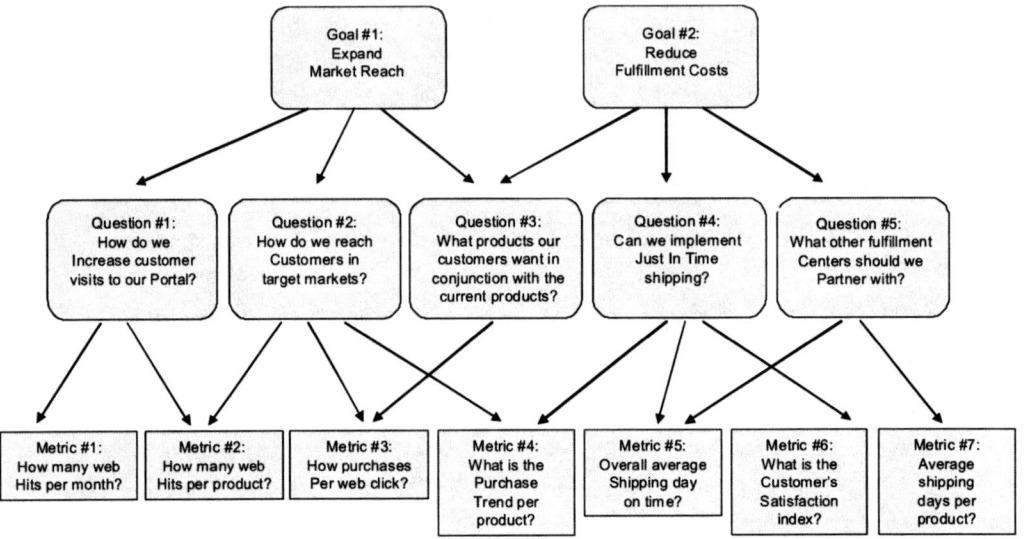

Fig 2.3 – GQM as a Governance Method - Example

Summary

Lean IT Leader brings the following characteristics to IT management:

- High velocity, high quality, high precision mindset to development and operations
- Partakes in defining business architecture a much as the IT architecture
- Is not afraid to tackle tough, complex IT problems
- Applies Lean methods to improve processes, Agile to improve delivery timelines and Six Sigma for quality design and control
- Leads through creating IT maxims, stratagems and culture of quality, service and value adding activities
- Delivers personal value, organizational value and trust
- Creates and leads the IT governance group consisting of C-executives
- Educates the CEO, CFO and other C-executives about information technology and its value adding capability
- Must go and see the problems and listen to the voice of the customer first hand.
- Attention to keeping IT inventory and operating costs low by applying Lean, Agile and Six Sigma methods described in the following chapters.
- Create governance structure using GQM to clarify IT direction and success criteria at the enterprise level

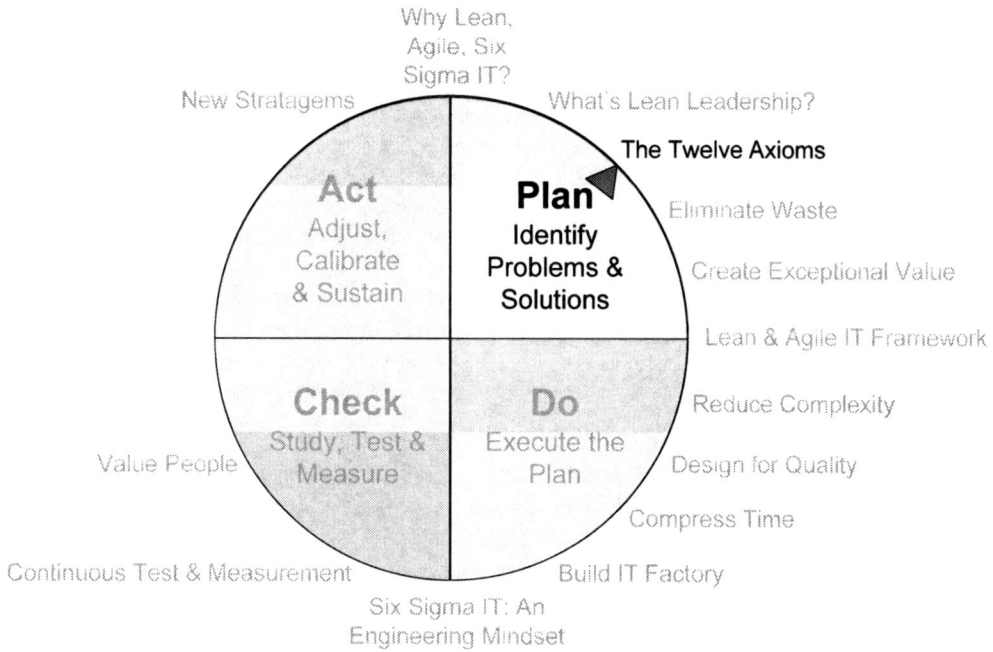

"The Toyota production system, however, is not just a production system. I am confident it will reveal its strength as a management system."

Taiichi Ohno

Chapter 3. The Twelve Axioms of Lean, Agile and Six Sigma IT Management

Lean thinking centers on 5 elemental principles: Identify *value*, develop *value streams*, determine the product and information *flow*, create a *pull* system of production, and strive to reach *perfection* in quality and process. We shall see that these principles take on a higher meaning when enabled by information technology or applied to IT management itself.

Lean principles are explained in detail by James Womack and Daniel Jones in their book, "Lean Thinking", but here is a brief explanation. *Value* is the sum of benefits, both tangible and intangible, that the customer enjoys as a result of product features or services. In the realm of information technology, customers can be internal or external. The value of information and information systems can be static, meaning at face value or can be highly powerful and strategic, if implemented accordingly. James Womack and colleagues[22] describe *value stream* as is a sequence of discrete steps that describe the flow of product, work in progress or services from start (raw materials) to the final step (finished product) for delivering the proposed value to the customer. IT applications enable value streams for the company. Likewise, value streams in IT come in many forms, from business analysis to application development to new technology solutions. They all create value for the IT customers.

---

[22] "Lean Thinking: Banish Waste and Create Wealth in Your Corporation", Womack, James P., and Daniel T. Jones, New York: Simon & Schuster. 1996.

Flow is about the rate and pace of productivity in a value stream. It's measured by *Takt time*. Takt Time is the time internal required to build one product to meet the customer demand. In other words, it's the frequency at which the production system must produce to meet the customer's order. A continuous flow, or single piece flow is ideal and can be attained when the production rate runs at Takt time. For example, the rate and tempo of releasing new functionality or application modules determines the Takt time for IT. We want takt time to be consistent and short. This is achieved by reducing development cycle time as we discussed in the last chapter.

Pull system is a type of flow where downstream customer or user pulls materials through the production system. The pull action generates a signal upstream notifying the system to resume production and flow. In contrast, a push system attempts to flow production from raw materials to typically inventory predicting a customer order. The goal of a Lean production system is to level out production to a constant production heartbeat, or Takt time. In order to level out the production, we must break large orders or large batches into smaller lots or smaller runs. For example, a large IT project would be broken down into smaller chunks of deliverables. When customers request a new application feature, they pull on the IT production system. But, when IT managers add the request to their portfolio of projects, or inventory of work in progress, they create a push production system. Ideally, we want customers to pull by requesting features and applications, not for managers pushing the project portfolio on to the IT organization. To Lean thinkers, the pursuit of *perfection* is a continuous improvement goal achieved through repeated application of Lean principles, in particular removing waste and defects, problem solving and process refinement. The goal of Lean production systems is to provide maximum value to customers at the lowest cost to manufacture. They argue that "value" is defined by the customer and that "value streams" start from the customer back to the producer. Production is governed by a "pull" system that cascades back from customer demand. To be Lean we would only replenish what the next step of operation requires at short intervals. "Flow" of value adding processes or materials move in one piece without interruption to the customer. To strive for "excellence" the producer must create a culture of continuous improvement.

Deming who is credited with the Total Quality Movement had a 14-point quality system. Deming's 14-points attempt to remove variation out of a production system, create a constancy of purpose towards improvement, and break-down of barriers between departments. Deming believed that once quality is built-into the process and variation is removed, inspections are not as necessary. Furthermore, Deming insisted on learning, self improvement and institutional education, in particular about its internal quality and processes. Deming's teachings had profound and lasting effect in cultivating quality movement in Japan. Lean production system principles developed by Toyota Motors were the reason for its global competitive advantage. This system rests on four stratagems or four "P"s:

1. Philosophy of long term thinking;
2. The right Processes to eliminate waste and create Just-In-Time Flow;
3. People, including partnerships, respect and stretch;
4. Problem solving which captures continuous improvement and learning.

According to some industry reports, in a single year, Toyota employees offered more than 700,000 improvement suggestions. This number represents about 10 improvement suggestions per employee per year. Toyota implemented more than 99% of those suggestions.

Jeffrey K. Liker lists 14 principles behind Toyota's Production System in his book, The Toyota Way[23]. **The 14 principles are:**

Principle 1:

Base your management decisions on a long-term philosophy even at the expense of short term financial goals

Principle 2:

Create continuous process flow to bring problems to the surface.

Principle 3:

Use "pull" systems to avoid overproduction.

Principle 4:

Level out the workload.

Principle 5:

Build a culture of stopping to fix problems, to get quality right the first time.

Principle 6:

Standardized tasks are the foundation for continuous improvement and employee empowerment

Principle 7:

Use visual control so no problems are hidden.

Principle 8:

Use only reliable, thoroughly tested technology that serves your people and processes.

Principle 9:

Grow leaders who thoroughly understand the work, live the philosophy and teach it to others.

Principle 10:

Develop exceptional people and team who follow your company's philosophy.

Principle 11:

Respect your extended network of partners and suppliers by challenging them and helping them improve.

Principle 12:

Go and see for yourself to thoroughly understand the situation.

Principle 13:

Make decisions slowly by consensus, thoroughly considering all options; implement decisions rapidly.

---

[23] "The Toyota Way, 14 Management Principles From the World's Greatest Manufacturer", Jeffery K. Liker. McGraw-Hill, 2004

Principle 14:

Become a learning organization through relentless reflection and continuous improvement.

In 2004, authors Mary and Tom Poppendieck wrote a book entitled, "Lean Software Development". In their book they offered seven principles for Lean development of software: Eliminate Waste, Build quality in, Create knowledge, Defer commitment, Deliver fast, Respect people, Optimize the whole[24]. While their perspective was focused on software development, many of the same principles apply to how we manage and deploy Information systems. What if we distilled the vast knowledge, best practices, success factors and experience about Lean, Agile and Six Sigma principles into a few axioms for achieving perfection? That was my initial attempt and motivation to write this book. I've been able to summarize them into 12 axioms. The following is a short description and highlights for each axiom. Chapters 4 to 19 cover each axiom in more detail. Let's briefly recap the 12 Axioms of Lean, Agile and Six Sigma IT management in more detail:

1. **Eliminate Waste: Perform Kaizen events to identify sources of waste and eliminate them.**

   The goal of this axiom is to define and document the key processes in IT. We need to identify the key value streams; Re-engineer processes to create continuous workflows; and eliminate non-value adding activities and instead apply freed up resources to high-impact tasks. We should strive to reduce any project idle time or wait time to achieve continuous flow of work and non-stop creative development. My advice is to make work flows and status of projects visible as they progress from one stage to the next. It's important that as IT managers we identify and remove barriers to continuous development and innovation flow in the IT organization. Barriers that disrupt development flow or cause projects to sit idle are common. They appear in form of inadequate tools, insufficient lab space, overly tight budgets, delays in testing, bureaucratic approvals instead of reviews that provide feedback, delays due to sick-leaves and stop-and-go styles of management. These sources of delay must be removed as we encourage rapid build-and-test cycles to eliminate wait times. Before solving problems Lean IT managers get the facts and data firsthand by looking at problems at the scene. Even high level IT executives should go and see the issues for themselves, so they can relate to the problem and understand the situation. IT managers should think and speak based on facts and personally verified data. In order to eliminate waste avoid duplication of efforts and re-inventing the existing solutions. Avoid developing from faulty designs, and faulty assumptions about customer requirements. For example, I participate in testing activities, even if it's only for a few minutes, so I can get a sense for the quality of applications being developed. During all system introductions or application releases, I make the effort to be present to observe the process. Right after the release, I talk to customers to get their feedback. If a problem continues to occur, it signals a process or quality issue. As a role model for my staff, I always committed to visiting the problem areas and observing

---

[24] "Lean Software Development", Mary and Tom Poppendieck, Addison Wesley Publishing, 2004. Also, see, "Implementing Lean Software Development, From Concept to Cash" by same authors, Addition Wesley Publishing, 2007.

the specific problems first hand. Often the issues were not exactly the same as the reports I was given. Subsequently, it was easier to relate to root-cause analysis and troubleshooting process, and the customers really appreciated to see my involvement. Waste is caused by partially done programs and churn in customer requirements. Waste can be eliminated by reducing development cycle time and by increasing the frequency of release cycles. Development cycles improve by reducing the inventory of partially completed projects and features that were not necessary in the first place. My advice is to avoid testing long after the code is completed because it results in longer test-and-fix cycles. Immediate testing after each development cycle reduces the chance of development churn. Eliminating waste starts with eliminating rework and the need for post production fixes in the field. Delayed projects inherently produce significant waste for the IT production system and the rest of the firm.

2. **Deliver exceptional value: Identify customers' value drivers and focus on delivering value beyond customers' expectation.**

If there were only one rule to apply to find and keep customers, it must be this one: Listen to the voice of the customer (VOC). Then earn their business and trust by understanding the customer's business and workflows. As IT managers, we must determine how IT can solve customers' problems and add significant value, strategic, tactical and operational value. We must focus on developing the customer-valued features and functions; Identify the value streams, value chain and how IT can produce value in each step of workflow. This principle advocates applying Information Technology to generate exceptional value for the customer, your customer's customers and the community at large. It promotes evaluating every activity and function in the IT organization to terms of ability to create value. IT organizations that have established the role of "business architect" have made huge gains in strategic alignment of business and IT. This role has typically been shared across senior IT analysts and business managers or even executives without the emphasis that it deserves. Lean IT places high importance on consolidating this role into what I call a "business architect". The business architect is an experienced senior business analyst, sometimes an IT consultant who can perform two critical functions: A) define key value streams and value drivers across organizational boundaries and B) translate those definitions and requirements into Information System (IS) solutions.

3. **Reduce Complexity: Manage complexity by reducing interdependencies and conflicting objectives.**

One of the characteristics that I offer for Lean leadership is the willingness to tackle the tough, complex problems. The Lean leader does not hide behind bureaucracy to avoid problems, instead confronts the complex problems, breaks them down into smaller pieces and then reassembles the pieces in form of a solution. The goal of this axiom is to remove interdependencies. Simplify and standardize architecture, project management, development, test and release processes. This is where we apply the "5S" method to reduce complexity; Establish IT governance to resolve any conflicting priorities or objectives; Simplify and streamline IT workflows and processes. Next, we form internal group of IT consultants who engage in business problem solving with IT customers and help them identify the right IT solutions for their needs. Mange change across multiple dimensions, in particular change management in IT and technology. Lean IT managers strive to solve Information system issues while they are small and solvable before they grow too complex and costly to fix.

4. Design for Quality: Develop processes for every IT task. Perform high-level and low-level designs followed by design reviews to ensure quality

The culture of high quality places high value on customer satisfaction. To achieve this axiom, Lean IT managers establish a quality culture for the IT staff and train the staff to have a high expectation for quality. My advice is to build a system and environment that reveals errors and defects early. The goal of design for quality is multi-dimensional: to mistake-proof solutions; to prevent error creep with better design, and remove errors by applying "permanent" fixes. IT management can achieve this by stage-gating development and building project plans that insist on well defined specifications, not necessarily fully completed specifications. Encourage periodic design reviews, code inspections and code walkthroughs, review of test plans and test results. IT staff must be empowered to move up quality related issues directly to the top management. Emphasize testing quickly after each phase of development is completed. Engage customers in testing to gain their feedback as early in the test cycle as possible. Building quality into the service and product begins with robust design, clear specifications and implementation methods that solicit user participation.

Every IT artifact should be designed before it is implemented. Too often, IT organizations spend a lot of analysis time and then rush into implementation, skipping an important step: design. High level design, low level design followed by design reviews are necessary to build for quality. Hiring IT architects and designers to augment the expertise of business analysts is a way to match the resources against the IT challenges. The goal of building quality is the discipline of inspecting for defects before releasing the application, not after. Keeping a defect list or issues log is OK. But such logs represent the unfinished work queue and thus waste in Lean production environment. The objective should be to have no issues or defects in the queue. To achieve this objective, we need to implement test-driven development. Similarly with IT implementations, we must think about developing the test environment and use cases for testing as we design the solution. We must ask questions like: "How will we test this application before release into production?" Similarly, a programmer before writing any code would ask: "How will I test my code?" Reducing the number of defects, will expand the available resource capacity to do other development projects.

5. Compress Time: Apply Lean and Agile methods to deliver IT solutions faster by reducing Cycle Time.

Rapid delivery of software applications, IT solutions and technology deployments in general will improve customer satisfaction and lowering risk. It also allows delivering solutions before user requirements or environment changes that affect product specifications. If the IT production system takes on a slow course, we run the risk of perpetually changing the application for ever and never releasing anything. To reduce complexity and accelerate delivery time, it's advisable to split the project into multiple releases: for example into a technical release and a business release. My advice is to focus on the 20% of solution that satisfies 80% of customer's requirements. Identify the critical customer requirements (CCRs). Perform design reviews and continuous testing to accelerate delivery time. Quite often this is possible by refactoring legacy applications. When appropriate improve the delivery time (and ROI) by re-using an existing solution. When I was hired as vice president of engineering at a firm, I observed this problem first-hand: an IT organization with limited resources attempting disparately to release a large, enterprise-wide application. To remedy the delays, I concentrated the development team on developing the core business functions and set a deadline to release the product rapidly. A second group tested the application on a daily basis as new releases became available. I also formed a third group, consisting of users to evaluate the releases on a weekly basis. That delighted the users since it gave them an opportunity to be involved in the process, and also to discover any wrong assumptions that developers might have made. The initial release of the application was received positively by the user community. Thereafter, each new release could adjust to customer changes quickly and at a low cost. The same is true of maintaining IT infrastructure. Slow updates and fixes result in accumulated queue of work, which add to the organizational stress and lead to inadequate or fragile infrastructure. We developed a standard Method of Procedure policy for rapidly applying changes at the earliest possible maintenance window. Standardization, eliminating wait and waste, testing and focus on key CCRs gave the IT organization the high velocity development framework it needed.

6. Build the IT Factory: Continuous Innovation in Practice

Building repeatable, stable and measurable methods in all IT activities has huge paybacks. A factory approach to IT means that all relevant processes, people and procedures are well understood, documented, and organized ready for deployment in advance. The goal is to have predictability, consistency and regular timing on your IT processes. This is fundamental to creating a system of flow and pull. Standardization applies to all tools for problem solving, software development, development environment, design methodologies, architecture, hardware, security, operations, networks and customer service. The IT managers, who have developed IT factories, create consistent processes and component-based development to deliver solutions at regular intervals. In Lean manufacturing environments, "pull" systems allow your downstream customers to get what they want, when they want it and in manner and quantity they want. They minimize work-in-progress, unfinished work and inventory by stocking small amounts of each product. In IT environments, "pull" is generated by customer demands for services and features. The goal of a pull system in IT must be to establish rapid delivery of services and response to customer needs. Minimizing analysis time, rapid problem solving and delivering "adequately done" solutions are the key enablers of this system. The "pull" system provides customers with immediate service and response from IT staff to address their issues.

It implies being responsive to day-to-day challenges that customers face. Providing rapid solutions, decision support reports, problem solving and application customizations or rapid handling of feature requests are the basic examples of creating a "pull" system. The entire IT factory and its flow are managed by a production manager. A production manager is someone who maintains the tempo of iterative releases into production while keeping the work leveled and monitoring the overall product quality. In the following chapters, we will review how establishing the production manager role, virtual Lean IT teams and matrix organizations can support the "pull" system for IT production system. Pundits advise that we create a work system to level out the workload to a consistent rate and avoid overburdening staff.

Eliminating waste helps reduce workload. While, eliminating root causes of failures and systemic weaknesses which cause system downtimes and service disruptions are steps towards leveling the workload. Mistakenly some managers engage in resource leveling exercises but miss the mark completely. It's wrong to level out resources. Instead we should level out the workload by properly assigning the tasks to the appropriate IT personnel. To level-out the workload appropriately we match the complexity of IT tasks to the skill level of IT staff. Within each IT organization, the skill level, ability to solve complex technical challenges and level of experience vary as much as 100 fold.

Assign the complex tasks to more skilled staff. Assign the high-risk projects to the more experienced teams. Depending on the situation, bring automated tools, contractors or smart-sourcing where appropriate to level out the workload. Identify and eliminate constraints and bottlenecks in the IT organization for delivery of solutions. An IT factory implements proven technologies rapidly. The work-cells have a clear idea of the processes that apply to their project, such as concurrent development, Agile testing methods and integration of components. When IT factories work with new technologies they develop a quick prototype first. A prototype should be done in less than 6 weeks, ideally in 2 weeks. Once the prototype is complete, the rest of the development effort is segmented and sequenced into repeatable and low risk iterative development cycles. Delivering a consistent, regular tempo of delivering solutions is the mark of an IT factory. IT factories are enabled by forming work-cells, component-based integration and developing by patterns. Work-cells consist of people who are trained to produce solutions consistently and consistent with pre-established rapid development processes. The necessary tools, framework, architecture and design methodologies have already been established by the IT factory production manager.

7. Continuously Test & Measure: Develop a culture of testing, gathering facts and measurement data about processes, applications and services.

Information technology must serve employees and their processes, not the other way around. Lean IT managers, avoid using or releasing unreliable technology and hard-to-use applications that impact flow. They reject technology and product choices that conflict with the quality culture or cause instability, unpredictability and reliability issues. They release solutions that have been adapted to your environment. Before releasing applications or changing infrastructure, Lean IT managers fully test the application through a pilot program.

They test all of the functions that the solution was intended for; maintain a lab that mimics the real world environment for comprehensive testing, verification and validation of solutions, all done before release. Based on the lessons learned, the experts suggest that we create visual displays and reports to show if any projects or processes are falling out of specification or expected range; Monitor all systems, applications, appliances and network devices to determine their status, performance levels and function; maintain logs of system downtimes and plot them on a time series graph, because we are interested in visually detecting patterns and trends. A culture of testing implies that we insist on continuous monitoring of key system parameters; set thresholds and boundary points for those parameters to alert of any degradation or threshold violation; use visual displays to indicate cascading impact of one or more system failures on departmental as well as global business functions. The philosophy of using visual controls applies similarly to visuals that indicate status of projects, workload, defect quantities, efforts to fix defects, trouble ticket backlogs, customer feature requests and customer tickets in progress and pending. There are more metrics to track and visually display. I've included some examples of metrics as I discuss Six Sigma methods in Chapters 11 and 12. To show visual status of information systems, effective IT managers provide corporate-wide online access to metrics such as system uptime metrics, current application response time, transaction volumes and similar operational IT statistics. We don't' know what to fix if we don't test and if we don't know about data and trends.

> 8. **Value People: Respect your people. Keep them accountable and trust them with the responsibility to make decisions.**

When it comes to managing people, a common stratagem that Lean thinkers suggest is around the trio of: Respect, Responsibility and Recognition of people. Lean IT managers grow leaders from within rather than hiring them from outside. In a Lean IT organization, all staff are expected to be leaders and role models to their peers and customers. They are expected to exemplify quality culture, service and the willingness to <u>own</u> business <u>*challenges*</u>. This is the responsibility dimension. IT Leaders must understand the daily work and know the customer's expectations in detail. They must exemplify, teach and promote the company's culture and values. They must be eager to meet with customers, see the problems first-hand, coach the IT staff; participate in problem solving and executing decisions flawlessly.

Since Information technology is a common thread across all organizational functions, we must use IT as the platform to achieve cross functional participation. Successful IT organizations promote team work and create virtual teams. As Lean IT managers, we must build teams to improve quality, productivity, customer satisfaction and flow; create shared vision and frames of context for IT staff to cooperate with one another and with customers. Is it important to encourage IT staff to participate in Kaizen teams formed by customers to solve technical and business problems? Absolutely, in fact we should welcome and lead such activities by forming IT user groups and meeting with customer leadership periodically to inform users of new developments and gather their feedback, requests and issues. People are inherently driven by the need to be recognized. Recognition is a major motivator. According to one of my colleagues, a doctor and behavioral scientist, "recognition is regarded as the most fundamental of human needs more than food, shelter and self actualization". Do you adequately and individually recognize and appreciate the IT staff in your organization? The principle of "respect for the individual" goes beyond employees and customers. Lean IT managers treat suppliers, solution vendors and providers with respect and view them as extensions of their IT organization. Just as they set stretch goals for their staff, they set stretch targets of quality, process maturity and standardization for their suppliers and solution partners. They are able to maintain a highly symbiotic and tight partnership with key vendors, those who supply the IT organization with critical software tools, contractors, and infrastructure equipment. Strong partnership and close relationship comes handy if you get in a bind and need their help. Leveraging this relationship, with every purchase, they are successful in using the vendor's resources as much as possible before using their internal IT resources for implementations. A sign of respect for individuals is to listen and value everyone's opinions and input. During major implementations or product development projects, I create virtual teams where every project participant is heard and is treated as equal partners in the business. When it comes to perform heroic tasks, the project members own the problems and accept accountability to complete them. Often they volunteer their weekend and holidays to work and finish the tasks ahead of schedule, since they own the challenges now. Similarly, when an issue or problem arises, the team does not focus on the individual but on fixing the process. The same mantra applies to code reviews, design reviews and peer reviews of MOP documents. As a result the team members feel secure and confident that their work is appreciated and are willing to give more.

9. Decide for the Long Haul: Maintain a long time horizon for IT decisions.

Making the right decisions must be undoubtedly one of the hardest things that IT managers are faced with. The problem is not just that the future is unknown, but because many facts about the present are also unknown. Often we feel the pressure to make quick decisions to save the day, but can't see past the immediate outcome and the potential unintended consequences of our decisions. Lean IT leaders establish information system plans with long term view of the business needs, technology forecast and market trends. We must consider all facts, scenarios and potential options when making decisions; discuss possible decisions with people who know the work and are affected; and follow methodical decision making process to find the optimal decision. They defer decisions to the latest time possible until more facts are available. And once the decision is made, they implement it with lightning speed. They recognize that flexibility is important to long term survival. So, they prefer those decision paths that offer the most flexibility through the solution's life cycle over those which limit future options and may lead to a dead-end.

Lean IT managers should seek the larger purpose and mission for IT organization in the firm; organize, align and grow the IT staff towards a common purpose that is bigger than the short term gains. It pays to establish a long range philosophical mission, one that goes beyond application releases and milestones as the foundation for the IT organization. To make sound decisions, we need facts. Often, our decisions about a project are either irreversible or very costly to change. It's best to defer such decisions until they are absolutely required. While planning is a useful exercise, plans must be flexible to change and adapt to the changing conditions. Often IT projects fail, because they make many critical decisions early in the project before adequate data and information about the implementation are available. Subsequently, traditional project managers make futile attempts to stick to the plan. Often they are held accountable to the original plan by the upper management. Such rigid commitments to strategic plans cause further digression from reality to become sure bets on project failure. Decisions that can be postponed to a later time should be deferred until more data is available. Too often IT managers make a short term decision that in the long run leads down to a costly dead-end. IT managers must keep the flexibility of decisions in mind. At the start of most initiatives and projects there are multiple decision paths available to a manager. The Lean IT manager must ensure that by taking a path which might seem optimal initially, they are not incurring future liabilities. In other words, take the decision path that keeps your future decision options open. Finally, traditional IT managers often make the mistake of choosing a course of action which has good short term return (or good face value) but on the downside the decision carries high risks that lead to huge costs and regrets. In other words, we must choose decision paths that have lower regret costs and ensure that a hedge plan is in place. I remember being asked to rescue an ailing project a few years ago. It involved implementing a new enterprise application for the company. It expected to serve over one thousand users. The Chief Technology Officer had chosen thin client devices for this application. On the surface, it was a good decision because thin clients were low cost and low maintenance.

But, since the application was yet to be completed and stabilized, there were many uncertainties associated with the technology components and revisions. Just as the application was being released, the thin client devices were deemed under powered. They had to be replaced at a huge cost and delays to the project timeline. But, they were replaced with only slightly faster version of the same thin client devices. Within three months, the new devices were again inadequate and had to be replaced - all two thousand of them. Finally after two costly rounds of thin client replacements, the IT staff deployed workstations that could be field upgraded to meet the application's requirements. The IT staff was finally able to manage the workstations as thin clients and perform remote upgrades which reduced the maintenance costs. The lesson from this costly rework was that the CTO did not consider the downside of the decision or the cost of regret. Had they chosen high-speed workstations initially, despite the initial higher cost, they could have avoided the costly thin client replacements. How could the CTO reach this decision without knowing the future? It's rather simple, by considering two stratagems: keep the future decision paths flexible and minimize the cost of regret. Fixed function, diskless thin client PCs offered the least flexible architecture for an application that was still in development. And, if there were a need to replace the fixed function thin clients, the replacement expenses carried a high cost of regret. A regular PC despite higher upfront cost was more flexible to upgrade, if necessary.

10. Learn Continuously: Implement IT projects with intent to create new knowledge and apply it to other projects.

I'm always amazed at how much my customers contribute with their new ideas whenever I provided them with a new technology or product. Studies have shown that customer could generate as much as 50% of new ideas and knowledge outside the corporate walls. To be effective, we must learn from customers about their business and from internal root cause analysis and Kaizen sessions. Only then we can accumulate and apply knowledge gained from root cause analysis, testing and defect analysis to add value to their business. Once we have eliminated waste and have created stable processes, we can reflect on the overall organizational effectiveness. IT managers must identify best practices and learn from them. Pursuit of perfection must be combined with cumulative learning at all levels of the organization. Training the IT staff and accumulating knowledge about business processes, customers' needs and quality improvement techniques are ongoing activities that come with problem solving. They occur when the IT staff applies itself to solving customers business and technology problem. Learning about user requirements and feedback from early releases such as prototyping add to our knowledge. When we frequently release enhancements, we increase the opportunity to learn and accumulate knowledge about the user requirements and release process. What we learn from each release cycle can be incorporated back into our knowledge base of standards and processes. Thus, new knowledge gained from each release helps with continuous process improvement. Faster, repetitive release cycles which are advocated by Agile methods, create more opportunities for this sort of learning. Finally we can create centers of excellence and emphasis such as quality circles and Kaizen events to enhance learning in targeted areas. Knowledge about applications, tools and products are continuously accumulated through emphasis on creating centers of learning and excellence.

> **11. Continuously Manage Risk: Continuously identify risks and mitigate them. Prepare risk response plans in advance.**

Agile methods inherently reduce risk. The notion of project portfolio is incomplete unless we identify potential risks associated with each project and devise risk response and hedge plans. Continuous risk assessment measures the portfolio exposure to risk, impact and probability of risk occurrence, in particular before starting implementation, and after each iterative release. Lean IT managers are good at developing risk mitigation plans and adjust them through the course of the project.

> **12. Build Intelligent Organizations: Create intellectual bonding by providing real time, relevant information to employees.**

Creating harmony between workers and between workers and their work is the beginning step toward creating intelligent enterprise. The point of this axiom is to make decisions that optimize the entire organization and global workflows, not just the local areas or departments. A common theme of this book is for IT to optimize globally, not just optimize in a local areas of the firm. Globally optimizing means two things: First the IT organization must consider how the entire firm's value streams are optimized across various functional groups and departments. Second, how IT can create an information systems environment where the expression "The whole is bigger than the sum of its parts" is realized. I've changed this common phrase to "How IT can transform the workplace so that the organization is more intelligent than the intelligence of its employees combined." Unfortunately, in many firms, lack of harmony and direction leads to produce less collective intelligence than the sum of intelligence in the firm. Chapter 19 explains the merits and some steps towards creating Intelligent Enterprise using information systems. I'll also build towards this goal by describing the purpose-driven IT management along the way. Optimizing the whole must start with the C-executives' vision for the firm and with collaboration of the CIO to determine where and how information systems produce the desired enterprise-wide results. This requires the IT team to know and understand the entire business drivers and workflows intimately. Strategic alignment and harmony can be created by applying Lean, Agile and Six Sigma methods such Hoshin Kanri and Balance Score Card.

Summary

- The 12 axioms are based on years of observations, research, experience and best practices of Lean, Agile and Six Sigma disciplines
- IT managers can be successful by building an IT framework based on these axioms
- Together these 12 axioms bring a culture of quality, renewed focus on customers and impetus to delivering highly valued solutions.

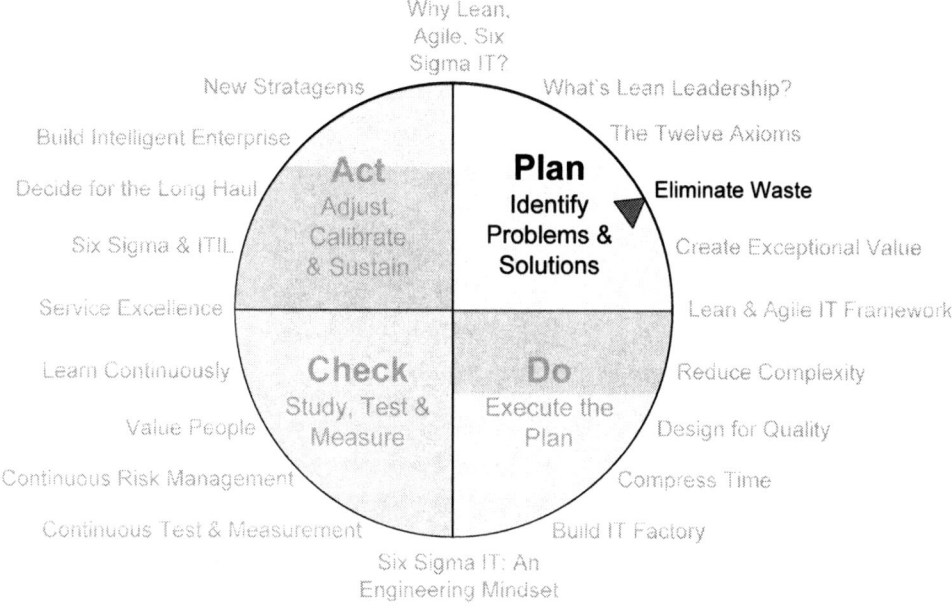

"Lean consumption involves solving customers' problems completely, not wasting their time, providing exactly what the customer wants, in a location they prefer and a timeframe they need. And finally it is helping customers reduce efforts to solve their own set of problems."

James Womack

Chapter 4. Eliminate Waste: First Steps to Recovery

Lack of focus by management is a major source of waste. What separates effective IT leaders from others is their focus on problems and problem solving abilities. Lack of focus leads to poor problem solving or poorly conceived problems, and that starts the path to waste at work. Over time, the problems get worse. Waste grows and hides the root cause of problems. Eventually, the problems grow to catastrophic proportions and that's when in traditional IT organizations, management pays attention. In Lean, Agile and Six Sigma IT organizations focus on problems and problem solving are everyday chores. The first step to recovery begins with focus on finding the problems and their root cause.

In this chapter, I'll review one of the most essential Lean thinking principles for IT management, namely eliminating waste. We'll review several concepts and tools including the *Theory of Constraints*, *Value Stream Mapping*, *Kaizen events*, and a sample of Lean problem solving techniques which are commonly used for eliminating waste.

Studies have shown than in most production systems, only less than 5% of total production time adds value. About 35% of the entire time is devoted to non-value adding but necessary activities and the remainder, 60% of the time are spent on wasted activities. As we shall see later, waste can be removed from IT activities in a step by step process.

I'm compelled to mention a very relevant philosophy of management called Theory of Constraints because it provides a scientific basis for problem solving in Lean and Agile methods. The Theory of Constraints (TOC) was developed by Eliyahu M. Goldratt in the early 80's. Goldratt introduced this theory in 1984 in his book, *The Goal*[25]. TOC deals with complexity in systems based on cause-and-effect and scientific reasoning. According to TOC, every organization at any given point in time, has at least one constraint that limits its performance relative to its objective. In order to improve the overall system performance these constraints must be identified and managed properly. Constraints can be internal (such as material flow or lack of information) or external (such as suppliers or market conditions). To understand waste, it helps to understand constraints.

Theory of Constraints & Systems Thinking

The principles of Theory of Constraint rest on systems theory. Any firm or organization can be viewed as a system. A system is an organized assembly of components, resources and procedures governed and joined by their connection or interaction with in a defined boundary. A system may consist of one or more sub-systems. Several systems can be combined to form a supra system.

Eliyahu Goldratt's theory helps streamline and optimize flow of operations. Goldratt provided five steps to eliminating constraints in his theory:

Step 1: identify the constraint (the process or issue that is causing the performance bottleneck in the system)

Step 2: Exploit the constraint (make sure the constraint is performing as best as it can)

Step 3: Subordinate all other processes to this constraint. (make other processes conform to reduce constraint)

Step 4: Elevate the constraint (increase the capacity of the constraint)

Step 5: As the constraint has been managed, another constraint must be found. Repeat steps 1 to 4 in order to find the next constraint in the system.

The consensus among experts is that as these steps are repeated, the organization improves its overall performance and odds of achieving its objective. Theory of Constraints is easy to understand and apply. It's a form of continuous performance improvement. As an example, let's apply this theory to a typical IT operation: handling a service request.

In Figure 4.1, I have illustrated an IT value stream and flow of work through several IT groups. Each group is a team of IT staff assigned to type of work they perform. The value stream encompasses programmers, systems engineers, business analysts, integration engineers, network engineers and so on. This diagram illustrates

---

[25] "The Goal: A Process of Ongoing Improvement", Eliyahu M. Goldratt and Jeff Cox. The North River Press, 1984

how work requests (raw materials) enter the system and flow through each group until completed. It also shows the productivity or throughput capacity associated with each group with a relative number.

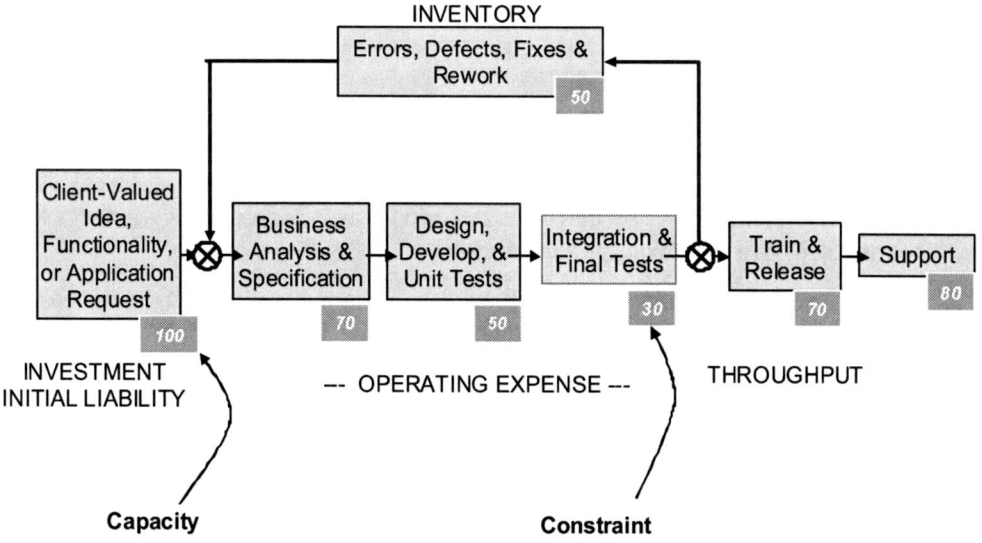

Fig 4.1 – Capacity & Constraint in an IT workflow

The throughput number is indicative of each group's capacity to handle demand. How many deliverables can be completed per month? Or, what percent of work requests can each group complete per month? For example, the capacity for handling incoming requests at 100% is quite good, as they can receive all new application or feature requests from customers. However, the ability of the next group (The Business Analysis Group) to analyze the requests and develop product specifications is only 70% of what is requested. In other words they can only handle 70% of the work load received from the prior group. The throughput number can be a percentage or ratio of completed deliverables versus work in progress queue.

The worst throughput is in the "Integration & Final Tests" group. With the capacity to test and integrate new applications at only 30% per month, this group is clearly a constraint.

The example in Figure 4.1 is actually a case from one of my consulting engagements. Further probing into this constraint showed that the integration team required two fundamental improvements: A) it needed additional resources and B) It lacked sound development processes. To remedy this constraint, the CIO agreed to hire more integration engineers and adopt agile development processes. Within a few months, this group was no longer a bottleneck. It improved its capacity to 80%.

The next constraints to remove were the groups that had 50% capacity: the "Design, Develop and Testing" group and the "Errors, Defects, Fixes & Rework" group. The productivity of the entire organization was now bound to the capacity of these groups, namely the organization was operating at 50% of its total possible capacity. After this assessment, the IT organization continued to make the necessary corrections and improve its productivity in both groups. Constraints cause delays which translate to "waste and wait" in other segments of the value stream. As long as serious constraints exist as shown in this example, it would be difficult to create a single flow, efficient workflow in IT.

Sources of Waste

There are three types of waste in the Japanese production management systems: Muda, Mura and Muri. Muda is a wasteful activity that obstructs smooth flow of an activity. Mura is any inconsistency in the system. Muri is physical strain on production workers. Any step that does not add value is regarded as waste (or Muda in Japanese). **There are two types of Muda**:

- **Type I Muda:** Any activity that adds no value, but is necessary for completing the value adding function
- **Type II Muda:** Any activity that adds no value and can be eliminated without impact on product

Lack of standards, poor calibration of equipment, system downtimes increase the variability of work that leads to inconsistency (Mura). When IT operations require constant firefighting and repair, it's a source of waste of resources, but also a source of strain for staff (Muri). One of the edicts in Lean thinking is "go look, go see", that is for one to see the problems first hand. To find the source of waste, a good practice for Lean IT managers is to observe the areas where value is being added and where wasteful activities occur. In their observations, managers should first look for Muda in people's workflows, first, then look for Mura and finally for Muri. After identifying waste, they perform a root cause analysis and eliminate the root cause of waste.

Traditional cost saving initiatives target all activities in IT organization. The notion of Lean is to apply cost saving initiatives to non-value adding steps immediately. Common sources of waste in IT are delays, rework, waiting and reinventing solutions which already exist. It would be interesting to note how much of IT resources actually deliver value versus waste[26].

Cases of Lean & Agile Success

When the new CEO at Acuity Brands Lighting company, a $2.4 billion concern decided to go Lean, the CIO began implementing and participating in five day Kaizen events to bring bursts of process efficiency. By applying Lean principles to IT, within two years the company was able to wean itself from 20 year old mainframes, build modern information systems and implement corporate wide VoIP. The IT team began to improve application development productivity by pair programming- multiple programmers working together on code. ...

---

[26] The next case study is based on "Learning to Love Lean IT", by Stephanie Overby, CIO Magazine, April 30, 2007

> ... Using Agile and Lean methods, CKE Restaurants built a point of sale (POS) system in-house, saving over $1 million in vendor costs. Through several continuous process improvements, the IT department reduced annual operating costs by 38 percent.
>
> According to the CEO, the IT department had transformed from "worst of company" to "first in company" as a result. CKE Restaurants employs 29,000 people with revenues of $1.4 billion. As far as Agile and rapid disaster responses go, Harrah's Entertainment is a good case to study. Harrah's Entertainment was faced with loss of telecommunications when fires struck southern California. But the management working with the IT department brought a casino online two days before normal utilities were available, avoiding $10 million in lost revenues.

IT Value Stream Mapping

In "Lean Thinking", authors Womack and Jones recommend defining customer value and organizing the firm around value streams. They suggest identifying value stream managers in the organization, managers who have complete responsibility for the value stream and answer to customers for overall customer satisfaction[27]. They add two more principles to complete their model for a Lean enterprise: Consider how value flows from the customer and strive for excellence. Kaizen events are a team approach to maximize value for a given work process.

Value Stream Mapping (VSM) is a method for value-add analysis by mapping production path, for delivery of services and technology solutions, and from start to completion.

The benefits of Value Stream Mapping are:

1. Provides a common language for discussing processes
2. Identifies sources of waste and eliminates them
3. Reduces rework, inventories, in-process and unfinished projects
4. Shows information flow, communication flow and linkage to production
5. Improved quality by 100% inspection, reviews or walkthroughs at the source
6. Shows how Lean concepts can be linked together
7. Provides basis for implementation

Developing VSM is a procedure for creating the ideal future production system. The goal of VSM is to identify the value-adding steps in a process and remove the non-value adding steps. The exercise is intended to improve lead times and

---

[27] "Lean Thinking: Banish Waste and Create Wealth in Your Corporation" ,Womack, James P., and Daniel T. Jones, New York: Simon & Schuster. 1996.

quality. To perform Value Stream Mapping, we can apply Shigeo Shingo's method. Shigeo Shingo was a Japanese industrial engineer and a major influence in Toyota Production System (TPS). He is best known for his books on TPS, poka-yoke (mistake proofing workflows and products) and rapid change over of production lines.

According to Shigeo Shingo, the value-adding steps are to be drawn horizontally in the center of the page. This provides the process map or the value stream across the page. The non-value adding steps are represented with vertical lines into the process map. These are called operational steps and regarded as waste. The operational steps are typically preparatory, set up or cleanup steps that allow a process to be completed. Shigeo Shingo suggests that process maps show the flow of materials while the operations lines represent the machine or human operators.

Consider a typical Help-Desk ticket for illustration. In most IT organizations, every customer request is logged into a ticketing system. All customers receive a tracking number for their ticket. In Figures 4.2A and 4.2B, the life cycle of a typical Help desk ticket is shown. I've drawn a diagram to show sources of waste using Shigeo Shingo method. Figure 4.2 shows the journey that the ticket took before it was completed at an IT organization.

Typical IT Workflow to: Create a network connection	Duration	Actual Time Spent on task
1. Get customer information. Open the ticket	1 hour	3 min
2. Assign the ticket to a network engineer	10 hours	1 min
3. Network engineer performs analysis	8 hours	7 min
4. Network engineer asks manager for approval	12 hours	10 min
5. Network engineer assigns ticket to operations engineer	10 hours	1 min
6. Operations engineer builds the network connection	10 hours	9 min
7. Operations engineer verifies network connection. closes the ticket	2 hours	3 min
8. Operations engineer closes the ticket	1 hour	1 min
Total Time spent	**54 hours**	**35 minutes**
Cycle Time Efficiency		*1%*
Value Add Efficiency		*57%*

Fig 4.2-A – Typical IT Workflow Cycle Time & Efficiency

The ticket was a request by a user for IT department to establish a network connection. Shown in the table, are the steps that a traditional IT organization takes to complete this request. I've shown the value-adding steps and the total duration for the entire effort in order to illustrate the waste. The total duration to complete this task was 54 hours, when in fact the value adding time (the direct time spent on the user's request) totaled only 35 minutes. Several steps such as steps one, two, four, and five could be eliminated if proper process and tools were already in place.

Cycle time and Takt time are somewhat related. For sake of simplicity we can assume that the Takt time is 35 minutes, namely we can complete one request every 35 minutes, or 68 such requests can be completed in a 40-hour week. However, due to delays in transferring tasks from one person to another, the duration is so long (54 hours) that achieving the Takt time is not practical. Therefore Takt time is bound by delays in cycle time for this workflow. The cycle time efficiency is 35 minutes divided by 54 hours, which yields only 1%.

The first table (shown in Figure 4.2-A) chronicles the life cycle of this trouble ticket through a typical IT organization. The cycle time efficiency is only 1%, namely only 1% of the entire Takt time is the value add delivered by direct labor. The rest is wasted idle time. If we compute the value adding efficiency, only 57% of the direct labor is adding value in this workflow.

Once we remove the non-value adding steps one, two, four and five, all efficiency metrics improve substantially (Figure 4.3). The Takt time is now reduced to 20 minutes and cycle time to 2.5 hours. That implies the total customer wait time is cut by 12X compared to the previous workflow. A drawing of this workflow using Shigeo Shingo method is shown in Figure 4.3.

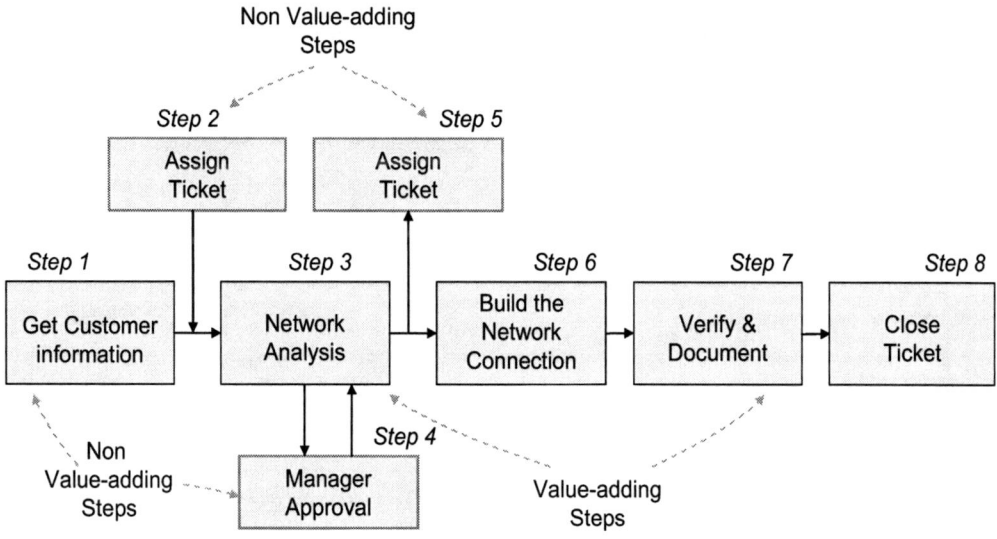

Fig 4.2-B – Initial Value Stream Showing Value Adding & Non-Value Adding steps

Steps drawn from left to right in Figure 4.3 are value-adding steps. Steps one, two, four and five drawn with vertical lines are waste. Before removing waste, the actual time spent on tasks was 35 minutes of which only 20 minutes involved value adding work. Similarly as the non-value adding steps are removed, the same ticket request can be completed in shorter time frame, namely 2.5 hours. Compared to the old workflow which took 35 minutes of direct labor to complete, the new workflow requires only 20 minutes to complete, a 43% increase in value-add efficiency.

By simply removing some non-value adding steps, we increased cycle time efficiency from 1% to more than 13%. There is still room to make this workflow more efficient. But, this is an opportunity for benchmarking your IT organization against efficiency of other IT organizations. Motorola for example, has a ticket resolution time of 1 hour on average. If we could decrease the duration of this ticket to less than one hour, the cycle time efficiency would increase to 35%.

Furthermore, let's apply the theory of constraints. Looking at the durations for each step, we find that Step 6 (Building Network Connection) is a constraint. If we could reduce the duration of that step by utilizing better tools, we could improve work efficiency even further.

Lean IT Workflow to: Create a network connection	Duration	Actual Time Spent on task
1. Network engineer performs analysis	30 min	7 min
2. Network engineer builds the network connection	30 min	9 min
3. Network engineer verifies network connection, closes the ticket	2 hours	3 min
4. Operations engineer closes the ticket	30 min	1 min
Total Time spent	**2hr: 30 min**	**20 min**
Cycle Time Efficiency		*13%*
Value Add Efficiency		*100%*
Cycle Time Improvement		*12X*
Value Add Efficiency Increase		*43%*

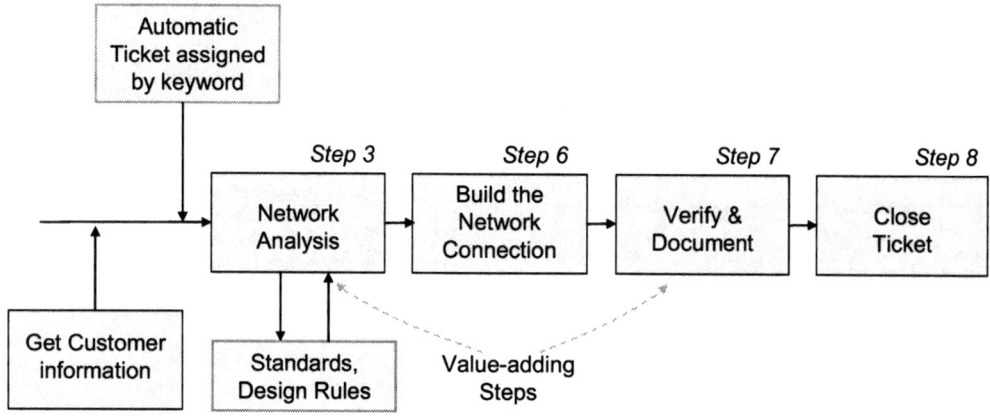

Fig 4.3-A&B – Improved IT Workflow has Eliminated Non-Value Adding Steps

In the improved workflow (Figure 4.3), the non-value adding steps are replaced by automation, standard design rules and employee empowerment. Thus manual interventions, hand-offs from one IT staff to another and wait times have been reduced. A side benefit of the improved workflow is that we have reduced hand-offs which reduces strain, idle time and puts us a step closer to mistake-proofing the workflow.

The obvious downside of this workflow is the amount of time that the customer had to wait to get a network connection, more than 2 days. The other negative aspects of this workflow are: too many transfers, or hand-offs as is called in IT circles, between people (four hand-offs) and the effort required to coordinate and communicate between each hand-off. Too many hand-offs is a waste in itself (Muda), but also can lead to inconsistency of work (Mura). Furthermore, multiple hand-offs between IT people causes interruptions as each person has to change their work context frequently. Each context switch is a source of waste as individuals require time to re-focus their mental activity. Too many hand-offs as shown in this workflow is a source of strain (Muri). Finally, quality and value have suffered in this workflow. In many instances, Agile organizations are so fast paced that they require IT work requests to be completed at an accelerated pace, in a few hours if not in a few minutes.

Clearly, this is not the ideal workflow. There are two metrics that we can use to actually measure the waste. The cycle time efficiency is the ratio of actual direct labor time spent, over the total duration to complete the customer's request. By eliminating the hand-off steps, we can reduce the direct labor time down to 20 minutes, as shown in Figure 4.3-A and 4.3-B.

We can calculate the value add efficiency as the ratio of the improved workflow time over the current time, namely 20 minutes divided by 35 minutes which give us a efficiency of 57%.

A Case of Eliminating Waste by Re-Use

A major bank in Texas was able to avoid purchase of additional bandwidth for its e-commerce applications using an interesting technical stratagem. It used its disaster recovery facility and network capacity to handle high call volume and website activity. In addition, the bank launched an e-business consultancy to create and implement customer e-commerce solutions which saved the bank thousands of dollars in operating costs.

From Kaizen Events to Lean IT solutions

Kaizen events are a cross functional method to bring process re-engineering and workflow change to the enterprise. When Kaizen events include IT staff, they can deliver powerful improvements. By participating in Kaizen events, the IT business analysts can understand and facilitate change, document requirements and propose IT solutions that can better support the new workflows. To be part of the solution, I recommend IT staff to participate and be active members of Kaizen teams.

Kaizen is a Japanese term for continuous improvement. Kaizen encourages small, incremental improvements instead of taking giant, quantum steps to change a process. Kaizen is performed by a team of people who are interested in the process improvement, a facilitator and individuals who actually perform the workflow as they are most familiar with it. The goal of a Kaizen event is to reduce waste, eliminate unnecessary steps (typically non-value adding tasks) and improve quality. The role of IT is critical as a change catalyst to implement the proposed improvements in the process. We should be ready to implement "light, Lean and disposable" IT solutions such as web tools, web forms, and bolt-on applications. Since they are easy and quick to develop, these applications come in handy for improving workflows rapidly. The goal of Kaizen is to bring about improvement by taking small incremental steps. When combined with Agile methods and Six Sigma tools, it can result in substantial quality and financial rewards. This is diametrically opposed to building IT solutions on large scale, multi-year, multi-million dollar projects which carry a huge risk of failure. The entire Kaizen event may take 10-20 days. The IT solution for the event must be developed and completed with in that general timeframe as well. There are two types of Kaizen events: A point Kaizen or a flow Kaizen. The point Kaizen focuses on a single work cell operation or a single department's workflow. The flow Kaizen considers enterprise-wide, cross functional processes. Kaizen events should be held on regular intervals. A complete workflow re-engineering must consider enhancing value-add as well as eliminating waste. I'll describe this idea in the next chapter on how to decompose workflows into their subcomponents and aggregate them back into the ideal workflow.

Stratagems: Assign at least one IT staff trained in Lean workshops to Kaizen events. Encourage the IT staff participate in Kaizen events. Maintain a portfolio of your organization's Kaizen events and the IT solutions required to enable the process improvement initiatives.

IT-Centric Kaizen Events

The goal of IT-centric Kaizen events is to combine business analysis and IT analysis with process re-engineering for the biggest impact. IT-centric Kaizen seeks to make small workflow changes that eliminate waste and automate as many tasks as possible by making minimal application changes. The following method is a simple 10-step approach to conducting an IT-centric Kaizen event towards eliminating waste.

Step 1. Convene the Kaizen meeting. Invite the stakeholders including individuals responsible for the work.

Step 2. Document the current process. Draw value stream mapping of the current process. Use Shigeo Shingo method.

Step 3. Use the value stream mapping to analyze the current process. Identify all issues and bottlenecks. Identify what customers perceive as value and how they want to receive it. What problems stand in the way of delivering that value?

Step 4. Identify the root cause of each problem that stands in the way of delivering the value to the customer. Build up the *fishbone diagram* by the 5-WHY process (Ask Why five times for each answer). This step is discussed in more detail in the next section.

Step 5. Define required process changes. You can perform gap analysis to identify new steps required and eliminate non-value adding steps. Outline the future state (ideal workflow). This is the new workflow to implement.

Step 6. Identify actors (customers, staff, personnel, etc.) involved in the process. Identify communication requirements between actors and method of communication. Define data elements generated, accessed or changed.

Step 7. Translate the new, ideal workflow in to Use Cases. Define dataflow and material flow. In essence capture the business logic that is implicit in the new workflow. Identify the functions and features required for the ideal value stream in the Use Case. If the required IT solution is a change to an existing application, document the proposed changes using Use Case notation.

Step 8. Design the IT solution using Use Case notation. Use a standard design language (such as Unified Modeling Language, UML) to document the design.

Step 9. Prototype the proposed IT solution. Present to the Kaizen team. Get user feedback.

Step 10. Build out the solution and run a pilot study based on the prototype. Identify any issues and tweak the solution as necessary for full production.

Finally, when the pilot program is completed, you can decide to put the solution into full production. In a Lean IT environment where continuous improvement is ongoing, the 10-step process repeats periodically at certain intervals or as business dynamics and information technologies change.

The facilitator should be experienced with conducting Kaizen events. In accordance with Agile IT methods, the participating IT team might consist of a business analyst and an application developer. Once step six is completed, steps seven and eight can be handled by IT staff without the rest of the Kaizen team.

A Simple Process Re-Design Approach

I have found the following approach to be a simple and effective method for eliminating non-value adding tasks. On a piece of paper or flip chart, draw a vertical line. On the left side list all the steps in the process that needs to be improved. On the right hand side write the time spent on each step.

Then for each step ask the following questions:

- Does the step change the item or the information?

- Does the customer want it? Does it meet customer's preferences?

- Does it get done right every time?

- Does it need to be transferred to another person?

If the answer to any of these questions is "No", then regard the step as non-value add. Those steps should be eliminated. More than likely, an application feature or slightly modified use of an existing information system can facilitate the workflow without them. Re-write the steps again. Add up the time for these steps. Determine the time saved by eliminating non-value add steps.

Emphasis on reducing waste and increased productivity come in two disciplines in Lean IT management:

1. To reduce waste, Lean IT managers encourage design for re-usability and maintainability. To keep costs low, re-factoring of existing applications and integrating existing off-the-shelf components make sense. Re-use of tools and applications increase productivity and reduce cost. For example, many of the decision support queries, data migration tools, system monitoring tools and interfaces are re-usable if designed properly. Typically, it is more advantageous and economical to re-factor an existing application than implement a new solution. Never develop a solution in-house if the equivalent is available off-the-shelf.

2. In order to maximize value and minimize waste, Lean IT managers transform the stagnant, non-value-add positions with dynamic, high-value-add roles in their organization. Surprisingly, I still find IT organizations that have vaguely defined positions. Here are some examples, "Customer Liaison", "Network Liaison", and "Security Compliance Auditor".

I believe such positions should be banned because their productivity and value-add are not directly measurable. These roles rarely produce deliverables or add value to the customer's value stream. These positions seriously lack clear lines of accountability and responsibility and therefore do not belong to a Lean, Agile and Six Sigma IT organization. They're difficult to measure and often create more separation than integration across functional teams. I prefer roles that have clear lines of responsibility and deliverable objectives.

In Lean IT organizations, these positions take on new roles such as "Process Analyst", "Network Engineer", "Security Consultant", or "QA analyst", as examples. To be more effective the role of "Customer Liaison" should morph into "Process Manager" or "SCRUM Master". While these titles do not include the word "customer", the output of their work directly serves the customer in form of deliverables that matter to the customer. The intent is to assign individuals with responsibility to foster and facilitate value-adding processes, standards, quality practices and consistent project management methodology during the course of a project. Lean IT organizations recognize the importance of roles such as "Application Managers", "Customer Satisfaction Managers", and "Value stream managers"; roles that assume shared responsibility with the unit business managers for the overall user satisfaction and value stream.

Problem Solving Tools – From A3 to Causal Models

During my consulting engagements, I still find a large percentage of IT organizations that lack standard decision making and consistent problem solving tools. Problem solving should be a core competency of a Lean, Agile and Six Sigma IT organization.

Fortunately there are many tools available to aid this process. Fishbone diagrams are considered one of the seven basic tools of quality management, along with the *histogram*, *Pareto chart*, *Check sheet*, *Control chart*, *Flowchart*, and *Scatter diagrams*. We will review only a few of these tools in the book, but there are many text books that describe these methods in detail. Alternatively, you can engage a Six Sigma Black Belt consultant to help you as needed. Among the problem solving tools used by Toyota are A3 method and Fishbone diagrams. In addition to these tools, I'll introduce two more advanced tools: *Causal diagrams* and *Cognitive maps*.

The A3 Method - Toyota Production System uses a tool called A3 frequently and for many problem solving purposes. It's called the A3 method because it simply uses the A3 paper size, equivalent to 11"x17". It is a visual aid built upon Deming's cycle of Plan, Do, Check and Act (PDCA). The paper is typically folded into 4 parts.

- Part one contains the title of the paper, background information and current situation. This part could also include some analysis about needs, gaps and the result of root cause analysis.
- Part two covers the Plan, what need to be done to correct the root cause.
- Part three outlines the implementation details.

- Part four includes discussions about what to inspect (Check) and how to correct any problems (Act). This part might outline what are the expected results, what to measure and how to check on the output.

The A3 method can be applied in the same manner as an IT-centric Kaizen. Part one outlines the situation and analysis. Part two defines the IT solution required to the problem described in part one. Part three determines a rapid and Agile development plan for implementation. Part four defines the release, validation and measurement plans.

Fishbone Diagram or Ishikawa Method

At one of the Kaizen events which I was a facilitator, the group's objective was to reduce application downtimes. The goal of the Kaizen event was to achieve zero-downtime of applications in their organization. It became clear that about 70% off downtimes at that organization were caused by the IT personnel making mistakes while performing simple updates, upgrades or configuration changes. The other 30% were caused by lack of and poor standards of execution. The participants used root cause analysis and drew the fish bone diagram to understand what is causing application downtimes. This is higher than industry average. Studies have shown that about 60% of all IT system downtimes are due to human error.

The Fishbone diagram (also known as the cause-and-effect diagram) was developed by Dr. Kaoru Ishikawa who pioneered quality management processes at Kawasaki shipyards in Japan. The diagram has been used since 1960's as a modern quality management tool.

Fishbone diagrams are used to identify the root causes of problems. This method is based on the notion that every effect has a root cause. Dr. Ishikawa believed that the root cause of problems can be traced to 6M's: Machine, Maintenance, Materials, Man, Method, Mother Nature (environment). An IT-centric model could include: Process (methods), People (staffing), Tools (Product, material and technology), Customer (user and work environment), Supplier (application and solution vendors) and Infrastructure (equipment, systems and networks). This model is shown in Figure 4.6.

There are seven steps to building a fish bone diagram and performing root cause analysis, as follows:

1. Draw a horizontal line. Write the defect or the problem (effect) on the right side of the line. Start working your way from right to left.

2. For a given effect, ask why it occurred, or what was the cause?

3. Draw a branch off the main line and write the answer.

4. If there are several answers, draw several branches off the main line and write the answer next to the end of each individual branch

5. For each cause, ask "Why" it occurred 5 times.

6. Continue to branch off from each line and write the answers.

7. The root cause(s) will be at the end of the branch.

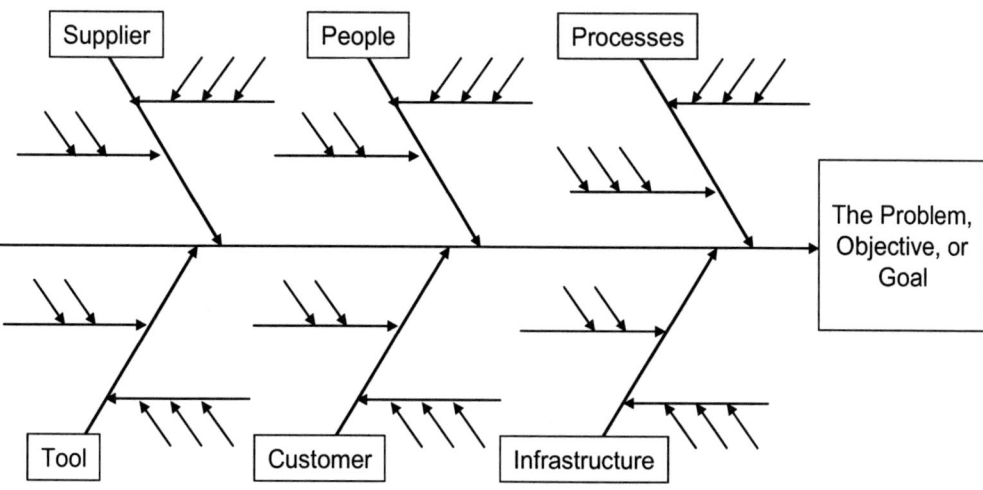

Fig 4.6 – Example of Fishbone Diagram Tailored to IT

Dr. Ishikawa envisioned that root causes could stem from five categories. The categories can be modified to fit an organization or specific industry. Particularly, one can apply the basic categories to fit IT-centric problem solving. Figure 4.7 shows the cause-and-effect model developed for the "zero-downtime" Kaizen meeting. The purpose for this diagram was to locate the cause of downtimes so the IT organization could eradicate them.

Armed with the influence weight for the root causes, the IT manager can devise some stratagems to eliminate the root causes. This is exactly what happened at the "zero downtime" Kaizen event.

After asking "WHY" 5 times, the Kaizen team identified two root causes:

1. They needed additional expertise that they did not have. This could be resolved by hiring the subject matter experts or consultants.

2. They lacked hardware standards. Simply, they needed to establish minimum standards for datacenter class servers that came with redundant fans, power supplies and higher meantime between failure (MTBF) ratings. As part of their purchasing standards, they specified a certain minimum MTBF ratings for all servers.

Overall, the IT organization lacked configuration management standards. To overcome the configuration management issues, they formed a change review group, insisted on change reviews and Method of Procedure (MOP) documentation before applying any configuration changes.

Causal Models

Because IT projects are inherently complex, chances are that more than one root cause is responsible for a given problem. There could be multiple root causes that influence other causes leading to the undesirable effect. These are called the indirect variables. The causes have cumulative and multiplying effect on each other.

To prioritize and identify which root cause is the most significant, you can use influence diagrams, also known as causal diagrams. A Causal Diagram shows how root causes are interrelated. It presumes that root causes are influencers. It applies weights to each root cause based on the degree of influence it has on the downstream causes.

Using simple math, we can measure the total strength of influence for a given root cause. Simply multiply the weights on each branch starting from the right side (effect) to the left (preceding causes). Add results to get the combined effect.

For the example in Figure 4.7, the total influence from "Lack of Expertise" on downtimes is computed as:

Total influence = 10%* 50% * 100% + 10%*100%*100% + 50%*100%.

The total equals 70%. *This means that the "Lack of IT Expertise" is responsible for 70% of the downtimes.*

The total influence from "Lack of Standards" on downtimes is computed as:

Total influence = 20%*100%*100% + 10%*100%*100% + 10%*50%*100%.

The total equals 30%. *This represents how much of downtimes are influenced by lack of standards at this organization. Finding the strength of influence is important in setting priority and level of investment to remedy the specific root cause.*

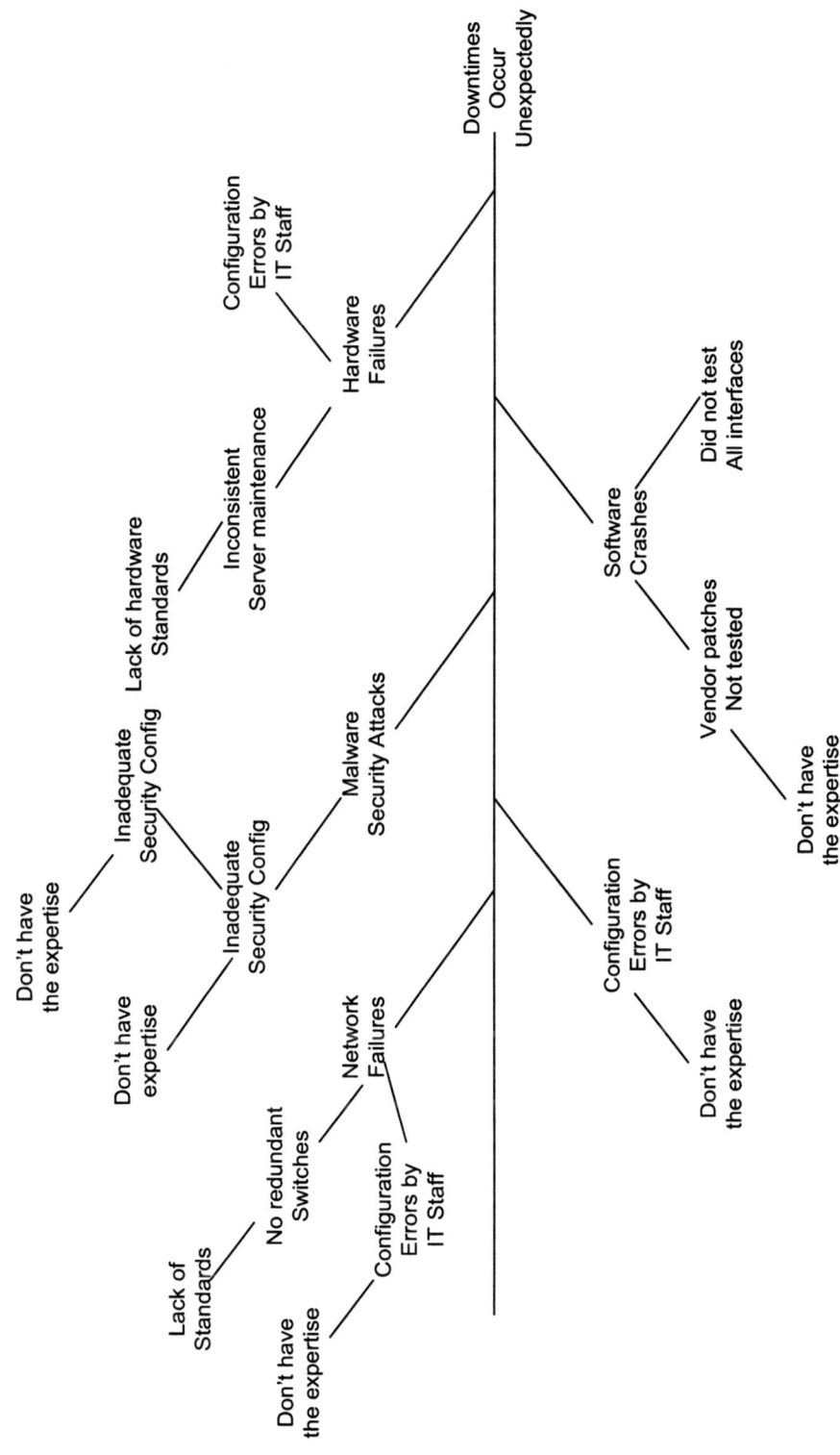

Fig 4.7 – Fishbone Diagram Example – "5-WHY Method"

To create a causal diagram, start on a new blank page and follow these steps:

1. List the root cause(s) on the left side of the page, and then list the downstream causes across the page in the order that they influence each other in time. It is important to position each box in the sequence and order that influence occurs, namely in the order of influence, listed from left to right of the page.

2. Draw a line connecting the root cause to the downstream causes to indicate influence. Direction of the line indicates direction of influence. Complete the diagram showing all causes and their connections.

3. Apply weights to each branch. Weights represent the degree of influence, also known as the strength of control. To apply weights we travel from the effect going back towards the root cause. Identify the weight of influence starting with effect, from the far right hand side.

   Apply weights between 0% to 100% until you reach the root cause. If a single cause influences only one other cause, the weight is 100%. If a single cause influences multiple other causes, you must determine how to split 100% among each cause. The sum of influence weights from prior causes to a particular cause must total 100%.

4. Once the weights have been applied, you can start from the final effect (at the right hand side of the page) moving backward (to the left) towards the root cause.

5. Identify the paths that have the most weight. When you reach the initial root cause, you have identified the most influential root cause.

6. You can repeat this to identify the second most influential factor and so on.

An example of this process is shown in Figure 4.8.

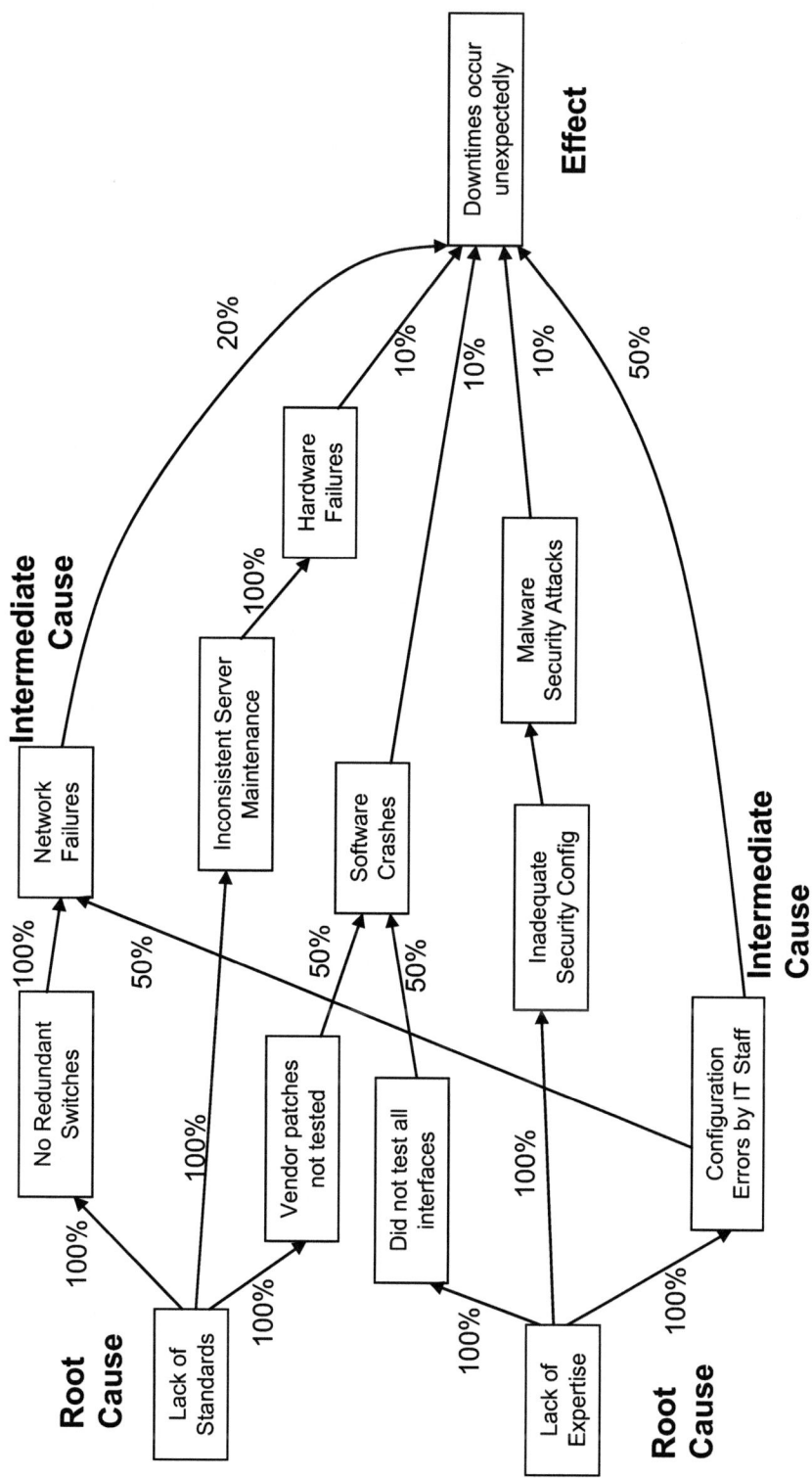

Fig 4.8 – A Causal Diagram with Weighted Influence Graphs

Cognitive Maps

Cognitive maps are a powerful tool for communicating workflows, describing IT problems, solutions, concepts and designs graphically and on a single page. Basically, they are maps that convey a description of thought in graphical form. They represent the problem-solution pair at one glance, in a graphical form and on a single page. There are many types of cognitive maps. They can be drawn on a small or large poster, some as large as 4'x6'. A cognitive map can illustrate the thought process that a user follows to complete their workflow. Another type can also illustrate a system with its sub components and their interactions at the sub system level. A cognitive map is typically a drawing, a photo, or a poster describing the problem-solution combo. An A3 sheet can be drawn in form of a cognitive map.

Story boarding is another type of cognitive map to communicate workflow and application changes. For example, to capture user requirements for features of a new application, one IT group convened a Kaizen event where users write down the desired application functions on a Post-it pad or a 3"x4" card. Then they arrange the cards in sequence according to their desired workflow.

Users typically paste these cards on a large roll of paper (or a 5'x7' poster). Sometimes screen shots of an application are used to illustrate workflow sequence through the application. Also called story boarding, the goal is to create a workflow poster, a cognitive map of users' workflows, step by step, screen by screen. These story boards give users an opportunity to walk-through their workflows and propose changes or application customizations. The maps help communicate workflow steps, identify any gaps and illustrate user experience before any part of the application is implemented.

There are other ways to use Cognitive Maps. IT consultants facilitate requirements analysis meetings with customers by capturing the results on a cognitive map. In such sessions, the IT consultant asks the customer to describe their problem by drawing it on the 5'x7' poster. Then, together they draw possible alternate solutions. Finally, they clean up the diagram and transfer the final draft on a new poster. This poster serves as a common visual aid of the problem-solution pair between the customer and the IT staff.

Figure 4.9 is an example of a cognitive map. It illustrates a visual map of the entire information system at a large healthcare facility including the applications, databases, the customer experience (front-end workflow) and backend workflows. In this example, the enterprise consists of a network backbone and a wireless network infrastructure connecting all users and applications. This enterprise maintains seventeen mission critical databases as shown.

The map conveys the internal back-office and external, customer-facing flow of work and information. It shows the customer's experience flowing through the system – drawn as a pipeline - as well as the backend and operational flow of information as work progresses from left to right hand side.

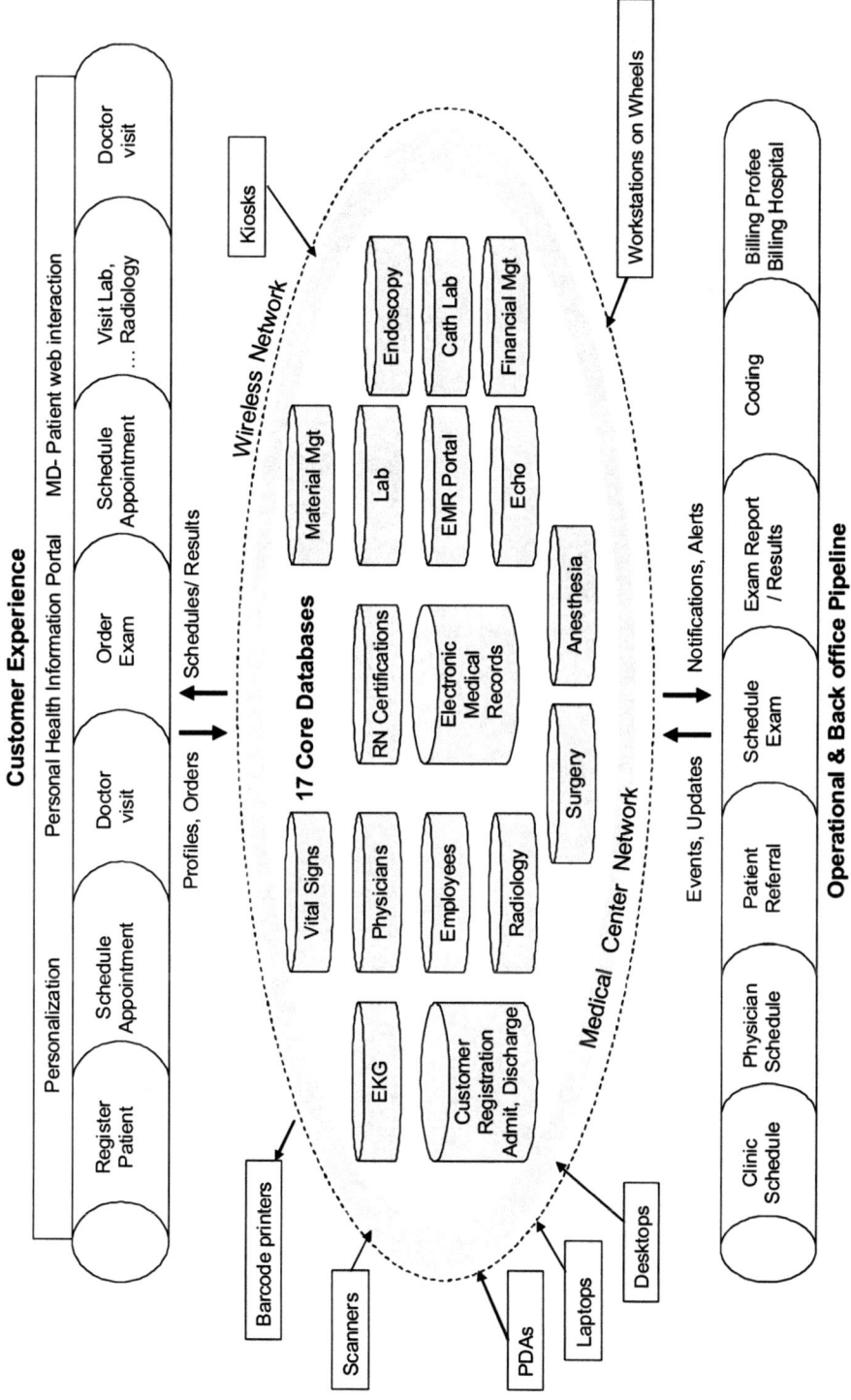

Cognitive Map of a Large Hospital Enterprise Information System

Fig 4.9 - "IT Ecosystem as Architecture" Cognitive Map (Peter K. Ghavami 2004)

One can draw a similar cognitive map but instead of using a workflow pipeline, draw the value-stream pipeline and demonstrate the interaction of applications with steps in the value streams. Other tools such as Venn diagrams and affinity diagrams are also noted in the literature, and used in practice.

> **Stratagem:** Use Cognitive maps to communicate problems, decisions and solutions with your IT customer and to gain mutual commitment to your proposal.

Cognitive maps can become living documents capturing a wide range of ideas, from a project life cycle to IT strategy formulation. They remain an invaluable documentation for capturing design, user interface definition, data modeling, and then later are used for building test cases and user training.

Summary

- Kaizen means "Continuous Improvement", or "to take apart and put back together in a better way"
- A short term project (1-2 days) to dramatically improve a process
- Lean IT uses Kaizen to improve IT and business processes using information technology
- Apply Kaizen events to eliminate non-value adding tasks.
- Use Shigeo Shingo method to identify non-value add tasks
- Eliminate Rework. Avoid temporary fixes.

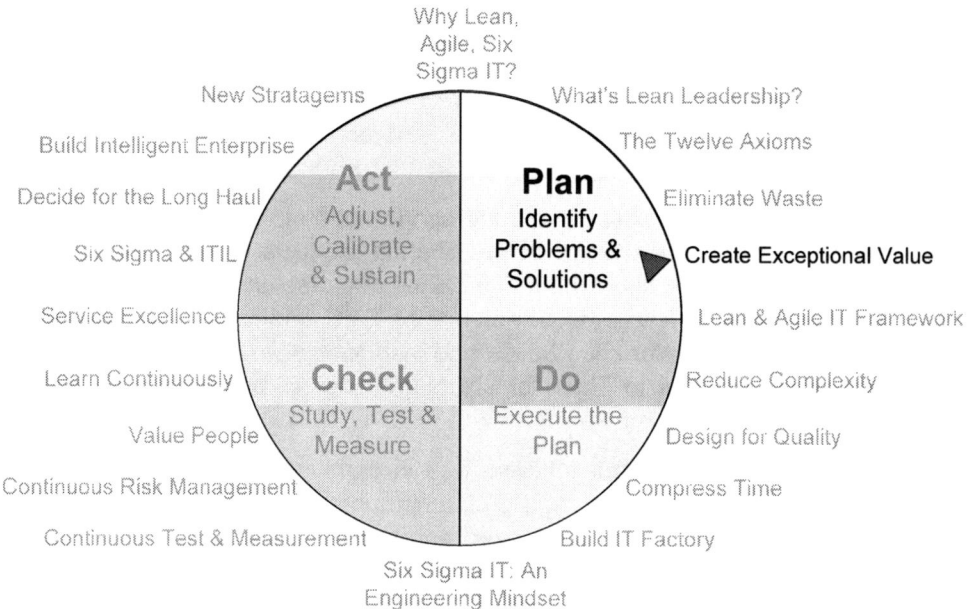

"You don't get paid for the hour. You get paid for the value you bring to the hour."
Jim Rohn

Chapter 5. Create Exceptional Value

Jeffrey Bezos must know something about creating value. Just in the last 5 years, his company, Amazon.com has returned more than 200% on its shareholder's investment. As the CEO and founder of the company, Jeffrey Bezos has transformed technology into a unique, high value service to its customers worldwide. Despite attempts from other me-too startups, Amazon.com grows strong, creating new market categories one after another, and dominating them. The company has implemented Lean thinking in several divisions and on various workflows. A key success factor of Amazon.com is how it extracts value from information technology by offering outstanding services.

Sakichi Toyoda, founder of Toyota Motor Corp, his son Kiishiro Toyoda and Taiichi Ohno, an engineer developed the Lean manufacturing system which ultimately resulted in Toyota's dominance of the automotive industry. Toyota is the largest automobile company in the world. Its profitability is higher than profits from all other auto makers, combined. Known as the Toyota Production System (TPS), it has reduced waste, costs and improved quality at the same time. The Lean methods offered by TPS in 1960's have revolutionized how we think of process optimization.

About three decades ago, around the mid 1970's, a professor at Harvard Business School asked his students to write an essay about Honda's business strategy. The essay question was "Should Honda Motors enter into the automotive market?" At the time Honda Motors produced motorcycles, typically smaller models and small engines. The unanimous students' response was "No. Honda could not compete with GM and Ford." But, in less than 10 years, not only Honda had entered the automobile industry it had become a major player and brand name in the market. The roots of the company's success go back to the time when company engineers visited U.S. to observe and learn how Americans drive. They observed, listened and learned about the American driving habits and preferences. Then, they translated those observations into automobile designs that tailored to those preferences.

In the world of athletic shoes and sports apparel, Nike is a major brand and world leader. In its nascent years, before offering products with its famous "swoosh" trademark, Nike imported shoes from Tiger Shoe Manufacturing in Japan. At that time, Tiger shipped shoes in plastic bags. Phil Knight, CEO and founder of Nike knew that American consumers prefer shoe boxes and tried to explain that preference to Tiger. When repeated requests to Tiger for shipping shoes in boxes were ignored, Nike started to build its own brand.

Another success factor for Nike was in crafting custom-made shoes for top runners and asking their opinion and preferences on several performance aspects of the shoes. They continuously customized and refined shoe designs for professional runners. They organized running clinics and test trials, basically conducting research on shoes that performed better.

Today, Nike has no factories. It does not tie-up cash in plant and equipment. Although it does not own factories, the company's 10 year plan calls for implementing Lean production system at its suppliers in Taiwan and elsewhere. Nike's strength is in research and development. Nike has mastered the art of value creation using technology, while remaining a Lean organization. These examples of achieving greatness have a common theme. The common DNA for success is creating value for customers. This is a key ingredient of Lean Thinking.

Value Chain, Value Streams

In general, value of something is how much a product or service is worth to someone relative to other things. There are several forms of value. There is intrinsic value, like the actual value of a gold coin if you melt it and get the gold out. There is the market value, what others are willing to pay for it. There is book value or legal value, the legally defined value of the item. And there is substitution value, the price of a substitute product or service. Ultimately, value is perceived by the customer. We all want to maximize value, -worth of our work, product and services. The simplest way to describe the value equation is the following interpretation: Value is the ratio of benefits divided by costs of generating those benefits.

$$\text{Value} = \frac{\Sigma \text{ Benefits}}{\text{Cost}}$$

The numerator, shown by the Greek letter Sigma is the "Sum of Benefits". Benefits are derived by features, solutions and services that the customers enjoy. The denominator, "Cost" is inclusive of all IT costs. It consists of the initial acquisition cost, implementation and maintenance, personnel, training, and related expenses to deliver those benefits.

The goal of Lean Management is to maximize benefits while keeping costs at a minimum. This is essentially the same as a Return on Investment model. Value corresponds to Return on Investment (ROI), benefits are translated to net revenues and cost is the expense outlays. Examples of Benefits in your organization can be spotted as satisfied customers, perfectly delivered applications that fit their workflows, high system availability and reliability, increased revenues, innovative solutions built upon effortless technology and opportunities to create exceptional value or competitive advantage. Not surprisingly these benefits are typically among what IT customers want.

Examples of Cost include direct expenses but also some soft losses such as the cost of failed projects, all sorts of downtimes, frustrated users, confused managers who can't make decisions due to inadequate operational and decision support data, applications that do not integrate, constant manual interventions to compensate for short-comings of IT applications, rework and poor quality implementations, late releases and run away projects that never finish. These and other IT tragedies are among what everyone shuns away from. Lean IT managers recognize the leverage points implied in this "value equation". To increase Benefits, they focus on enhancing their service levels, automating workflows, innovating and delivering strategic solutions. To reduce cost, they focus on *Kaizen* (Continuous improvement), *Quality* and compressing *Time*. Generally speaking, the numerator is typically enhanced through Innovation and technical leadership, the denominator by embracing process improvement.

As we attempt to eliminate poor service we can rely on *value chain analysis*, *value stream mapping*, *Feature Driven Development (FDD)* and Six Sigma techniques like *Quality Function Deployment (QFD)*. Value chain is the progression of materials or work in progress from a provider to a customer who in turn adds value and provides it to the next customer in the chain. In every step, a customer of the previous step is the service provider to the next work in the chain. Every chain is likely to have a long succession of customers, but only one is said to be the *keystone customer*.

The keystone customer is the one that makes or breaks the entire chain. This customer's satisfaction is key to the success of the entire value chain. Lean IT leaders deliver value in 3 ways. These are the same factors that impact IT effectiveness in the enterprise:

1. New Product Introductions: Rapid delivery of products at high quality and low cost that meet or exceed customer's expectations

2. Service Excellence: Provide services that satisfy users and customer's needs

3. Enable Business and Clinical Processes: Participate in Kaizen events. Define and engineer Information Technology into customer processes that enable automation and mistake-proofing workflows

There are generally two perspectives of value creation. I've applied both views when applicable while keeping an eye on how information technology can improve or drastically enhance value at each step:

1) Value Stream: how the sequential flow of work adds value at each step of workflow until the work is completed. Each worker adds value by performing his or her task and transfer work in progress to the next worker in the stream.

2) Value Chain: How a worker in the current step of workflow enables the worker in the next step to create value for its customer. At each step, the worker is the customer of the previous step. The goal of each worker in the chain is to enable the next worker to create value for its customer.

Generally, the value stream perspective fits the manufacturing and industrial sector businesses, while the value chain perspective fits the professional, service and web-enabled sectors of business.

For example, Nucor Corporation, one of the largest steel producers in the U.S. might choose the value stream view to improve its efficiency. In contract, Amazon.com might choose the value chain view as it enables its customers to create knowledge and feedback to each other about its books and content, thus customers are able to create value for each other.

Value streams and value chains can be identified with in IT workflows. On both the supply-side and demand-side of IT, we can identify how the progression of work from one IT staff to another adds value for the next person in the chain and finally for the end customer. The CIO must assign responsibility of an entire value stream to individual IT managers (in a matrix organization fashion) to make their work visible and the lines of accountability for the related IT systems clear. For example, in the past, I've designated managers to be responsible for the customer satisfaction related to an application and the entire value stream.

Each manager was responsible for the delivery of value for that stream with focus on the efficacy of the information systems. Did the system availability and customer satisfaction improve as a result? Did IT activities get aligned with the business activity? The answer is yes and the results were remarkable. Such responsibility includes all aspects of an IT value stream. For example, a value stream of maintaining and updating an application is a value stream that includes business analysis, customer training, system monitoring, application updates, business continuity, testing and debugging.

But, only one individual, the value stream manager was responsible for ensuring that the entire value stream provided the intended results. The asset theory of IT encourages us to think of investments in IT and process improvement as corporate assets. When these assets are used strategically in the organizational processes, only then will we see enhanced organizational effectiveness. A detailed look into several IT case studies shows that firms which measured and improved their intermediate metrics were most successful in achieving the overall business objectives.

An in depth review of IT case studies reveals that three levels of corporate-wide metrics are critical to determining the impact of business process redesign through IT.

These levels are:

- High-level organizational variables such as profitability, productivity, and Return on Investment;

- Intermediate variables such as turnaround time, capacity utilization, automation, informational transformation, coordination, and cycle times;

- Low-level variables such as headcount, new customers, orders received, customer satisfaction and defective or returned products.

Other studies have shown that information systems which improve the intermediate metrics are likely to make the biggest impact on the high-level measurements.

A thesis by John Mooney at University College in Dublin and his colleague in the U.S claims that: "Firms derive business value from IT through its impacts on intermediate business processes. Such intermediate processes include the range of operational processes that comprise a firm's value chain and the management processes of information processing, control, coordination and communication"[28].

For example, let's consider two leading computer manufacturers, Dell and Hewlett Packard. Both companies deliver exceptional value to their stock holders. To steam line its sales and fulfillment operations, Dell developed a data warehouse with customized application interfaces and user-friendly front end that allows Dell employees query the warehouse with complex questions. The system is based on a four-tier architecture combining standard based and open-source software which has reduced the technology life cycle costs.

Hewlett-Packard Corporation combined its IT and global operations to build an integrated supply chain and e-business solution. The IT group developed a business-to-employee portal that standardized HR functions worldwide, saving the company $50 million with a six month return on investment. The same portal is able to deliver internal financial data reporting to management.

Virtual But Dedicated IT Workcells

Several years ago, while managing several simultaneous product development efforts, I had to create a balanced but focused team approach to handle the concurrent demands and fast pace of the projects. Up until that time, a project was driven by the project manager and a series of workorders (or tickets) for various IT staff to perform one task or another. There was no consistent flow of development, test and release.

---

[28] "A Process Oriented Framework for Assessing the Business Value of Information Technology", John G. Mooney, Vijay Gurbaxani, Kenneth Kraemer, The DATA BASE for Advances in Information Systems, Spring 1996 (Vol. 27, No. 2)

Quality and productivity suffered. This was more true when an engineer received several workorders and had to decide which was higher priority. A lot of arguments went on to decide priority and a lot of time was wasted on re-prioritization. So, I created workcells that worked on various projects in parallel. Each workcell was a virtual group. It consisted of engineers, developers and other professionals integrated as a virtual team dedicated to a project. But these individuals were shared resources among the workcells on their projects. This organization model increased productivity and created a flexible form of matrix organization.

After each project was completed, and the product went into production, I created a different workcell to maintain the system and manage the value stream for each application. Each workcell was a virtual team dedicated to a specific value stream, led by a value stream manager, typically the lead application manager. Each workcell consisted of individuals with diverse IT skill sets and expertise. Customer complaints were rare and if they occurred, the IT value stream manager was responsible to resolve the issue.

The value stream manager regularly met with the business unit managers to identify opportunities for application enhancements, change and modification requests. These requests were based on findings from Kaizen events or value stream mapping analysis. The benefits that resulted from this approach were simple but highly cost effective.

Unless a Kaizen event was held, the value stream manager and customer representative defined the value adding features in upcoming upgrades. Quality and consistency were ensured by using a cohesive workcell of IT professionals. An application designed for delivering value in a chain must pay attention to value-enabling features. The features that consider value chain and value streams are likely to ask for additional data fields or application features that may not have been identified otherwise.

A Healthcare Case Study

In this case study, let's consider the workflow at a diagnostic radiology clinic located in a hospital. I've illustrated the value stream and value chain perspectives for a patient visit to this clinic. The workflow is initiated by a referring physician, likely a family doctor who orders a radiology exam for the patient.

A value stream (as shown in Figure 5.1 and Figure 5.2) can be described as work in progress starting with Schedulers, who schedule the patient for the exam; moving on to Technologists, who scan the patient according to the type of requested exam; and on to Radiologists who render a reading off of the image; finally to transcriptionists who type the dictated report into a document for the referring physician.

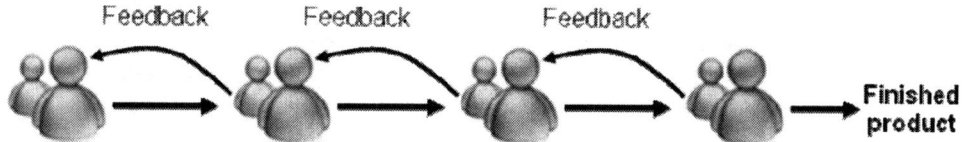

VALUE STREAM
Value is added as a sequential enhancement to a deliverable, a work package or process

At each step:
1. Inspect work package received from prior step
2. Send feedback to the person at prior step
3. Perform task (add value)
4. Send work package to the next person in the value stream

Fig 5.1 – Value Stream

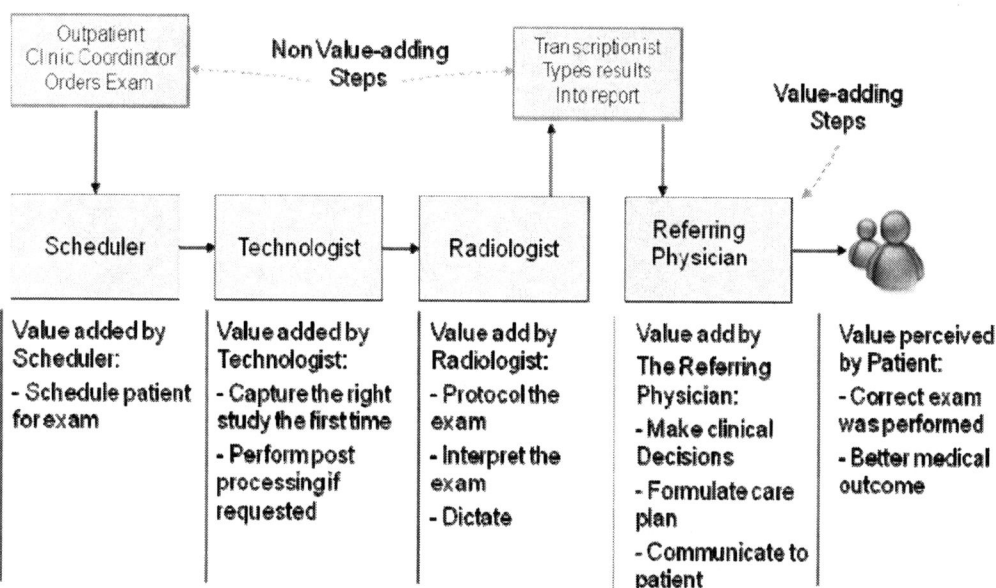

Fig 5.2 – Value Streams. Non-Value Adding Steps Identified

Value is added in each stage as work flows to completion from one individual to the next. IT staff can add value in a variety of ways at each stage, such as: automating tasks, eliminating paper and film, reducing time to perform each task, or by improving quality. This view is a value stream approach.

We can automate the steps by implementing certain applications or features. If we apply Six Sigma Quality Function Deployment (QFD) techniques, we would list the critical customer requirements and give high priority to those design attributes that are most influential on meeting the customer requirements. Alternatively we could apply an agile method such as Feature Driven Development (FDD) to develop these solutions. FDD and QFD are explained in the upcoming chapters.

As the diagram illustrates, the value-adding steps are drawn horizontally. The non-value adding steps are drawn vertically with arrows that show the direction of control or flow of information. A Kaizen event would seek methods to eliminate the non-value add steps. In a properly structured value stream each worker gives feedback to the previous worker in the stream. This feedback is important to adjust and control the variables of the previous task.

But, in the value chain perspective, each worker is a client of the previous worker. The intent is for one worker to maximize the ability of its client to create value for his or her client downstream. An example of this value chain is shown in Figure 5.3 and Figure 5.4.

In the value chain perspective the flow of value is perceived differently. What enables a value chain is information; immediate feedback from the downstream client, the keystone customer and all clients along the chain. The keystone customer is the one who can make or break the deal, or in this context the chain. Feedback can be captured via information systems and input into the process upstream.

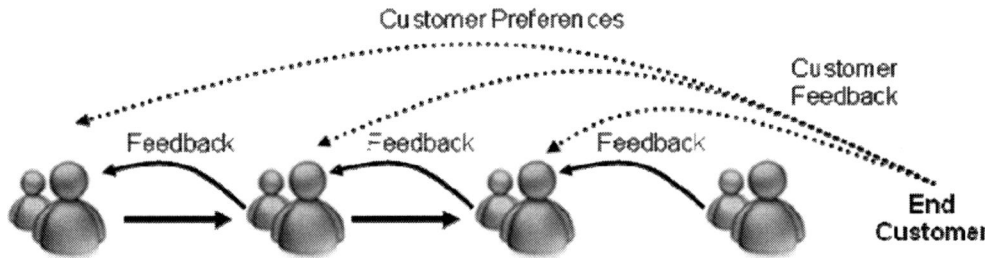

VALUE CHAIN
Value add as enabling the next person to create value for his/her customer

At each step:
1. Inspect work package received from prior step
2. Identify how and what the next person wants to create that is of value for his/her customer
3. Add appropriate value to enable the next person create value for his/her customer
4. Send feedback to the person at prior step
5. Perform task
6. Send workpackage to the next person in the value chain

Fig 5.3 – Value Chain

As illustrated in Figures 5.3 and 5.4, value flows from the end-customer (in this example, from the patient) back toward referring doctor and on to the Radiologist. The end-customer is the patient, although some may argue that the insurance provider is also an end-customer. The referring physician is the keystone customer. It is important to note that perceived value drivers are determined by the keystone customer[29,30].

This value chain perspective transcends the scope of IT beyond the walls of a single department across the entire continuum of healthcare in the hospital. It requires delivering solutions that impact a series of users inside and outside of the Radiology clinic.

Value Chain as each individual enables the next person in the chain to create value for their customer

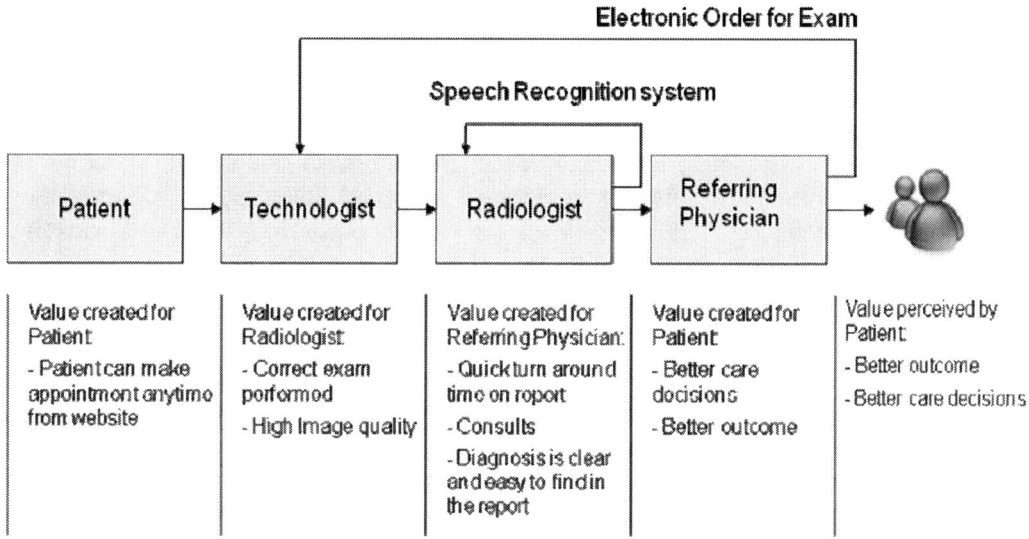

Fig 5.4 – Value Chain Example

A Lean IT manager must consider supporting users, applications and services that encompass the entire value chain. Given this case study, can you spot the non-value adding steps? Can information technology transform this value chain into a more efficient and effective workflow? A Kaizen event at a healthcare facility identified two non-value adding steps and used information technology to remove them: order entry and transcription.

First, the referring physicians can directly enter their order into an electronic order entry application without the intervention of the clinic coordinator. The second opportunity for eliminating waste is to use speech recognition technology. This application allows Radiologists to directly capture their report into the electronic

---

[29] "Evidence-Based To Value-based Medicine", by Melissa M. Brown, Gary C. Brown, Sanjay Sharma, American Medical Association

[30] "Perceived value of computer-based patient records among clinician users", Wager KA, Ornstein SM, Jenkins RG. MD Computing. 1997 Sep-Oct;14(5):334-6, 338, 340.

medical record without using transcribers. The net effect of these changes can benefit the keystone customer tremendously.

Not only the direct labor costs are minimized, the chances for errors are reduced and the turnaround-time from ordering exam to receiving the report are drastically reduced. But there is a third opportunity for increasing value. What if patients could schedule their procedure themselves through an online application without the need for a scheduler to intervene? A patient web portal could easily accomplish this goal. The portal could display all open time slots on a calendar and the patient could choose the time slot. A day before the scheduled procedure, an automated voice response application would email and call the patients to remind them about their appointment.

Improving Value Streams by Kaizen

By introducing the automated speech recognition software, the healthcare organization was able to save over $4 million per year in transcription labor costs. Prior to the Kaizen event, Radiologists dictated their reports into an analog phone system and several hours later, a medical transcriptionist would listen to the recorded report and type it into the hospital electronic medical record. This process added delays and costs for personnel. The outcome of the Kaizen event was that by eliminating the transcriptionist step, reports could be completed in a few minutes instead of a few days. The Kaizen meeting called for a speech recognition application where Radiologists would dictate directly into it.

Quick turn-around time on Radiological reports can be achieved by eliminating the time spent by transcriptionists typing physicians' reports from a tape recorder. Report turn-around time can be virtually instantaneous if Radiologists dictate directly and generate their reports using a speech recognition system. Because there is no wait for typing a report, the referring doctors are able to receive their reports as soon as they are interpreted by a Radiologist. Previously, the report turnaround time at this healthcare institution averaged 36 hours. Today, the average turnaround time is 4 hours.

The rapid turnaround of reports has built a strong loyalty among the referring doctors. They prefer sending their patients to this healthcare facility because of the faster report turn around. Finally, the most valuable aspect of implementing the new workflow is the net effect increase in patient care quality. The sooner the radiology reports become available the sooner primary care physicians can make care decisions about their patients' health. Primary care physicians are the keystone customers.

> **Stratagem:** To maximize your value as an IT executive; Identify the keystone customer. Apply both perspectives of value streams and value chain for your customer's business.

Once the value drivers have been identified, the Lean IT managers may use Agile methods plus industry standard Tools, to implement IT solutions that deliver the desired "value", from concept through implementation to final release. Interestingly there is side-benefit to this automation: since the application generated reports were more structured, it was easier for the referring physicians to understand them, and find the important results in the report.

In turn, investment in these applications enabled referring physicians to deliver higher value to their patients by delivering faster and more accurate medical care.

> **Stratagem:** Lean analysts should map workflow steps to application functions, and vice versa. They identify tasks that can be eliminated. These are usually the non-value add tasks. Then they identify and develop the application features that can automate the new value adding tasks.

Conjoint Analysis of Value

One direct way of assessing value is to ask the keystone customer in a value chain. Surveys are good tools to ask customers about their wants and preferences. A technique called conjoint analysis can capture customer preferences and rank them by dollar value.

Let's assume we want to determine the conjoint value analysis for patient preferences visiting this hospital.

An example of questions that we could ask in this technique might be:

1. If you normally wait 2 days to get medical test results, how much extra would you be willing to pay if your wait was shortened to one day?

2. Would you be willing to pay $50 to get a DVD of your Radiology Exam for your personal records?

3. Which one would you prefer: A discount of $300 per day for a double occupancy room or single occupancy room at regular price?

4. If we could offer a second opinion on your test result, what is the maximum you would be willing to pay out of pocket?

Similar questions apply to almost any industry and for almost any Kaizen event. The answers will give clues about perceived value held by end customer and the keystone customer about a particular workflow. Knowing the monetary value of the customer's preferences helps us appropriately develop and price the value adding steps in the new workflow.

In the context of information technology, the following line of questions illustrates conjoint analysis, as we ask customers:

1. Which application feature is more important to you, feature "A", or feature "B"?

2. Adding feature "A" delays application delivery timeline and raises cost. How much would you be willing to pay extra to get this feature?

3. Faster delivery of an application by 1 month will cost 20% more. Would you be willing to pay the extra money or wait one month for delivery?

Of course the metrics and dollar amounts in these questions are hypothetical, only to illustrate the comparative aspect of conjoint analysis. You can substitute your specific questions and metrics instead.

Another technique for analyzing customer preferences is the Kano model, a powerful tool for identifying customer expectations. It was developed by Dr. Noriaki Kano, a Japanese quality expert. I'll cover the Kano model in Chapter 8.

We can draw graphs to show the monetary value placed on application features and functions, versus cost to develop them. Each feature does and can be mapped to one or more revenue generating value streams.

In Figure 5.5, I've used a scatter plot diagram to show the customer's sensitivity to cost increase in exchange for adding a feature. (This is by the way an example of the scatter plot chart). It's likely that features with higher perceived value will be implemented first. These are the features that are along the trend line or above it.

Lean and Agile framework encourage us to implement the highest value adding features first. For example, from Figure 5.5, we would implement features "D" and "J" before implementing features "H" or "B".

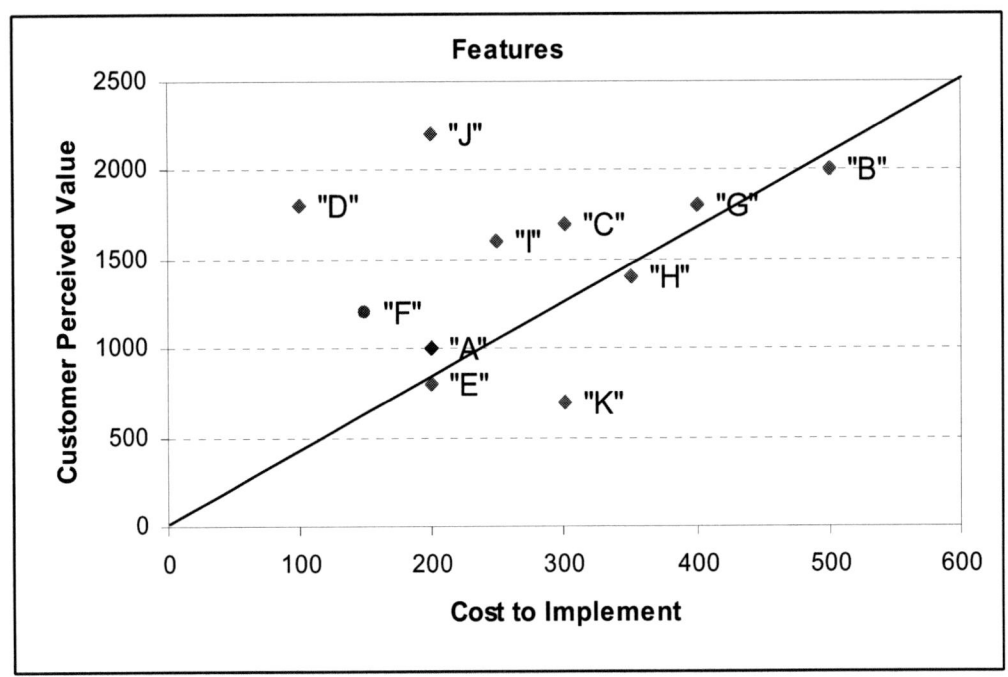

Fig 5.5 – Scatter Plot of Features: Cost versus value

Measured Value as Return on Investment

Let's discuss how value can be measured in form of return on investment (ROI). Before conducting a Kaizen event, we can estimate the benefits in terms of savings or increased revenues. Similarly, after the Kaizen event is completed, we can measure the actual benefits.

For each value stream, we can relate the application features to value stream benefits, and convert benefits into dollars. The challenge is to translate the intangible benefits into dollars just as we do with tangible benefits.

For example, continuing with the case study of speech recognition application, I've computed a 5-year return on investment model for this IT project in Figure 5.6.

IT PROJECT ROI ANALYSIS						
PROJECT: Speech Recognition System						
ITEM	**DESCRIPTION**	**YEAR 1**	**YEAR 2**	**YEAR 3**	**YEAR 4**	**YEAR 5**
COSTS:						
Software	Software licenses	$ 455,000	$ 80,000			
Hardware	Servers, monitors, rack, microphones	$ 427,000				
Professional Fees	Implementation costs	$ 200,000				
Internal Labor	Four IT staff required for 6 months	$ 400,000				
Annual Maint.	Software maintenance	$ -	$ 60,000	$ 60,000	$ 60,000	$ 60,000
Annual Maint.	Hardware maintenance		$ 30,000	$ 30,000	$ 30,000	$ 30,000
Total Costs		**$ 1,482,000**	**$ 170,000**	**$ 90,000**	**$ 90,000**	**$ 90,000**
BENEFITS						
Value stream 1:	Faster physician reports - 2% savings in time	$ 60,000	$ 120,000	$ 120,000	$ 120,000	$ 120,000
Value stream 2:	Increased revenue from better medical codin	$ 42,500	$ 85,000	$ 85,000	$ 85,000	$ 85,000
Value stream 3:	Reduce surgery wait time by average of 1mir	$ 480,000	$ 960,000	$ 960,000	$ 960,000	$ 960,000
Value stream 4:	Savings for eliminating paper	$ 125,000	$ 260,000	$ 265,000	$ 270,000	$ 275,000
Value stream 5:	Reduce transcription expenses	$ 45,000	$ 90,000	$ 90,000	$ 90,000	$ 90,000
Value stream 6:	Savings from retiring old analog system	$ 17,000	$ 34,000	$ 34,000	$ 34,000	$ 34,000
Total Benefits		**$ 769,500**	**$ 1,549,000**	**$ 1,554,000**	**$ 1,559,000**	**$ 1,564,000**
Net Income (Loss)		**$ (712,500)**	**$ 1,379,000**	**$ 1,464,000**	**$ 1,469,000**	**$ 1,474,000**
NPV	Net Present Value @ 8%	$ 3,767,657				
IRR %	Internal Rate of Return	195%				
Break Event Point - Months		18				

Fig 5.6 – ROI Analysis considering Value Stream Benefits

The model captures all capital and operating expenses; quantifies the benefits derived from each value stream; and return on investment. The model assumed an 8% net present value rate as cost of money. Here is a brief explanation of the line items in the spreadsheet in Figure 5.6:

Capital Cost: The upfront cost of acquisition including hardware, software, vendor implementation costs, training and internal labor for implementation.

Operating Cost: Includes the ongoing cost of maintenance, internal labor for customer service, cost of backups, upgrades and repairs.

Value Stream: Each value stream line item captures the dollar value realized (or projected) from implementing the application for that value stream.

In this model, we estimated benefits for several value streams as the result of implementing the speech recognition application, including:

1. The time saved by Radiology Physicians per case.
2. Increased revenue as a result of better medical coding
3. Reducing the surgery wait time. Each minute of surgery wait time can cost as much as $100/hour.
4. The benefits associated with becoming paperless. This hospital believes it can save $1 per exam by eliminating paper.
5. Savings associated with reducing medical transcription budgets
6. Savings from retiring the old analog system

As illustrated in the ROI model (Figure 5.6), the total upfront investment for implementation is $1,482,000 and the total benefits come to $769,500 in the first year. The net income (actually loss) in the first year is $712,500. But after an 18-month break-even point, the IT solution delivers positive cash flow as the costs of maintenance and upgrade are offset by benefits from all 6 value streams.

The total 5-year net benefit discounted at 8% is $3,767,656. Not bad at the first glance. But, is this a good investment? How would a project like this compare to the other project proposals at your organization? To compare this investment to other investments, you can compare the IT ROI to your company's internal rate of return requirements. You can also determine the overall rate of return on your company stock or from your company's other investments.

The return on IT investments (such as implementing new applications) must outperform the company's internal rate of return, namely return on equity. Are you looking to justify additional resources to the C-executives for implementing a new project? If the ROI can show an excellent return on investment, justifying the project and staffing become easier.

> **Stratagem:** Are you planning to implement a new project and struggling to convince the C-executives to give you additional resources? Just use a language that they understand. Show them the pro-forma ROI statement and let the numbers do the justification.

Just for illustration, let's compare this project to 3 other stocks: Boeing, Microsoft and Starbucks. On average these stocks had a return of just over 100% over 5 years. The return on this IT project is 195% which makes it a better investment than investing in a portfolio of these stocks. So, is this IT project a good financial decision? Clearly in this instance if we compare the ROI of 195% from this project to the average stock returns of three public companies, the answer is yes. But again, we must compare the internal rate of return of each IT investment to the company's required internal rate of return.

COMPARABLE INVESTMENT ROI ANALYSIS					
Comparables	2002 Investment Value	2007 Investment value	Return On Investment	2002 Stock Price	2007 Stock Price
Microsoft Corp(MSFT)	$5.5M	$7.50M	36.36%	$22.00	$30.00
Boeing (BA)	$5.5M	$12.87M	134.15%	$41.00	$96.00
Starbucks (SBUX)	$5.5M	$14.5M	163.69%	$9.86	$26.00
IT Project Protfolio	$1.48	$3.77M	195.00%	N/A	N/A

Obviously, for an IT investment to be acceptable, its ROI must exceed your company's internal rate of return. How can we quantify the value stream benefits for implementing an application? Fortunately, IT customers are often willing and eager to provide a list of benefits and quantify them for us.

I have seen many benefits mentioned and quantified from participants about the proposed IT applications during Kaizen events.

A common list includes:

1. Improved cash flow from reducing accounts receivables
2. Increased revenue from improved billing accuracy
3. Improved cash flow and inventory cost reduction from same day shipping
4. Reduced staff time by eliminating paper and faxing from one dept. to another
5. Reduced staff time by using Interactive Voice Response
6. Reduced staff time by creating a self-help portal for customers
7. Increased sales due to certain application implementations

Summary

- Customer is the final arbiter of value
- Listening to the voice of the customer and understand what customers value
- Define your value proposition by analyzing customer preferences through conducting conjoint analysis
- Value Chain and Value stream mapping allow IT staff to align solutions with the business objectives and the customer expectations

- Information Technology is a core value generating engine for the enterprise. IT can deliver exceptional value by being effective in three dimensions:
    1. *New Product Introductions:* Rapid delivery of products at high quality and low cost that meet or exceed customer's expectations
    2. *Service Excellence:* Provide services that satisfy users and customer's needs
    3. *Enable Business and Clinical Processes:* Participate in Kaizen events. Define and engineer Information Technology into customer processes that enable automation and mistake-proofing workflows

Stratagem: Those IT organizations that involve and engage the keystone customer in their applications and solutions are likely to add the most value.

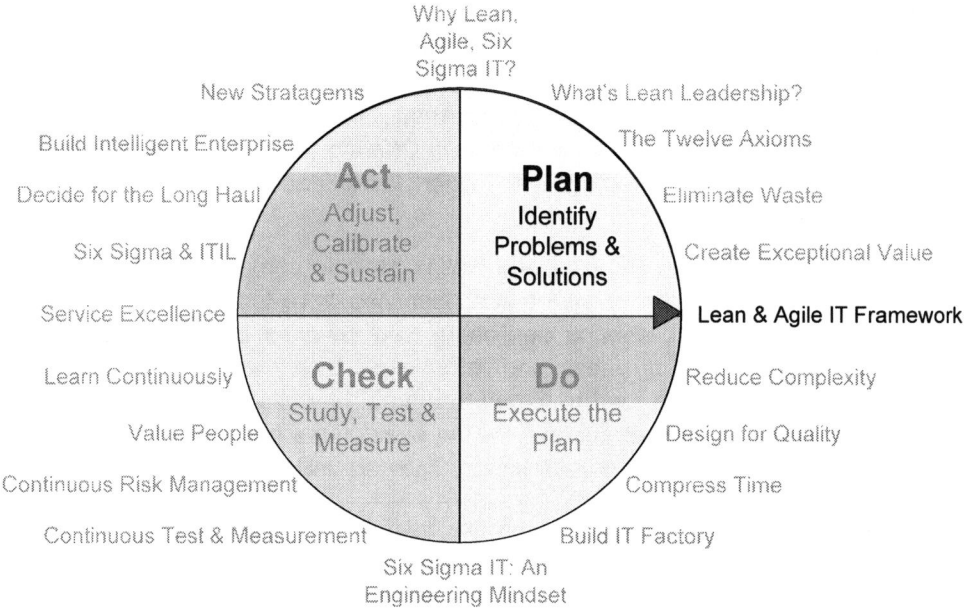

"Your most unhappy customers are your greatest source of learning."

Bill Gates

Chapter 6. Lean & Agile IT Framework

When Sergey Brin and Larry Page, the founders of Google.com met at Stanford University, they clicked right away. In the mid-Nineties, Sergey Brin had worked on data mining techniques and formed a research group at Stanford for data mining. Up until that time, search engines like Yahoo! and Alta Vista gave search results based on alphabetical directory and whatever their editors selected as related websites.

In 1996, Larry Page and Sergey Brin began analyzing web links. They built their search engine on a distributed system built from surplus and old PCs that Stanford did not need[31]. They started to count how many times a link was accessed. Viola, came up the idea to rank search results based on frequency of access, proximity of phrases and links pointed to a particular website. Thus they could sort sites based on their popularity. Around 1997, they had created a PageRank system. It worked well, but when they tried to sell it to Excite, Yahoo!, or AltaVista, or license the technology, there were no takers.

That was until the first investor showed up. The very first investor in the company liked not only the technology but also and the way Brin and Page were running their company. Essentially, they did not waste money on advertising or high-end expensive equipment. Instead they wanted to buy mother boards and other

---

[31] "The Google Story", David A. Vise, Bantam Dell, New York, NY, 2005

equipment to inexpensively build computers themselves. In 1998, Brin and Page left Stanford and set up a 24x7 datacenter at a fellow Stanford student's garage. At the time their search engine was handling 100,000 searches per day. In 1999, with only 8 employees and a massive network of cheap PC parts, they were serving 500,000 searches per day. Jeffrey Bezos, CEO of Amazon.com invested in the company. By the time the company offered its Initial Public Offering (IPO), its financial position was staggering. The firm was getting ever bigger, faster and cash rich by seconds with virtually no debt.

What do Google, Amazon and Netflix have in common? They have a keen ability to extract and create value-adding services from technology. They all bring value to consumer by delivering applicable web services built from mostly off the shelf technology. Their business and information technology architectures are so morphed together that it's hard to separate them. They use meta data often supplied by the consumer, in form of surveys, online evaluations and real time click imprints. They are the new arbitragers of information. They are all Lean IT organizations

> **Stratagem:** To be Lean, IT architectures must be morphed into routine business activity. The mark of achieving this morphological goal is found when it is difficult to distinguish between the business activity and Information Technology. The Lean IT architectures must match the business blueprint. The organization's DNA must be ingrained into its IT architecture.

The biggest opportunities for Lean IT management are in focusing on service excellence, operational efficiency and effective project management. The advice that I often get from successful CIOs are that:

1) The IT staff must be engaged with the strategic mission at the workplace and their work must be visible.

2) To ensure operational effectiveness the IT managers must be involved in problem solving with their team.

3) Flexible architectures powered by Agile methods are needed to keep IT in a constant state of readiness to respond to technical and business turbulence at all times.

Jeffrey Liker in his book, The Toyota Way quotes a Toyota manager saying: Always supplement the system information with "go look, go see"[32]. Lean IT managers follow this advice. They are visible, accessible and hands-on, ready to identify and resolve operational issues alongside with their staff. They meet with their customers often to see their IT problems first-hand. They participate with their IT staff in trouble-shooting process and resolving user issues.

Being hands-on allows the Lean IT manager to spot problems, trends and patterns which can be collectively resolved or preferably prevented. Problems are often best understood at the location that they occur and can be resolved at the local level at the lowest possible expense.

---

[32] Known as "genchi genbutsu" in Toyota Way: 14 Management Principles From the World's Greatest Manufacturer", Jeffrey Liker, McGraw Hill, 2004

I wrote this chapter to emphasize that IT must be effective. IT must be completely morphed into the daily business activity as well as propel the firm to reach its long term strategies. When IT is not effective, it can be cast away as a cost center. To be effective, IT must look at its own performance in three dimensions of product, process and service.

Since the half-life of most technologies are rapidly decreasing, the effective IT organization must adopt a rapid and agile implementation of new products. To design effectively, we must abandon our old silos and methods of design; doing business analysis or use cases for the sake of doing design. To be effective and competitive, we must incorporate a wide range of ideas and disciplines into our IT activities[33].

Cases in Agile and Lean Success

Agile IT principles propel companies into leadership positions in their industry. Consider the case of Warner Music Group1. The company embarked on a music digitization process to provide legal music downloads and launch ringtones. Digitizing vast collection of music required massive storage, network and server capacity. Every month over 500,000 pieces of music are downloaded doubling the company's market share. NBC with revenues over $6.7 billion and 6,000 employees has to be Agile and Lean because timely news matters. The company devised a "TV station in a box" server model with enabled fast setup of remote news bureaus. When it acquired Bravo, it migrated to a new integrated platform, resulting in doubling its net revenues.

Another Agile example is O.C. Tanner Company, with 1,800 employees and revenues of $300 million used Agile software development methodology to implement more than 1,000 business system enhancements in one year. IT enhancements to manufacturing, supply chain and customer facing processes reduced customer calls in half. Agile Information Technology management is often focused to delivering tangible results in a limited time. Take for example, The PNC Financial Services Group in Pittsburgh. The company employs 23,000 and generates $5.3 billion in revenues. In response to new federal regulations, the company had to retrain about 3,800 branch and phone center employees in five months. It rolled out a new teller system in eight months which started positive return on investment in one year. One goal of mature IT organizations should be to standardize information systems across similar value streams. Consider the case study from Celanese a chemical manufacturing company. The company was able to save 40 percent of its IT cost through a consolidation and standardization program. It also believed in flexibility by building customizations through configuration flags in its applications. By turning certain features on or off, Celanese could adapt a system to any of its business units. Celanese Chemical Manufacturing...

---

[33] The case study is based on "100 Most Agile Companies Honored. Which Companies Lead in Agility?", Edward Prewitt, The CIO Magazine, August 2004

> ... began a standardization and consolidation program to reduce its IT costs and streamline business systems. During the four year program, the company was able to consolidate seven data centers into one and replace 13 ERP systems into one application.
> The major business units consisted of base chemical group and plastics group. But the IT leadership recognized that the business workflows are essentially identical between the two groups. The company was able to serve both business groups using common functions in one system, but tailor them to each business line. Celanese IT organization is regarded as Lean and Agile. It's business units are focusing on module processes within an enterprise-wide architecture. According to the Celanese CIO: "Companies can be agile only if they can turn specific [application] functions on and off".

The goal of a Lean IT framework is to deliver information systems and solutions that support and enable the strategic and operational objectives of the enterprise. Continuous improvement implies rapid changes in the organization, processes and re-configuration of information flow. For a Lean IT framework to support continuous improvement it must be flexible and Agile. Companies whose IT frameworks advocate modular design, incremental development, re-usability and maintainability, structured processes, metrics and measurements are likely winners.

In this chapter, we'll review the elements of Lean and Agile IT framework through the lens of IT architectural framework and IT effectiveness.

Elements of Lean & Agile IT Architectures

There are many traditional architectural models in practice today. Among the more established and popular models are Booch, Zachmann, Rational's 4+1 View, and variations of object oriented approaches. Zachmann's model has been an industry standard for defining IT solutions for some time. It's strength is to define function, application, data and workflows that are to be delivered[34]. Zachmann's model serves as an excellent "*Descriptive*" model. It's a good tool for describing the present state and the ideal state (or future state) of the IT architecture. But, Zachmann's model has serious shortcomings. For one thing; it's rigid and static. It does not give directions to reach the future state, either. In contrast, a *Prescriptive* model delivers more architectural direction. Descriptive models explain how something works. But, Prescriptive models state *what must be done*. They have a higher degree of successful implementation since they connect the dots from architectural design through release of product.

In summary, a model to enable Lean & Agile solutions should consist of three frameworks:

1. *Business framework:* collects and analyzes workflows, Kaizen events and business needs that deliver the expected value.

---

[34] "IT Architecture Toolkit", Jane A. Carbone, Prentice Hall PTR, 2006

2. *Design framework:* provides a roadmap for creating IT solutions, design and components that deliver the objectives defined in step 1. This section also deals with evolutionary model of maintenance, operations and low-cost. This framework can include Design for Six Sigma principles which we will review later.
3. *Implementation framework:* Implementation strategies, process and best practices that enable the actualization of the IT framework defined in step 2.

Because IT services are foundational to Lean IT management, the appropriate IT framework must be based on a model that can transform application function points into service and service into value. The appropriate IT framework must deliver value swiftly. Hence, Service Oriented Architectures (SOA) and Software As A Service (SaaS) have gained popularity as alternatives to traditional models like Zachmann.

SOA architectures attempt to link distributed applications and data to service consumers (or end users) so they can receive those services on-demand, across diverse domains, ranging from legacy to new applications. Service Oriented architectural models deliver real, tangible benefits at a low cost. They deliver services based on modular programming and re-factoring existing, legacy applications. As a result these architectures deliver quick functionality to the service consumers, qualifying them ideal approaches for Lean IT.

Service Oriented Architectures have two other benefits. They allow transforming technology into services that generate value, and they allow modular development. Both of these benefits bring cumulative advantages, such as keeping the overall costs down, faster implementations and flexibility to change applications rapidly.

SaaS is associated with the Application Service Providers (ASP). Its purpose is to deliver hosted applications to customers over the internet. The initial SaaS applications were available as single tenant hosts. Today, there are multi-tenant SaaS applications available and many can be installed onsite. The number of companies who offer SaaS applications has multiplied in the recent years since the term was coined in 1999. Oracle, Google, SAP and Microsoft are already major players and have plans underway to offer additional SaaS applications.

SaaS and SOA are two sides of the same coin. SaaS allows rapid application deployments at very small startup costs. Both are excellent models for Lean and Agile IT environments.

Enterprise & Mission Critical Applications

So you might ask "how can you apply these methods to enterprise systems implementations?" This is a valid question for several reasons. The enterprise system implementations typically require large groups of analysts and implementers. The average implementations can take anywhere from 18 months to three years, but some have gone as long as five years or more.

According to industry reports, software and hardware expenditures on enterprise systems exceed $15 billion annually, plus another $10 billion for professional services to implement them. Large corporations such as Intel report that their entire expenditure for their enterprise systems will exceed $1 billion before completing the project.

Can Lean, Agile and Six Sigma methods help with large enterprise applications? The answer to this question is a definite yes. These methods are excellent tools for managing large scale, high-risk, high-stake mega projects.

Enterprise systems started as "back office" applications, but gradually moved to front office and store front environments. Today, enterprise systems support a variety of applications from Enterprise Resource Planning (ERP) and Supply Chain Management to Sales Force automation, customer relationship management and those that actually drive the workflow for the enterprise. In the recent times, enterprise systems are packaged with complementary third party software called "bolt-on" systems. Intranets and service oriented applications blur the distinction between back office and front office. Web-enabled applications some packaged as bolt-on systems present the appropriate data and functionality to the user while enterprise systems store, retrieve, and maintain data as back-end systems. These web-based applications are easy to modify and integrate across the enterprise.

Case Study: UPS delivers

Take UPS as an example. UPS at one time was regarded as an example of a well-managed transportation company. In reality as it's becoming evident, UPS has been a well-managed information system company all along. The company's executives invested over $10 billion dollars in enterprise systems over a course of 10 years but with clear vision and strategic intent.

Implementing enterprise systems are intertwined with big change, big project and big risk. But, it does not have to be so. Lean and Agile methods can provide solutions that meet the majority of customer required functionality rapidly. Lean encourages us to segment a "big" enterprise project into separate implementations. We have also come to realize that most such "big" implementations consist of multiple, smaller sized projects. An enterprise system project actually may consist of at least three distinct but overlapping implementations. Managing each implementation requires a different set of IT stratagems, approach, tools and skill set.

The three implementations are "physical implementation", "technical implementation" and "business implementation". The physical implementation might include facilities preparations in the datacenter, installing servers, work-stations, mobile devices and the necessary network infrastructure. The technical implementation includes the software, data, application and integration aspects of the implementation. It also covers the non-functional aspects of implementation including performance, security, data warehousing and disaster recovery considerations. The business implementation considers user workflows, training, support, and mapping features to specific business functions; namely, operationalizing the IT solution. The most successful project managers have recognized these three activities as three distinct set of projects.

Lean and Agile methods also promote resolving complex issues that matter first. One of the insidious problems of implementing enterprise applications is the consistency of data definitions. For example, the term "patient" or "customer" must be consistent across multiple functional business areas or even divisions. The problem becomes more complex as implementers consider the term "address" for the "customer" as it could denote billing address, ship to address and other address definitions which must be consistent across the firm.

Terms such as "account balance" or "blood pressure" might mean differently at different points of service and might be recorded by different metrics. The Lean and Agile implementers strive to abstract for consistency at a level to define services and objects instead of specific data elements. Reaching decisions about standards, consistency and complex questions early in the project lifecycle will help steer the project in the fast track direction. Ultimately, the true measure of IT success and its frameworks are gauged by their effectiveness. Can you tell how effective is your IT organization? Are you getting the products and services that you envisioned? The answers to these questions take us to the topic of IT effectiveness.

IT Effectiveness: Product, Process, Service

The effectiveness of Information Technology is a direct influence of *Product quality*, *Process maturity* and *Service excellence*. The ultimate measure for IT effectiveness is determined by user satisfaction. When we consider the basic concepts of Lean, Agile and Six Sigma from an IT perspective, we are interested in making IT an effective instrument of change. Change comes naturally with continuous improvement and is necessary for transforming your firm into the new vision. We are interested in measuring and improving IT effectiveness across multiple dimensions of *Product*, *Process* and *Service*.

Grasping the basic concepts and frameworks for product, process and service are critical for IT managers to develop a common agenda among their staff and customers. Here is a basic overview:

Product: is concerned with applications, IT infrastructure and functions delivered to users. IT management meets this dimension by researching, analyzing, evaluating and selecting solutions. The topics considered relevant to "Product" are about function, form and fit of applications, workstations and network infrastructure. The focus is on attributes and characteristics of the IT solution.

Process: creates methods and standards for operations, development, project management and trouble resolution. Process maturity of an organization grows as it demonstrates ability to define processes, consistently perform them, measure and optimize them.

Service: is about what users want and expect from IT. Service activities deal with user concerns, issues and assistance. User satisfaction is a key indicator of IT effectiveness. This chapter will cover each of these dimensions in turn.

Product Dimension

Before opening the topic further, let's address two questions that often face CIOs. The first question is whether to outsource all or portions of IT services. The other extreme is to insist on handling all IT activities in-house.

In 2007, Cingular decided to outsource its IT organization to IBM. Washington Mutual Bank, one of the largest banks in the U.S. has been on the out-sourcing roller coaster a few times. It outsourced its IT organization in the 90's to IBM. Then it brought the internal IT organization back. Later around 2005 decided to outsource to IBM once again. This lack of internal strategic direction combined with poor financial decisions and difficulties with its subprime mortgage loan practices forced Washington Mutual to be acquired by JPMorgan Chase. Smart-sourcing is a stratagem. It means partnering with the right vendor to perform certain IT functions or projects for your firm at a lower cost, better or faster than your IT organization can deliver. However, those functions should not be core competencies of your firm or critical competencies that will be needed in the long run. In situations where the IT organization is unable to deliver or support core competencies, the stratagem is to do the opposite. That is to bring external expertise, such as consultants or subject matter experts inside to work and transfer knowledge to the internal IT staff.

The second nagging question is whether to acquire an integrated solution or the best of breed application? Clearly it would be a waste of internal resources, a very "un-Lean" idea to re-invent the wheel by building an application if a commercial, off-the-shelf application is already available. With respect to integrated solutions, clearly they promise to be the option with the lowest cost, most sustainable with faster delivery schedules.

The fallacy that IT managers often fall for is the delusion that single vendor solutions come integrated right out of shrink wrap. Not so. Single vendor solutions are not necessarily integrated! Many vendors have acquired IT applications through mergers and acquisitions and have not gone through the pains of integration yet. Be aware that if you are the first customer to undergo the integration process, the costs and risks will be substantially higher than expected. Thus, the two ends of the extreme for selecting applications are integrated solutions on one end and best of breed on the other end. Any veteran of IT world has learned the harsh trials of integration and interface development between multiple applications. The traditional wisdom is to stay with an integrated package even if its functionality lacks customer's expectations. But there are exceptions. There are a few reasons for an IT organization to opt for a non-integrated solution.

The reasons are a need for either new technology or unique functionality or both. Unique functionality means that the application has a high degree of specialization or specific features that are vital to the highly profitable segment of the firm's operation. New technology implies situations where the technology is still emerging and has not been fully assimilated through vendor's integration plans. In these situations, if the cost of integration can be out-weighed by the benefits of acquiring a best of breed, - or a best-in-class application, then it's appropriate to do so. The next diagram illustrates the decision matrix for application selection. Despite our desire to consolidate all business functions into one application, there are certain highly specialized or novel requirements that cannot be met by an integrated, off the shelf application. Consider the case of TD Banknorth.

The company found some of its business units looking for more sophisticated products to compete. The CIO had to innovate with new IT capabilities with the same level of resources due to serious cost pressures. The company was able to achieve this goal by a number of Agile, Lean and Six Sigma methods, as explained in the next case study.

	Technology & Application Arena are Well Established	Emerging Technology, or facing Highly Specialized Arena
Low Financial Impact	Integrated	Integrated or Bolt-on
High Financial Impact	Integrated or Bolt-on	Best of Breed

Fig 6.1 – 2X2 Technology Acquisition Decision Matrix

Case Study: Creating specialized solutions through Continuous Innovation

TD Banknorth is a leading banking and finance company located in Portland, Maine. Given the competitive trends in the industry, it required more sophisticated products to compete. The CIO had a challenge to create new specialized solutions but with the same level of resources. The IT organization decided on a two pronged approach. It focused on enterprise data architecture and standardization as well as increasing IT efficiency so it could free up resources to work in the new solutions. Looking at data strategy across multiple functional areas helped plan and evolve an enterprise data strategy.

To align IT with business, the CIO designated IT staff who entrenched themselves in the lines of business and act as relationship managers with their business colleagues to ensure IT business alignment. The success from this approach has rewarded TD Banknorth nicely. The company has moved towards standardized governance of IT architecture, business process development and technologies across the enterprise.

Finally, there is a visible fissure between what vendors think as "the product" and what IT perceives as "the product" they are getting. This issue is at the heart of vendor management, technology management and product management. Figure 6.2 illustrates this chasm.

To vendors, technology features and functions are their product. Other aspects of the product such as service, maintenance, training, customizations and integration with existing applications are seen as add-on bells and whistles. They are merely after-thoughts.

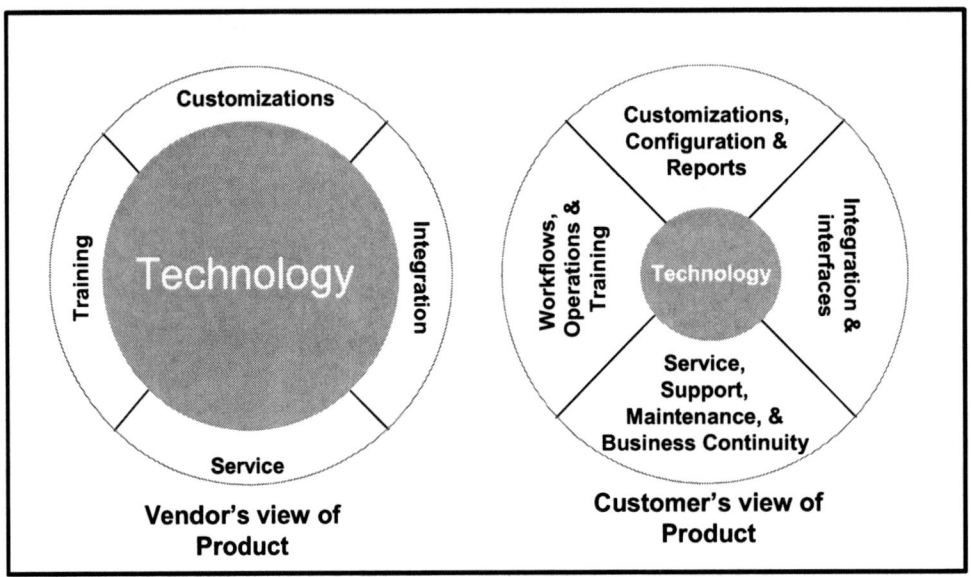

Fig 6.2 – Vendor's View versus Customer's View of Product

However, in IT department's view a product must come with all the niceties of tailored service, customized application, training, turn-key implementation, decision support reports, and interfaces unique to the firm and other soft services. The end-users' perception of product is less about technology and more about what the technology can do for them. IT must bridge this gap. Not many application providers understand this chasm. And, no wonder so many customers get buyer's remorse after implementing their IT applications. This gap illustrates the importance of managing information technologies from a customer perspective.

Finally, a word about an old rule of thumb, the rule of $1/3^{rd}$. It states that the upfront cost of a product is only $1/3^{rd}$ of the entire cost of ownership. The other $2/3^{rd}$ are implementation, maintenance and upgrade costs. No matter how perfect the vendor's solution, your IT organization will spend some level of effort, -sometimes small, but often immense amount, to make the solution work for the customer. Delivering good product is possible through Six Sigma techniques such as Taguchi method, Kano's model and Design for Six Sigma (DFSS). I'll explain these techniques in the ensuring chapters.

Stratagem: Every off the shelf solution will need to be adapted to your company's needs, objectives and environment. Consider using Six Sigma techniques such as Kano model to ensure best product fit, functionality, quality and low cost implementation.

Process Dimension

Having deep understanding of the firm's workflows is just as important as understanding the technical aspects of information technology. True that IT is a catalyst for change and a great enabling tool for workers to automate their work. But, workflows are becoming increasingly more complex. While we often see workflow and process used synonymously, we will shortly see their distinctions. For IT to be effective, we must revisit the old ways of doing analysis. In some cases we must abandon the old techniques. In other cases, we must combine multiple disciplines and perspectives in our analysis. I'm offering this section not as the only gospel on process design, but to show examples of how IT-centric workflow analysis can be performed to achieve new workflow models and insight with intent to enhance the value stream.

To begin with, I'll focus on workflow design with an eye on combining value streams, function-point analysis and use cases. In the following sections, we'll combine old flow chart techniques with use cases and function-point analysis. But, I encourage IT managers to apply their tools in any way that fits into their objectives and problems.

For example, in one instance I applied function-point analysis by considering the monetary value contribution from each function to determine whether it should make the development list or not. I called this "Function Value Analysis". It allowed my customers to see the value of each function (along with its cost of development of course) and decide if they want the function developed or not.

Now, let's head back to IT-centric business process redesign to make IT effective. We'll begin with an overview of IT-enabling workflows. Workflow is a combination of four elements: *Process, Practice, Protocol, and Path*; and three business modeling constructs: *Event, Rules* and *Entity*. As Lean IT experts, we are required to understand the language of workflow and process re-engineering. There are several outstanding books that discuss business process re-engineering for your reference.

Flowcharts have been used since their development in 1920s to describe flow of materials, data or state of a system. Flowcharts show the schematic representation of work or an algorithm. The building blocks of flow charts include: start and end, shown by an oval or circle; tasks shown by rectangles; flow of control, shown by arrows, decisions or conditions, shown by a diamond (rhombus). Because of increasing workflow complexity, we need additional tools for workflow design and re-engineering. We can apply new tools from Systems Theory, Lean, Agile and Theory of Constraints. Defining workflows can be accomplished by decomposing it into a series of tasks connected from start to finish by directional arrows indicating the flow of work in progress.

Typically each task is shown by a rectangular box; decisions by a diamond box; start and stop by a circle. There can be variations using other shapes. But the goal is to create a diagram that is self documenting, i.e. it explains what is happening in the workflow. Because work complexity is increasing, describing a workflow in terms of process, practice and protocol has become a necessity. This is true when we consider workflows that require collective teams working together.

For example, a surgery operation requires many tasks to be performed by several actors with different specialties such as doctors, nurses, technologists and other roles. Each actor follows their distinct workflow which must be orchestrated and synchronized together with other actors in an optimal fashion. Other examples include aircraft manufacturing, military operations and auto races. Multiple actors come together knowing exactly what must be done, when and how in order to complete the work.

I'm presenting only one of many possible workflow re-engineering models here. If this model appeals to you, great, if not, you can choose among other methods and standards. But, there are two practical advantages for using this model: A) you can use it to simulate the proposed workflow and determine if the effects of changes are acceptable before implementing, and B) you can translate this model directly in to a design that can easily and quickly be programmed or implemented. Let's review the basics of process, practice, protocol and path below:

Process answers questions to *what* and *how* a task is to be performed. A process definition answers questions such as "What tasks are to be done?" And, "How should the task be performed?" A process is a set of steps that are taken to complete a task. We can use a simple box as shown in Figure 6.3 to denote the process activity and any inputs and outputs related to that activity. The Process "P" contains a definition about the tasks that are to be completed in this task. This diagram explains what's the Input, and what's the expected Output from the process. Notice the process box allows the concept of Input and Output as measurable items, resources, information or material flow.

Practice answers questions to *when* and *who* should perform the task. For every task, we ask: "When should the task be done and by who in this task?" or "What should be communicated to who and when?" Practice definition can describe when a particular action is required and who will be performing that activity. A simple box as shown below can denote the role of actor (the person who carries a task), and parameters as input and output. Input parameters might include Time of activity, quality thresholds and tolerances, and other input variables. Output parameters might include quality data, time of completion, or other observed data. You may identify other types of Events, time-stamps, quality parameters and actors depending on the nature of work that is being studied.

Protocol answers questions that remove ambiguity about the task in a particular situation. A protocol is an agreed upon set of rules or guidelines to carryout a task in a specific circumstance. For example, in medicine, it's a set of treatment rules on how a patient should be cared for. In diplomacy it's about standards of behavior. In computing it defines how computers interact or exchange data. A protocol definition may describe the agreed-upon mode of behavior and response to a given situation. It's a critical piece of workflow definition. We use an oval or circular shape connected to a process or practice box to indicate that a particular protocol regulates the mode of performing the workflow.

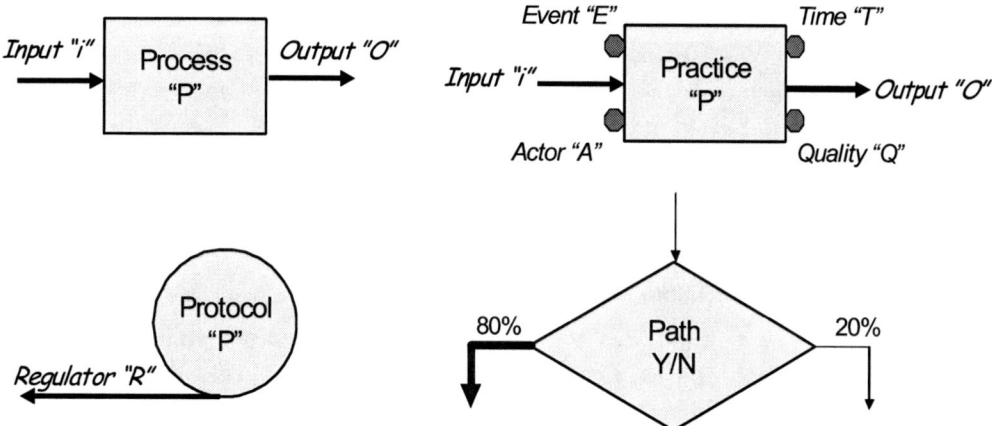

Fig 6.3 – Building Blocks for Workflow Composition

Path typically contains Yes/No or True/False conditions. It is represented by a diamond (rhombus) to denote "decision" or "choice" in flow charts. The symbol as shown below has two arrows indicating the path that will be taken if the condition is Yes/ No. Each decision arrow shows the probability, namely the likelihood that the path will be taken. Notice the more probable path appears as a thicker arrow. Good workflows should minimize decisions and alternate paths as much as possible.

All four workflow components above, must encapsulate three modeling constructs: *Business Entity, Business Rule, and Business Event*:

Entity means the item, artifacts and data generated or required for each type of workflow. For example, "accounts receivable", "address" and "customer order" are business entities. Workflow documentation must define the business entities.

Rules also known as the business rules typically define or constraint an aspect of workflow to guide or control certain decisions and behaviors. They are typically written as "IF ___ THEN _____ applies", where a business can fill out the blanks. Business rules often focus on access control, decision criteria and triggers. For example, IF car is driven 3,000 miles since last oil change, THEN schedule an oil change, is a basic rule about oil change.

Events are triggers that activate other workflows. A trigger becomes valid if certain condition or threshold is met. Business rules trigger events when a certain condition is met or a threshold is reached. For example, IF sales are less than $2M, THEN offer promotion of 10% discount on second purchase, is an automatic business rule that can apply to a web store pricing.

All seven workflow components are important to capture business functions and to design information systems that support them. From this model of self-documenting workflow diagrams we can develop designs that can easily and quickly be implemented in an IT solution. There are plenty of options available depending on our goal and development process. We can write a use case from a workflow diagram. If you are considering an off-the-shelf application, the workflow diagram provides the necessary details to adapt the application precisely to the workflow. Some may prefer to translate the workflow diagrams into a Unified Modeling Language (UML) model. I'm one of them.

UML is an excellent design tool that can capture these workflow definitions and provides a built-in mechanism to capture use cases. There are many books available on UML. I've included two examples of Use-Case driven workflow diagramming at the end of this chapter which illustrate the methodology and power of process re-engineering for IT implementations.

Case Study: Use-Case Driven Workflow Analysis

When managers of a clinic decided to implement an application for recording their medical procedures, they had no workflow documentation. Without a workflow description, they could not define their application requirements.

First, they had to document their workflow and prepare a requirement specification. Once this step was complete, IT staff was able to issue a Request for Proposal (RFP) and solicit proposals from potential vendors. Documenting the workflow was done by an extreme programming method: the clinic manager and an IT analyst met in one session. The IT analyst documented the workflow as the clinic manager narrated her ideal workflow in a 3-hour long meeting.

When completed the workflow definition looked a lot like the diagrams in Figure 6.4. It delineated the process, protocol, practice and path in detail. The model was reviewed later through joint meetings between users and a systems analyst. This example illustrates how a graphic notation can be easily used by IT staff to build a "use-case" driven design of the ideal workflow and corresponding application. The diagram serves several purposes: It serves as a common descriptive model of workflow among workers; it serves as a design template; and it establishes a contract between the stakeholders and IT as to what the IT staff will deliver to them.

The model was presented at a Kaizen meeting. Final comments and changes were gathered from the meeting. The diagram captured the flow of activity in a surgery room for certain "angiography" procedures. The safety, legal and regulatory requirements are that for each surgery the procedures must be recorded, tracked and documented in detail and in a single application. This final workflow shows what actions must be taken, when and by who. It captures the sequence of process steps, time stamps and quality parameters at the start and end of most tasks. It includes a few protocols shown by "C", "D", "E" to denote the type of "Checks", "Delays" and "Events" that are necessary protocols for each task.

What is noteworthy about this diagram is that it allows rapid prototyping and development of the application since it shows exactly what is really happening in the procedure room from start to completion of ...

... a case. It shows parallel process steps for different actors: the physician, the technologist and the patient. The results were remarkable. An application software was purchased and configured according to the use-case design to handle the specific protocol, business rules, practice, protocol and various events.

From the data collected during medical procedures, the clinic manager can generate a vast amount of quality metrics, utilization statistics and measurements.

As a result of this application, the surgery clinic has learned when to schedule the right mix of inpatient and outpatient clients and to be more efficient. The department has reduced idle time and delays during and between surgery cases, thus increasing its capacity to handle more medical procedures by 25%. This represents a significant financial improvement for the surgery department both in terms of additional revenue and also reducing the capital expense (costs of adding more surgery rooms are substantial and the surgery department avoided the capital expense).

Prior to conducting the Kaizen event, each actor documented her procedural work independently and in free text. There was no consistency among actors across the workflow. Data captured was not in consistent scale nor normalized. It was nearly impossible to perform any quality improvement without dependable data.

The events, checkpoints, time stamps and delays which should be recorded consistently and on time were often missed. The user workflow and requirement seemed complex and confusing. After the Kaizen event and the Use-case driven workflow was created, clear specification and actionable requirements emerged which were incorporated into the new application successfully.

Looking at the diagram we can trace the workflow and how the software application should orchestrate activities among multiple actors. Quality values that must be recorded in the application are shown as Q1 and Q2. These are the quality comments that physicians enter into the application.

Time values are shown as T1 to T10. The time stamps are automatically recorded by the application. Checkpoints such as "pre-procedure verification" are recorded by C1 and C2.

Stratagem: Define & document the workflow associated with each value stream in terms of *Process, Protocol,* Practice and *Path*. Use these building blocks along with *Events*, *Entity* and *Business rules* to frame the workflow automation and orchestration for the organization.

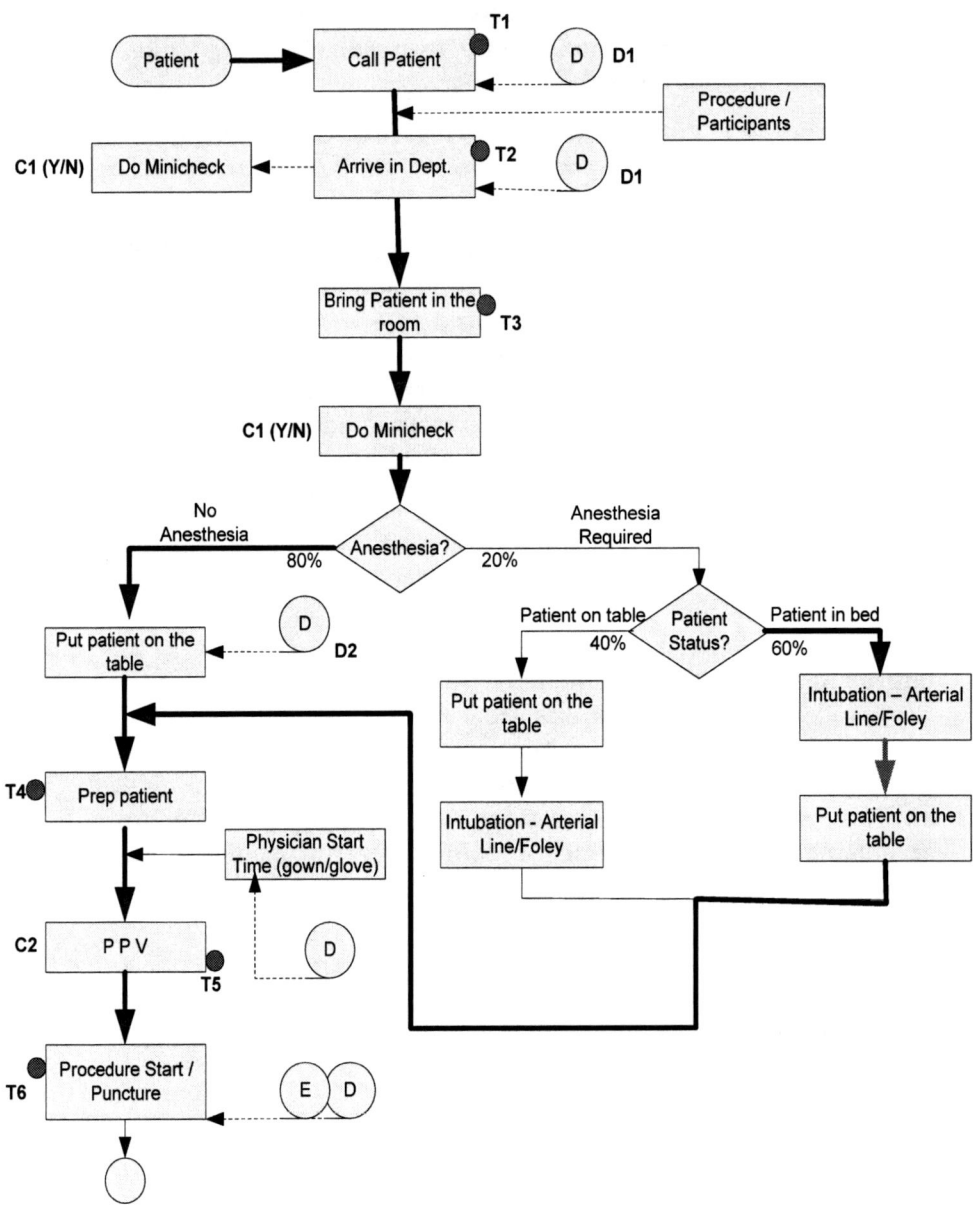

Fig 6.4 – Part 1. Sample Workflow Diagram Depicting Process, Protocol & Practice

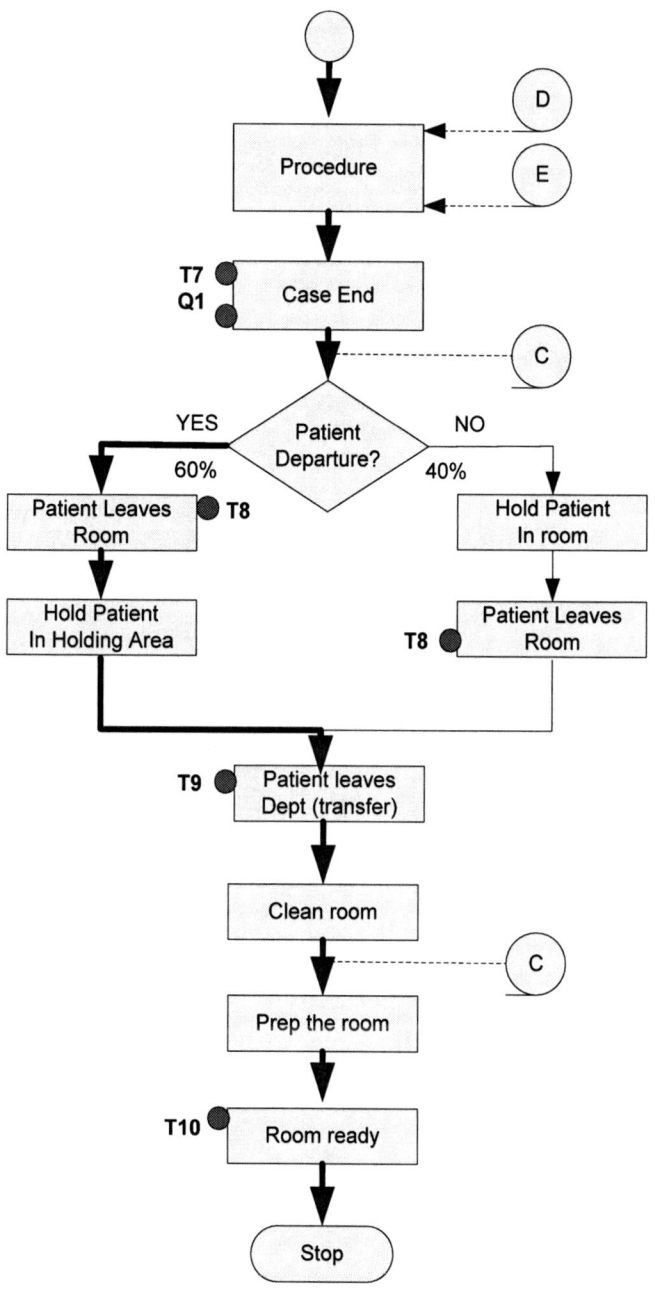

Fig 6.4 – Part 2. Sample Workflow Diagram Depicting Process, Protocol & Practice

As an illustration of how a Kaizen event can produce a blueprint for information technology and a detailed design let's review another use case (Figure 6.5).

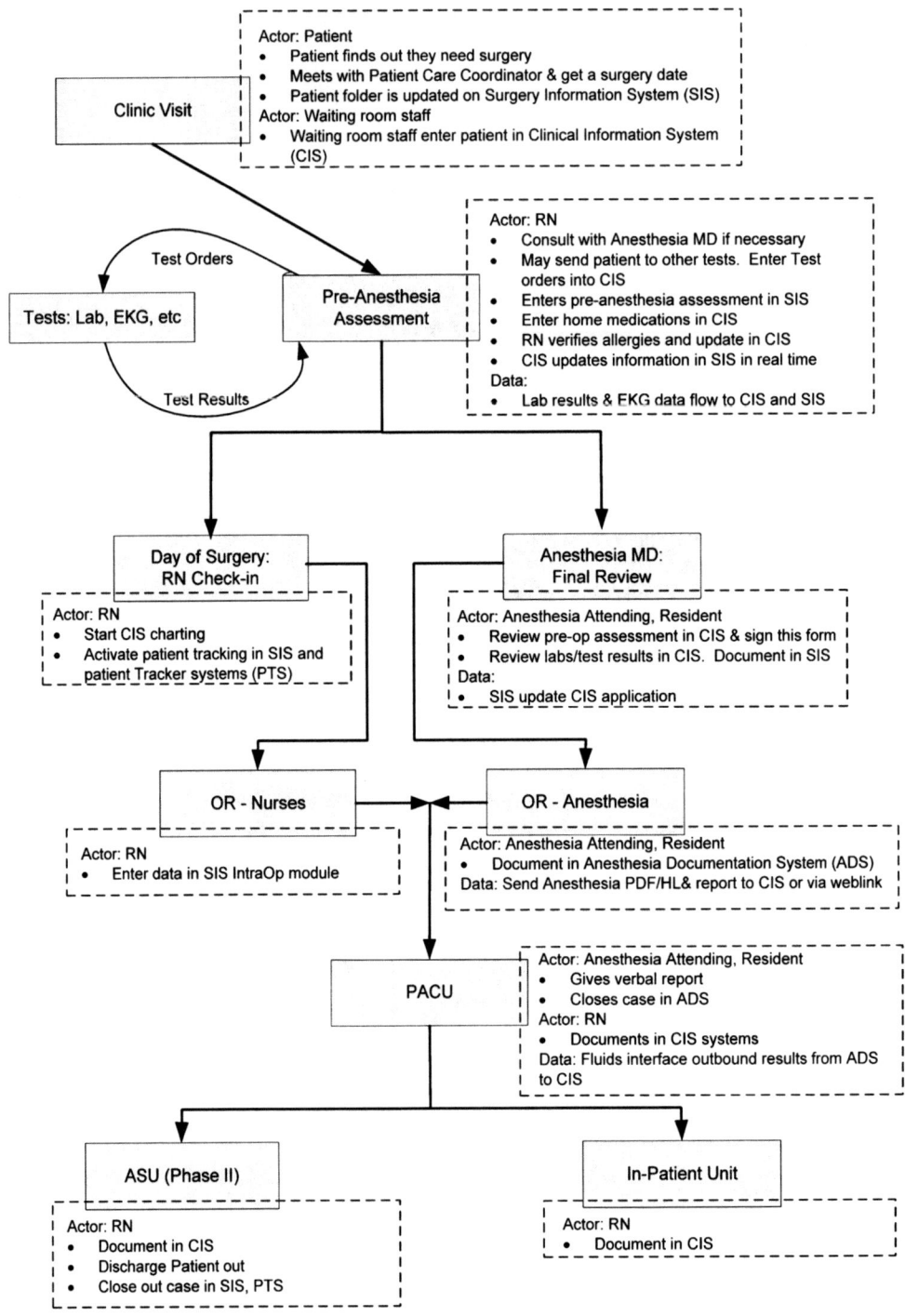

Fig 6.5 –Sample Workflow Documentation in Use-Case Design Notation

The diagram shows a low-level design for a rather complex, multi-actor clinical workflow. This workflow describes the value stream for a patient's surgery case, starting from pre-operating procedures to discharge from operating room. The diagram shows how such data must be recorded, when and by who. It represents the combination of process, practice and protocols. The purpose of this example is to illustrate how a design as a result of a Kaizen event can actually be achieved. Using the Use-case driven workflow analysis, it's fairly straight forward to develop an application or configure an existing application to enable this new workflow. As you may have noticed already, the functions described in each box are value adding steps only. These are the steps that are to be automated via the software application. The list of functions and features in the application will directly focus on these value adding steps. The entire workflow actually spans over eight different applications: A surgery scheduling system, a nurse charting application, a registration system, lab application, the cardiology system, the electronic medical record and the anesthesia charting application. Note that each process box has a dashed box next to it that defines the interaction between Actor (user) and the applications. It defines the Data and Functions in each box. The take away from these examples are that in-depth analysis of value adding steps are necessary. Also, workflows can span multiple databases and applications. The IT analyst must understand the workflow, data elements and functions by conducting use-case driven analysis of workflows.

Using the Function Driven Development (FDD) methods a library of functions from these use-cases can be prepared. Assembling a library of such functions can lead to building re-usable services that enable such workflows. This is the starting point of service oriented applications which will enhance re-usability and productivity for the IT organization.

Service Dimension

Service quality can be defined as the difference between what customers expect for service performance and their perception of the service they actually get. Proponents of this definition, argue that Information Technology function is a service function and consequently the attitudes of users as primary customer are credible indicators of IT effectiveness. The gap between what users want and what they actually receive can be measured. Research in this area suggests a gap analysis model as a conceptual framework for achieving user satisfaction.

I recall one IT manager in a presentation to company executives referred to IT users as his colleagues, not as customers. The IT manager was quickly challenged by the executives and later by the user community. Users and corporate executives justifiably expect certain performance and service levels for their investment in IT. They want to see some level of IT commitment to service, support and implementing applications that achieve corporate objectives. In relation to the IT organization, should users be viewed as colleagues, customers or clients? Is there a difference between these perspectives? In this context, let's take the term "users" to mean the user community, including managers of those communities. Some definition of these relationships might help set the right tone in the organization.

Users as Colleagues: In this model, users and IT staff have a symmetric, fluid relationship, often undefined or undocumented. Users' expectations from IT staff can vary from user to user, as the type and quality of services vary depending on situations and timeframes. This is an ad-hoc, unpredictable (as in unreliable) service model. IT is satisfied with delivering basic and minimum, often inconsistent services. Users are for the most part left to make their own IT decisions and acquire what they need. Often in order to satisfy an IT need, users resort to hiring outside contractors to handle certain services not delivered by the IT organization. In return, IT staff should expect minimal funding. Less mature and unsophisticated IT organizations tend to be content under this model. Since IT processes, capabilities and management have not matured, there is no service level agreement (SLA) in place with users. Delivering IT services in an ad-hoc manner is acceptable to users. Consequently, IT governance either does not exist or is ineffective. IT is not used with strategic intent. This model does not meet the Lean and Agile principles.

It would be inappropriate for the firm because it does not commit to any target of performance and does not bring process and service quality to the organization. In one case, I saw each business unit hire its own staff because the central IT organization simply ignored the business unit's needs and did not commit to any service levels. Such IT organizations are likely to be fragmented and miss on the real strategic advantages of information technology.

Users as Customers: This is the most common view of users in IT industry. It underscores IT's role as a service organization. Customers, user communities that allocate financial budgets, fund the IT organization, and in return, IT staff delivers services to those users. The level of service varies based on the funding levels. But, both sides have a set of pre-agreed service level agreements (SLAs). Customer satisfaction is usually a key measure and IT management is committed to serving its customer's needs. Those needs are assessed regularly. Users, collectively represented by department managers or C-executives, participate in forming the IT direction, short term and long term IT plans. IT delivers its services as products that fit the customer's needs and expectation. Often status of IT projects are reviewed by the executive management team or steering committees where customers have a voice, and IT managers listen to the voice of customer.

Users as Clients: This model encourages partnership between IT and users at all levels of strategic, organizational, and business operations. IT staff are expected to create and deliver superior value to other departments and individual users. Value can be created by IT staff in a variety of forms; by enabling strategic initiatives; delivering business solutions that significantly increase profitability, productivity and overall strategic achievement; access to new markets and usher new products.

In this model, IT staff step in as consultants who take on responsibility and ownership of the client's problems and bring solutions to them. IT staff are encouraged to know their users' business, their workflows, factors that affect their work and how IT solutions can solve their problems. One Lean IT manager summarized her mantra as:"If you want to be a consultant to your clients, you must know your client's business inside and out, even better than them." C-executives have a high degree of trust in the CIO and in the IT organization. They regard IT as a partner and include IT managers in formulating the corporate and departmental strategies.

User Satisfaction: A Service Metric

There are a number of methods for measuring user satisfaction. With the advent of web-based systems, several metrics for user satisfaction and IT effectiveness are available online. User satisfaction is a key indicator of IT's effectiveness. We are interested in improving factors that affect user satisfaction in three tiers: individual users, community of users or groups, and the enterprise.

Typical satisfaction factors at user level include the following:
1. System availability
2. System response time
3. Ease of access to information
4. Number of clicks required to perform a function
5. Information accuracy and consistency
6. Availability of self service functions
7. Intuitive interface and ease of use
8. Number of defects or failures encountered during each session

The factors that affect Service quality drivers include:
1. Help desk or Service desk responsiveness
2. Knowledge level of staff.
3. Staff's ability to resolve user issues
4. How quickly the user problem is resolved

At the group level there are other metrics of interest that affect user satisfaction. They can include the following factors:
1. Ability to improve communication with other team members
2. Ability to enable and improve workflows
3. Analytical and decision support features
4. Groupware tools that facilitate collaboration on a common project

The drivers of management and executive satisfaction with IT are driven by level of IT alignment and its effectiveness in meeting corporate goals. The factors that affect the management and executive satisfaction at enterprise level include:
1. Enabling corporation to meet its objectives
2. Availability of decision support information
3. Application of IT to streamline operations
4. Partnership to solve problems
5. Delivery of IT solutions with in time and within budget

Stratagem: Customer satisfaction is a major indicator of IT effectiveness. If your IT organization could only deliver one thing, that would have to be the best service possible.

Let's review the E*Trade case study below[35].

Case Study: E*Trade Trades in for Lean & Agile Methods

E*Trade is regarded as a leading internet companies in the world. In 1990's the company began by offering low cost online trading to traders. But eventually, it sought to be the destination portal for diverse investors. The companies' objectives were to attract new investors, create multiple revenue streams and increase customer cost of switching to other online brokerage firms. E*Trade began a strategic technology initiative to expand its technology base and reduce online trading problems. It was reported that while securities brokerage companies had enjoyed rapid growth based on technology, as much as 45% of trades were mishandled in the industry. Customer complaints were handled by email or phone but neither mediums were satisfactory to customers.

E*Trade wanted to stand out as the trading company with the best customer service. Despite investments in information & communication technologies, there were many glitches due to network routing, peak transaction volumes and software problems. A transaction that would normally take a few seconds would take up to 20 minutes during high web traffic. The company executives had to be Agile as they recognized the volatility of securities market and the fierce competetion to expand online investment services. Management accelerated development of its trading system and website. It overhauled its C++ based system with a system based on BEA System's Tuxedo Architecture, a distributed, component based environment. It implemented several Netscape Enterprise Servers connected by Cisco System Local Director for web traffic load sharing and balancing. The BEA Tuxedo system manages transactions while the Netscape servers manage user sessions. After the technology re-architecting, the application reliability and performance improved drastically. By 1998, E*Trade was adding 2,000 new customers and handling around 40,000-50,000 transactions per day. To coordinate system changes quickly the chief technology officer called for daily change management sessions at 5:30AM, one hour before opening of the stock markets in the U.S. In 1998, the company spent $75 million on upgrading its systems including its Destination E*Trade Website and E*Trade technology architecture. As a result of these changes, the company could handle 150,000 simultaneous customer orders. Next, it focused on building partnerships to enhance its products and services. For example, it partnered with ISP service providers such as AOL to give customers easy access to E*Trade services. Similar partnership with Microsoft allows Microsoft Investor service and MS Money application direct access to E*Trade's online investing services.

---

[35] This case study is based on "E*Trade Securities, Inc., Pioneer Online Trader, Struggles to Stay on Top", Adam T. Elegant, Ramiro Montealegre, in Cases on Electronic Commerce Technologies and Applications, Mehdi Khosrow-pour, Editor, Idea Group, Inc. 2006

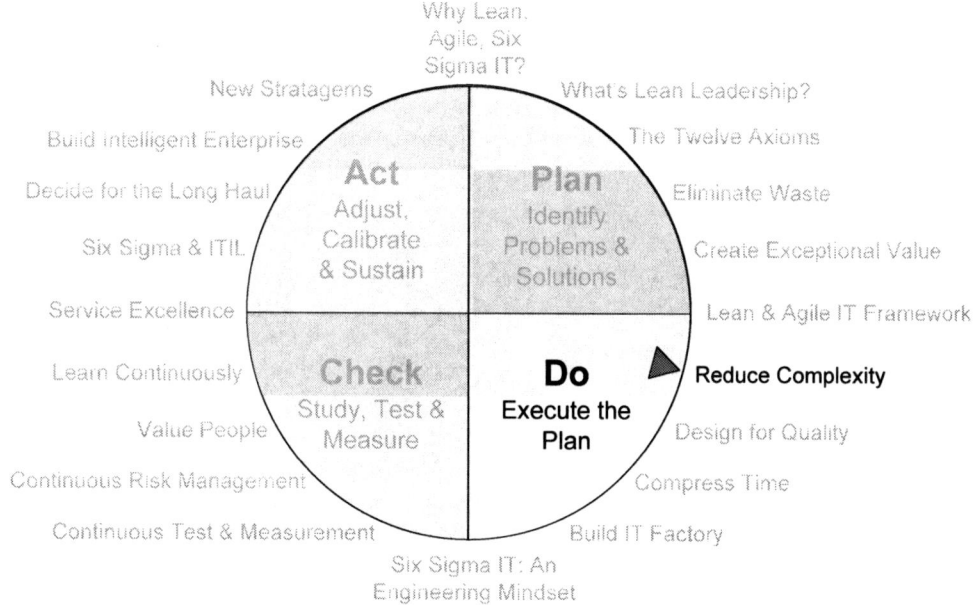

"Almost all quality improvement comes via simplification of design, manufacturing... layout, processes, and procedures."

Tom Peters

"One of the key outcomes of creative thinking is simplicity. Time, mental stress and money can be saved by simplification. Therefore, I believe a drive towards simplicity should be a key part of any organization's policy."

Edward De Bono

Chapter 7: Reduce Complexity

A popular concept of Lean thinking that eliminates waste and helps continuous improvement is 5S. 5S is about "Sort", "Set in order", "Shine", "Standardize", and "Sustain". Companies who have applied these 5 steps have created safer and more productive work environments. This is due to the increased organization in the workplace. Edsger Dijkstra who is a well known pioneer and author of many computer programming books once stated: "Simplicity is prerequisite for reliability". 5S can be used to reduce IT complexity quite effectively.

Waste in IT comes in several flavors. Unfinished and partially completed application releases top the list. Too often project hand-offs from one group to another, causes repetition of tasks or misunderstandings that result in defects. Implementing extra features that are not necessarily adding value, also known as gold plating are another source of waste. Interdependencies between tasks cause delays which lead to longer project lead times. Delays and Defects are other sources of waste. Finally, unnecessary task switching results in lingering unfinished tasks because it forces the IT staff to repeatedly break their concentration and reset their mind as they switch between tasks. Studies have shown that knowledge workers are most productive if they work on 3 tasks simultaneously, and no more. But when the number of simultaneous tasks increases to 5, their productivity actually decreases due to the restart cost associated with task switching.

Using Five "S" To Reduce Complexity

Most companies who start Lean initiatives begin with implementing 5S at the work place. The goal of 5S is to create a clean and organized work environment. This involves basic housekeeping and rules for keeping the production floor clean. Its objective is to organize, sort and create visual controls of the inventory, reduce waste, improve work in progress and quality. Developed in Japan, the 5S is broken into 4 activities and one conviction as follows:

1. Sort: This step is intended to sort all equipment and materials based on frequency of use. It removes items that are not used out of the work area. Its goal is to leave only the equipment and materials that are necessary to perform daily activities. For IT managers, this is synonymous to prioritizing projects and tasks; knowing how projects consume different resources at different phases of their life cycle. Priority of tasks must give IT a streamlined operations and balanced flow of application releases. IT managers may decide to give priority to a particular project over others if the project is near completion or if other applications are waiting on its completion. It also means sorting through the unfinished projects and completing the critical ones rapidly. For the systems manager, it implies sorting through systems and applications; retiring old systems and reports that are no longer needed; creating as-build documentation of the current infrastructure; Clean up of log files; backup of old files and removing any unused applications or scheduled jobs.

Sort attempts to take an inventory of projects, problems, and deliverables, then prioritize them. In this step we prioritize application backlog, feature requests, work in progress according to customer-valued ranking. Furthermore, we retire old applications and servers that will never be used. We make a list of IT issues, problems and complex decisions. This forms an inventory of demands for IT. In one firm, after we sorted the applications based on their number of users on a bar graph we discovered a long tail problem. Aside form a few enterprise applications a group of departmental and division-level applications with smaller user base emerged. It became clear to the IT executives that their processes for handling enterprise applications and departmental applications had to be different. The long tail applications were going to be managed by Agile and Lean methods. This is shown in Figure 7.1. Similar graphs about many IT metrics can reveal simple "aha" picture of the problem that make tacking the problem easier.

Another sorting tool is the binary sort that we've long used in computer algorithms. A binary approach to sorting divides a list into two parts based on certain criteria and then repeats the process until the item is found. When we divide the network infrastructure into zones, or when we try to isolate bugs to a particular segment of the network by applying binary rule, we approach the root cause of the problem most rapidly. As another sorting tool we use the Pareto rule repeatedly in sorting. If we apply Pareto's 80-20 rule, we can separate 20% of systems that represent 80% of the complexity. Applied once more to the 20%, we get 4% of the systems that need to be focused on, replaced or modified to resolve the complexity.

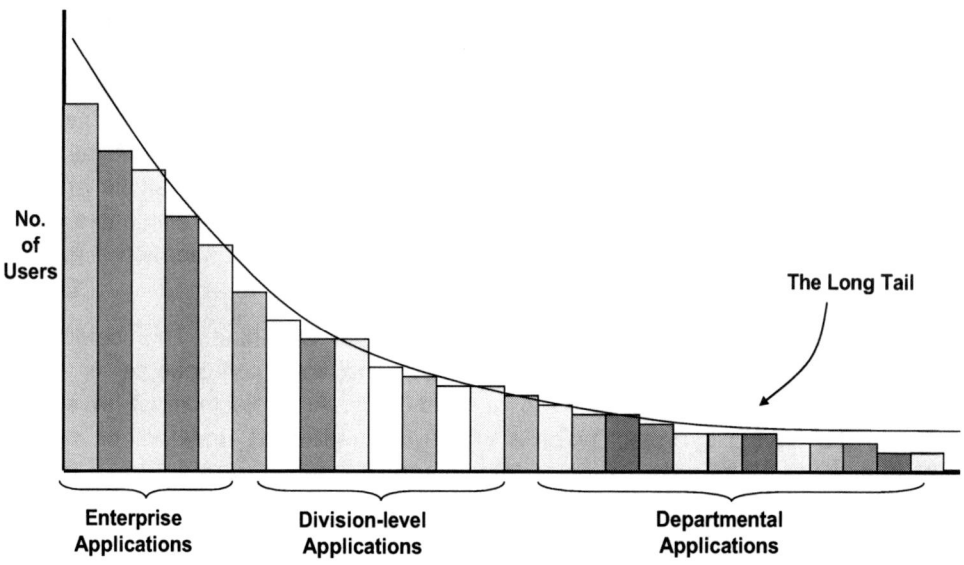

Fig 7.1 – The Long Tail As a Sorting Tool

2. Set in Order: The second stage of 5S is intended to orderly arrange all materials and equipment. In the context of IT environment, sorting and setting in order might include shelving and properly placing items in pre-designated locations. These item include tools, test fixtures, documentation, workbench, cables, etc. It could also imply sorting software tools, organizing and sorting storage by category, implementing document management systems, and version control and application virtualization. In this step, we arrange the IT assets, designs and solutions and match them to issues, complex decisions and problems identified in step 1. This step attempts to define enterprise architecture and standards including patterns for design, development, integration and testing of individual applications. This step segments complex problems and large projects into sub components and removes interdependencies between them.

One IT organization created a common test lab where test fixtures could be reserved and borrowed by different development teams using barcode scanners. When testing was completed, all test equipment was returned to designated locations. Before setting the lab equipment in order, each group wasted a lot of time searching for test space and equipment, which often led to confusion and conflict between different development teams. After implementing 5S, the lab was kept in pristine and usable condition. Less time was wasted on finding space and lab time, and more time could be devoted to testing by the development staff.

3. Shine: The goal of shine is to keep the workplace tidy, clean and organized. It prevents clutter and dirt in work areas that can be messy and cause hazardous work conditions. The purpose of shine is to keep scrap, shavings, cutting and dirt from falling on the floor in the first place. Within the context of IT, the goal is to remove old equipment, scrap cables and monitors from the work environment that should be purged. The same is true for the server and application management.

Retire old applications and servers as soon as they are replaced by new systems. (A new system must obsolete the old one. Never get in the situation of maintaining a legacy and a new system). Periodic spot checks of server and database log files, database storage compression, disk de-fragmentation, and security logs are examples of shine and are good systems management practices that fall into this category. The benefits of shine are that the equipment and applications are always ready to use. Routine system hygiene is part of daily activity that eliminates the need for major spring cleaning. For the IT management, eliminating paper is a step towards universally creating tidy workplace.

Infrastructure clean up is another example of Shine. This could include replacing poor performing or poorly installed network components or software applications with the correct patch level or updates. All projects must have a visual display, like having a project website where their status is updated, or dashboard where detailed status information is maintained. IT managers must track issues list and resolve issues that recur frequently. Such issues are typically obtained from the trouble ticketing systems or user work requests. Maintain a clean board either electronically or on a white board listing user work requests that are pending completion or are still open. Test applications or solutions immediately after they become available. Perform simulated or mock go-live tests. Resolve issues, defects, and warnings associated with the mock-go live. Perform production readiness checks before final go-live. Create and maintain a library of tools, scripts and documents. Create and maintain a knowledge base of troubleshooting trees, infrastructure updates and logs of application updates and changes.

This step removes any features and projects that are not valued by the customer. Our focus should be on developing the 20% of the solution that satisfies 80% of customer's requirements. The intent of shine is to release any unfinished work in progress that can be easily completed. In other words, the goal of this step is to clean up the backlog of tasks and unfinished applications.

4. Standardize: The fourth stage of 5S promotes orderliness at its core. This is achieved by adopting standards for labeling, color coding, and other methods of creating structure. The intent of this step is to develop standards and processes for all facets of IT tasks including hardware, software, troubleshooting, purchasing, project management, reports, disaster recovery, and help desk across the enterprise

In the context of Information technology management, standards apply to several areas:

Communication: Regular status updates from staff and groups; regular announcements of system downtime plans and maintenance plans; a 3-month rolling schedule of future application releases and planned downtimes.

Change control: Notify and obtain change approval before updating, upgrading or releasing new systems into production environment. We will review Change control in more detail when we discuss ITIL standards in the coming chapters.

Hardware and Software Tools: Specifications for hardware and software tools that ensure low maintenance operations and high uptime.

Infrastructure management: Specifications and standards for datacenter management, such as class 1, 2 or 3 datacenter, network infrastructure, cabling, data closet wiring, and switch fabric standards.

Systems integration: Specifications for security, IP addressing, development environment, desktop and mobility devices.

Development: Specification for testing standards, development process, quality inspections, prototyping, pilot programs such as alpha and beta releases. Maintain standard naming conventions, coding standards, error logging and security standards.

Data: Standardize on database structures, dataflow diagramming, file formats and structures, database reports, data migration tools and query optimizations.

5. Sustain: Learn and retain knowledge from steps 1-4. Train and maintain 5S discipline by repeating steps 1-4. The last stage of 5S is commitment and discipline to maintain an orderly work environment that is clean and always ready for use. The intent of this stage is to train staff to keep the prior 4 steps in mind and to prevent the work place from reverting back to chaos and clutter.

Outside the IT department, to standardize and sustain 5S, information technology can offer excellent solutions such as bar coding, RFID tags, electronic whiteboards that are visible in the entire enterprise, and workflow orchestration software.

Simplification through 5S – A Heuristic Approach

5S has been a great tool to organize manufacturing shop floor. In IT, 5S can bring structure, organization and clarity to daily management as well as short term and mid-range planning and execution. 5S can be applied to operations, decisions, problem solving and customer services. We'll review 5S several times in this chapter to apply its principles to multiple aspects of IT management. 5S is a valuable problem solving and plan setting tool. The complexities that plague IT are multi-dimensional and sometimes non-linear in nature. As a result, there are often multiple, seemingly conflicting perspectives about what should be done next; which decision or alternative action should be followed.

Fortunately, Kaizen and Hoshin methods have simplified the process by simply focusing on what customers value most. Whether we are fixing a problem or seeking to plan and execute an objective, the process should focus on the customer-valued topics. We can apply 5S to either solving big, complex problems or to determine a stratagem to reach certain goals and objectives.

The purpose of this section to describe how big, complex problems can be simplified and organized through 5S. Similarly, the same principles can be applied to big, complex objectives or Hoshin plans. In that event, we would ask questions such as: In order to achieve this objective, what specific tasks or projects must be completed successfully? The answer will construct the branches of the fishbone diagram.

1. Sort: The goal of this step is to sort out what does not add value or is not valued by the customer. We can form a 2x2 matrix to find the high impact problems or objectives. It basically means sorting problems (or objectives) by complexity or size and by the value of solving the problem.

For example, the 2x2 matrix shown in Figure 7.2 sorts the problems by size and by their value to the customer. Using this matrix, we can narrow the list of problems to just a few high-impact items, those that are high value, complex and big. The smaller, easier high-value problems can be resolved through Kaizen events. Those that are not valued by customers should not distract employees and management from the high-impact problems. The few, big and complex problems are then decomposed in the next step. In the diagram, big problems are shown as big circles and smaller problems as smaller circles. Managers can assign a "problem statement" to each circle.

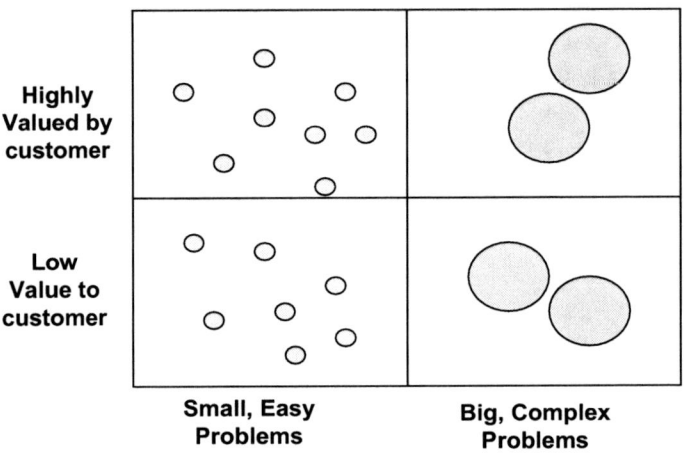

Fig 7.2 – 2x2 Matrix to find the high-impact, big and complex problems

2. Set in order: We apply root-cause analysis or an influence diagram to decompose every high impact big problem into smaller problems. A fishbone diagram can be used to diagram the root cause of the problem. The process of decomposition or de-aggregating the complex problem starts with asking two questions: Why does this problem exists? And, what problem needs to be fixed first before we can solve this problem. The answers construct the branches of the fishbone diagram. This approach attempts to decompose the problem into its subcomponents.

For example, the diagram in Figure 7.3 starts with the high-impact complex problem on the right side of the page. Why does this problem exist; and what problems need to be resolved in order to fix this problem? The answer is we need to resolve problems "A", "H" "J" and "E". In order to resolve problem "A", we need to resolve problems "B" and "C". The process continues until the end branches are decomposed into simple problems. The items closest to the main branch are tier-1 problems. By adding branches, we move from first tier problems to second tier problems and so on. There could be many tiers. The outer most items, typically the fourth and fifth tier problems are the root-cause of issues. During this process, it's conceivable that some of the smaller problems on the fishbone diagram are repeated and some might have been spotted in the 2x2 matrix. That's Most managers attempt to tackle a complex problem without identifying the underlying issues and their interdependencies. The fishbone approach identifies the root cause problems and sets in order the sequence of resolving them.

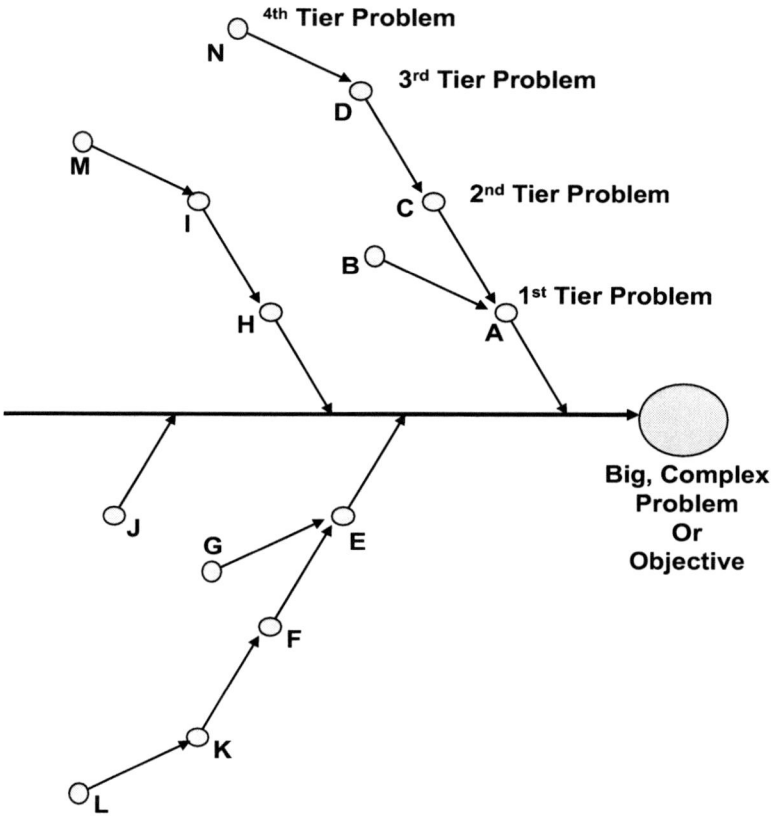

Fig. 7.3 – Fishbone Diagram as a Problem Decomposition Method

The sequence of tackling the smaller problems is determined by listing the highest tier branches of the fishbone diagram first. These are smaller problems that must be resolved first before we can resolve a lower tier problem. These problems can be resolved independently via Kaizen or other methods such as Design for Six Sigma (DFSS).

By glancing at the fishbone diagram, we find problems "H", and "L" at the highest tier. We should resolve those before tackling third tier problems "D", "K", and "M". After addressing the third tier, we will resolve problems in the second tier: "C", "B", "I", "G", and "F".

Each problem can be assigned to different individuals to teams. The process continues until the first tier issues are resolved. The layered concentric diagrams show the root-cause problems in the most inner circle. The sequence of execution is from the most inner circle to the outer circle.

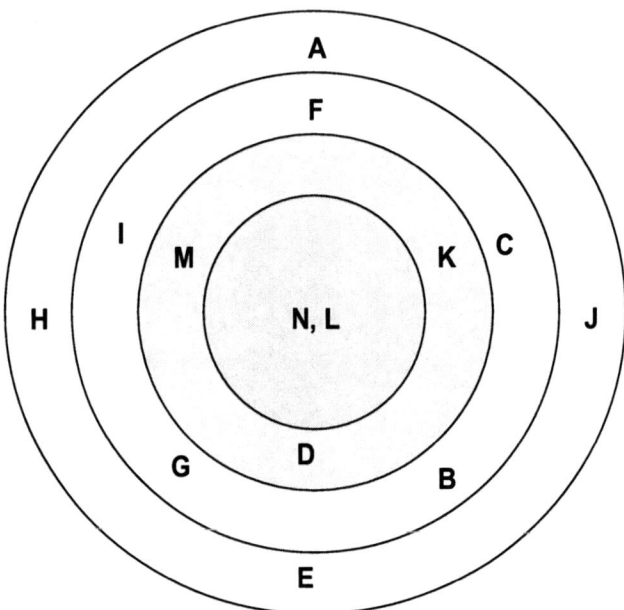

Fig 7.4 – Set In Order the Sequence of Resolving Issues to Solve the Complex Problem

3. Shine & Inspect: Once all first tier problems have been eliminated, we can begin to re-aggregate solutions to solve the big, complex problem. The purpose of Shine is to re-aggregate the solution and put the integrated solution into motion. The third S, also means Inspect. Management must validate that the integrated solution works properly as expected, and clean up the remnants of the big, complex problem. Similarly, if 5S were instead applied to achieving a complex objective, we would re-aggregate the solutions to meet the objective. The tool works the same, but managers can apply them for different purpose: either solving a big, complex problem, or to reach a big, complex objective.

4. Standardize: When we apply 5S process to reduce complexity, one benefit is insight into what are the problems and the order of resolution. The result is a transformation across operations, products and services which eliminate the complex problem. However, the new insight must be institutionalized and consistent across the organization. Standardization begins with documentation, education and communicating the value of consistency to employees. Standardization is a major tool for control and reducing deviation. The solutions that have been developed must be standardized so the big, complex problem does not re-occur under the guise of a new problem.

5. Sustain: To sustain problem solving, managers must repeat the 4S steps on the next complex problem until all big, complex problems are resolved. Sustain is a key step in continuous improvement. The entire company employees at all levels of the organization must be trained on 5S and be encouraged to apply it to their work. Employees must be encouraged to report small issues. Managers must keep a list of these small issues and treat them as early indicators of larger, more complex problems. According to Pascal Dennis in his book "Lean Production Simplified", there is a hierarchy of system and machine downtimes that foretell of future problems[36]. The "Machine Loss Pyramid" is a concept of tracking breakdowns, minor stoppage, minor failures and hidden failures.

In a 1931 book, entitled "Industrial Accident Prevention", Herbert Heinrich argued that for every serious injury, there are 10 minor injuries, 30 property damage incidents and 600 near misses. In the context of information systems, we observe servers, workstations, operating system, network and application failures leading to major downtimes. The "Service Loss Pyramid" shown in the next diagram (Figure 7.5) is adapted from Pascal Dennis' text. It illustrates the frequency of incidents that foreshadow major breakdowns.

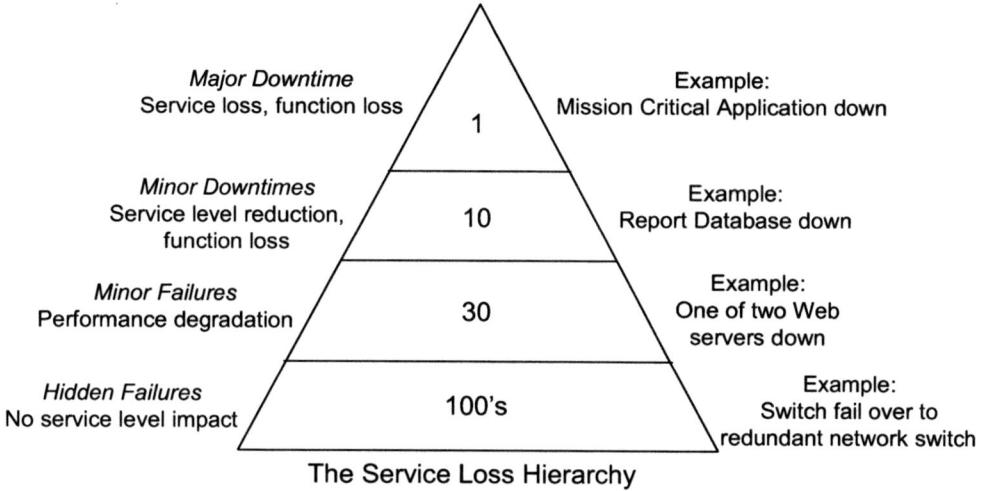

The Service Loss Hierarchy

Fig 7.5 – Service Loss Pyramid

The pyramid tells us that to prevent major downtimes, we must track and prevent the hundreds of hidden and minor failures in the IT infrastructure. To reach zero downtime quality, the IT processes and operational margins of error must be tightly defined and controlled. Minor failures, hidden failures and near-misses must be tracked and analyzed by IT management. A Pareto analysis combined with root cause analysis will point to patterns and trends that foretell of future downtimes. In addition to the 5S method, some Lean practitioners have suggested additional principles including "smart-sourcing", "safety", "simulation", "segmentation" and "symbiotic" relationship with suppliers. When considering information systems and IT management, we could consider these other principles. They include:

Synergy: partnering with vendors to develop and support applications reduces maintenance cost and overall cost of ownership. Vendors sell commodities, but partners really share your vision and take part in your business success. I encourage my staff to develop business and technical partnerships with vendors for a variety of reasons. Here are a few to consider: Synergy between IT staff and vendor partners allows access to the partner's skilled and talented developers. It also provides a

---

[36] "Lean Production Simplified", Pascal Dennis. Second Edition, Productivity Press, New York, N.Y. 2007

channel to get their assistance on difficult or complex architectural questions. At times of emergency, partners already know your business and IT environment and as a result they can actively and immediately be helpful. Partners are a great source of knowledge.

My staff often asks vendor partners about their experience at other sites. Among common questions we ask are: "How are your other customers doing this?" and "What are the best practices out there?" or "Could this be done in a better way?" I've often brought partners into a project to get extra tools, resources, assistance, and logistics help at virtually no cost. Often, I encourage my staff to perform disaster recovery drills with involvement of vendor partners.

Smart-sourcing: Smart-sourcing means outsourcing with strategic intent. It's advisable to outsource only certain activities to outside firms or to contractors, not everything. Smart sourcing can reduce direct and indirect costs significantly. For example, it can reduce the cost of inventory (the accumulated investments in unfinished projects and work in progress) and operating expense. But, there are 3 rules to smart-sourcing:

1. Never outsource an activity that is a part of or is directly your firm's core competency.
2. Outsource to a company or contractor who can do the activity better, faster and at a lower cost.
3. Outsourcing must free-up management attention such that your firm can focus on its core competitive advantage.

Simulation: The goal of simulation is to help management predict the impact of their decisions or workflow changes on the value stream and company performance before implementing those decisions. The same principle applies to many IT decisions.

Often complex IT decisions have to be made with inadequate data and facts. Simulation allows analysis of complex dynamic multi-variable scenarios before implementing a new work process or a decision. The role of simulation is to analyze outcomes for multiple scenarios. Even when perfect information is not available, we can use surrogate data (for example low, medium or high and probabilities about future occurrence of some events) to validate our assumptions and approximate the effect of our decisions.

Segmentation: This is also an Agile methodology. Its goal is to separate, partition and segment any aspect of information technology in order to simplify and control IT complexity. For example, when we segment we partition a development project into manageable chunks.

The focus is on developing the 20% of code that delivers 80% of the customers' critical requirements. When we divide a network into virtual LAN partitions, we are segmenting the infrastructure into more manageable segments. The idea behind segmentation is to decompose complexity into smaller, more manageable sub-systems (or sub-problems) where the cause-effect relationships and the vital facts can be defined more clearly. This is where architecture and framework become so useful as they segment while at the same time unify the problem-solution space.

Symbiotic: The goal of symbiotic relations is to build partnerships with vendors where IT department develops new applications or innovative solutions that are used internally and also can be licensed by the vendor. The IT department can collaborate in development with another partner or exchange solutions with a vendor under this arrangement.

Safety: The goal of safety is to use IT solutions to make workflows safer and mistake-proof. This includes application functions that prevent hazardous situations or targeted testing that prevents software defects that might cause adverse safety problems for users. The Japanese term for mistake-proofing is *Poka Yoke*. IT promises a vast opportunity to mistake-proof workflows, most of it is yet to be discovered and developed.

Sizing: The objective of sizing is to harmonize the IT solutions with the user demands. When I was consulting for a large firm, the CEO asked me to identify areas of improving productivity in the enterprise. I applied the theory of constraints to identify areas where productivity was low. I looked for the low hanging fruit, the productivity bottlenecks in the enterprise.

An immediate opportunity that I spotted was the poor sizing of workstations installed throughout the organization. The IT department had issued identical PCs to all staff and only laptops to managers. Many of the employees who spent their entire workday on the company's billing and revenue generating activities were disadvantaged because they required faster PCs than what the IT department had installed. This was particularly true because the company's financial applications were highly CPU and memory intensive.

Clearly these knowledge workers needed higher speed PCs at their desks to increase productivity. These departments had acknowledged huge backlog of work due to inadequate IT tools. When I sized and ranked the company's job roles based on PC power requirements, the CIO agreed to provide faster PCs to certain class of users according to their application requirements. As a result, the backlog of work decreased as productivity increased. Similarly, sizing should be applied to all aspects of network bandwidth, firewalls and storage capacity as well as server and workstation speed to create a balanced work environment.

Succession: Another name for iterative process. This approach promotes fast and repetitive cycles of application releases that delight the customers. Rather than using long development-and-test cycles followed by a big-bang release, try successive releases. "Succession" encourages faster development turns on incrementally releasing new features over time.

The goal of succession is to release a solution quickly typically in 2-6 weeks to meet the basic and fundamental customer needs first and then add additional features in the subsequent releases.

Summary

1. IT complexity is rooted in the multi-variable, often non-linear nature of IT work. Train staff on 5S principles so they can simplify their work.

2. IT complexity can be reduced by applying 5S technique:

a. Sort and segment big problems into smaller chunks. Maintain a list of issues as they arise. Use Fishbone diagram to separate and remove interdependencies between smaller problems.

b. Set in order by prioritizing tasks and problems. Set the sequence of problem resolution in order

c. Shine by removing non-value add tasks, features and problems from the backlog

d. Standardize all facets of IT activities: analysis, design, development, testing, release and support

e. Sustain by tracking small issues as they are early indicators of big, complex problems to come. Resolve small issues rapidly before they become big, complex IT problems. Prevent big, complex problems from stirring up. Employ Kaizen teams to resolve small problems before they compound together to become big problems.

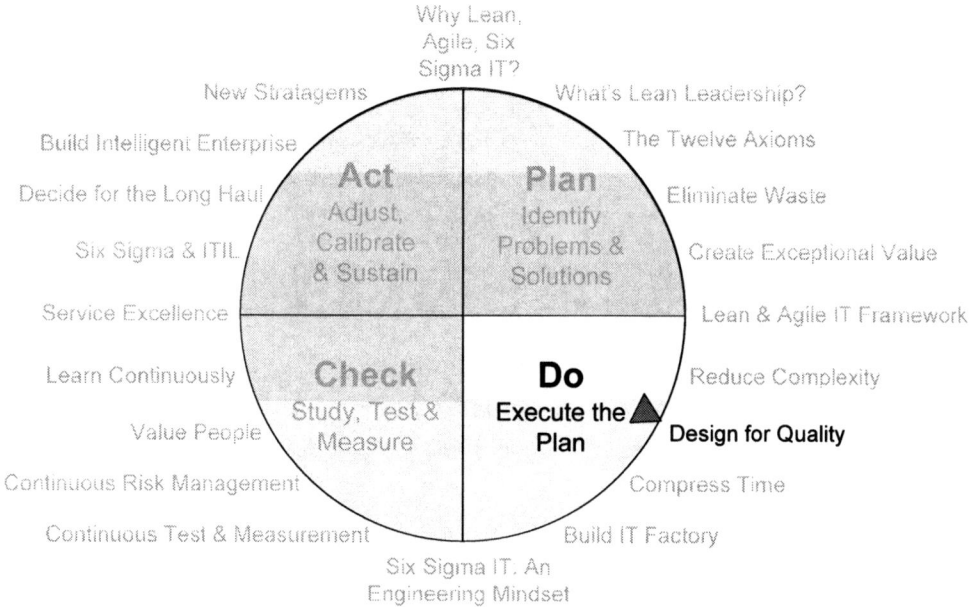

"Design is so critical it should be on the agenda of every meeting in every single department."

Tom Peters

"Quality is not a project based variable, but a corporate asset"

Ken Schwaber

Chapter 8: Design for Quality

In Lean, Agile and Six Sigma IT environments, nothing is built unless it's designed. IT staff conduct their work not as analysts or programmers but as engineers. The engineering mindset is a cultural change for many traditional IT organizations, but it's necessary if we strive for perfection. A survey conducted by Forrester Research in 2004 found that 84 percent of companies surveyed had centralized enterprise architecture groups of fewer than 10 people regardless of company size. If we are to be responsive and accommodating to the diverse and changing needs of our IT customers, Lean thinking guides us to consider establishing an IT architecture advisory group where quality and design can be underscored. The same principle motivates us to promote Service Oriented Architectures (SOA) as an underlying architectural model, and SaaS (Software as a Service) solutions. This chapter covers the elements of design for quality. We'll review topics such as FDD, Kano Model, PDCA, Communication Matrix, Information flow diagramming and Lean Architectures.

Feature Driven Development (FDD)

Feature Driven Development consists of 5 activities:

1. **Develop Overall Model.** This activity begins with a high level study of the requirements, scope and deliverables. The result is a proposed groups of

domains that together complete the solution. The domain area models are assigned to small groups which present to peer groups for discussion.

2. **Build Feature List.** Identify a list of features for each set of business activities. The features are defined in terms of <action> <result><object>. For example, "Compute Balance for an Account". Each feature is sized to be completed within 2 weeks.

3. **Plan by Feature.** Prioritize and plan development from list of features. Assign classes of features to different chief developers.

4. **Design by Feature.** The chief developer designs each feature and the overall model for those features. Then assigns development of each feature to a developer on the team. The developer completes the feature in two weeks.

5. **Build by Feature.** Conduct an overall design inspection by considering all features. After unit testing and code walkthroughs are completed, the feature is promoted to the main build.

If the intent of the workflow diagramming is to improve the workflow, we can apply the Kaizen method to eliminate non-value adding tasks. The next chapters explain the Kaizen procedure.

Lean Design & Architectures

To ensure quality and consistent implementations, Lean IT puts a huge emphasis on design and architecture. Similar to scaffolding during a building construction, Lean Architecture attempts to build flexible, modular and incremental solutions. Built in layers, laid one on top of another, the modular architecture delivers solutions early in the project life cycle and continues to expand functionality through scaffolding while maintaining flexibility to adapt to changing requirements. Design can take either an empirical approach or a deterministic approach.

The deterministic approach is a recount of the strategic planning school which has been shown to fail more often that to succeed. It attempts to define in detail the exact product requirements before completing design. In contrast the empirical approach begins with a high level product concept and after carefully defined repeated feedback loops converges towards the final interpretation of the concept and the design.

For example, Toyota's Prius development did not specify the size of the engine or even the fuel type and hybrid engine. It did not specify the dimensions of the vehicle either. However, it did specify a specific fuel economy metric of approximately 47 miles per gallon and a roomy interior for passengers. These conceptual design objectives later translated into specific type of engine and shape of the car. The preference for empirical development approach is not in conflict with six sigma design methodology. In fact it reinforces Design for Six Sigma (DFSS) methods which we will discuss in the coming chapters. Empirical approach is better suited to changing regulatory, customer or competitive requirements, because it can adapt better than the deterministic approach. This flexibility must be built into IT framework and architecture.

Service Oriented Architecture: An Enterprise IT model for Lean Thinkers

Studies conducted by MIT Sloan Centre for Information Systems Research (CISR) based on 456 enterprises between 1995 and 2006 identifies four distinct architectural stages – Silos, standardized IT, standardized business processes and business modularity.

These studies, "IT Architecture as Strategy" and "IT-Driven Strategic Choices" conducted under Jeanne W Ross, the principal research scientist at CISR, found that most of the enterprises are at stage one and two. The studies hint that when an enterprise has reached the fourth stage of IT architecture, it can most benefit from an SOA framework. According to Ross: "Each stage takes about five years to get through, although some firms are able to mature faster than others."[37]

In stage one, where departments approached IT in silos, they create a vast array of disjointed and rigid solutions that amount to islands of information. This led most enterprises to adopt standard technology platforms and common frameworks wherever possible. For example, they began to develop common standards for servers, databases, workstations and their configurations in stage two. Advanced enterprises that have standardized business processes are at stage three. IT management is regarded as a partner and ally in forging strategies and implementations. Information technology is viewed as an enabler and accelerator of business functions.

The fourth stage of architectural maturity is based on business modularity and agility. At this stage, workflows and their supporting information technologies become modular that can be re-used and replaced easily and rapidly as business requirements change. Going from stage one to two is within the confines of IT management and relatively easy to implement. But going from stage two and three to four require organizational change and executive leadership vision to implement. As mentioned earlier, SOA attempts to bring IT services to customers from myriad of ways. Leading enterprise architects believe that SOA can help businesses respond more swiftly and economically to the changing business landscape. Let's consider the IBM's utility model of IT for a moment. In a city, you do not receive all services from a single service company.

Similarly, in the SOA model, you should be able to access your desired IT services from any sources that make it available. In the enterprise IT city planning, SOA combines web services, legacy applications, and messaging to deliver a set of customer-valued functions. All IT services are aware of each other and collaborate to form what's known as a Federation. A service is a piece of software that can be accessed via a network to deliver functionality to a service requester which can be a user or another software component. Services can be used autonomously or can be

---

[37] "The Four Stages of Enterprise Architecture", Galen Gruman, CIO Magazine, Feb 07, 2007.

integrated to provide higher level services. Services communicate with their clients by exchanging messages. SOA is a design framework, not an implementation.

SOA represents an *open, extensible, collective* architecture that promotes integrated web services across diverse new and legacy applications in the enterprise. Service Oriented Architectures are comprised of *autonomous, Quality-of-Service capable, vendor diverse, interoperable, discoverable*, and *potentially reusable services*. SOA has come to be synonymous with a computing platform that is based on web service technologies and service-oriented principles. Use of web technology is an important principle of SOA for delivering those services. The SOA approach to architecture blueprint is that it unifies business processes by structuring large applications as a collection of smaller modules called services. These applications can be used by different groups of people, whether they are inside or outside the company, and through a mix of services derived from new or legacy applications.

SOA is about implementing standardized service abstraction layers and loosely connected relationships between business logic and application modules. Changes in either business logic or application technology are easily handled because of loose integration between the two. This fundamental approach promotes IT flexibility and agility. SOA is also evolutionary in its approach to application implementation, which underscores the points about prototyping, joint application design and incremental development processes. At the most fundamental level, SOA is built upon XML data representation.

XML documents and accompanying schema passed between applications standardize format and data typing in communication. It promotes creating common enterprise vocabularies. Since XML carries self-descriptive information, it makes it easier for developers to maintain, understand and trace data messages. SOA allows integration of existing legacy and best of breed applications because it can create a vendor-neutral communication framework. Thus it relieves IT departments from proprietary interfaces and expensive to maintain middleware. SOA goes beyond web service architectures. It abstracts the backend processing so it can evolve and execute independently by each application. Other fundamentals of SOA are Coordination, Discovery, Orchestration and Choreography.

Early in the evolution of SOA, a standard is used to specify a registry of all web services available and to allow all applications to discover these services. Coordination provides a framework for interaction of services, their context and activity life time in a state-less manner. Discovery means that services register their capabilities and can be discovered by other clients and services on the network. Orchestration is the function of a software architect to define and link services together to enable certain workflows and value streams in the appropriate sequence. In the process of orchestration, a software architect associates services in a non-hierarchical arrangement using a special software tool that contains a complete list of all services and their characteristics.

All these design elements are important because they allow modular, component-based, layered approach to building IT solutions. Lean and Agile production systems can be implemented when the "chunks" of deliverables get smaller. Services can participate in a workflow such that the order of messages affects the behavior of operations performed by a service. This is called service choreography. In an enterprise, services advertise such details such as their capability, interfaces, policies and communication protocols. Details about their implementation, such as programming language, operating system or hosting platform are not of importance to clients and are not revealed. Services are loosely coupled with each other, meaning that they exchange information through messaging that can be one-way, synchronous or asynchronous.

The benefits of SOA are flexibility, scalability, re-usability and replaceability. The other advantage of SOA designs is that they can capture business logic effectively and consistently by well-defined interfaces, loosely coupled federation of services and ability to encapsulate business functions. Service-Oriented Modeling Framework (SOMF) is a blueprint, a map depicting the diverse components that contribute towards a successful service oriented modeling approach.

SOMF was developed by Michael Bell as a service oriented development life cycle methodology. SOMF provides a common language to describe the collaboration requirements between modular business and services. As a framework, it helps identify the elements of service design schema and what each element is to deliver. SOM analysis is a key starting point for this framework. The next diagram depicts a process for SOA design. One of the interesting advantages of SOMF is ease of traceability and governance. The IT governance is easy since business objectives can easily be traced to services being offered through SOA designs.

Rapid Business Function Deployment with Service Oriented Approach

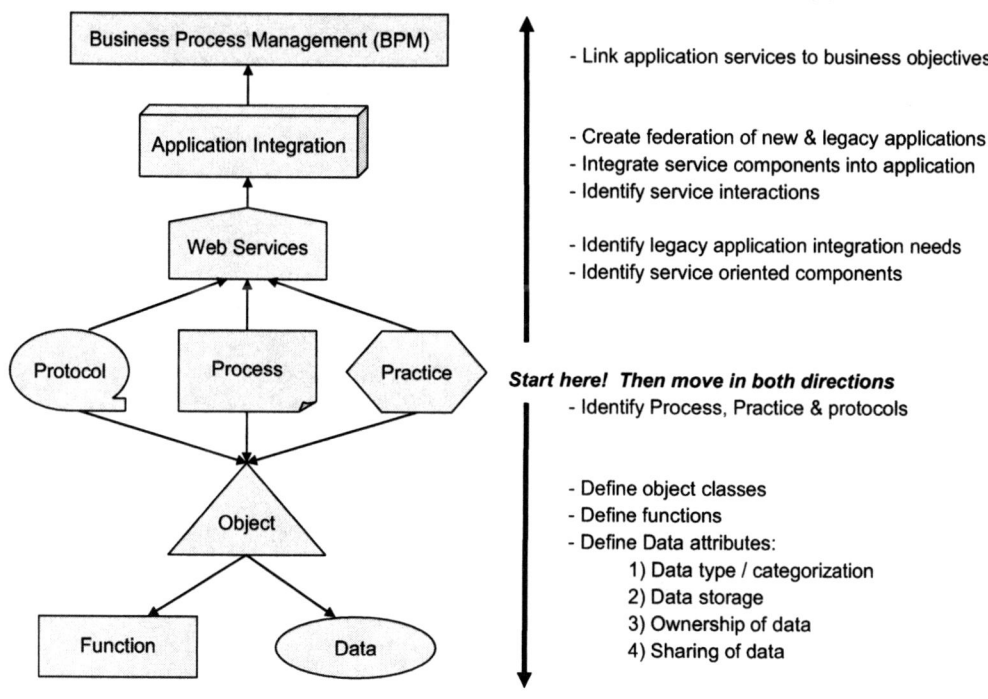

Fig 8.1 – Service Oriented Modeling Process.

Details of SOMF and SOA design methodologies are outside the scope of this book, but the reader is encouraged to review texts including Michael Bell's books on this topic.

Software As A Service (SaaS)

In a recent survey conducted by McKensey & SandHill Group in 2008, more than 800 CIOs were questioned about trends in IT industry. More than 56% believed that SOA and Software As A Service (SaaS, typically pronounced 'Sass') are the most important trends[38]. When asked why they might consider a SaaS application model, the most prominent decision factors were the speed to deploy the application and lower cost of implementation.

SaaS is a model of software deployment where the application is hosted as a service provided to customers over the internet. This eliminates the need to install and host the application on the customer's servers, thus shaving lots of upfront cost and time associated with facility preparation, server setup, installation and server management. Most SaaS solutions are priced as subscription (monthly or annual fees) or per usage.

Today many ERP, CRM, Video conferencing, finance and accounting, online office applications are available from SaaS providers. Some SaaS software providers offer development toolkits that allow the customer IT staff to modify and add functionality to fit their business needs.

Some of the limitations of SaaS solutions are the poor perception of security over the internet, performance, availability and portability of data to other applications. Portability issue is raised about 'vendor lock-in' factor which makes switching vendors a barrier.

But despite these limitations, SaaS offer many benefits that outweigh these limitations. Not only the cost of building these applications are at a fraction of in-house implementations, the operating costs are much lower.

The result is lower IT Liability and Operating Expense which increase the return on IT investment. SaaS vendors will cover the cost of hardware, software development and hosting. Moreover, applications delivered over the web or through virtual terminal (terminal emulation) place less demand on the client workstations. Thus the IT department can extend the life of its workstations longer. Some SaaS vendors offer 'try before you buy' plans which further reduce the risk to the customer.

IT managers can selectively adopt SaaS applications in two main areas:

1. **Functionality:** Where best of breed functionality is available from SaaS vendors, and when compliance with new laws and standards are important
2. **Lower Cost:** A typical SaaS deployment costs 60% less than a traditional single vendor deployment

---

[38] "Enterprise Software Customer Survery, 2008", McKinsey & Company, and SandHill Group, 2008.

Using a SaaS application should be a serious consideration for Lean IT organizations that need to deliver a semi-shrink wrap solution rapidly and at a low cost.

Design by Layers – The Layered Pyramid Model

One of the simple metaphors for handling complex designs is to consider the product from multiple perspectives and in layers. Multiple perspective teaches us to consider the product (or IT solution that we wish to design) from the perspective of the user, customer, organization and technology. Each perspective gives us a new set of design parameters and constraints. The layered approach is similar to making a pyramid by scaffolding in layers.

We design the solution by considering all layers from infrastructure at the bottom layer to back-end, middle tier and user front-end. The point about the layered approach to design is to separate complexity and consider design attributes for each layer and again as a whole.

For example, when we are considering adding a new module, we think about security, performance as well as objects, data and functions. Design attributes for each of these design parameters must be considered at the network level, server level, database data tables, integration (middle tier), web distribution and web presentation (user interface) and client devices (desktops, mobile devices)[39].

This model shows the foundation as the infrastructure consisting of networks, datacenter and telecommunications components. Just above that, the platform layer consists of servers, operating systems, desktops and mobile devices. The middle tier sometimes referred to as the middleware consist of choices for interfaces, messaging between platform components and translations between the platforms. The application layer provides the user with features and functions that support the workflows.

The highest level is the knowledge creation layer. This layer enables users to access information, create knowledge and carry out the business workflows. A similar model to this is a layered cake model shown in Appendix B. The layered cake model is fundamentally the same idea, but with slightly different separation of layers. The layered pyramid model also allows scaffolding, a major concept in Lean IT management. Scaffolding allows new solutions to be built, modularly upon existing solutions. The goal is to avoid the vernacular "re-inventing the wheel."

Figure 8.2.1 illustrates the layered pyramid metaphor by showing the use of both layers and scaffolding. My clients like the simplicity of the layered design approach. Basically, when we design in layers, we discover omissions and issues associated with each layer as well as the entire hierarchy of IT solution.

---

[39] Another layered model is the 7-layer ISO stack. It is similarly a good checklist for network design engineers.

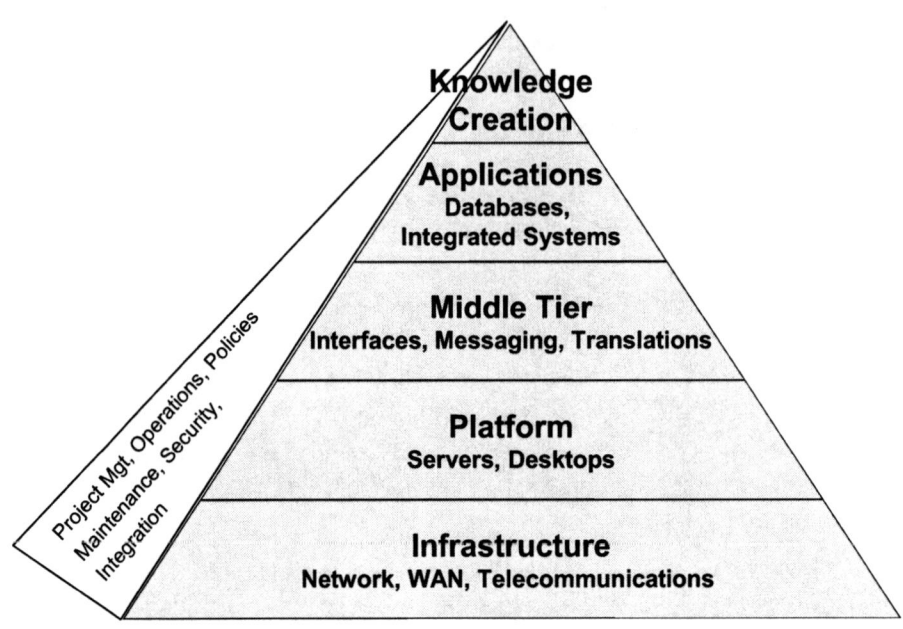

Fig. 8.2.1 – Layered Approach & Scaffolding in IT solution design

DFSS: Design for Six Sigma

Although we've not discussed Six Sigma concepts yet, Design for Six Sigma (DFSS) deserves an early mention. Six Sigma approach to design is fact-based. It considers the key variables that are critical to the outcomes that customers expect from the IT product. These are the critical-to variables. The design team must have an understanding of what these critical-to variables are. For example, in one IT organization critical-to variables might include Critical-to-Quality, Cost of ownership, and Maintainability, shown as CTQ, CTC and CTM. In another IT organization, critical-to variables might include Critical-to Performance, and Uptime, shown as CTP and CTU. Key to DFSS is capturing the voice of the customer (VOC). As a result, DFSS identifies customer needs before starting the design and prioritizes customer requirements in terms of critical to quality CTQ and other CTx's. In the next chapter other benefits of DFSS for IT are discussed including faster time to release applications and lower cost of maintenance. Studies have shown that as much as 70% of the cost of ownership is influenced by design. Having designers and architects on each project is a key success factor in IT Design for Six Sigma. One of the most powerful tools offered by Six Sigma design is Quality Function Deployment (QFD). We will review the QFD method with an example at the end of this chapter.

Design for Six Sigma is a set of methodologies to build and introduce new products, services or processes successfully. Meeting and exceeding customer expectations are key to its success. Many new product introductions fail because either the customer requirements are ill-defined or that they do not follow rigorous design process methods.

DFSS is a simple procedure as outlined below:

1. Capture customer requirements.
2. Analyze customer requirements. Identify must-have versus nice to have features and functions.
3. Develop a straw-man design including sub-system components.
4. Review design and evaluate any gaps and issues. Meeting customer requirements must start from the top and flow down to sub systems.
5. Build a prototype or simulation of the design to validate it.
6. Track the capability of the product or service at each step of development and identify any gaps that must be resolved.
7. Develop a control plan.

Kano Model for Design

To satisfy and delight IT customers, we must recognize Kano's model. It outlines three drivers for customer satisfaction. The three drivers are: basic needs, performance and unspoken requirements. The basic needs are those product and service attributes that are absolutely required by the customer. These are "must-have" expectations. In other words, their absence is a source of dissatisfaction. Performance attributes are measures of function or features that reward the customer. Higher performances translate into higher value. Customers will pay more to get higher performance.

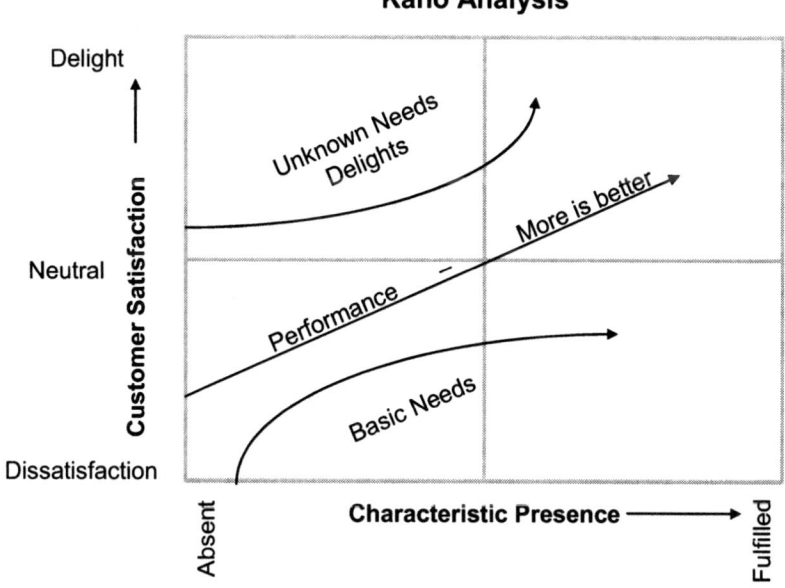

Fig 8.2.2 – Kano Model for Design Attributes

The unspoken requirements are attributes that delight, surprise and excite customers in a positive way. These are a source of competitive advantage. The next diagram illustrates this concept based on the Kano Model. The model was developed by Japanese quality expert Dr. Noriaki Kano. Applying the Kano model to IT services motivates us to listen to the *voice of the customer (VOC)*. This voice should resonate with IT as we frequently ask for customer input; conduct surveys; observe customer behavior as they use IT solutions, facilitate Kaizen events and joint application design forums. The first step in Kano analysis is to list all customer requirements in a spreadsheet and classify them with "S", to denote Satisfier, "P" to denote Performance or "D" to denote Delight pertaining to the customer expectations. We can then apply weights to these requirements and prioritize them.

The Kano model comes in handy for a variety of uses, including Design for Six Sigma, Quality Function Deployment (QFD) analysis, and building quality into IT products in general. Emphasizing Design, using a common design language and testing methodology should be key standards of implementation. Fortunately we have UML. Unified Modeling Language (UML), is a great standard to document and communicate designs. Some components of UML support workflow modeling (known as activity-based UML model), some support Use-Case designs and others enable Package-based designs[40]. In all, they are forms of UML, an industry standard modeling toolkit that helps build designs. Why Designs are a key contributor to success and reducing risk? Some of the top reasons for project failures are characterized as "insufficient or ill-defined user requirements" and "lack of cohesive design". Designs in form of Use cases, data modeling and workflow definitions, followed by reviews allow stakeholders to give feedback, correct and adjust the initially perceived requirements. Design reviews alone can hugely improve quality, increase the odds of success, and reduce costly rework and risk.

Case Study: Design Flaws that Prove Costly

In 1996, the European Space Agency launched the massive Ariane 5 rocket into space carrying 4 satellites from the agency's center in French Guiana. Within 40 seconds after launch, the rocket's internal guidance systems sent diagnostic error messages to the onboard computer responsible for directional steering. The computer mistakenly took the messages as flight data and concluded that the rocket had made a sharp turn. In attempt to correct it, the computer signaled the rocket boosters to swivel their exhaust nozzles to extreme angles. This caused the rocket to tear apart from the aerodynamic pressure and start the self destruction sequence.

Developed over ten years at a cost of $7 billion, the Ariane 5 blew up thirty nine seconds into its flight, destroying the four uninsured satellites. What was the cause of this failure despite tens of millions hours of human labor and innovation? The inquiry after the crash revealed that the guidance systems malfunctioned when they tried to convert velocity data from 64bit to 16bit format. Software engineers had decided that internal error correction was not necessary because the velocity figure would never get large enough. The head of Ariane 5 project admitted...

---

[40] "UML Distilled", Martin Fowler with Kendall Scott, Addison-Wesley, 2000

... that "very tiny details can have terrible consequences. It's not surprising, especially in a complex software system such as this." At the time, this programming error was probably one of the most expensive software bugs in history. It was nevertheless a design flaw which could have been corrected at a detailed design review. The Y2K problem is another example which reportedly cost corporations $250 billion worldwide to fix. A recent bug caused by the adoption of the new standard day light savings time change is interesting to note. In 2006, Congress enacted the law to change the daylight saving time to March and November. Many computers which were built before 2007, automatically adjusted their clocks in April and October. They had no knowledge of the new daylight saving dates. Caught by surprise, Microsoft hastily released a patch to correct the automatic time change. ...

The patch correctly changed the spring and fall daylight savings times in March and November. But, forgot to prevent the previously stored program to automatically change the system clock in April and October. Consequently an older computer with this patch would be two hours ahead. Microsoft quickly released another patch to correct the earlier software bug. The consequences of a simple defect can prove to be disastrous for many businesses.

Built For Quality

The salient point from the case studies is to recognize that often design flaws result in unintended and costly consequences. The IT manager should not be satisfied with a high level design but also demand low level designs which consider and answer detailed questions about the artifact under development. For quality to be upheld, it must be everyone's responsibility, but visibly at the highest level of organization. The CIO must be the Chief Quality Officer for Information Technology organization. Aside from insisting on low level design and performing design reviews we should focus on test driven design. Testing is a vast and exciting field for those interested in advancing quality. The purpose of testing is to find defects before the customer finds them. Therefore everything must be tested before release to the customer, and everything should be designed for testability.

Every IT organization who is in pursuit of perfection must give adequate attention to testing. There are at least **three good stratagems to employ:**

1. **Establishing adequate testing infrastructure, tools and processes.** The infrastructure might include a mock, isolated network of systems that mimic the actual production environment consisting of at least 3 environments: staging, testing and pre-release systems. The processes would define the steps and procedures for conducting tests. Automated test tools improve tester productivity.

2. **Hiring skilled people who are experienced in testing.** It's said that "test engineers must be the smartest people you hire". This is because to be effective, test

engineers must think in terms of writing test plans and test cases that find and isolate most defects in the shortest time.

3. **Design systems for testability.** The best programs have testability, diagnostic mode and self testing features built-in. The process of testing begins with user requirements and use cases. This is where having detailed documentation of user requirements pays off in shortening the project schedule. Test engineers can convert user requirements in to test scenarios. Each test case should exercise as many scenarios as possible to test all possible program paths. Conducting stress testing, longevity testing and margining are highly recommended. Test cycles should immediately follow each iteration of deliverables.

Toyota Production System advocates using Andon, a visible display of current production status. Following the Andon principle, test results must be visible or accessible by all stakeholders including the customer and the CIO. Test results are summarized into quality dashboards which can be reviewed by the director of QA, project manager and project team members. It is important to gauge users' tolerance for defects before releasing an application in advance. Typically, a meeting with project sponsors and user community allows IT management to disclose the quality level of the product. The "Go-NoGo" decision, whether to proceed with roll-out or not is made with user participation and input from project sponsors. With respect to quality, there are two distinct stages: The incoming quality and the outgoing quality.

When we acquire a new application or technology, it's imperative to examine the vendor's product quality, release notes, test process maturity and quality standards before purchasing the goods. This is incoming quality. While we may have little control over a vendor's product quality, we can influence the vendor's quality process. The best practices recommend that we ask vendors for their product's "release notes". A release note is a full disclosure document that a vendor releases to customers notifying them of any known defects or functionality issue in their product. Now-a-days it has become vital to review these release notes before starting a project. If a vendor cannot furnish release notes, it's a sign of dreadful quality problems ahead. Considerable due diligence goes into evaluating a vendor's product, process and technology before acquisition.

We must evaluate the technology to ensure that it is proven and properly applied by the vendor. We must ensure that the vendor practices strict version control and change management mechanisms. Outgoing quality is what the IT organization releases to its customers. Outgoing quality depends on process maturity and quality of testing performed by the IT organization. Having an IT QA director is a role that underscores the importance of quality. True that quality should be everyone's concern. But, the QA director sets the standards and programs for quality. The QA director is also concerned with statistical interpretation of test data. The statistical interpretation seeks to determine:

1. Which components are more defective than others?
2. Which critical customer requirements are affected
3. How severe is the impact of each defect on quality and functionality?
4. Does the test coverage adequately cover all aspects of the application?

5. Does this level of quality meet the project sponsor's and users' expectations?

The project manager is concerned with the scope of defects and impact of fixing them. The impact analysis seeks to define:

1. What is the impact of fixing each defect on the project schedule?
2. What features or functions may not be adequately fixed or tested before release?
3. What will the project sponsor and users accept as the minimum quality standard?

The project team is concerned about which defects must be fixed first and the depth of defects. Here is the explanation of these factors:

1. What is the priority for fixing defects
2. Which defects should be fixed and which defects can be remedied by a workaround?
3. Which defects stem from poorly defined customer requirements, design flaws or architecture oversight? These defects tend to require the most resource and introduce the most fundamental changes.

Elements of Requirements Analysis: Plan, Do, Check, Act

The 2x2 matrix shown on the next page is a simple tool to guide the IT business requirements analysis activities. This tool is ideal whether we are starting to define the business requirements from scratch, or participating in a Kaizen event to explore a problem and identify its root causes. In either case, this tool allows capturing the problem statement and then defining the ideal solution desired. It's based on Deming's Plan-Do-Check-Act cycle (Figures 8.3 and 8.4).

In the first diagram, the rows define the current and target (future) state. The columns define the system "Description" (in terms of input and outputs), and "Analysis". The Description column describes how it is done today versus how it should be done in future state. Analysis column breaks down the system into its subsystems and sequences what the interrelationships between the subsystems should be (how does it work, or what is the process & technology components).

In the second diagram we analyze the requirements with Plan, Do, Check, and Act steps. In Figure 8.4, the first quadrant (PLAN), describes the current state of workflow. This is the plan, including results of a root cause analysis or Kaizen event. The second quadrant (DO), analyzes the issues with the current state system. It searches for any short term solution, workaround or low-effort fix to the problem.

The third quadrant (CHECK), describes the future state that we wish to create. This is synonymous to Check in the Deming's cycle. The fourth quadrant (ACT) outlines how the future process will be enabled by the IT solutions.

Context → View ↓	Description (Problem Statement)	Analysis (Solution Statement)
Current State	**1** - What is the problem? - What is the root cause of the problem (apply 5-why technique) - Perform influence diagram & identify factors that influence root cause - Gather data & metrics	**2** - What are the obstacles in resolving the issues in current state? - Are there workarounds? - What is the backup plan? - What can be done to change the current state?
Target State	**3** - What is the ideal workflow or result? What is the ideal outcome? - How will the root cause be eliminated? - How will the influence factors change? - What are the desirable or target measurements we want to achieve?	**4** - What IT solutions are needed? - What technology options are available? - What is the feasibility of each option? - Which options offer better lean advantages? (flexibility, reliability, maintainability, form, fit, function)

Fig 8.3 – 2X2 Requirements Gap Analysis

Context → View ↓	Description (Problem Statement)	Analysis (Solution Statement)
Current State	**1** **Problem Statement (PLAN)** About 20% of exams are typed by transcriptionists. This adds several hours to report turn around time. Reports are recorded by analog phone system.	**2** **Short Term Solution (Do)** The current Speech recognition application uses an older speech engine technology. It is inadequate to recognize the unique subspecialty words, thus becomes a productivity inhibitor for some Radiologists
Target State	**3** **Ideal Solution (CHECK)** 100% of exams are done via Speech Recognition software. No typists are involved. Report turn around time is under 8 hours. Improve productivity by using report templates. Radiologists will be able to dictate remotely from anywhere (including home office).	**4** **Action Plan (Act)** Speech engine's recognition capability must improve considerably. Need to overhaul or acquire a new speech engine. Implement a Radiology dictionary, macros, structured reports. Implement web architecture to allow remote access.

Fig 8.4 – 2X2 Requirements Gap Analysis Matrix using Plan, Do, Check, Act

To illustrate this framework, we can apply it to the "Speech Recognition" application as shown in Figure 8.4. After a team of IT and end-users carried out this analysis, they realized that their current application was no longer able to meet their requirements (Quadrant-2). They defined the ideal features of a new application (Quadrant-3), issued a request for proposal (RFP) and acquired a new system.

Workflow Automation Categories

Workflows depending on their characteristics can generally be divided into four categories. A 2x2 matrix comes in handy to sort out the four categories. The rows divide tasks into creative or routine. The columns divide tasks into one of a kind (unique), and repetitive. Examples and stratagems for automation of each quadrant are listed below. It's important to recognize this workflow classification so we can create appropriate IT solutions that match each genre of work properly.

Quadrant 1 - Creative and Unique Work: Application examples for this category include: Research applications, image processing, and web publishing. Users typically include physicians, engineers, architects, writers & artists. This group typically uses Macintosh or specialized workstations. For this class of users we recommend providing the requested level of support. Most users in this category tend to be self sufficient and prefer self-service IT support. There are exceptions however, as some class of users might expect full service and support. To be Lean, we maintain platforms as needed. If the workstations are unique and not mainstream, we could consider outsourcing support. For example, one IT organization supports Intel-based workstations but outsources Macintosh support to an outside service company.

Quadrant 2 - Mundane but One of a Kind Work: Applications in this category include certain unique tasks or tasks that are in reaction to unexpected events. Users typically include workers whose work is not well defined and are in state of constant flux. For this class of users we want to organize and structure their work into well defined routine and repetitive types of work. Otherwise, this kind of work is not easily automated and might be a good candidate for outsourcing.

Quadrant 3 - Creative but Repetitive Work: Applications in this category include developing sales proposals, conducting analysis, certain desktop publishing, and writing ad copy. Users typically include specialists, physicians, marketing staff, IT staff (Mac and PC clients), sales and marketing personnel. For this class of users, it makes sense to offer the best of breed applications. Solutions that not only improve productivity by also offer features to enhance creativity. For these users, integration becomes a secondary decision factor.

Quadrant 4 - Mundane and Repetitive Work: Applications such as word processing, scheduling, billing, and accounting are examples of this category. Users typically consist of roles such as Administrative assistants, accounting staff, order fulfillment and inventory control personnel. The workers in this class of work typically use PC or thin clients. To improve productivity of this group, we automate and standardize workflows using IT solutions. The repetitive and routine (mundane) genre of work is the low hanging fruit for automation (as shown in the diagram below).

Workflow Automation Classification		
	Unique Work	**Repetitive Work**
Creative Work	*Quadrant 1:* *Creative & Unique Tasks*	*Quadrant 3:* *Creative but Repetitive Tasks*
Routine Work	*Quadrant 2:* *Mundane but One of a Kind Tasks*	*Quadrant 4:* *Mundane & Repetitive Tasks*

Fig 8.5 – 2x2 Workflow Automation Classification Tool

Stratagem: Lean IT managers consistently are on the look-out for opportunities to automate and innovate workflows. To reduce organization's overhead, IT managers must understand the nature of work that's being carried out in the organization.

Communication Matrix: A Cross-functional Design Template

IT plays a pivotal role in collaboration and communication. The key element of a knowledge-based workplace is communication between staff. In complex work organizations, take for example healthcare or finance, accurate, timely and complete communication are essential. User interfaces are a mode of communication. To be effective, Lean IT framework brings user communication needs along with application integration requirements to focus.

Knowledge workers interact in three primary ways: communications, transactions and collaborations. Knowing the nature of worker interactions and their requirements across functional areas are necessary to select the appropriate technology. Communication is an exchange of information between two or more participants. Transactional interactions involve exchange of information or items between parties in such a way that they alter relationship between the parties. Collaborative interactions involve participants using their relationships to alter a common entity (the converse of transactional interaction).

Lean IT encourages building IT solutions that support single-flow processes considering all three means of interaction. In most environments, workflows are facilitated by communication. Information Technology can and must play an enabling role in facilitating "high-bandwidth" communication. A high bandwidth communication is a high value-adding exchange of knowledge and information. This is the sort of communication that carries rich, timely and coherent communication, free of error and waste. Analyzing workflows through communication analysis can be accomplished by forming a communication matrix. This by itself can serve as a requirements analysis and design tool. It is done by observing communication flow across the organization, roles and workflows. One of the effective tools that I've used for enterprise level Kaizen is the Communication Matrix. Communication Matrix defines how knowledge workers interact with each other, how information is exchanged and in what form; and what is the source, intent and flow of information. Communication Matrix is role based. It can be a small 2x2 matrix, if there are only 2 people or 2 departments involved, or an NXN matrix if there are N roles in the collaboration. For wider reaching Kaizen events, it can be a large matrix, encompassing all departments and functional roles. In general, facilitating communication among professional staff is one of most under-utilized applications of IT in the industry.

Communication matrix is a tool to capture all existing and required interactions, messages & communication between members of an organization as they fulfill their function and carry their daily work. In its basic form, the Communication Matrix defines the message type, frequency, time and method of communication between various roles in the organization.

Within the context of process re-design, a message is considered communication if it meets the following criteria:

- It must be between two parties
- It must be repeated as part of work process
- It must convey information

Communication can be in any form: a phone call, a face to face meeting, a text message, fax or preferably by other electronic means. Of course, for sake of process improvement, we would want to minimize waste and time spent on communication. Our goal is to make communication digital, efficient and "high bandwidth" carrying highly meaningful information; send and receive a massive amount of pertinent, useful information, which can be actionable. In other words, the person receiving a high bandwidth communication can make an intelligent decision and take the correct action. When IT managers develop and understand the communication matrix for their customer's organization, they will be in a stronger advisory position.

Here is another example from the healthcare sector: In a hospital, Communication Matrix can capture the interactions between many role pairs: patient to nurse, nurse-to-nurse, doctor-to-nurse, doctor-to-doctor, and so on. The message type describes the context and content of communication. Frequency defines how often that particular communication occurs. Method can be "Phone", "pager", "Fax", "Paper", "Instant Message", "email" or other electronic formats.

For illustration, the sample matrix in Figure 8.6 defines communication between various roles in a medical clinic. The diagram started with documenting the current state and later was updated to show the desired future state as shown. Each square where the row and column for each role intersect explains the nature of communication between the two roles. Squares that are crossed-off imply that no communication occurs as part of the routine workflows between those two roles. This basic framework facilitates further understanding and architecture for Information systems. It brings to focus the type and level of communication between knowledge workers. In this example, it documents the current mechanism for communication between Patient, Nurse, Physician, and other roles in a hospital.

A Medical Center's Communication Matrix: Routine Office Visit (Future State)

Describe Type, Context and Frequency of information being exchanged between one role to another role

Role	Patient	Nurse	Attending	Resident	Patient Care Coordinator
Patient ↑	None	Symptoms [V,Ph,W] Meds [V,Ph, W] Allergies [V,Ph,W]	Symptoms [V,Ph,W] Educate patient [V,W]	Symptoms [V,Ph,W] Educate patient [V,W]	Schedule patient visit [V,W]
Nurse ↑	Symptoms [V] Meds [V,Ph, W] Allergies [V,Ph,W]	Shift change info [V,E,W]	Test results [V,E] Patient vitals [V,E] Meds history [V,E]	Test results [V,E] Patient vitals [V,E] Meds history [V,E]	Med orders [V,E] Test orders [V,E] Exam orders [V,E]
Attending ↑	Symptoms [V,Ph,W] Educate patient [V,W]	Med orders [V,E] Test orders [V,E] Exam orders [V,E]		Review [V,E] Report [E,Ph]	Med orders [V,E] Test orders [V,E] Exam orders [V,E]
Resident ↑	Symptoms [V,Ph] Educate patient [V]	Med orders [V,E] Test orders [V,E] Exam orders [V,E]	Review [V,E,W] Report [E,Ph,W]	Shift change info [V,E]	Med orders [V,E] Test orders [V,E] Exam orders [V,E]
Patient Care Coordinator ↑	Schedule patient visit [V,W]	Patient exam schedule [V,E]	Test results [V,E] Patient vitals [V,E] Meds history [V,E]	Test results [V,E] Patient vitals [V,E] Meds history [V,E]	Shift change [V,E] Patient case info [E]

Fig 8.6 – Using Communication Matrix as a Design Tool

Tracking how knowledge workers interact in this matrix reveals the opportunities for improvement, eliminating waste and errors. As we analyze how information is created, stored and exchanged in this matrix the elements of data strategy and design begin to emerge. For example, there are reports that 30% of patient safety incidents are caused as a result of communication errors during shift changes. A shift turn-over between nurse staff requires communicating end-of shift information (orders, instructions, precautions, etc) from one nurse to another. Although, such exchange of information occurs only once for each shift change, clinically it's vital to continuous flow of care. The method of communication for shift turnover varies from hospital to hospital. The inadequate mediums are verbal or hand-written paper pad. The more desirable method is digital, using either an application form, a note in the electronic medical record, a weblog or digital message board or some other IT solution. The point is that the matrix highlights the needs for IT solutions to facilitate those interactions. In the communication matrix, the communication methods are shown by codes such as: Verbal (V), Phone (Ph), Fax (F), Paper (P), Electronic App (E), and Web App (W). Your institution may utilize different or additional codes for this analysis. The future (ideal) state is shown on a different matrix on the next page. The future state matrix shows where Web and other digital medium can be used to streamline communication.

In the future state matrix, there is no fax and paper. All orders, results and communication are digital; which means they are stored and accessible by multiple staff at anytime, anywhere. It also means that all data can be mined, searched and used for better decision support. At one medical center, a Kaizen event was conducted to address the "shift change communication" issue. It recommended creating a simple web application with a web form as front-end. This is how it would work: at the end of each shift, a nurse documents all turn-over instructions for the next nurse, in a web form. The instructions have hyperlink to detailed patient data in the electronic medical record. The new web application is based on service oriented architecture. It's aware who the next nurse is, (from a link to the staff schedule application), and requires the next nurse to review and sign-off on the instructions upon log-in. The new application also ensures each nurse has read and signed-off on the clinical notes, is presented with necessary precautions and instructions before starting a work shift. At the enterprise level, architects can similarly apply the communication matrix to show data interaction requirements between applications. From this matrix, "Information flow", and "data flow" diagrams can be developed as the next steps in information system design.

Information Flow Design

Since the goal of Lean IT is to maximize value for the customer, it pays to consider the information flow and data associated with a customer's life cycle through the firm. Information flow diagrams show the evolution of data for a customer between applications across multiple functional domains and workflows, from start to finish. They are a useful tool for Information Technology design staff to identify required integration points between their applications. There are many data flow analysis tools and methods to choose from. A high level view is the model of tracking a customer through the workflow and tracking information flow as shown in the example in Figure 8.7. This diagram, borrowed from a Health Information Strategy document, shows the flow of information between applications by tracking a patient's journey through the continuum of care at a hospital facility[41]. The diagram shows the current (present state) dataflow to highlight the weak integration points. This design methodology provides the IT architect with the elements of design to build more seamless, integrated applications to create a single-flow work process. The diagram shows functional areas of care on the left and Time as its horizontal axis. Each box shows a single workflow. The arrows show the flow of patient and information for the entire care process. Lack of integration at this healthcare system has created a data fragmentation problem. The problem was caused by piecemeal, independent implementations of clinical applications. To remedy the situation, the hospital has adopted a service oriented approach to solve its data fragmentation problem.

Whether you use the Communication Matrix or an information flow diagram, your customers will appreciate the clarity of approach and the ability to see the entire process on one diagram. Similar diagramming techniques such as A3 (used by Toyota) and Cognitive Maps are used to illustrate the bottlenecks or issues associated with the current process and allow Kaizen event participants to identify the ideal process. A similar data flow diagram was developed for an Anesthesia Documentation application at a medical institution. The data flow illustrates the events in time and data movement between various workcells. It maps data flow and clinical workflows across diverse functions of care delivery such as: pre-anesthesia, lab department, intra-operation, post operation and intensive care unit. Another advantage that can be gained from an information flow diagram is to determine any interface requirements between various applications in advance of starting the design phase. The dataflow in the diagram above shows how patient information touches three separate applications during the workflow continuum. The other model is based on tracking information flow and application interactions by tracking a customer through a lifecycle of doing business with the firm. In either approach, using a Service Oriented Architecture, a federation of these applications could be developed. This federation can be accomplished by a web-based front-end portal that interacts with all three applications shielding the user from their nuances.

Quality Function Deployment (QFD):

QFD is rooted in a matrix approach to finding and sorting critical customer requirements. It is a tool totally committed to satisfying the customer by creating "positive quality". It starts with listening to the *Voice of the Customer (VOC)*. Voice of the customer can be heard through customer complaints, surveys, focus groups, interviews and online feedback. From the voice of the customer, we can generate the critical-to quality (CTQ), Critical Customer Requirements (CCR). In Six Sigma methodology, cause and effects are shown by a transfer function $Y = f(X)$. Y is the effect, the outcome or the result of causes. Causes are variables represented by X's. Once the customer's CTQ requirements are documented, we can analyze and organize them into a *CTQ Tree*. A CTQ Tree is formed by listing the requirement and branching out into its components, typically the causes that influence the customer's requirement.

---

[41] From "INFORMING HEALTHCARE IMPLEMENTATION STRATEGY" document October 2006, Health & Social Services Committee, NHS, Wales.

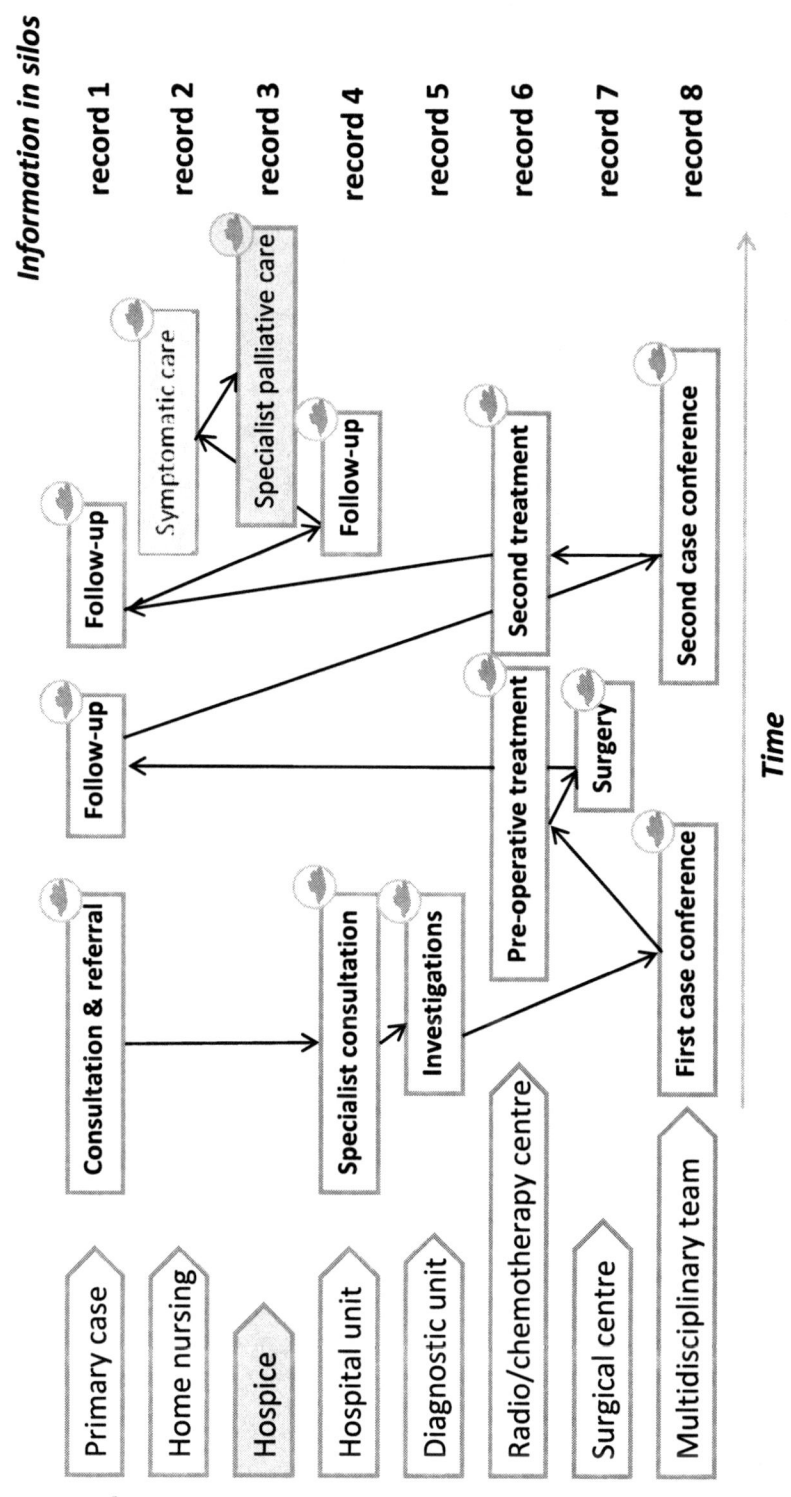

Fig 8.7 – Information Flow Diagram to Identify Application Integration Needs

The customer requirement is Y, and that is satisfied by functions or features, denoted by X's. QFD can be instrumental in prioritizing feature and function design. For illustration, we can consider the speech recognition application discussed in Chapter 5. The QFD starts with a relationship matrix, then adds a correlation matrix and ends with what's known as the House of Quality as shown in Figure 8.9. The House of Quality represents the $Y = f(X)$ transfer function. The Y's are the critical customer requirements (CCRs) or Critical-to items such as critical to quality (CTQ). These are known as the whats: "What is needed?". The X's are the design or process requirements, also known as the hows: "How do we do it?" The IT analyst can create a house of quality for each project from a set of business requirements and design attributes. The house of quality is a template that looks like a house, consisting of a table and a triangular matrix on top. The rows reflect the customer requirements. The requirements are listed in the next column, and prioritized from 1 to 10 (10 being the most important) based on their importance to the customer. We can use Dr. Kano's model to sort the requirements as shown in the third column. The letters 'S', 'P' and 'D' denote the customer reaction to these requirements as 'Satisfy' (the customer will be dissatisfied if the feature is absent), 'Performance' (what customers are willing to pay additional price for), and 'Delight' (the features that excite and pleasantly surprise the customer), respectively when the feature is offered.

In the column headings the analyst places either the design attributes (design characteristics) also known as the design criteria. Each cell represents the cross section of customer requirements and design attribute. These are responses to "How do we do it?" In the row immediately below the column heading, the analyst places the desired measurements. Each measurement is shown by either an up-arrow, a down-arrow or an "O". If an increase in a design attribute is desired, the analyst places an up arrow. An up arrow indicates that "more is better'. If a decrease in the design attribute is desirable, the analyst place a down arrow. If the design attribute must be an exact measurement, we place an "O". To populate the matrix cells, the analyst begins by asking "what is the importance of the design attribute (column) to the customer requirement (row)"? A number between 1 and 10 is assigned representing the significance of the design criteria on the requirement.

When all cells have been filled, the analyst tallies the final score at the bottom of each column (The total Importance weight). The columns with higher scores have priority over the other columns. In other words, the design criteria that produces the highest score take precedence over lower score design criteria. As an example, let's consider the speech recognition application again. The House of Quality shown on the next page lists the customer requirements on the rows and design characteristics in columns. We can use QFD matrix to evaluate multiple competing applications based on their ability to meet the design characteristics. At the top of the matrix the correlation between designs attributes are depicted by a tilted matrix.

Since the top matrix gives the shape of a pitched roof shape, the QFD matrix is called the House of Quality. The cells in the correlation matrix may represent any of the following relationships: strong positive correlation, positive correlation, and no correlation, negative or strong negative correlations. By using the House of Quality, the IT team knows the strength of relationship in $Y=f(X)$ transfer function, between every design or attribute and every customer CTQ requirement.

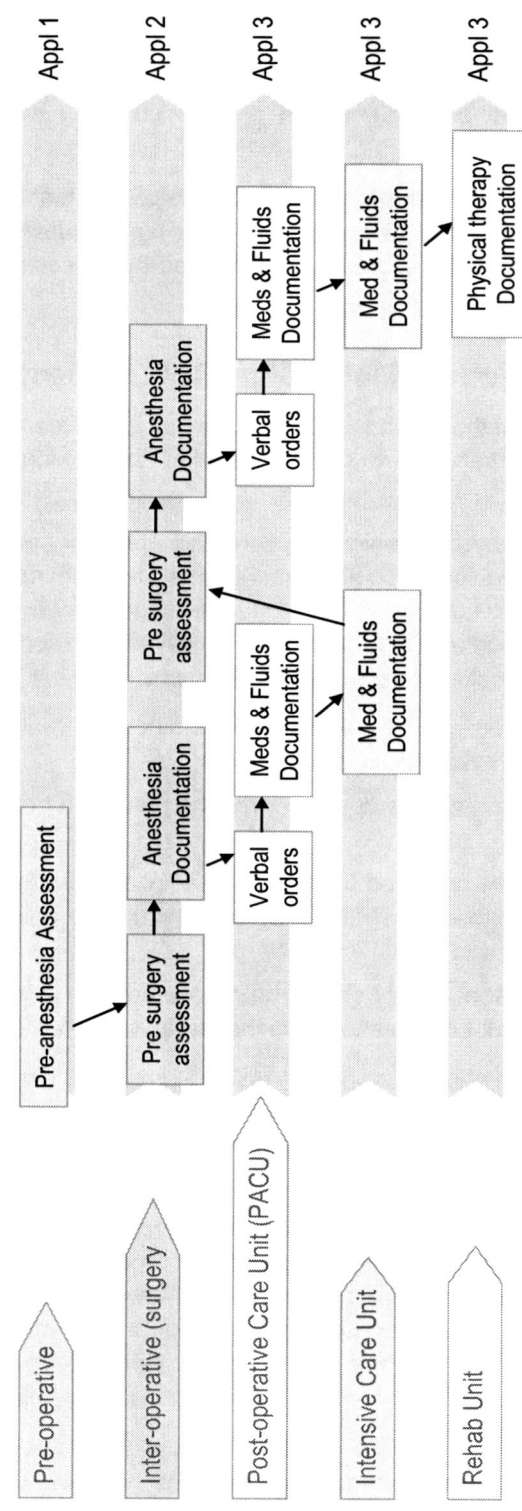

Fig 8.8 –Information Flow Across Multiple Application & Workflow Domains

155

So the team is aware of which design X's are most important to the CTQ Y's and how the design requirements are interrelated. The other use of QFD is to develop the right application features. QFD matrix can prioritize which design characteristics must be implemented first, which can clarify direction for an Agile implementation.

The total score demonstrates that three design features are most important to satisfy the customer's requirements: 'Speech Engine Quality' with score of 288, then 'Macro Functionality' with score of 285, followed by 'Speech Microphone Quality' with score of 255.

The role of Taguchi Method for Robust Design

Taguchi method is based on Design of Experiments. Its primary mission is to optimize design variables to reduce variation and eliminate causes for defect early in the design cycle.

Pioneered by Dr. Genichi Taguchi, this method can reduce cost of ownership by reducing noise factors such as environmental variation, manufacturing variation and component deterioration during the product's usage. Known as a technique for robust design, this methodology is known to have saved hundreds of millions of dollars in diverse industries including software development.

Taguchi's beliefs have been applied since 50 years ago to product design. Taguchi's method had a few simple concepts:

- Quality should be designed into the product (or process) and not inspected into it.
- Quality is achieved by reducing deviation from the target. Products should be designed such that they are immune to uncontrollable environmental factors, and
- The cost of quality should be measured as a function of deviation from the standard. Losses should be measured system-wide.

Taguchi method considers *Noise*, *Signal* and *Control* variables in design. These factors are illustrated by a P-Diagram as shown in Figure 8.10. IT managers interested in high precision, high quality implementations can apply Taguchi method to identify the optimal application design and implementation plan.

For example, let's suppose we are contemplating implementing an enterprise application. Taguchi method encourages thoughts given to the effect of environmental noise such as, network jitter, network latency, interruptions in to the messaging layer, failures of neighboring applications, and sudden surge of user transactions, etc. We could add user computer literacy levels and virus attacks to that list. Our goal is to use Taguchi method to design IT solutions that are immune to these factors during the life of the solution.

In environments where noise factors are stronger, more robust design and application testing are required. This is to help us better understand and manage the control variables. Other factors to consider are input signal and control variables. Input signals are factors such as user diversity, workflows or different departments (finance and marketing might use the application quite differently).

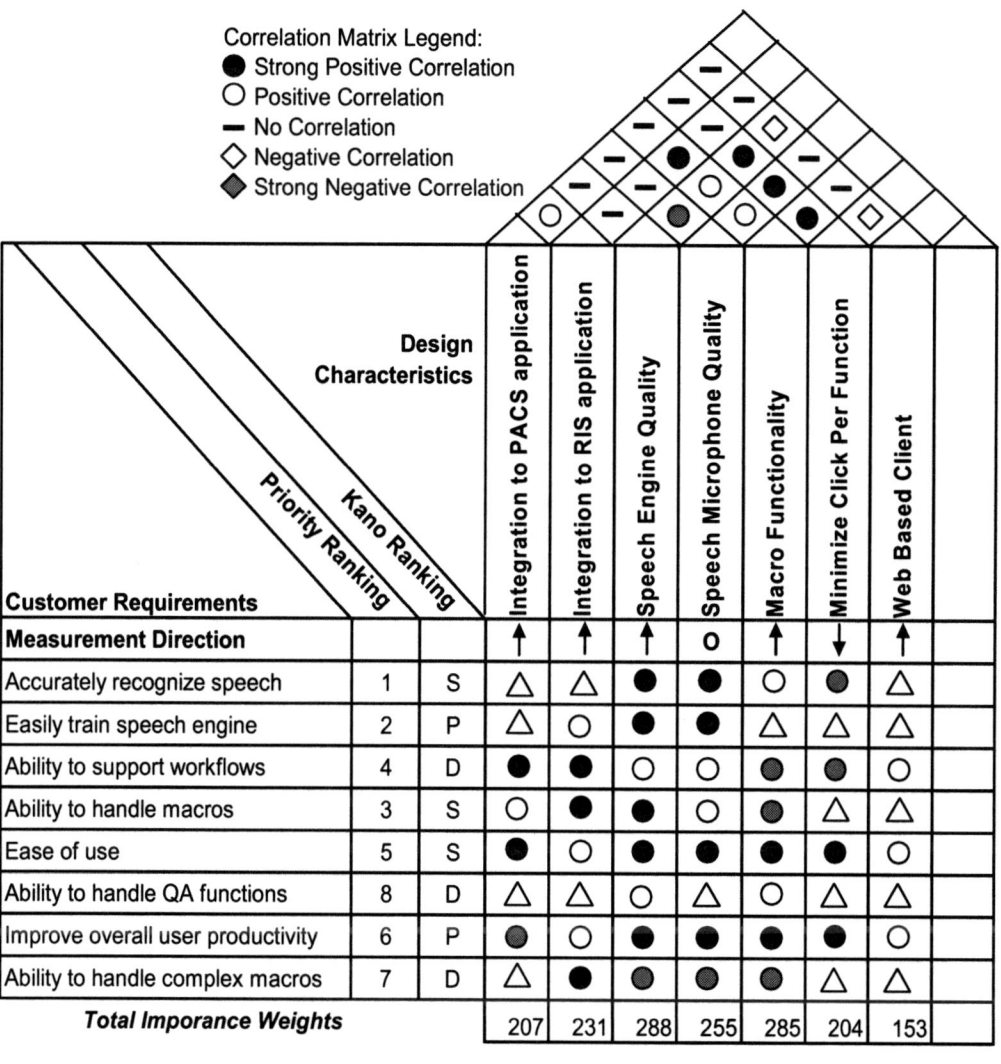

Fig 8.9 – House of Quality – DFSS Example

Finally, control variables are factors that we can control in the implementation. For example, we might consider releasing the application to finance department first, or we might decide to release a limited functionality as pilot or a beta release before heading on to full production. Taguchi method strives to reduce costs by finding problems that occur with a product and fixing the immediate causes. Similar to design of experiments, this method conducts various tests to the product design and measures the outcome. Each experiment varies the control variables while applying noise and then measures the result.

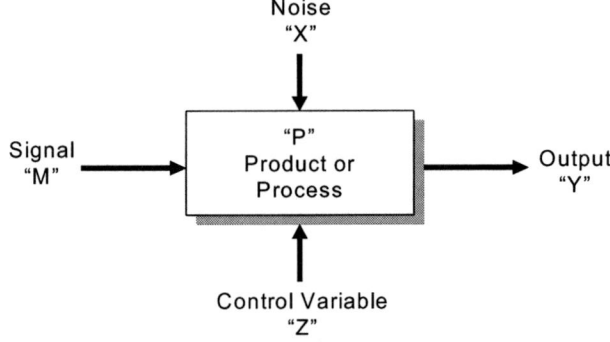

P-Diagram for Dynamic Problems

Fig 8.10 – Taguchi P-Diagram for Solving Dynamic Problems

The idea behind these experiments is to continue design modifications until a more robust design is found. To illustrate, a P-diagram like the diagram below is used. "P" is the product or process; "M" is the Signal that decides the Output "Y"; "X" is the noise factor; and "Z" is the control variable.

The goal of this process is to minimize the output variation even in the presence of noise inputs. Taguchi method divides all designs into static or dynamic categories. Basically, there are 4 steps to this method:

1. Plan.
2. Design experiment.
3. Conduct matrix experiment.
4. Evaluate results to determine the best levels of control factors.

The matrix experiment is based on orthogonal array of control variables and other variables forming a matrix. Once the orthogonal array tests are completed, the results are tabulated in the matrix and can be compared to identify the "best" design. The best or optimal design is the design that has the most consistently desirable behavior when subjected to noise and external variables. Simulation tools can be used to perform the matrix experiment analysis.

An example of orthogonal array tests is presented in a case study in the next section. The case study demonstrated the effect of software process decisions on project outcome (product quality, project duration and development cost) using a matrix of control variables. It determined that conducting low-level design was an appropriate decision for that particular project.

Using Taguchi design method, it's possible to reduce the test cycle times. This method can be applied to new product development as well. For example, consider the design of a new web-based application. When applied to a web application, it's plausible to consider a number of elements on each web page; and one or more design alternatives for each element. Then we can compare all possible combinations of outcomes for those elements. Similar studies have been performed to find the "best page design" by determining which combination of elements on a webpage increase the likelihood of converting a visitor to a customer.

Taguchi method has many applications in testing, data design and modeling. It promotes quality designs that are resistant to wide ranging variability in data, unreasonable use and severe application conditions. For example, an analyst who is creating a web form to capture user information would consider incorporating self-correcting data fields to make the data fields immune to noise (or bad data). For example, the input data field for "Date of Birth" would only accept positive numbers between present year and present year minus 130. The data field must automatically reject any non-integer (numbers with decimals), negative numbers, zero, any numbers that are higher than the present date, or that result in age over 130 years. Test plans should also test for these scenarios.

Simulating Projects: A Project Manager's Flight Simulator

It has been shown that simulation can be a useful tool for predicting the results of project manager decisions and selection of the appropriate process for a particular project. Results of a simulation study demonstrating the value of simulation for project management were presented at a conference in 1999. The study used the waterfall model as the development process[42]. It simulated the effects of decision choices about design, test and coding on the project outcome. Since project managers have the option to raise or lower levels of activity on design, coding, testing and other phases of development, they face a dilemma.

Which level of activity will produce the best results? In the simulation study, there were 6,561 possible decision scenarios and each decision produced a different outcome. The outcomes were measured by cost, number of defects and project schedule delays. The simulation compared results for all 6,561 different possible scenarios of software development processes for a given project. The simulation equations were initially based on a TRW initiative and Barry Boehm's COCOMO-II model. Barry Boehm developed COCOMO to analyze software productivity and economics[43].

In the study, the simulation program was calibrated using outcomes of prior projects and history of IT projects at the institution. As a result the simulation program could mimic the capabilities and characteristics of the firm. Then the project manager was given the opportunity to model a new project in the simulation program. The project manager could enter specific data about the project, such as number of function points, size, the expertise level of the development team, and number of application screens into the simulation program and run the program.

---

[42] "Using Data Envelopment Analysis for Evaluating Alternative Software Development Process Configurations", Timothy R. Anderson & Peter K. Ghavami, PICMET '99: Technology & Innovation Management: Setting the Pace for the Third Millennium, pg 41

[43] "Software Engineering Economics", Barry Boehm, 1981, and "Software Cost Estimation with COCOMO II", Barry Boehm, 2000. Barry Boehm developed Construction Cost Model (COCOMO) as a calculus to determine project effort, cost and development time while he was Director of Software Research and Technology at TRW.

A few minutes later, the results were ready. Simulation results for some of the decision configurations are shown in the following table (Figure 8.11). The outcomes of these decisions are shown in terms of number of defects at the release time, the duration of the project and the overall cost of implementation. Scenario #1 is the worst decision because it carries the most defects, duration and costs. The best scenarios are those that have the lowest defects, duration and cost. The simulation model was based on prior work sponsored by a major software company. Each of the 6,561 different process scenarios represented different decisions on levels of effort, for each phase of the project. The levels of effort were either, High, Medium, or Low. Since there were 8 different implementation phases and 3 possible effort levels, there had to be 3**8, or 6,561 different scenarios. The simulation program was so successful that it eventually became a sort of flight simulator for IT project managers in the firm. It allowed the project managers to evaluate results of their decisions in a laboratory setting before starting the project. Because of its power to explain and emulate real life situations, this program became a great problem solving tool. The simulation program provided insight which helped with resource planning and risk management for each IT project.

For example, the simulation program compared results of scenarios where the project manager could decide on a high degree of design but with low levels of testing. Alternatively, what would be the outcome of the project if we considered minimum design work, combined with low efforts on testing? What about other scenarios that put more effort on complete specifications and High-Level Design (HLD), but no effort on Low Level Design (LLD)? What if we were content with a medium amount of testing, and vice versa? Each process schema was simulated using Monte Carlo methods to measure the quantity of defects and duration of project. Monte Carlo method was developed in the 1940s by physicists working on nuclear weapon projects in the Los Alamos National Laboratory. It's suitable for study of problems where system components have a wide degree of freedom[44].

Monte Carlo methods are used for simulating physical and mathematical systems by applying repeated computation and random or pseudo-random numbers. In its Monte Carlo calculations the simulation program considered 10,000 possible random iterations of chance for each of the 6,561 scenarios. The simulation results were astounding and supported by actual results discovered later. The scenario where the manager applied more effort to high-level design produced better outcomes than the scenario which ignored design all together. Likewise, scenarios where more testing were done showed faster completion time and lower costs.

The simulation results showed that decisions where greater amount of resources to high-level *and* low-level design were applied produced higher quality software and finished faster than all other scenarios. The lesson for the project manager was to emphasize the importance of low level design to her team. Many of the design flaws and uncertainties about the application were discovered during the low level design phase and that alone saved the project a large amount of expense and rework.

---

[44] The term Monte Carlo Methods was coined by physics researchers Stanislaw Ulam, Enrico Fermi, John Von Neumann and Nicholas Metropolis to use randomness and repetitive nature of the physical properties of atom. The term is a reference to similar activities in a casino, but reportedly named after the famous casino in Monaco where Ulam's uncle would borrow money to gamble.

Development Phases / Simulation Scenarios	Requirements	Specification	High Level Design	Low Level Design	Code / Implement	Test	Verification	Validation	Release	No. of Defects at Time of Release	Total Project Schedule (Weeks)	Total Project Cost ($k)
Scenario #1	Low	Low	Low	Low	Low	Low	Low	Low	Low	1650	208	$6,320.00
Scenario #2	Med	Low	Low	Low	Low	Low	Low	Low	Low	1540	196	$5,980.00
...	...	...	...	...	...	...	...	...	...	...	...	...
Scenario #1873	Med	Med	Med	Med	Med	Hi	Med	Med	Med	346	176	$4,835.00
...	...	...	...	...	...	...	...	...	...	...	...	...
Scenario #3085	Hi	Hi	Hi	Hi	Med	Hi	Med	Med	Med	320	160	$4,457.00
...	...	...	...	...	...	...	...	...	...	...	...	...
Scenario #5103	Hi	Hi	Hi	Hi	Hi	Hi	Med	Med	Med	320	162	$4,665.00
...	...	...	...	...	...	...	...	...	...	...	...	...
Scenario #6560	Hi	Hi	Hi	Hi	Hi	Hi	Hi	Hi	Med	310	170	$4,980.00
Scenario #6561	Hi	Hi	Hi	Hi	Hi	Hi	Hi	Hi	Hi	308	172	$5,040.00

Fig 8.11 – Construction and results of Simulating a Development Project before starting the project (Uses Waterfall Process)

> **Stratagem:** More often than not, a low-level design is the best stratagem to get the benefits of quality, lower cost and short schedules. Strive to detail out a high level design to create a low-level design. Low level designs followed by design reviews are secret ingredients that produce quality products in shorter time period.

Summary:

- Design promotes quality, customer satisfaction and shortened project times. Quality should be built into the product and process.
- Ensure every development effort includes design followed by a design review.
- All operational tasks such as patches or upgrades require a method of procedure (MOP) which must go through vendor and peer reviews before being applied.
- Apply feature driven development techniques (FDD) to sort out scope of project and the order of implementation.
- Every IT activity must have a process and every process must be re-engineered to eliminate waste and chances for mistakes.
- Plans to release solutions must be engineered and planned with customer involvement.
- Do not be content with high level designs. Encourage low level design.
- Establish a common, corporate information design and architecture
- Define, adopt and agree on a universal set of information standards for the integration of information systems across the enterprise
- Apply communication matrix method to design the ideal communication mediums across value streams for delivering value to-customers
- Testing is a good measure to find defects. But, a better measure is to have safe-guards against errors early in the development cycle.
- Mistake-proofing: Identify where a process might produce an error or defective product, then modify the process to eliminate chances for error.
- Give users opportunity for iterative feedback during the course of project.
- Perform iterative design reviews and code inspections before testing.
- Immediately test after each component completion. Test quickly and fiercely to find defects.
- Gather metrics from your testing. Components with higher failure rates should get further testing.
- Perform root cause analysis. Ask Why 5 times for each cause of defect. Example: What is the root cause of system downtimes?

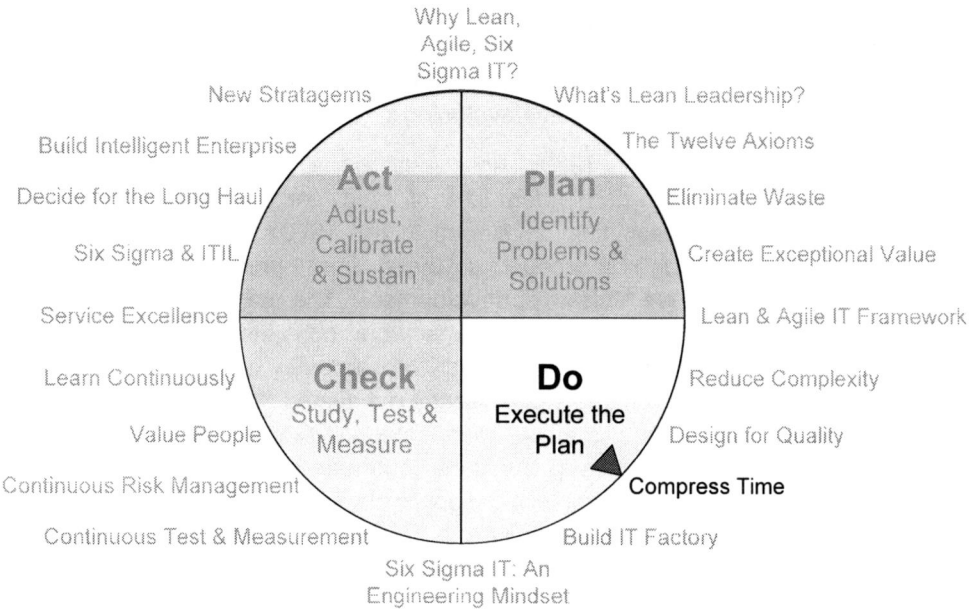

"Time stays long enough for those who use it."

Leonardo Da Vinci

Chapter 9: Compress Time: Applying Agile Principles

To eliminate waste is to manage time. Rework, fixing recurring errors, constant fire fighting, responding to recurring reliability problems all pilfer precious resources and time. Managing time, or compressing it as I've called it, opens up capacity, expands space and reduces costs. Time is frequently mentioned by CEOs along with quality, innovation and productivity as a potential strategic weapon.

In their book "Competing Against Time: How Time-Based Competition is Reshaping Global Markets", authors George Stalk, Jr. and Thomas M. Hout argue that when corporations compete, those who can reduce development time, sales time and service times will win[45]. This is fairly intuitive, in particular in zero-sum situations. The first mover can capture a substantial share of the market and establish the norms and rules of the game in the industry. Similarly inside the enterprise, when time to release an application is reduced, the ability for the institution to capture benefits earlier will improve the bottom line. The inherent benefit to the IT organization is that reducing time, opens more capacity for other projects. This creates compounding positive effects for the IT organization. I described the benefits of Agile methods through the "J-curve" concept in the summary chapter.

I also addressed eliminating the common causes of waste (in form of rework as a result of defects) by employing high level and low level designs. Effort spent on design will reduce latent defects and rework in all facets of IT from software

---

[45] "Competing Against Time: How Time-Based Competition is Reshaping Global Markets", George Stalk, Jr. and Thomas M. Hout, The Free Press, New York, NY, 1990

development and systems integration to network and infrastructure implementations. Agile methods form a conceptual framework for rapid software engineering and development. They contain a number of tools and methodologies that minimize risk and increase the odds of success by developing software in a short amount of time.

Developed in the mid 1990s, Agile methods were a reaction to the strategic planning approach which demanded lots of rigid and micro-managed planning. Strategic planning approach first developed in the 1970's, demanded unnecessary bureaucratic, slow and non-productive tasks from programmers which were inconsistent with effective software development. The same is true of strategic planning approach in IT. Most such plans were obsolete soon after they were conceived. Many strategic planning projects ran aground when most of the project schedule, resources and funding were already exhausted. In its May 21, 2007 issue, The CIO magazine reports of a survey conducted in 2006 by the Agile Alliance[46]. In the survey respondents who used traditional methods said only 29 percent of their projects were successful. Conversely, respondents who used Agile techniques, said 81 percent of their project were successful.

According to a survey conducted by Forrester Research in 2006, only 17% of North American and European enterprises use Agile development processes. But the same research reports that popularity of Agile is on the rise as more IT executives have expressed plans to adopt its methodologies[47]. In this chapter we'll review traditional and Agile development process models, SCRUM, JAD, RAD and other Agile methods.

Development Process Models

In many ways, software development processes parallel the information system life cycle; they present a useful backdrop to how we implement IT solutions. The traditional software development and most IT projects follow the waterfall model. Some IT managers have ventured into prototyping and using iterative models to deliver solutions faster. Most recently, other software development models such as the spiral model have gained popularity.

Before describing the Agile IT principles, let's review conventional models first. We need to reiterate that information system projects are increasingly becoming a combination of software development, infrastructure development, business process reengineering and systems integration of diverse information technologies. More than ever, they are cross-functional efforts. Thus, a typical IT project's life cycle follows these activities:

1. Business process reengineering – business architecture, business model definitions
2. Cost-benefit and Risk assessment
3. Project scope and specification

---

[46] "How Agile Development Can Lead to Better Results and Technology-Business Alignment", Thomas Wailgum, CIO Magazine, May 21, 2007
[47] "Enterprise Agile Adoption in 2006", Forrester Research, 2006

4. Systems architecture and conceptualization
5. Systems requirements
6. High level systems design
7. Low level systems design
8. Unit development
9. Unit test
10. Systems integration & testing
11. Installation at site
12. Site customization
13. Site testing
14. Training & documentation
15. Implementation
16. Acceptance
17. Maintenance

Most IT projects follow a waterfall model, basically executing tasks in a sequential manner. There are some models that emphasize feedback and control more than others. No single model fits every project or all situations. As IT managers we strive to manage IT projects to meet the project objectives on the three dimensions of schedule, cost and quality. Essentially, it's the role of the IT managers to choose the right model for the project at hand. Selection is influenced by the manager's prior experience, knowledge and the organization's skill level and process maturity.

Waterfall model: This is a sequential approach to development and implementation. The process begins with requirements definition, systems definition, design, code, testing and implementation. The inherent problems associated with the waterfall approach are that at the start of the project there is a great deal of uncertainty. Scoping the project before design is completed can lead to wrong project plans because design influences so much of the development activity. Most projects in the waterfall model tend to take longer to complete. The risks are often discovered at the later stages of the project, sometime just before production release. Waterfall model is still the most commonly used approach for IT implementations. A simple modification of the waterfall process can produce higher quality deliverables: simply add an inspection or review step at the end of each stage in the waterfall process. This is called "Stage Gating". For example, after Requirements stage, conduct a Requirements review and sign-off. Similarly after Specification stage, conduct specification review, and incorporate changes. Some reviews can be informal while organizations that practice strict quality guidelines prefer formal reviews.

Here is a list of recommended reviews after each stage:

- After each design phase, conduct a design review.
- After coding you can perform a code inspection or walkthrough.

- Before testing, review test plans for completion and adequate coverage.
- After testing, review test results. Notice test metrics and perform Pareto analysis to find defect concentrations.
- After verification, identify defective areas. Prepare release plans.
- After validation, perform gap analysis. Prepare support and maintenance plans.

Agile Methods

Agile methods are based on iterative development processes. Software developed during one unit of time is referred to as an iteration. An iteration may last from 2 weeks to 6 weeks. Mega projects that include more than 20 people and over 6 month in scope are good candidates for this method. Agile thinking strives to break down the scope into several smaller and manageable iterations. Each iteration is an entire IT project including: planning, requirements analysis, design, code, test and release. At the end of each iteration, the team re-evaluates the project plan and priorities. Agile methods are a departure from the traditional "big-bang" and high risk implementation approaches.

Agile methods prefer face-to-face communication over written documents. Agile teams are located in a single open office. The team includes the customer or a representative, a business analyst or product manager who intimately knows the customer's business and needs. Agile methods are results driven. In contrast to traditional software economics which measured lines of code, or function points, the Agile methods emphasize working application as the measure of progress. Methodologies conforming to Agile include Scrum process, Joint Application Development (JAD), Rapid Prototyping, Crystal Clear, Extreme Programming, Adaptive software development and Feature Driven Development. IT can gain huge leverage from these methods in its project implementations. Agile methods are adaptive. They allow quick adaptation to changing realities. Because Agile methods are iterative, they can scale up to handle large projects and requirements changes. In contrast the waterfall process like most traditional heavily plan-driven methods relies on predictive planning.

In 2001, a number of software development luminaries met in Colorado and issued a manifesto for Agile development. The manifesto set a different priority for software developers. Among them, the Agile Manifesto calls for preferring:

Individual interactions	*over*	*processes and tools*
Working software	*over*	*comprehensive documentation*
Customer collaboration	*over*	*contract negotiation*
Responding to change	*over*	*following a plan*

This is not to say that process and tools are not important. In fact IT organizations that are weak on processes and tools should not use this manifesto as justification for their lack of process maturity and inadequate tools. Such organizations must first reach a level of Lean implementation before considering Agile methods. Agile is not to be confused with chaotic implementations either. There is a distinct order and control mechanism embedded in Agile methods, such as Scrum project management.

The Agile Alliance founders believed that while there is value in the right hand side items, they value the items on the left hand side more. Based on the Agile Manifesto, a number of Agile methods that apply to IT management have been developed including the following stratagems:

Stratagems:

1. Customer satisfaction is achieved by continuous and fast delivery of useful applications and solutions
2. Providing working solutions and applications that are maintainable is the principle measure of success
3. Deliver solutions and applications frequently in weeks rather than months
4. Create a culture of close, daily interaction and cooperation between the IT staff and customers
5. Late changes in requirements are acceptable
6. Projects consist of motivated and committed individuals
7. The team participants have high trust in each other
8. Simplicity is preferred over complex designs.
9. Teams are self organized and driven to complete tasks with high quality.
10. Plans and methods are flexible and can adapt to change
11. Expect uncertainty and manage through it by implementing iterations and adaptation
12. Stimulate creativity and innovation by setting stretch goals and providing tools and equipment

---

Agile methods deliver higher return on investment by making continuous flow of value and solutions to customers. As IT managers engaged in Agile projects, we want to boost individual performance by building team accountability for performance and results. Let's look at some Agile lifecycle development models for IT:

Iterative model: This model divides the project into smaller deliverables. Each part is developed and delivered using a mini-waterfall process. Feedback from completing a part is fed into building the next part. As soon as a component is completed it is ready to be placed into production. The lifecycle of each part includes requirements analysis, architecture, design, unit development, integration, testing, site-testing, followed by release. Iterative model delivers application releases in several phases. While the iterative model solves many of the problems associated with the waterfall model, it does present new challenges of its own. Additional informal requirements might arise during the course of development. These unplanned requirements are also known as the "feature creep" or "scope creep" in the industry. Iterative models are susceptible to feature creep, but at the same token, they are ideal to absorb these requirements. The difficulty arises when feature changes must be applied to components already in production. Managing new features is critical to success of this model. The iterative model is a valid model for Agile development. Similar to Agile development, this model requires user community involvement throughout the project.

Spiral model: This is an iterative model first introduced by Barry Boehm in 1988. It combines prototyping, waterfall risk assessment and iterative methods to handle large, complex and expensive IT projects. Also known as the spiral lifecycle model, the model consists of four distinct iterations:

1. Define requirements and objectives
2. Build a prototype as a form of design and perform risk assessment
3. Detail the design, code, test and implement
4. Release and plan the next iteration

Depending on the scale of the project, each iteration is presumed to last six weeks to six months. At each risk assessment, the stakeholders are able to determine the risks and uncertainties that are exposed through prototyping. They can determine whether they should proceed forward with the plan, or modify the plan to reduce risk. At one time in my career I oversaw a development effort to build an online trading system. My team included 20 developers and engineers. Because of the uncertainty and lack of clear requirements, we chose the spiral model. We began every iteration by building a prototype and showing it to the executive team. Nine months and three iterations later, the executive team really liked our deliverable, but came to realize that it was missing some key features. The market conditions had changed. Online trading had evolved. They wanted the ability to trade many different commodities globally. The executive team agreed to market what we had created for the time being, but wanted to change the course of development. Because we were using an Agile method, it was relatively easy to plan the next iteration according to their objectives. Without risk assessment in each iteration, we would have proceeded blindly to build the wrong application and miss the opportunity to build the ideal product. You can apply scrum project management to either iterative or spiral model. Scrum, an Agile project management method uses short two to six week iterations and begins each iteration with sprints to achieve deliverables in each iteration.

What comes after Lean? Extreme Agility

Not every IT organization can reach agility. You must have mastered Lean principles first. Agile methods are suitable for IT environments that:

1. Include senior and experienced IT staff;
2. There is high trust between customer and IT;
3. Requirements change often;

4. It's possible to create small teams and culture thrives on chaos.

In contrast, plan-driven methods are a better choice when IT staff are junior; requirements don't change often; culture demands order, bureaucracy rules, and large number of participants are involved in the project. The worst form of plan-driven methods is manage-by-committee models that we often see in government IT organizations. Don't expect these organizations to be a role model for IT as they often cannot complete projects within budget or allotted time.

An Agile IT framework called Dynamic Systems Development Method (DSDM) was developed in the UK in the 1990s based upon Rapid Application Development. DSDM uses iterative development and incremental approach combined with continuous user participation in the IT projects. DSDM combines the best practices from its consortium of vendors and experts in information system development. The goal of DSDM is to deliver information systems on time and on budget.

There are many similarities between DSDM and the spiral lifecycle model. This method recognizes that projects have limited time and resources and plans accordingly to meet the business needs. In order to achieve these goals, this method follows seven phases:

1. Pre-project phase

Life cycle phase begins with:

2. feasibility study
3. Business study
4. Financial model iteration
5. Design and build iteration
6. Implementation and release
7. Post project phase

In addition to the 12 Agile stratagems discussed earlier, DSDM offers additional edicts. Among these edits are: higher emphasis on testing; 80% of functionality are delivered by 20% of the system requirement; and that all decisions during the development are reversible. Testing is expected to be carried out throughout the entire project life cycle. This is the basis for a "Test-driven development".

Applying the Pareto principle, DSDM starts implementing the first 20% of system requirements that deliver 80% of customer requirements, thereby providing solutions early. This might be good enough for a release to production. The remainder of the functionalities are added over time by the next iterations. In DSDM, project management and development techniques are incorporated.

The project manager and application manager are often the same or they work closely together through the entire project. This methodology is quite congruent with the "A"-Frame model which will be discussed in Chapter 10. DSDM rewards the team based on product delivery rather than completing tasks. Project risk assessment and scope of work are based on business functionality instead of task completions or lines of code completed.

Higher Standards – Faster Execution

So far we have discussed Lean and Agile methods, their theory, process reengineering and project management disciplines. There is also an IT framework for implementation. There is a stark difference between Lean IT and the traditional IT management. The traditional IT management relies heavily on Strategic Planning, Application Portfolio management and costly measure to reduce risk[48]. As a result traditional IT organizations struggle with their stigma as a cost center in the firm. Strategic Planning approach which was first introduced by Stanford Research Institute (SRI) in the 1970's has shown to fail, and for a variety of reasons, due to:

1. Its monolithic, rigid approach
2. Ignoring other critical factors such as creativity and process[49]
3. Adding to complexity rather than simplifying the project
4. Inadequate attention to managing technology, process and quality

Lean IT management, on the other hand is a key value adder and strategic-enabler for the organization. Lean IT by itself can be a strategy that differentiates your organization from the rest. As I'll explain in the following chapters it encourages small teams, distributed development, service-oriented architectures, portfolio of services, compressing time, and low-cost approach to implementing IT solutions.

According to a study published by the National Institute of Standards and Technology (NIST)[50], the majority of defects are introduced during early phases of requirements and coding. However, the majority of defects are detected later in the project cycle after coding and testing. Experience has shown that fixing a defect later in the project costs much more than fixing the same defect in the early stages of the project.

As the table in Figure 9.1 depicts, the amount of defects introduced and detected at each stage of development vary. Note the relative cost of fixing defects at each stage progressively increases as the project moves forward to later stages. For example, according to the NIST study, the cost of fixing a defect during the beta test is ten times the cost of fixing that defect at the requirements phase. The ideal quality program strives to introduce zero defects and the ideal testing program strives to detect 100% of those defects at each phase.

The economic impact of this study is that Lean and Agile IT organizations must strive to control introducing defects while detecting and fixing defects in the early phases of their projects. To achieve this objective, high level design, low level design, design reviews and testing are emphasized.

---

[48] "CIO Wisdom, Best Practices from Silicon Valley's Leading IT Experts", Dean Lane, Prentice Hall PTR, 2004
[49] "Jack Welch and GE Way", Robert Slater, McGraw Hill, 1999. Also see, "Strategy Safari: A Guided Tour Through the Wilds of Strategic Management", Henry Mintzberg, et al. 2005, The Free Press.
[50] NIST Economic Impacts of inadequate Infrastructure for Software testing, May 2002

	Requirements & Analysis Phase	Coding & Unit Testing Phase	Integration Phase, RAISE system Test	Beta Test Phase, Early Adopter Feedback	Post Release, Production Phase
Percent Defects introduced in each Phase	30%	58%	12%	0%	0%
Percent Defects Found in each Phase	7%	42%	28%	13%	10%
Time Required to Fix each Defect	1.2X	4.9X	9.5X	12.1X	15.3X

Fig 9.1 – The Economics of detecting & fixing defects during project lifecycle

Lean IT management considers the long-term effects of decisions, technology and applications. Despite slightly higher upfront cost and effort, Lean IT managers encourage their staff to follow these pearls of Lean management:

- Reduce risks and waste by building solutions incrementally. Use JAD, RAD, SCRUM and other incremental processes that involve users and allow adaptive solutions.

- Build solutions that last. High level and low level designs are key contributors to quality. Invest in testing and validate solutions by prototyping or through pilot programs.

- Avoid temporary fixes that frequently break down and require IT's attention. This is a source of waste. Fix the problems at the root cause level and in a systemic way. Do not be satisfied with a "band-aid" fix or a work-around. While workarounds are acceptable as temporary solutions, staff must be encouraged to eliminate the root cause of technical problems in a systemic way.

- Develop tools to improve staff productivity and to compress time. Emphasize personal productivity tools and streamline IT processes to reduce execution time.

- Catch and Fix defects early. Catching a defect and solving a problem in the early stages of development costs far less (sometimes by an order of magnitude) than in later phases of implementation, as we saw in the NIST study. Therefore, always define, architect, engineer and design solutions at the early stages of the project.

- Build quality into each stage of your project. Follow each stage with a quality review; simply a review of test results and quality metrics. Finally, develop the roll-out or engineer release plan for a perfect fit into the customer environment. Rehearse release process through mock-live scenarios or pilot programs.

- Define standards for design, workflow re-engineering, communication, testing and IT workmanship. Adapt a standard toolkit like UML as common language for specification and design.
- Accumulate knowledge by documenting solutions, procedures and services. Documentation is a form of design. Over the long haul accumulated knowledge will reduce error and rework. It will bring consistency of knowledge to the IT organization.
- Understand and study the customer's workflows. Analyze workflows; map tasks to product functions and vice versa. Determine the side-effects of functions, and never use an application's side-effect for a workflow function.
- Be opportunistic: If a solution already exists, do not recreate it. If you make a solution that adds value for one user, find out if it can do the same for the rest of the organization by turning it into an enterprise service or solution.
- Reduce time to perform any task, whether it's for IT staff or for clinical staff
- Perform tests eagerly. Reward testers for finding bugs and defects. The quantity and severity of bugs hint at quality of the application or service. If you find a lot of defects, test more. If quality is poor, fix the development process before proceeding to the next stage of development or release.
- Eliminate waiting and delays. Create a single flow development environment.

The Agile implementation framework covers multiple dimensions of project management, process, people and standards. The Lean approach emphasizes processes that produce results faster and uncover problems earlier. Among Agile and low cost processes, you can try Joint Application Design (JAD), Rapid Application Design (RAD), SCRUM and Rapid prototyping as best practice standards. Traditional processes that are heavily "Waterfall" or "Strategic Planning" driven are not advised. The problem with traditional implementation processes is that the implementation team does not recognize the true risks and proper design choices early in the project. Most of the projects that fail using traditional implementation processes find out about the problems after 80% of the project cost and time have been exhausted. By then, it's too late to fix major issues that should have been caught in earlier phases of development. Next, let's review Agile Implementation processes briefly.

Joint Application Development (JAD)

Designed by IBM and successfully applied for many years, Joint Application Development prescribes participation of users and capturing their input throughout the development process. The key success factor in JAD is that implementation begins with understanding the user-system interface and workflow functions. JAD allows the user interface, namely the front-end to drive the initial stages of implementation, i.e. it lets the front-end to define the middle-tier and backend. The traditional approaches that start with the back-end or database design and later develop the user functionality find themselves surprised by higher costs and disappointed users, because user front-end changes will impact the back-end database structure and are likely to introduce rework. In JAD, development begins with defining the user screens first. From there the services, objects, along with functions, methods and data elements are defined.

These can form the basis for the design of integration points and business logic layer (middle tier) and database (backend). At each phase of development, users are allowed to provide feedback to the implementation team.

Rapid Application Development (RAD)

Rapid Application Development is another methodology that promotes incremental development using modular, component based building blocks. RAD can begin with a skeletal solution which gives users basic workflow functionality. The functional features or additional modules are then added incrementally. RAD advocates releasing a solution when reaching 80% completion rather than waiting for full implementation of all functions. This methodology often uses prototyping to reduce implementation time. RAD process is suitable for both well-defined projects and ill-defined projects. It can be a fast, low-cost and Agile technique for delivering solutions. To make RAD successful, form a small team of subject matter experts and highly skilled IT staff to build the first instance of the solution.

SCRUM Project Management

Project management has become a multi-disciplinary and vital component for introducing change. Effective project management is now regarded as a critical success factor in most industries. Proficient project managers must be able to tolerate a stressful environment and diverse range of issues while making decisions about resource coordination, apply technical principles and manage deadlines and cost. The Project Management Institute, PMI has published a standard for project management called Project Management Body of Knowledge (PMBOK). The institute offers project management certifications such as PMP designations which are highly recommended. Hiring PMP certified project managers is a wise first step towards ensuring consist project management principles are applied. But, following PMI's structured approach is not necessarily a guarantee for project success.

On another front, the International Organization for Standardizations (ISO) has published a series of project management standards for different industries. The ISO-10006 is a quality in project management standard which underscores the importance of project scope, cost, time and attention to management when new technologies (such as information systems) are involved. In 2007, ISO launched a workgroup to develop ISO-21500 standard for project management. One useful aspect of the ISO-21500 standard is that it allows multinational firms to coordinate their project management processes consistently across the globe. ISO standards emphasize transfer of knowledge between projects and sharing lessons learned to improve project management.

Case studies of failed ERP (Enterprise Resource Planning) implementations, offer a few interesting lessons to be learned. Among them: keep the scope of deliverables small so they are manageable; grow the scope only after implementing the initial deliverables. From lessons like these, Scrum project management was born. This methodology is a departure from the Project Management Institute's structured and predictive approach to managing projects. In 1995, Jeff Sutherland and Ken

Schwaber introduced Scrum at the OOPSLA95 conference[51]. Scrum was developed as a method to contain cost and time in implementation[52] by maximizing agility and ability to handle complex projects. This process is iterative, adaptive and has excellent quality controls. It consists of three roles: A Product Owner, a Scrum Master and a Team.

Scrum operates this way[53]: The project is sub-divided into a number of major deliverables or iterations with specific time table. The team begins each iteration as a *sprint*. At the start of each iteration the team reviews what it must do. It defines what it can deliver by the end of the iteration. At the end of the iteration the team meets again to evaluate its accomplishments, inspect quality and performance. Any adaptation or changes are decided at that time. The Product Owner represents the interests of all stake holders in the project. The Scrum Master is responsible for teaching and facilitating the Scrum process. The team is self managing and self organizing. Every day (or once a week), the team meets and reviews its deliverables. Each team member must answer 3 questions: *What have you done since the last Scrum meeting? What do you intend to complete by the next meeting? And, what are the inhibitors preventing you to reach your goal?*

At the end of the sprint, the team meets with the Product Owner and demonstrates the functionality it has completed and prepares for the next sprint. Scrum Master maintains a backlog of tasks that are to be delivered. I've seen SCRUM process used successfully for many projects. I've trained my staff on Scrum project management. Aside from using it for rapid implementations, SCRUM process has been an exceptional process for resolving major quality defects or problems caused by a vendor's product or infrastructure failures. For example, if you would recall the speech recognition application project from the earlier chapters, we can review the Scrum project plan for it. The Product Owner identified five distinct sprints for implementing the speech recognition application. A sample of the project plan is shown in Appendix C. Using SCRUM, the project team was able to complete the project in four months, two months ahead of schedule.

Extreme Programming

A branch of development called extreme programming has been influential to Agile method. Created by Kent Beck in 1996, Extreme Programming was a methodology to rescue the struggling Chrysler Comprehensive Compensation (C3) project. A typical Extreme Programming session involves a programmer and customer sitting face to face. The customer verbally describes what she needs and how she wants to use the application. While the customer explains her workflow in a narrative like telling a story, the programmer designs and codes. The programmer may pause to ask clarifying questions. At the end of the session which may last several hours, the programmer shows the result of the running code to the customer. Specifically, in the "Test-driven development" (TDD) practice of extreme programming, programmers are

---

[51] ACM SIGPLAN International Conference on Object Oriented Programming, Systems, Language and Applications, 1995.
[52] "The New New Product Development Game", Takeuchi and Nonaka, Harvard Business Review, Jan-Feb 1986
[53] "Agile Project Management with Scrum", Ken Schwaber, Microsoft Press, 2004

encouraged to write automated test tools and perform unit and integrated tests throughout the development cycle. In TDD development, programmers write short test cases and repeat their tests periodically. They perform regression testing, namely repeating tests to verify any previously fixed defects. Many successful IT organizations use variations of extreme programming and are delivering rapid solutions to their customers.

More Tips on Time Compression

Time compression is a powerful stratagem for amplifying IT resources, resulting in higher productivity and perceived customer value. One of the aims of Agile IT management must be compressing time by completing tasks faster. Compressing time creates more capacity, expands space and amplifies the resources ability to produce more. Left unchecked, time can slip away at tremendous costs and cumulative risks. When projects and even small tasks slip into failure, they turn into a liability and risk for IT. More often than not, projects fail because they are not managed to complete within allotted time.

Loner projects carry higher risk of failure. Losing control of time, lack of time management, leads to higher risk of failure. Lack of closure on tasks and projects eventually escalate up to paralyzing levels, making IT team ineffective, torpid and powerless. Since information technologies *and* user requirements change over time, run away projects seem to never complete. They get trapped in a vicious cycle of perpetual development, thus failing indefinitely. The high inventory of unfinished projects, work in progress, fixes pending test are major sources of cost for IT. Such projects devour resources and money until eventually aborted by executive management, or turned around by major shift in management.

Managing time, getting closure on tasks on time is essential to governing both change and technology. Managing projects at a high velocity will reduce time and hence increase productivity. A secret to achieving shortened project timelines and compressing time is to apply an *"eager"* approach towards performing tasks. Being "eager" means more than being proactive. Lean thinking promotes the concept of pull and just in time. The pull method propels us to "start working on tasks as soon as they hit the work queue". The "eager" approach applies to all deliverables and work in progress. As soon as a portion of the project is complete, it must be tested and released immediately. The common wisdom in traditional management has advocated a "lazy" approach to performing tasks: "Wait until the customer screams for it and then start working on the task".

The traditional *"lazy"* approach creates disjointed workflows and accumulates a large inventory of work-in-progress. But, the "eager" approach creates a single flow of work and thus paves the path to success. If we applied the "Lazy" approach to manufacturing airplanes, in order to assemble the plane we would wait until all subcomponents, such as the wings, fuselage, engines and tail, have arrived at the assembly line before we would assemble anything. That leads to the high inventory levels that we are trying to avoid. Surprisingly many information technology organizations approach development in the same fashion. They build all subcomponents first (notice the long wait) and begin integration only after all pieces are ready to be joined together (late verification means late discovery of defects).

> **Stratagems:**
> 1. Compress the time required to complete each task in the project.
> 2. Eliminate delays and non-value adding tasks.
> 3. Start working on tasks *asap* and complete them in a shorter time than scheduled.
> 4. Re-use existing solutions and tools before building a new one.

More surprisingly, still many traditional IT organizations implement every new application from scratch as an entirely new development effort. This would be as outlandish as if Boeing Company manufactured one airplane at a time from scratch, each as a new development project. The Eager approach dictates that assembly should begin as soon as two subcomponents can be assembled. IT projects are similar to this example. In order to compress time in IT projects, parallel work and immediate assembly of various components are recommended. Clearly the Eager approach to integrating IT components will result in faster completion time. The potential assembly issues are uncovered earlier and hence the problems are discovered sooner at a lower cost to fix. The other benefit of eager approach is the ability to deliver partially completed solutions which allow earlier user feedback and can meet user requirements enough to be deployed into production. Projects that take a long time to complete suffer from high costs, outdated technology, and missing new user requirements.

Summary: Tips for Time Compression

- Use rapid development techniques to deliver fast:
    - Rapid Application Development (RAD)
    - Joint Application Design (JAD)
    - Feature Driven Development methods (FDD)
    - Use SCRUM project management
- Outsource to a partner who can do it better and cheaper
- Break the project into smaller deliverables. Rather than spending months working on a large deliverable in a big-bang release, use multiple iterative, and incremental releases.
- Reduce Cycle time:
    - Even out the arrival of work
    - Minimize the number of steps in Process
    - Minimize the size of tasks in Process
    - Establish a regular tempo for regular releases
    - Limit work to Capacity
    - Apply Eager approach to tasks. Use Pull scheduling in your projects
    - Avoid time-consuming strategic planning approaches. Instead breakdown projects into smaller chunks and apply iterative development cycles.
    - Test as soon as possible, and test fiercely to break the product. Testing reduces time-to-release.
- Implement rapid Build-and-Test cycles.
- Apply eager work habits. Begin work on new tasks immediately.

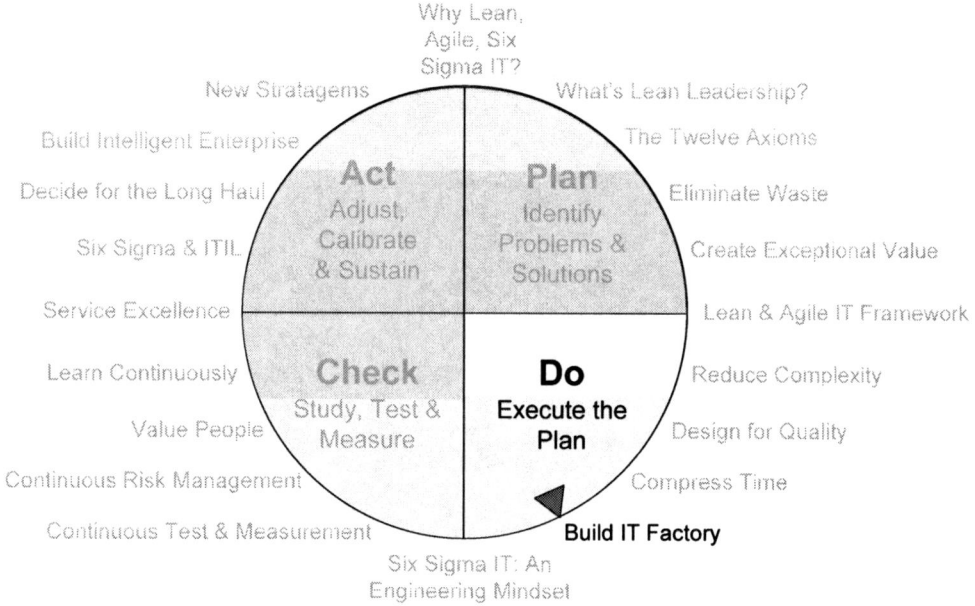

"The Toyota production system, however, is not just a production system. I am confident it will reveal its strength as a management system."

Taiichi Ohno

Chapter 10: Build IT Factory

In the previous chapters, we reviewed several traditional and Agile implementation processes. A characteristic of a factory approach to IT is repeatability, re-usability, consistency and predictability of project outcomes. The goal of IT factories is to provide quality services and products at the lowest cost, risk and timeframe possible, but consistently. That implies using a consistent development process, integration, testing and service delivery while minimizing changes to the IT assembly line formation.

The nature of information technology work, in general is different from manufacturing, but sound manufacturing principles can be used successfully by IT organizations. IT work lends itself to creative activity, constructing and integrating solutions from various technology components. This is the kind of work that's highly non-linear and non repetitive. But there are always patterns, re-usable sub components and standard processes that can immensely reduce IT costs and waste.

A few years ago, when I was the vice president of engineering at a custom software development company, I created a consistent process for building applications. It was an application factory consisting of several small work cells of engineers. We built applications based on patterns, re-using pre-developed software components and integrating those components. It was an amazing success. We could reasonably predict the quality and timeline for release of the functionality. The work cells consisted of a few people about five to ten, consisting of developers, a designer, testers, a technical writer, and a Scrum master.

All work cells developed solutions based on common and consistent processes and patterns. The basic paradigm of IT factories is creating a consistent flow of innovation at low costs, lower risks and standardized production model. The production model for IT factories consists of the following building blocks. We'll review the building blocks throughout the book:

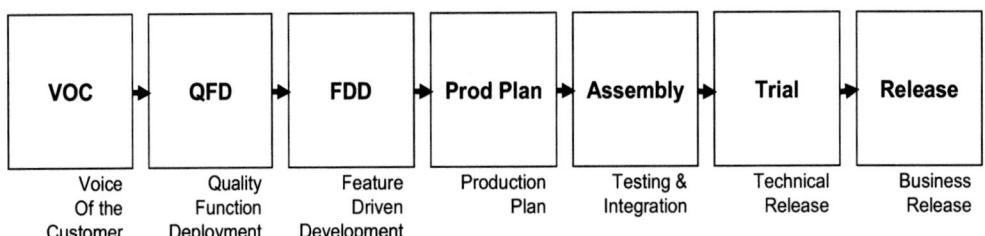

Fig 10.1 – The Building Blocks of IT Factories

Application Factories: IT as a Production Process

Software development and IT implementations in general can be viewed as production processes. Research and publications such as "Software Factories"[54] and "Software Product-Line Engineering" compare software development to manufacturing cars[55]. Just as cars can vary by engine type, upholstery, seats and interior options, IT implementations can vary but follow a similar process. In this chapter, we'll review the basic frameworks for IT factories: implementing solutions by assembly a set of common application components. Our discussion will cover the Zachmann model, the I-frame, T-frame, and A-frame assembly line.

In Toyota's Lean Manufacturing model, the concept of SMED, Single Minute Exchange of Dies, is a process of retargeting the assembly line for major variations. Using SMED, a manufacturer can quickly re-purpose its assembly line to build different models of the same product. The IT production process can be similarly retargeted for building different solutions rapidly. When we view IT implementations as a production process, we must ask where are the bottlenecks on the production line? Our goal is to create a uninterrupted, single flow of innovation and development. The bottlenecks are typically caused by dependencies between deliverables, poor design, defective vendor applications, and organizational challenges where development teams are not integrated.

Research has shown that inspecting deliverables can be an effective aid to identify and measure potential bottlenecks. Inspections of vendor applications are possible by reviewing application release notes, site visits to other customer sites and reviewing test results. It can be more intensive by conducting internal pilot tests or testing at a vendor's lab environment. In the realm of extreme programming and Agile methods, "building the simplest things" that add the most value will produce the most

---

[54] "Software Factories: Assembling Applications with Patterns, Models, Frameworks and Tools", Jack Greenfield, Keith Short, Steve Cook, Stuart Kent, John Crupi, Wiley Publishing, 2004
[55] "Software Product-Line Engineering: A Family Based Software Development Process", Weiss, D. and Lai, C.T.R., Addison-Wesley, Boston, MA, 1999

deliverables rapidly[56]. We must strive to deliver the most value early in the implementation cycle. So, it's easy to plan a production system that gives highest priority to features that deliver the most value first. The diagram below shows the order of production priority:

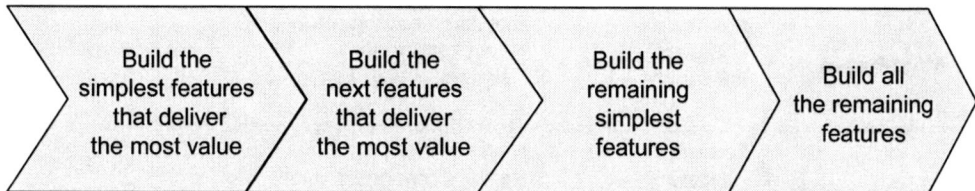

Continuous Innovation: Development as Production System

Fig 10.2 – Development Priorities in a Production System

The production plan shown above provides a continuous stream of deliverables. The implementation plan can be conceived in terms of four short duration phases. The production plan begins with implementing the 20% of the application that satisfies 80% of the customer-valued requirements. The plan proceeds to implement the next set of features that are most valued by the customer. Next, it builds the remaining simplest features, and finally builds all the remaining functions. Notice that the role of the project manager or program manager is not mentioned here. Instead, I emphasize the role of the production manager who not only manages the project, but also sequences the delivery of components to customers.

To build a production plan we can start with an FDD approach. Once the scope of the project is defined, then we list and rank features by their value and customer priorities. The production manager with the aid of project stakeholders classifies the features into three groups: "Must-haves", "Nice-to-haves", and "Gold-plated". The gold-plated features do not add much value and are not essential to the value streams.

These features can be immediately removed from the production plan (see Figure 10.3). We also list the subcomponents required for each feature. We want to identify existing subcomponents that already provide the services. When we view IT implementations as production systems the role of the project manager changes to that of a *production manager*. She must plan ahead to remove bottlenecks in advance.

Bottlenecks cause "wait time" or idle time. Common delays due to lack of materials, software, equipment and also management approvals are avoidable wait times. The production manger must identify both the risks as well as the bottlenecks. She must exercise risk mitigation as well as bottleneck elimination plans. This requires some elements of pro-active thinking and planning. For example, notifying all project participants and stakeholders of what will be coming in the next few weeks is just as valuable if not more important than reporting what was accomplished in the last few weeks.

---

[56] "Repository Mining and Six Sigma for Process Improvement", Michael VanHilst, Pankaj K. Garg, Christopher Lo, ACM, May 17, 2005

Development List Priority (High, Med, Low)	Feature, Function Description	Sub-Component: Services, Classes & Patterns (software, network, application, services)	Difficulty (Hard, Medium, Easy)
Must-haves	Feature D ---- Feature B ---- Feature M ---- ...	Existing Component available New Component Existing Pattern available ...	Easy Hard Hard ..
Nice-to-haves	Feature G ---- Feature K ---- Feature A ---- ...	New component Partial Component available New Component ...	Medium Easy Medium
Gold Platted	Feature C ---- Feature E ---- ...	Do not implement Do not implement ...	N/A N/A

Fig 10.3 - Production Planning Based on Feature Driven Development

A traditional project manager typically reports what has been accomplished in the past. Conversely, a Lean and Agile production manager announces what deliverables and actions are expected from project participants in the coming weeks. This type of notification allows stakeholders and project participants alike to prepare and remove potential bottlenecks. This method creates a pull for deliverables. Scrum project management which we discussed in the previous chapters offers the right constructs to do this type of future notifications. A factory approach to IT implementations requires higher quality deliverables early in the production cycle. This is intended to reduce latent defects and rework. The inherent danger with releasing defective programs are that they disrupt the continuous flow of deliverables, they make the program increasingly fragile and brittle; and they introduce potential dependencies with other segments of development.

Software Development by Pattern

One of the disciplines in application factories is developing software by pattern. The notion of software patterns is derived from object oriented development. A Pattern is an abstraction from a specific form which can be reused or keeps recurring in other contexts.

The most notable advantages of using patterns are re-using proven designs, making design easier and faster. Within the context of Information Systems, a pattern represents instructive information about an essential structure of IT systems. Among patterns that are easily recognized, we can spot user interfaces, data mining, decision support, and data exchange between applications has having common structures that keep on recurring in our development efforts.

There are three types of patterns: architectural patterns, design patterns, and coding patterns. Architectural patterns describe a fundamental structural organization or schema for information systems and relationships between them. Patterns are subsystems that specify their purpose, function, and interconnections with other subsystems. Typical examples of architectural patterns in information systems include server security, service oriented architectures or web-based data exchange between applications.

Design patterns deal with schema and rules for detailing a subsystem or software component. They define the input, output, functions and inner-working of the design in such a way that it can be constructed. As an example, consider a design pattern for integration of various desktop software and hardware components that captures office, mobile phone, and fax and printer functions. Coding patterns define the low-level programming, scripting or procedures for implementing a specific component or function. A typical example is scripts for tape backups that can be re-used as a pattern. Literature refers to the production view of software development and IT implementations by software factory, application factory and software development by patterns. All references describe the concept as creating work cells that follow clearly defined development and management processes. Using fundamentals of industrial manufacturing principles such as standardized components, parallel processes, consistency of quality, software factories can produce predictable results at lower costs.

Use of light weight computer aided design and development (CAD) tools are encouraged but only to the extent that they assist with managing the production flow and not "super size" the development effort. The success of Application Factory in IT organizations depends on several approaches as follows:

1. Apply the "eager" approach to gathering requirements and basically high quality requirements definition
2. Understand production cycles and typical durations of specialized tasks such as architecture, design, coding, testing and release
3. Perform skills assessment of staff. Knowing the complexity of tasks and assignment of those tasks to the appropriately skilled IT staff.
4. Create a library of tools, patterns and standard off the shelf components and emphasis on reusability
5. Create a library of documented standards for all IT activities to create consistency across all functions
6. Form matrix organizations for application factory: create small work cells dedicated to a specific project while its members belong to specialized fields of IT.
7. Develop modular architectures that can evolve and adapt at subcomponent level as changes emerge including new technology, new business requirements, and new vendor solutions

Microsoft has published its standards based on .NET architecture for software factory implementations. Called the Enterprise Framework Factory (the EFx Factory), Microsoft promotes common naming conventions, common application blocks and component library standards as the basis for its factory. What's positive about EFx Factory is that Microsoft emphasizes the service oriented architectures in its factory. Namely, all components must be conceived in terms of their intended services during development. In this section we will review the "I" frame, "T" frame, and "A" frame representing different Implementation models. Each frame has its advantages and disadvantages. It is up to the IT manager to determine which model best fits the particular problem or situation. Before describing these models, let's discuss and evaluate a traditional architectural model called Zachmann to establish a baseline[57].

> **Cases of Agile and IT Factory Success**
>
> HealthMarket.com has revenues of $90 million and 133 employees, located in Norwalk, Connecticut. HealthMarket uses an evolutionary process known as "creeping elegance" employed for systems development. The IT group relies on standards-based, component-driven architecture that allows successful migration to open systems. L-2 Communications Integrated Systems provides aerospace services and products. With revenues over $1.2 billion, the company needed an integrated ERP system that supported unique workflows required in its business. The information technology group launched a wireless aircraft inspection system to reduce inspection cycle time. The system was integrated into ERP which saved hundreds of thousands of dollars because it allowed the ERP to generate immediate estimates and for customers to review service orders remotely.
>
> Business needs and operational challenges at Ruby Tuesday with revenues nearing $1 billion and 38,000 employees can change rapidly. The company's IT department set up a help desk alert system that allows help desk grow from 12 staffers to 100 seats as necessary. To keep agile, the IT organization maintains a 90 percent of staff level of analysts, allowing frequent changes in their responsibility. CompuCredit headquartered in Atlanta, Georgia, is a leading financial company.
>
> The IT department developed an XML-based business information gateway which accelerated the company's collection efforts. The company's new portfolio of credit card accounts is serviced in 60 days, half the time of previous portfolios. W.W. Grainger of Lake Forest, Illinois is a $4.7 billion company with 15,000 employees. It implemented a customer inventory availability tool utilized by its sales staff supporting 20,000 transactions in a one-month trial.
>
> The net increase in sales from the trial was over $180,000. Similarly, the end-to-end supply chain improvement cut cycle time by 30 percent. Acxiom Corp in Little Rock, Arkansas, used Agile, open and component based approaches to improve processing capability. The company developed a grid computing platform to manage data across the enterprise while reducing costs and failure rates. This approach allowed customers to buy customer information to acquire computing power inexpensively and incrementally.

---

[57] The following case studies are based on heavily borrowed case studies from CIO Magazine and Annals of Cases in Information Technology, Editor Mehdi Khosrow-pour, Idea Group Publishing, Information Science Publishing, 2002-2007

Zachmann Model

The Zachmann model is a traditional architectural model that attempts to define all aspects of an IT solution. This model can be viewed as a matrix: The rows explain tiers of view from perspectives of customer, department, enterprise and IT staff. The columns answer questions about Who, Why, When, How, Where and Whom. The diagram in Figure 10.4 illustrates the model in detail. Each component of the model are defined as follows:

- **"Data"** means key facts and entities about the business, customers, partners, patients, and whoever your company is interacting with, plus information generated by users and what is communicated between staff.

- **"Function"** means key operations, tasks and unit of work performed by users. This is typically then broken into specific function points which describe a single action by the user. For example, in manufacturing, entering an order into the order entry system is a workflow that includes several function points: Select product, verify customer, select delivery date, Change quantity, etc. For example in healthcare, entering a patient referral into the scheduling system is a function which might consist of several function points (actions), such as select a procedure, select a physician, enter allergies, precautions and patient visit schedule.

- **"Platform"** refers to all aspects of technology, such as: physical (network, storage, equipment), logical (business logic, middle tier, messaging, interfaces) and conceptual (plans, security, access, integration).

- **"People"** means IT customers. In the context of information systems, all users are Information workers, i.e. they are both consumers of information and generate information for other users.

- **"Whom"**. I like to call this column "Services". It means services and levels of services delivered by the application, the infrastructure and by the IT staff to users.

- **"Workflow"** refers to work procedures and process to complete a task. Workflows should capture the trio of process, protocol and practices.

Using Zachmann, early in the project cycle, the architects must emphasize the first row of the model. They attempt to understand "Customer" workflows, activity list, and data entities used or created. Most IT projects fail in general because they do the opposite. They start with the back-end or database components first, and then spend the effort to analyze the process and user front-end. What's attractive about Zachmann's model is that it offers a "table of elements" perspective that spans the entire spectrum of IT planning.

A simpler and more practical variation of this "Table of Elements" approach is a "feature-driven" model that shows subcomponent development activities in layers. Figure 10.5 illustrates the layered approach to production planning. As shown in the diagram, each customer-valued feature is listed and then prioritized as High, Medium or Low. Then each feature is analyzed in layers of Value, Workflow, Front-end, Middleware and Backend.

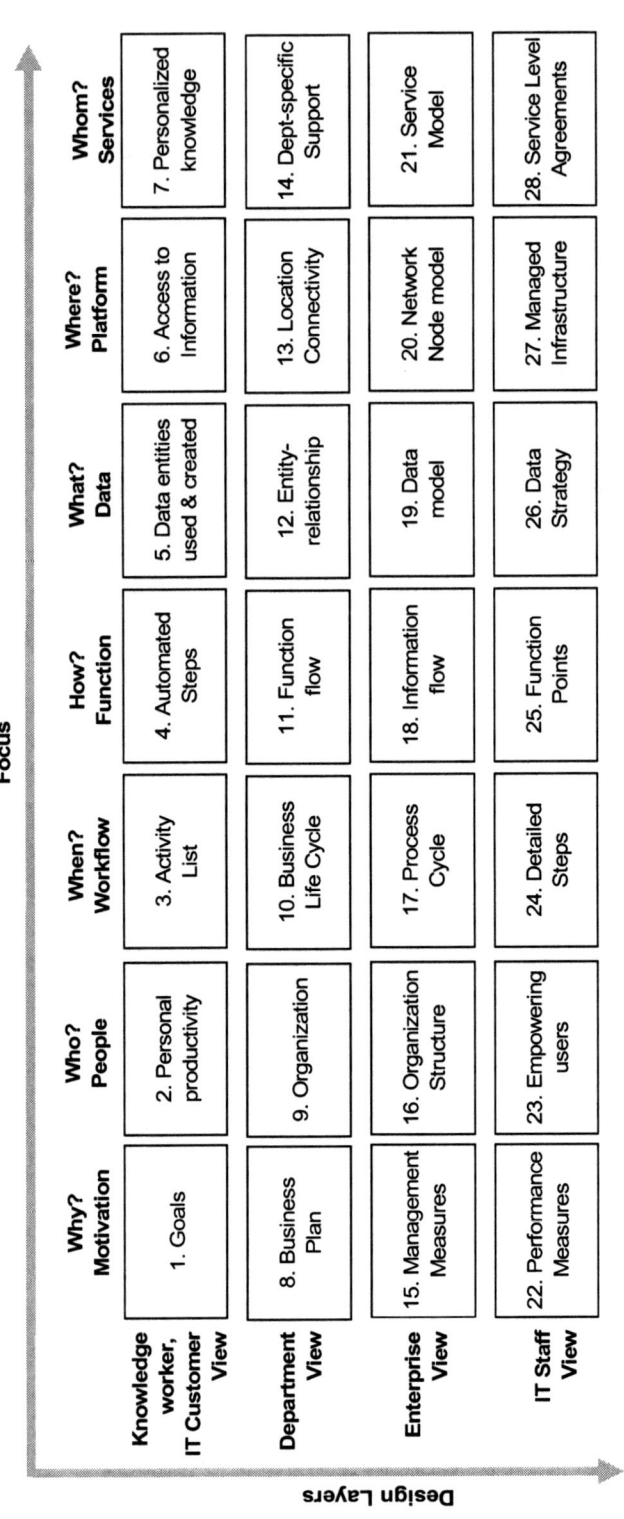

Fig 10.4 – Zachmann Model for IT Framework

At each layer, starting from the value stream and going towards the backend, the requirements and impact for each feature is analyzed. When completed, the matrix collectively represents two things: the scope of work required to implement features and the order of implementation. The order of implementation flows from the high priority to low priority features.

Layers	Feature A	Feature B	Feature C	...	Feature N
Priority: High, Med, Low					
Value Stream, Value Proposition					
Workflow: process, protocol, practice					
Front-end, user interface					
Middleware, integration, interfaces					
Backend, database					

Fig 10.5 – Layered Approach to Production Planning

Now we are ready to review each of the architectural models for Lean IT, including the "I", "T", and "A" frames. We are borrowing these concepts from industrial engineering discipline and apply it to IT.

The "I"-Frame Model

As the shape of the letter "I" indicates this is a linear, feed forward model of development. This is analogous to what's known in the software industry as the "waterfall" process. In this model, development flows from one stage of development to the next stage. The stages start with requirements definition, design, development and test. A unique feature of the "I" frame model is stage-gating. Stage gating enforces strict quality check points at the end of each phase, and fixing defects before starting the next phase. Quality check points can be formal or informal reviews, inspections and test result evaluations. This approach attempts to deliver high quality products, but can fail to meet the cost and schedule targets. But, this model is rather rigid because as projects progress, it becomes increasingly more difficult and costly to make changes after each phase is completed.

Using the "I" frame implementation model, we must be certain that each phase is completed to the customer's complete satisfaction before moving to the next phase or new features. In the Agile and Lean approaches any administrative activities that do not add value to the development are removed. The goal of Lean IT project management should be "one piece flow" development. In other words, keeps the development going without interruptions. This approach calls for user participation to focus on requirements definition and performing quality checkpoints such as reviews at the end of each stage and even integrated testing. There is a bigger emphasis on activities that lower the project risk. Another variation of the "I" frame model is concurrent engineering & development. This model attempts to shorten the long development cycle by allowing work to start on multiple phases in parallel before prior phases are completed. For example, before the analysts complete the requirements phase, another group starts the specification phase. Similarly, after the specification phase has finished, designers can start design from a partially completed specification.

The "T"-Frame Architecture

The "T"-Frame model is an extension of the "I"-Frame model. It's founded on the premise that once you have completed a product, you can release multiple variations or extensions of the product to serve other customers. To illustrate, I use the analogy of an oil refinery. In an oil refinery the process converts crude oil into multiple weights of oil sold in cans for automobiles.

The refined oil is inherently obtained from an "I" frame process, but making specific weights, for example what we purchase as W10-30 or W10-40 weights are products obtained at the end of the T process from a common basic material, the crude oil. Similar to the "I" frame model, this approach requires a "big design upfront". The big design upfront is necessary because we want to be absolutely sure that the requirements and design are correct before proceeding with implementation. Despite this weakness, these models can be retrofitted to meet Lean and Agile principles. The concurrent development model is one example. These models are suitable for smaller, less complex projects which are under six months in duration and involve less than ten IT staff.

> **Case Study: Microsoft Vista Operating System**
>
> For years, starting with Windows Operating System, Microsoft developed each new generation of operating systems using the "I"-Frame and "A"-Frame models. Using the "A" frame model, Microsoft had considerable success. However, when developing its Vista Operating System, the company faced difficult choices that resulted in costly delays. Microsoft admitted at least twice to postponing the release date of Vista.
>
> Two years into development, Microsoft halted development and restarted the project from scratch. With the previous operating systems, Microsoft built the core system first and incrementally added new features over time by releasing new versions. With Vista Operating System, however, Microsoft engaged in a "T" frame architecture by creating 6 versions of Vista, including the Vista Home, Vista Business, Vista Enterprise, and Ultimate, plus 32-bit and 64-bit versions. The company insisted on a complete package release of all versions at once. The development took 5 years, longer than any other operating system released previously by the company. If we consider the development time that Microsoft spent on developing NT, XP, and now Vista, and if the company were to use the same development model ...

... we can extrapolate the next operating system to be available in no less than 9.5 years. Surely, the development model has to change if 9.5 years is deemed too long. Other architectural models such as the "A"-Frame which we will review next, might have served Microsoft better. With Vista, the company could have released a 32-bit version first and then the 64-bit version later. Alternatively, the company could have released the home and business versions first and the enterprise version later.

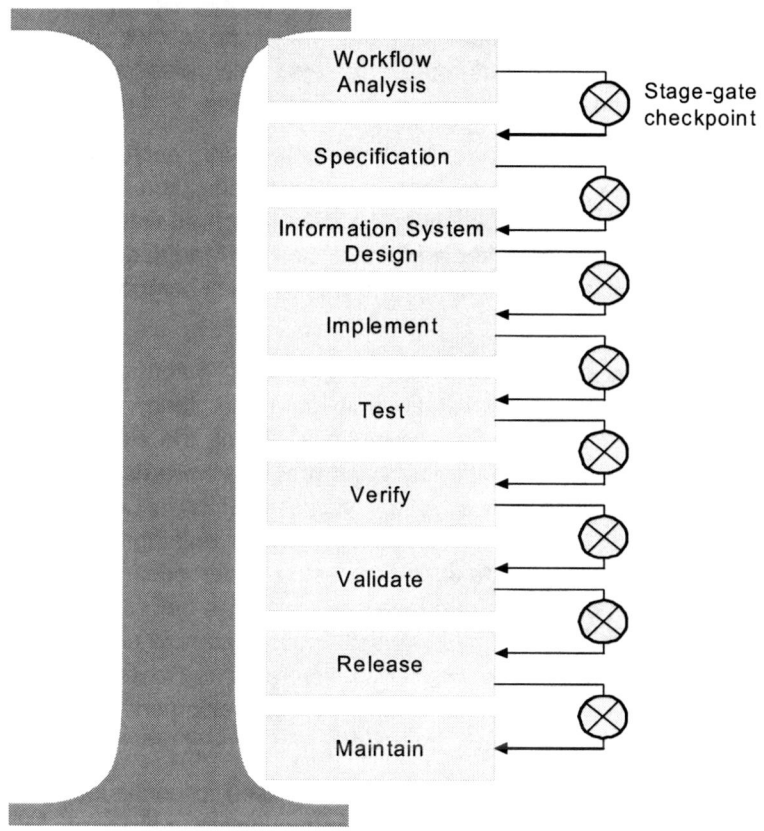

The "I" Frame Diagram:
The "I" Frame Implementation Model With stage-gating

Fig 10.6 – The "I" Frame Production Model – Adapted from Waterfall Model

Both "I"-Frame and "T"-Frame models are regarded as non-incremental architectures. The "A"-Frame model offers the best of both worlds. It can be iterative as well as integrative of IT work packages. It's flexible to adapt and integrate re-factored legacy applications as well as new and bolt-on solutions.

The "A"-Frame Model

The "A-Frame" model is analogous to building an airplane. It's suitable for complex, large, multi-team mega projects. An aircraft manufacturing company builds planes by building aircraft components separately and in parallel, all under consistent enterprise-wide design standards, then assembling the components to complete the plane. This approach enables Agile, concurrent, Lean and rapid development approaches for software, IT and systems integration projects. Similarly, an IT organization can implement a solution by building the sub-components in parallel according to common standards and processes. When completed, each component is unit tested and then incrementally integrated into the sub-assembly. As sub-systems are completed, tested and integrated, they are released into production to meet the basic needs of users. When components are incrementally assembled (that's the peak of A-Frame), the final integrated testing and roll-out occur. This incremental and consistent release tempo reduces long waits and allows users to begin using applications early. As new features are incrementally released, the gradual impact of change on users and operations are more manageable.

The priority and order of development for each sub-assembly can be motivated by specific value streams in the organization. We identify and begin implementation of features that deliver the most important value streams first. A similar development process model, known as the "Cellular Manufacturing Process Model", is used by some organizations to define the way in which components are integrated into a target solution.

A project is broken down into a number of "manufacturing cells" which take delivery of, or make components and integrate them into larger aggregates (subsystems, systems, or packaged solutions). Along the way, metrics that measure the quality of the supplied components and progress towards project completion keep us abreast of production status. A key success factor in Lean IT is to start the IT framework with a "Customer" perspective. This is nothing new, but how it's done makes the difference. Understanding the customer perspective starts with discussions about user requirements, user interface and workflows before creating the back-end & database schema framework. We want to understand how users will use the solution and how can they create value. Namely, which features create value for the customer? Years ago, IBM developed its Joint Application Development (JAD) methodology, in a way to involve and capture users' input early and throughout the development process.

This is an iterative process that lends itself to continuous improvement over time. The design process begins with a simple question to the user, "What is your ideal workflow?" The process continues with function point analysis, mapping functions to application features to determine what is feasible, all the way to the interfaces and backend database. Then the reverse takes place: given the functionality available from the application, what other value streams and benefits are possible. The analyst must then present to users the workflow options feasible. The difference between user's wants and what is feasible, is the gap. Often to bridge the gap, the IT staff request feature enhancements to the vendor for future upgrades. When designing a sub-assembly, the designers must be mindful of the long-term plans for what this sub-assembly will be integrated to and how it will evolve.

Long term view inspires architects to keep maintainability and re-usability in mind, so their designs will be modular and flexible. The A-frame architecture can be built either top down or bottom up. The layers of A-Frame are: Workflow, Function, Component, Integration, System, and Service. They are defined as:

Framework: The "A-Frame" begins with identifying process or workflow "steps" in "zones" of work. A process step is a task that is performed by one individual in a single mental decision or motion. A "Zone" is a process segment, or in Kaizen terms a work cell, where a collection of workflow steps occur. It encapsulates process, protocol and practice steps. Typically, materials or information are transferred or communicated between work zones. Information systems provide functions to handle process steps and facilitate transfer of information between work zones. The goal of this activity is to streamline the workflow and remove non-value adding steps. IT business analysts who invest in learning about process optimization and process redesign are likely to produce the best results. Analyzing the process steps and how zones are to be interconnected by Information systems will produce the ideal IT solution. As an example, a zone in a medical institution might include steps to register patient, verify insurance, capture allergies and medications. At a bank, the loan processing zone consists of activities that include consumer loan application processing, credit history report and loan-structuring. The metrics associated with work zones are key to establishing requirements. For example, a bank might set a processing time target to process an online loan application.

Function: Next on the "A" frame ladder is function. Here IT analysts attempt to map the necessary application function points for a work zone. The analyst identifies the back-end data requirements for each function point.

Component: A collection of function points that can be used, tested and packaged for a particular work zone. When completed, the component can be released into production as a stand-alone application, or as an incremental addition to an existing system. This is the sub-assembly level where each component can be represented by a stub. When definition of the sub-assembly is complete, each sub-assembly is tagged and stored in a library along with its set of data, function and workflow definitions. Other analysts are able to re-use this component for other workflows. Implementation of sub-assembly can begin immediately and often it can be put into pilot production.

Interface & integrate: This is the stage of assembling components and integrating functions to create a single-flow process across the enterprise. Until every component has been developed, the architect can integrate the components (sub-assemblies) as stubs. This layer is a cross functional bridge between sub-assemblies. It can be a data exchange server, a translation layer between multiple sub-assemblies, or the middle tier. More than likely, this is a messaging layer and can consist of a service oriented application layer.

Application System/ Environment: Refers to the collective application either as a central system, portal or place to gain access to application functions. This is the capstone of development and allows modular replacement of sub-assemblies as required. The system can present the components in different sequence for different workflows. It is generally the common application that governs the process & information flow across the entire process continuum.

Service: Defines those services that users are able to receive from the application or from other staff as a result of the application features. These services produce the value streams that your organization has sought after. Services are the result of transforming a feature into a product or solution that customers want.

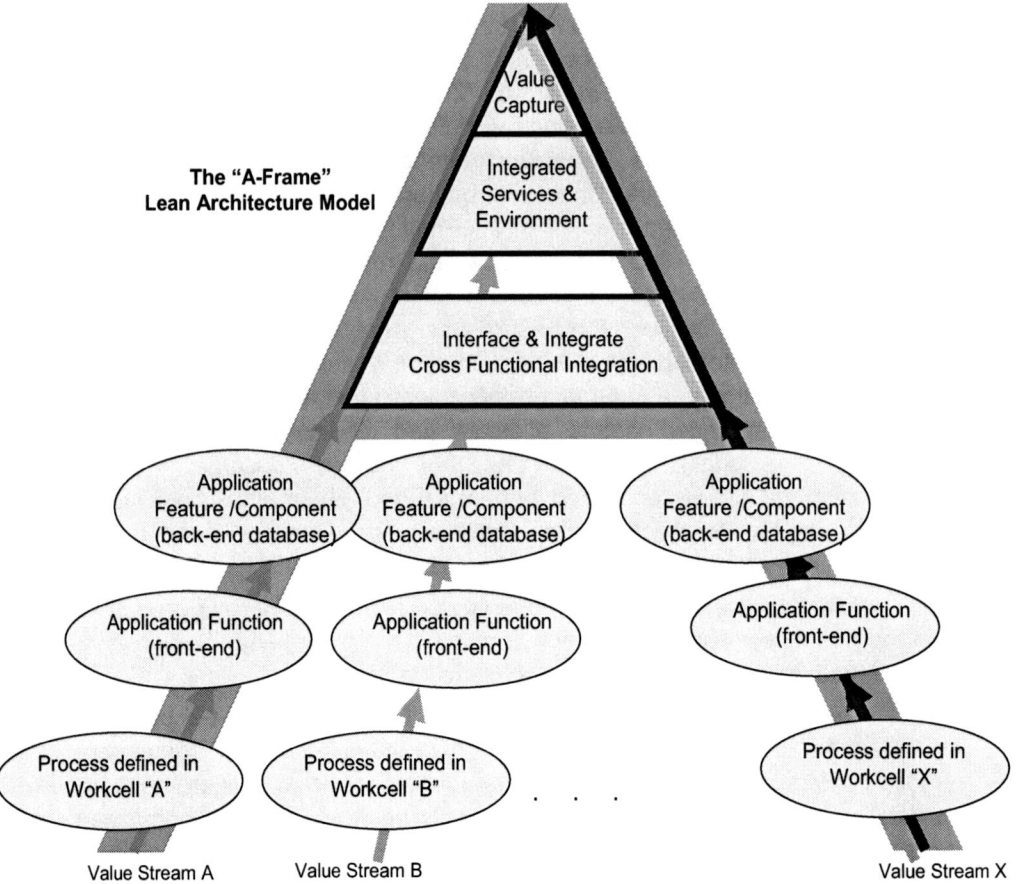

Fig 10.7 – A component-based Production System: The "A"-Frame Model

Stratagem: Derive as many services from application features as possible. The cost of developing the feature is already absorbed. Any new services mean "almost free" new benefits.

Summary

- Build IT factory: Create a consistent tempo of releases based on the I-Frame, T-Frame or A-Frame assembly model
- Create a production plan using Feature Driven Development and Agile ranking of features
- Identify sub-components that can be re-used
- Create a pull mechanism by concurrently developing and testing new subcomponents
- Breakdown projects into smaller deliverables. Deliver solutions through iterative releases
- Build new release by integrating new sub-components into existing application

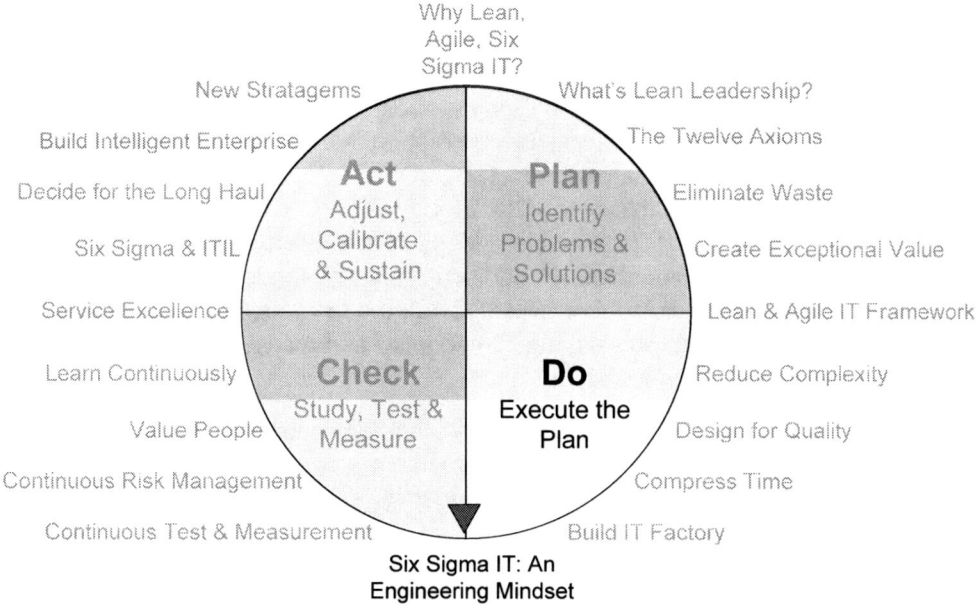

Six Sigma IT: An
Engineering Mindset

"CEO's have always left quality to chance or to committees, never to people high-level enough to make decisions."

Dr. Joseph Juran

Chapter 11. Introduction to Six Sigma

If you applied the Lean and Agile IT methods that we discussed in previous chapters, by now you have achieved a highly responsive and effective IT organization that is adding value at all levels of the firm. In this chapter, we will discuss how Six Sigma principles can help IT become far more deliberate and focused to deliver higher quality and performance.

I have seen far too many clients who missed wonderful new technology introduction opportunities due to poor design and inadequate release planning. Applying Six Sigma to IT brings an engineering mindset and higher level of precision to IT activities. Most of IT processes gain a disciplined and structured level of implementation from Six Sigma: The traditional requirements analysis becomes requirements engineering; releasing applications is no longer an activity that comes after testing, but it is a design activity called release engineering. The key to success in new product introductions is high-precision design at the front end of projects and release engineering plans that are precisely set by the project team before go live of an application.

Aside from striving for flawless execution, Six Sigma attempts to eliminate defects by promoting data-driven fact-based decisions. This has two interesting implications. It underscores the value of real-time and even predictive data for the decision makers regardless if they are in the C-suite or on the shop floor. Furthermore, data-driven decision making helps IT streamline its own internal operations towards creating defect-free products and workflows for its customers. IT managers will act upon facts not opinions.

One of the goals of Six Sigma is to identify variables that are critical to management objectives, such as Quality, Cost or Customer Satisfaction. These variables are regarded as critical in contrast to non-critical variables. The critical variables have designations such as CTQ (Critical to Quality) or CTS (Critical to satisfaction) or CTC (Critical to Cost) and so on. Six Sigma process allows management to identify CTx variables. Many of the Six Sigma methods attempt to define these critical-to variables. In addition, these methods attempt to capture and prioritize critical customer requirements (CCRs), the key requirements expected by the customer. These CTx variables should be adopted and measured as part of fact-based decision making for IT management.

Variation is a source of inconsistency and deviation from target objective, be it quality, cost or functionality. Six Sigma attempts to identify and remove causes of variation. Variation is any fluctuation in a process. Variation is measured over time by recording fluctuations.

Fluctuations can represent data about process. Here the cause and effect are at play. Fluctuations are caused by variations in variables which directly or indirectly affect the outcomes (The Critical-To objectives such as quality, project schedule, cost, etc). In the IT realm, as an example, customer satisfaction "Y" is the result of application performance variable "X". Then we might record application performance (such as response time) at different time intervals. Each recorded result is a function of variables, shown in a formula as $Y = f(X)$. This is the Six Sigma transfer function. It's interpreted as "Y" is a function of "X". Each "X" represents a critical variable that affects the process behavior and variation.

Process behavior is charted using any of several common tools such as bar charts and control charts. A control chart is a time-series chart that shows the process behavior with respect to two limits representing upper and lower boundaries. The upper boundary is known as Upper Control Limit (UCL) and lower boundary as the Lower Control Limit (LCL). Process variation is recorded between these two limits (Figure 11.1). For example, keeping the temperature in a data center between 60 degrees and 70 degrees establishes the upper and lower control limits of the operating temperature.

There are two causes of variation: *Common* and *Special*. A Common cause also known as random cause is any source of unacceptable variation that is inherent in the process. Common-cause variation is also called inherent variation, noise and with-in group variation. Special-cause variation is any source of unacceptable variation that comes from outside of the process.

Variation from common causes is regarded natural and variation from special causes unnatural. Any variation between UCL and LCL is regarded as natural (common) variation, and any variation above UCL or below LCL is unnatural (special) variation. Recording variation data points provides statistical data for further analysis. Let's consider the following case study as example.

Case Study: Microsoft MSN Support Hotline

Microsoft has located its MSN support centers across the globe in different continents. Centers A, and B have recorded the time they spend on resolving a particular type of customer call to the center. Each center uses its own process for handling this particular problem which we will correspondingly call them process A and B. Below is the measured time to resolve the customer problem through each process:

Support Center A Process (minutes):

9.3, 11.5, 9.8, 10.7, 12.1, 8.9, 11.3, 14.2, 8.9, 10.3

Support Center B Process (minutes):

7.4, 10.2, 9.6, 14.3, 11.5, 9.4, 8.6, 11.5, 9.3, 12.6

From this data set, we can compute Mean, Mode, Range and Standard Deviation. The Mean or simply average for process A is 10.7 minutes and for process B, 10.44. From this data we can tell which process on average is faster but we cannot tell which process varies more. Median provides the midpoint in the data set. The median for process A is 10.5 and for process B is 9.9 minutes. We can calculate the most frequent value in the data set called Mode. In process A, the mode is 8.9 (two times) and 11.5 (two times) in process B. Range shows the spread of data points between the lowest and highest. Process A has a range of 5.3. Comparing that to process B which has a range of 6.9, implies that process A has less spread. So common sense tells us that the process A values vary less than process B.

To calculate variation, the best method is using standard deviation. Standard deviation quantifies the degree that the data varies from the mean. It is shown with the Greek symbol "σ". The data values are shown with letter "X". The mean of a variable "X", is shown with letter "X", and a bar over it, also known as X *bar*. Mathematically, the sum of values is shown with another Greek letter, capital sigma, "$\sum$". The following formula describes how we can compute standard deviation:

$$\sigma = \frac{\sqrt{\sum (X - \overline{X})^2}}{n}$$

Where "$\sum$" means the sum of; X represents observed values; $\overline{X}$ is the arithmetic mean, and n = the number of observations. Using this formula, we find standard deviation for process A to be 1.65 and for process B, 2.04. Larger standard deviation implies bigger variaion. Since process A has lower standard deviation, it is more predictable than process B. Standard deviation is a measure of data spread over the range of data. With a large data sample, if we plot all data points, the distribution of values will appear in some form of a bell-shaped curve where it's highest around the mean and then dwindle off on both sides. If both sides of the curve are symmetrical, the distribution is regarded normal. Normal distributions have important characteristics such as:

- They can be represented by two values: mean and standard deviation
- The distribution is symmetrical around its mean
- In normal distribution, the mean, the median and the mode are equal.
- One standard deviation from the mean represents 68% of values (±1 sigma)
- Two standard deviations from the mean represent 95% of values (±2 sigma)
- Three standard deviations from the mean represent 99.73% of values (±3 sigma)

Until Six sigma was adopted as the standard for quality, the standard process variation of 3 sigma was acceptable. Historically, if a data on the normal distribution curve landed within plus or minus 3 sigma from the mean, it was regarded good enough. In other words, 99.73% of process values were acceptable. For example, a data center that operated at three Sigma (3σ) level, would experience about 24 hours of downtime per year; not very comforting to IT managers of mission critical applications. Namely, it still allows 2,700 defects to be out of spec, or 2,700 defects per million opportunities (DPMO). But, Six sigma has changed that standard.

If a process produces outputs that are within the upper control limit (UCL) and lower control limit (LCL), that are inside the specification, the process is regarded capable of meeting the specification. Process capability is a measure of the ability of a process to stay within those specifications. Short term process capability is considered the ability to stay within specification for a short while. But over time, it's recognized that processes shift from the center. Thus, long term process capability is important to sustaining quality. This is accomplished by controlling the special cause variation of a process. Special cause variations are factors such as environmental conditions, unexpected changes that are external to the process. Six sigma equates to 2 defects per billion opportunities or .002 defects per million. The founders of Six Sigma at Motorola opted to allow 1.5 sigma from upper and lower control limits to allow for long term variations. Thus we accept 3.4 defects per million as the standard for six sigma today.

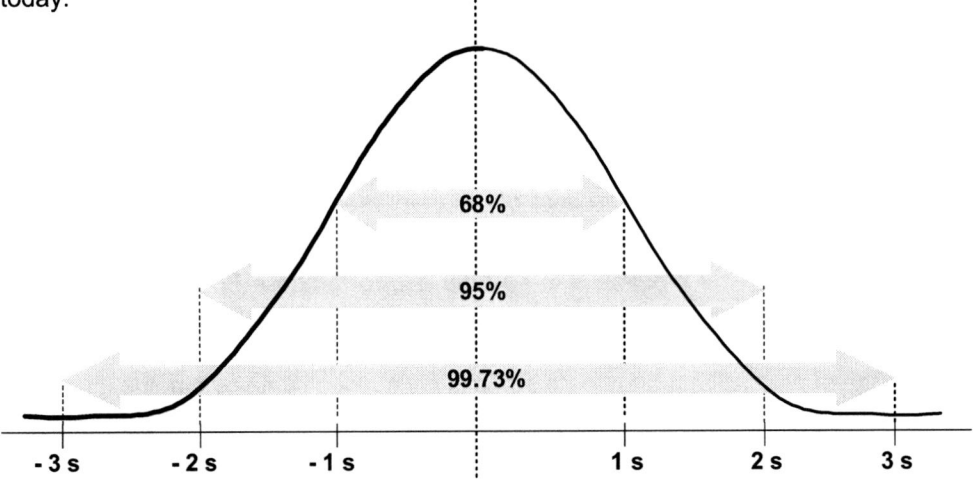

Fig 11.1 - Normal Distribution

Business Metrics

To succeed in almost any Six Sigma program, collecting relevant and consistent data is vital. Delivering real time data and the kind of analytics that can predict the future behavior of business parameters are even more valuable. Data about Critical-To variables and root-cause variables that influence Critical-To variables are more relevant. Enabling business metrics and measurements are key IT value drivers for the organization. There have been a number of successful corporate-wide metrics programs. One of the well known success stories is the Hewlett-Packard's (HP) program. At HP, the collection and use of data occurred at several levels of the organization and for distinct purposes at each level. As data begins to accumulate, businesses are able to determine key success factors.

Strategic management has a vested interest in corporate-wide metrics. In intelligent organizations, strategic management makes high-level long term decisions to ensure overall success of the business enterprise. Members of this system make decisions about policies, core competencies, markets, outsourcing, mergers and acquisitions. For this purpose, strategic management requires business intelligence, highly summarized data about product lines or large segments of the organization such as business units. It may need data and forecasts based on metrics to set goals, objectives and establish corporate programs.

Collecting data across multiple disciplines and functional boundaries has proven difficult. Some organizations, led by their IT leadership have formed "metric user groups" to identify the required data, its universal definition frequency, level of detail and its flow across business units. One such group, consisting of 35 members and representing 15 business units was successful in defining relevant business metrics at multiple levels of the firm. Most existing systems are unable to support corporate-wide metrics program. In this case, IT managers were able to create the needed application to maintain the data and provide decision support reports to strategic management committee. The data collected has been used for benchmarking, quality improvement and identifying the weaknesses in products and systems. The goal of Six Sigma is to reduce standard deviation of a process variation to the point that 6 sigma (six standard deviations) can fit within specification limits. Thus measurements are important to six sigma analysis and design. The implications of Six Sigma are that proper metrics are defined. Finding the appropriate metrics starts with the customer.

The IT industry is at best performing at 3 sigma accuracy today. Much of the IT analysts work with in a wide range of analytical parameters that allows high variations in quality and results. Procedures for operations and maintenance have a wide degree of variation as well. These factors contribute to the high variability and unpredictability of IT performance across a wide range of IT functions; be it project outcome or application uptime, or customer satisfaction. That's why I'm advocating a transformation of focus from the IT analyst approach to the IT engineering discipline. I'm promoting the concept of IT engineers coupled with focus on design and testing to deliver high velocity, high quality and high precision work.

For IT managers, it's vital to know what the customers want and what they regard as critical. Leadership must be involved in defining how these metrics link to the strategy. Metrics such as CTQ (critical to quality), CTS (critical to satisfaction), CTF (critical to finances) and similar metrics might be appropriate and apply differently to different organizations. But the common theme is to eliminate defects by controlling "Critical-To" variables. *Again a defect is any deviation from customer's expectation.* Once you have identified the Critical-To factors, you can focus on the transfer function: $Y= f(X)$, where "X" represents the control variables that affect "Y" the output of the process.

Take for example a transfer function that defines the control variables to CTP (Critical-To Profitability) for an ecommerce application:

$$Y = w_1 X_1 + w_2 X_2 + w_3 X_3$$

Here the variables X_1, X_2 and X_3 represent the independent variables that affect Y:

X_1 : is the application availability

X_2 : is the application performance

X_3 : represents the number of customer valued features

Parameters w_1, w_2 and w_3 are the weights, also known as the strength of the variables. We obtain these weights through customer surveys and conjoint analysis sessions. While the weights are constant, the value of Y (Profitability) follows the value of X_1, X_2 and X_3. It rises or falls as variables $X1$, $X2$ and $X3$ rise and fall. Once key business metrics have been identified, IT managers must seek to establish measurement criteria, methods for data collection and creating the baseline. A baseline is a standard for comparing the current status of performance and future status as a process improves. Once the base line has been established, IT managers can display ongoing process output visually using a dashboard. Six sigma tools offer a number of graphs such as bar graph, histograms, box plot, Interval plot and other graphs. Managers can also benchmark their process performance against other similar IT organizations. Benchmarking shows how a process performs relative to other similar organizations. For example, if you are managing IT in the e-commerce industry, you should benchmark your process output against other IT organizations in the same industry. You can benchmark your system uptime, response time and product features against other firms in e-commerce. Once data is available, you can perform gap analysis to identify which process outputs are deficient. Six Sigma offers a number of tools for analyzing data and identifying the control variables that have the most impact on your process output.

Process Capability

When analyzing data, we are interested in several attributes as shown by the graph in Figure 11.2. We are interested in spike and spread, in deviation from average and in skewness. Each is important and known as the process capability index. One capability index is the process performance index. Shown as Cp, it's a measure of variance, or the width of distribution of data. It tells us how consistently we can produce the same output, but not how far we are from the average.

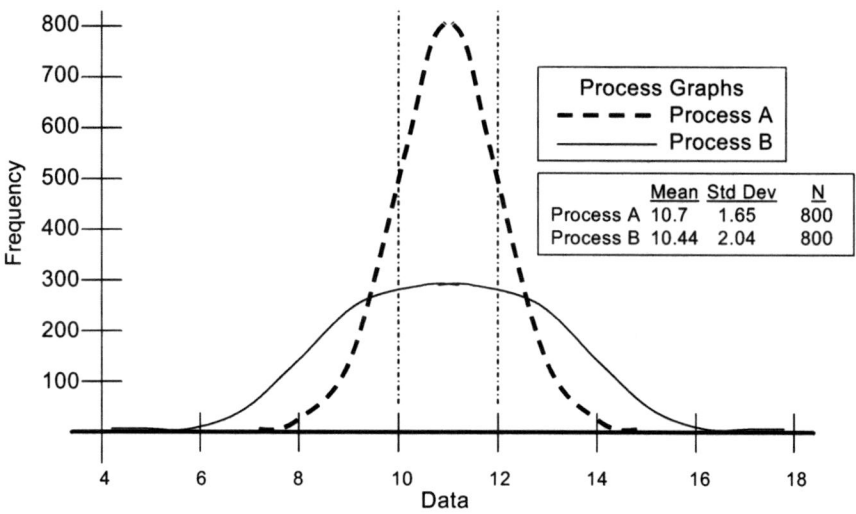

Fig 11.2 – Variation, Skewness, Central Tendency

Another capability index called process capability determines how close our average value is to the target value. Shown as *Cpk*, it measures how well the output data is centered on the target value. Continuing with the Microsoft MSN case study, let's assume that we have collected 800 data samples. From looking at the following graph, it's easy to discern that Process "A" has less variation than Process "B". The same conclusion can be made from standard deviation values. Process "A" has a smaller standard deviation. If we were able to record hundreds of data samples for Process A and B, a density distribution graph like Figure 11.2 can illustrate the Cp and Cpk graphically.

To calculate both Cp and Cpk, we need *specification width* and *process width*. Specification width is the difference between the upper specification limit (USL) and lower specification limit (LSL). We set these limits as boundaries within which our process must operate. These limits are also known as upper and lower tolerances. Any output outside of this range is unacceptable. The process width is the difference between the upper control limit (UCL) and the lower control limit (UCL). It is simply calculated by multiplying standard deviation by 6. The Cp can be calculated as:

Cp = specification width/process width or Cp = (USL – LSL) / 6σ

Higher Cp values indicate less variation. For example, comparing Cp for process "A" to process "B", all else being equal, since process "A" has smaller standard deviation, it has a higher Cp.

A Cp value greater than 1 is desirable and indicates good process capability. A Cp value of 1 is acceptable, but any Cp values less than 1 are unacceptable. Higher Cp values are indicators of higher precision. It is customary to set the upper and lower specification limits at ±3 sigma from center line. A Cp value of 2 corresponds to Six Sigma.

Let's consider the Microsoft MSN case study again. We can establish an USL of 11 and LSL of 9. This implies that the center line or the ideal mean is 10 minutes. You'll note that we have set the upper and lower specification limits at ±1 minute from the ideal mean. This implies that to reach a 6 sigma level, the standard deviation for both Process A and B should be reduced to 0.40. Cpk on the other hand is regarded as a long term capability index and a measure of demonstrated excellence. It measures how centered the outputs are compared to the ideal mean. It is calculated by the less of the following two values:

$$\text{Cpk} = \text{lesser of } (USL - \text{Mean}/3\sigma) \text{ or } (\text{Mean} - LSL/3\sigma)$$

If Cpk is exactly on midline, then Cp and Cpk will be identical.

One of the simple Six Sigma tools is the *Control chart*. Control charts are useful for *Statistical Process Control (SPC)*. SPC was developed initially to control process outputs over the long term. It is used to control the Critical-to variables such as Critical to Cost (CTC) and Critical to Quality (CTQ). Within the realm of IT management, we are interested in measuring additional process variables such as Critical to Delivery (CTD), Critical to Satisfaction (CTS), and Critical to Uptime (CTU).

When we observe these critical-to variables over time, it's called Statistical Process Monitoring. A control chart shows the process variations over time. As shown in the diagram below, the vertical axis of the control chart represents the scale of statistics associated with the critical-to variables. The horizontal axis represents the chronological groups of output data over time. Two horizontal lines establish the upper and lower control limits. They are ±3σ from the centerline. Each group of data samples includes its mean, range and standard deviation. The centerline is a real time average of all sample points. Each subgroup is shown as a dot on the chart and the dots are connected chronologically. Each dot represents the mean of the subgroup. It is advised that each group contains as many as 20 data samples to start the control chart. The initial 20 data samples are called the *trial control limits*. They show if the initial process conditions were within control when the process started.

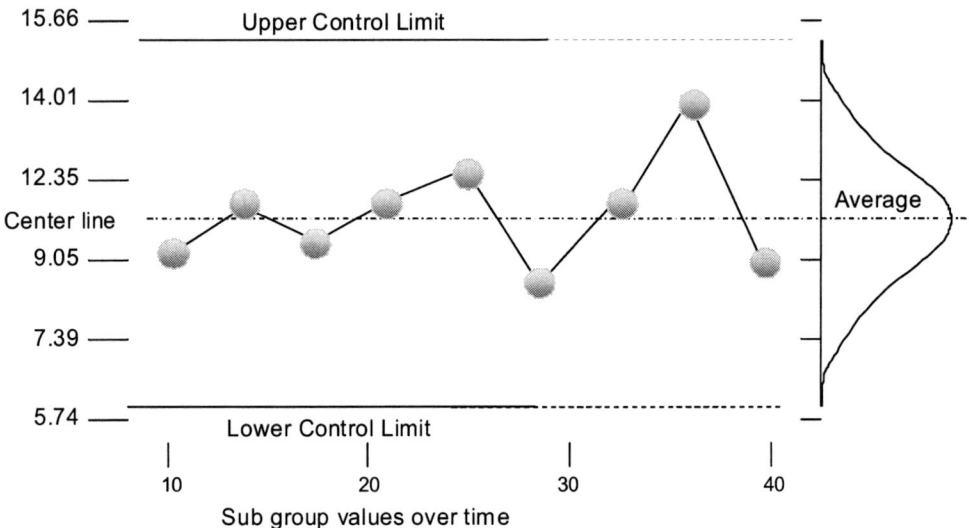

Fig 11.3 – Control Chart with Upper and Lower Control Limits

Let's assume that we have adequate data collected from the MSN Support Case we reviewed earlier. The control chart below shows subgroup data plotted over three major bands. The band between the control limits denotes random variation. The two bands above and below the control limits represent the nonrandom variation. We regard a process in control when all the points fall inside the control limits. By looking at a control chart, it is easy to discern process patterns that indicate a process is falling out of control. The control chart above shows that the process output is moving out of control mostly due to external or random variation.

IT managers must consider process optimizations not just at scattered local areas but across the enterprise. IT operations such as help desk and support come with random variation and structural variation. Not all activities are necessarily random. They might appear random, but a scatter diagram can show patterns in data. Often a distribution curve and central tendency be identified for those activities. For example, the time to resolve a user issue can be in a range but typically with 95% certainty can fall into a distribution curve.

The patterns of IT systems utilization usually peak around 9:00-10:00AM, subside around noon and then peak again around 2:00-3:00PM. Random and structural variation impact capacity, lead time and inventory levels. The call volume coming to a help desk might seem random, but it is likely to follow the usage peak patterns. Structural randomness occurs usually on certain days of the week or certain departments (For example, on the day after usual patches or preventative maintenance have been applied). The goal of Lean and Six Sigma is to prevent the need for users to make a help desk call in the first place. Simulation can highlight the weaknesses in the system.

Greg Brue and Rod Howes in their book, "Six Sigma" reference a Statistical Quality Control Handbook published by Western Electric which defines four rules that apply to control charts[58]. Based on industrial experience, the rules state that a process is out of control if any of the following conditions are present:

- At least one point is outside the three-sigma control limits
- Two out of three consecutive points are more that two sigma away from the centerline, on the same side
- Four out of five consecutive points are more than one sigma away from the centerline, on the same side
- Eight consecutive points are on the same side of the centerline

The Six Sigma principles and rules are important to high precision IT operations and implementations. For example a good metric to track in a control chart is the time to resolve IT trouble tickets. The centerline, Upper and Lower control limits can be established by IT management or through a *Service Level Agreement (SLA)*. The Service Level Agreement can be an informal internal statement of commitment to customers or a formal contract. In either case, the SLA can specify the control chart parameters for application availability, response time and time to resolve a particular set of IT trouble tickets. Another metric to track is the number of defects from inspection and testing. For illustration consider Myers' law based on his book entitled, "The Art of Software Testing". Myers' law states that the number of defects identified

---

[58] "Six Sigma", Greg Brue and Rod Howes, McGraw-Hill , 2006

before release is comparable to the number of defects after release. Though may sound counter intuitive, the interpretation of this law is that the number of defects identified before release is a measure of quality of that software. Finding more defects does not imply that a software package is getting cleansed of bugs, rather it implies the software package is inherently "buggy". The number of defects found before release is an early indicator of the software quality after release.

Metrics that give measures of defects per line of code, or defects per function points, and per module are commonly used in the industry. Number of defects per module gives a relative measure of quality of one module compared to other modules. Other metrics that can be tracked in a control chart are the number of trouble tickets generated after a new application release. If a new application is converging towards stability, the frequency and mean time to failures should decrease over time.

Six Sigma Organization

Six Sigma methods bring an inherent organizational structure to the firm. This structure consists of:

- **Steering Committee:** consisting of senior level executives. It's responsible for identifying projects and opportunities, allocating resources, monitoring progress, identifying black belts, and establishing implementation goals.
- **Champions:** are key management personnel who provide guidance and resources for the process. They must have in-depth understanding of their process and methods used in Six Sigma including measurements and quality control.
- **Green Belts:** are introductory participants in the Six Sigma process. They understand the concept of data collection and data interpretation.
- **Black Belts:** have been thoroughly trained and often full time participants in Six Sigma initiatives. They have proficiency in analysis tools. They act as teachers, coach and facilitators in the process. They can be leaders of teams responsible for each Six Sigma project.
- **Master Black Belts:** are proficient and have demonstrated prior successful implementations with proven results. These individuals achieve their title as recognition for outstanding performance. They mentor and teach Black Belts.

The 5 phases of Six Sigma Process

Reaching Six Sigma in IT is accomplished through the use of two methodologies: DMAIC and DMADV, or generally DFSS. The DMAIC, is a five phase process (Define, Measure, Analyze, Improve, Control), a tool for improving existing processes that fall below specification or service Level Agreements. The DMADV process (Define, Measure, Analyze, Design, Verify) is used for developing new products or processes. DFSS, Design for Six Sigma is the general methodology for new product or service development. It incorporates tools and methods that enable Six Sigma development processes. There are other forms of Six Sigma methodologies. A particular added phase to DMADV methodology that fits IT activities is the focus on release of products into production, namely Release engineering. Some of the other notable processes that fit IT are:

- IDOV – Identify, Design, Optimize, Verify
- DCOV – Define, Characterize, Optimize, and verify
- DMEDI – Define, Measure, Explore, Develop, and Implement
- DADIVR- Define, Analyze, Design, Implement, Verify, Release

Let's review each phase of the DMAIC methodology briefly:

Define: The key question in Six Sigma initiative is to answer: What is the problem? In this phase, we define the project goals, customer requirements, expectations, internal and external deliverables, gaps between current state and desirable state, a problem or an opportunity.

Measure: Measure current process to determine performance. In IT, measurement could cover system uptime, mean time to repair and metrics such as response time or number of software defects. It is defined by a transfer function: $Y = f(X1, X2, \ldots Xn)$. For example, uptime is a measurement "Y" and also a function of several input variables "X" that represent elements such as "hardware", "software quality", "datacenter factors", "security" and so on.

Analyze: Analyze and determine the root cause of defects. You can use the 5-Why questioning method (also known as the fishbone diagram or Dr. Ishikawa's method) to determine root cause. Analysis must produce definitive, fact-based understanding of choices available and trade-offs between those choices.

Improve: Determine the gap between current measurement and desired (target) measurements. Define the process changes that eliminate defects. Propose a set of "X" variables that produce the best possible solution.

Control: Determine how the critical input variables can be maintained in the modified range, to prevent the problem from occurring in the long run. Devise mechanisms to control future process performance. The tactics might include training, monitoring and implementing feedback between systems or users for control.

As mentioned above, DMADVR is derived from Six Sigma methods for achieving perfection in developing new IT products, new technology adoption or application implementations. It encompasses the following six phases:

Define: Define the project goals, customer requirements, use-cases, data flow, workflow and user interfaces. Result of this methodology is a requirements document.

Measure: Strive to measure and specify customer requirements. Be specific about user requirements by providing what is included in the scope and what is out of scope.

Analyze: Analyze the process options and alternatives with the customer. Evaluate pro-and-cons about different implementation approaches, features, functionality and data models.

Design: Create high level design and review with customers. Once accepted by the customer, proceed with low level design. This step includes the design of workflows, the data flow model, user interface, database schema and entity relationships, security model, and all 7 layers of the ISO model. (Also see the layered design pyramid discussion in previous chapters). You may consider the Taguchi method for creating robust design that withstands internal or external variations (noise). The goal of Taguchi method is to reduce variability. By reducing variability one can prevent failures in downstream stages. In other words, during design stage, of all design options select the one that has the least variability, and at the earliest design phase.

Verify: Review low-level design with the customer and users or the user representative. Make corrections and refinement before implementation. In an iterative or incremental development process, this step is analogous to testing the code.

Release: Defines engineering steps for releasing a product into production with consideration for training, customization, adaptation of IT solution to the environment. In this step, pre-requisites for releasing the product are identified and completed. The goal of this step is to define the release activities step by step and identify roles and responsibilities of participants.

> **Stratagem:** Every new IT application, solution or upgrade must increase reliability, uptime, performance and functionality, while reducing variability, cost of ownership and cost of maintenance per function point over the previous IT solution that it replaces.

Aside from its great problem solving tools, Six Sigma encourages IT managers to document their processes, measure, analyze and improve them. Managers at all levels must demonstrate leadership and commitment to Six Sigma, in particular as their emphasis on metrics might come under question initially by peers. Note what Joseph M. Juran who used the *Pareto principle* suggests about the vital few variables. Applying the 80-20 rule, Juran said "there are a few variables that represent 80% of variation. The key is to find those variables and manage them." In the long run, fact-based and data-driven management of IT will prevail as improved results demonstrate the advantages.

Pareto Principle is founded on the notion that 80 percent of problems, defects or requirements are introduced by 20 percent of the causes. Similarly, it applies the notion that 80 percent of customer requirements can be satisfied by 20 percent of application functions. Pareto principle also applies to IT portfolio management. There are 20 percent of the projects that consume (or waste, depending on your perspective) 80 percent of IT resources. Increased quality and customer satisfaction achieved through Six Sigma methods will give your organization the leading edge and the strong foundation to stand above all others. There are in total seven DMAIC tools of which we have reviewed only a few so far. For more details you can read any of the Six Sigma texts including "Six Sigma" by Greg Brue and Rod Howes[59]. The seven tools of quality control (QC) are also known as Ishikawa QC tools.

The complete list of Six Sigma tools includes:

1. **Flow charts:** Graphical representation of input, output and units of activity. Flow charts show the entire performance of a process or workflow in one graph.

2. **Check sheets:** Data tables that that allow collection and analysis of data on critical to variables (X's). For example, common check sheets in IT might include measurement tables that record frequency of factors that cause downtimes or other quality problems.

3. **Pareto diagrams:** Pareto chart is a bar chart in which the bars represent the items being measured and compared, ordered by size or frequency.

4. **Cause/Effect diagrams:** A diagram to identify the root causes of effects. Typically uses a fishbone diagram for illustration.

5. **Scatter diagrams:** or scatter plots are graphic tools that show relationship between two or more variables as dots plotted in a graph.

6. **Histograms:** graphical representations of frequency of occurrence of continuous data values. The graph of frequency shows the shape of the graph, spread of data and skewness.

7. **Control Chart:** a graphical tool for monitoring variation and changes that occur in a process to determine the in-process variation (common cause) from environmental variation (special cause).

Impact of Metrics & Measurement on IT Service & Application Quality

Six Sigma IT is a doctrine motivated by data-driven decision making, design and measurement. It's not surprising that metrics and measurements are a big part of the management activity. Much of the prior studies on reliability and quality metrics that have been conducted about software, also to some degree apply to IT. Such metrics have dealt with number of program loops, lines of code, mean nesting level and comments volume ratio. But, of more interest to IT are metrics that measure the appropriateness of functionality to a process and the capability of the solution to meet the firm's objectives at all levels of the organization.

Studies have shown that collecting data about software metric actually helps companies develop better applications. In 1995, I conducted a study to evaluate the impact of measurements on software quality. In a survey of 80 software companies, those who measured software metrics showed a strong correlation with higher customer satisfaction and software quality. Another study proposed measuring what it called the ten dimensions of quality: reliability, user-friendliness, integrity, portability, correctness, understandability, extendibility, economy, efficiency and verifiability. It's

---

[59]"Six Sigma", Greg Brue and Rod Howes, McGraw-Hill, 2006

appropriate to introduce additional metrics, such as: maintainability, maintenance life cycle cost, user satisfaction index and utilization patterns. Generally, there are five categories of IT metrics: measurements about operational, productivity, service, strategic and quality variables. Below are some sample metrics you might institute for each category in your firm:

Service Metrics:

- Number of service calls received per hour or per day at Service Desk, categorized by criticality, urgency, importance or severity
- Number of service calls resolved within 1-hour, 2-hour and so on for each category (this can be drawn in a histogram)
- The Pareto chart of "time-to-resolve" service request for each category of trouble tickets
- Number of log-ins per day. Total hours of usage per application per day.
- Number of dropped sessions or application failures per day by application
- Response time by application, by time of day
- Number of transactions per application, per hour and per day
- Number of service calls per application, per desktop, and per department (or group of users)
- Average length of time to resolve customer tickets per day
- Number of service tickets received per application and by feature

Productivity Metrics:

- Total number of tickets received versus closed by Help Desk per day, per month
- Number of features released per month for a given project
- Number of applications released per month
- Number of design reviews or inspections per month
- Number of bug fixes completed and tested per month (or per week)
- Number of server patches and workstation patches applied per month

Quality Metrics:

- Number of defects or errors reported for each application or subsystem in production
- Number of defects and errors reported for each application or subsystem before release to production
- Number of failed upgrade attempts per month

Strategic Metrics:

- Number of current corporate initiatives supported

- Number of strategic objectives met
- Ratio of firm's strategic initiatives supported by IT over total number of strategic initiatives in IT backlog

Operational Metrics:
- Number of security incidents (hacks, etc) per week
- Number of incidents, problems and errors by application, subsystem and service category
- Number of downtime occurrences. Duration of each downtime.
- Correlation analysis of downtime occurrences
- Downtime or incident impact: Number of users affected by each downtime or incident
- Time to repair for each downtime

ISO Standards for Quality

International Organization for Standards (ISO) has published a set of documents for software quality that encompass these metrics. Here is a brief overview of the ISO metrics:

Reliability: Refers to the product attributes that maintain its operations according to the specification and intended function. The factors that contribute to reliability are: security, integrity, coherence, functionality and absence of errors.

Efficiency: is defined as a set of attributes of the IT solution that provides a level of performance or output based on the amount of resources used. ISO divides efficiency into two metrics: Time behavior which is related to response time and throughput rates, and resource behavior which refers to the amount of resources required to perform a function.

Portability: refers to the amount of effort required to run the application on different computer platforms or reconfigure the application for other stated processes. Portability is based on generalizability and adaptability factors.

User-friendliness: refers to the ease of learning, operating, data entry and navigation of an application. The factors that affect this metric are ease of use, accessibility and help features.

Economy: is defined as the return on investment for an IT solution. It is concerned with cost of developing the IT solution and its impact on profitability.

Verifiability: refers to ease of testing the application to ensure it performs as intended. Testability of an application is a factor that affects its verifiability.

Maintainability: is the set of attributes that characterize the effort to make modifications, customizations, fixes and patches over the life of the application. The factors that affect this metric are: modifiability, flexibility, and compatibility.

Understandability: is the characteristic of understanding what the application does and how its subcomponents interact with one another. Factors that affect understandability are modularity, clarity, uniformity, structure, conciseness and informativeness. The metrics in the above dimensions total 23 factors. When evaluating purchase of an application or quality of an in-house solution, IT managers can use these factors to score and compare each solution.

The Six Sigma doctrine of IT management demands that any work performed by IT staff must have a defined and documented process. The processes must have measurable attributes, meaning metrics must be identified and reported regularly (if not in real time). This applies to all facets of development, operations and services from applications performance, system availability, response time to ease of use. Once you have identified the Critical-To variables that affect quality, performance, and critical customer requirements, you can begin to define specific metrics that fit your business environment.

Additionally many Lean IT organizations maintain metrics and measurements on new applications before and after release. These metrics includes:

- Number of design defects found in each stage of application life cycle (design, code, integration, test, validation, alpha release, beta release, post-release)
- Number of defects found in unit tests (at component level)
- Number of defects identified during each stage of development
- Amount of rework required to fix each defect at each stage of application life cycle

Quality Dashboards

Quality check-sheets or dashboards often rank defects based on severity, complexity and amount of rework required to fix. Following the Six Sigma methods, managers apply Pareto analysis to the list of defects. It is common for a quality assurance manager to rank application modules or sub-systems by number of defects reported.

Those subsystems that have higher rate of defects are likely to be poorly developed and require further testing or even re-design. As an example, the spreadsheet in Figure 11.4 shows a Pareto analysis of an application before being released into beta program. In the first column of this table, the subsystems are listed. In the following columns the defect count is shown for each subsystem. The defects are sorted in three categories of severe, minor and complex.

The 'Average Days of Re-work per defect' is the number of days required to fix a defect on average. This is an important metric which can be used as a forecasting tool to determine how long future fixes will take by category or by component type.

Quality Improvement Dashboard						
Application Component Metrics & Measurements						
Area	No. of Severe Defects	No. of Minor Defects	No. of Complex Defects	Average Days to fix A Defect	Total Defect Count	Total Days to Fix Defects
User interface	4	6	3	2.7	13	35.1
Database Tables	6	8	4	2.6	18	46.8
Report Writer	2	7	0	2	9	18
HL7 interface & links	3	6	1	3.2	10	32
Document Mgt System	4	11	1	1.8	16	28.8
Encryption module	3	5	2	2.2	10	22
Network stack	2	3	1	2.4	6	14.4
Event Handler	1	5	0	3.5	6	21

Fig 11.4 – Quality Improvement Dashboard for a Particular IT Application

Figure 11.6 illustrates one of many dashboards possible for this example. From this table, IT management can estimate the cost of the lead time to fix defects in each area and for the entire project.

The chart shows quantity of defects and total days required to fix by component. Clearly the 'database tables' area is the most defective component but the 'user interface' area is the most costly to fix. The last two columns show the total defect count and cost in resource days required to fix each component.

Internal versus External Measurements

When gathering application metrics, we are interested in internal and external measurements[60]. Internal metrics measure attributes like "line of code" or "function point" analysis which are derived from the application itself. External metrics measure attributes that are derived from the application behavior, such as number of defects or response time. Internal metrics are regarded of little value unless they are linked to external metrics. Among external metrics, test-driven metrics are of importance to application quality.

Given our goal of building intrinsic quality in to the product, we are interested in the following metrics:

- **Test Coverage Measure (M1):** Number of test cases/source lines of code.

- **Test Completeness Measure (M2):** Number of test cases/number of requirements.

- **Test Coverage Measure (M3):** Test lines of code / source lines of code.

- **Cost Authenticity Measure (M4):** Number of lines of code changed / total source lines of code.

---

[60] "Good Enough Software Reliability Estimation Plug-in for Eclipse", Nachiappan Nagappan, Laurie Williams, Mladen Vouk, Dept. of Computer Science, North Carolina State University, IEEE, 1998

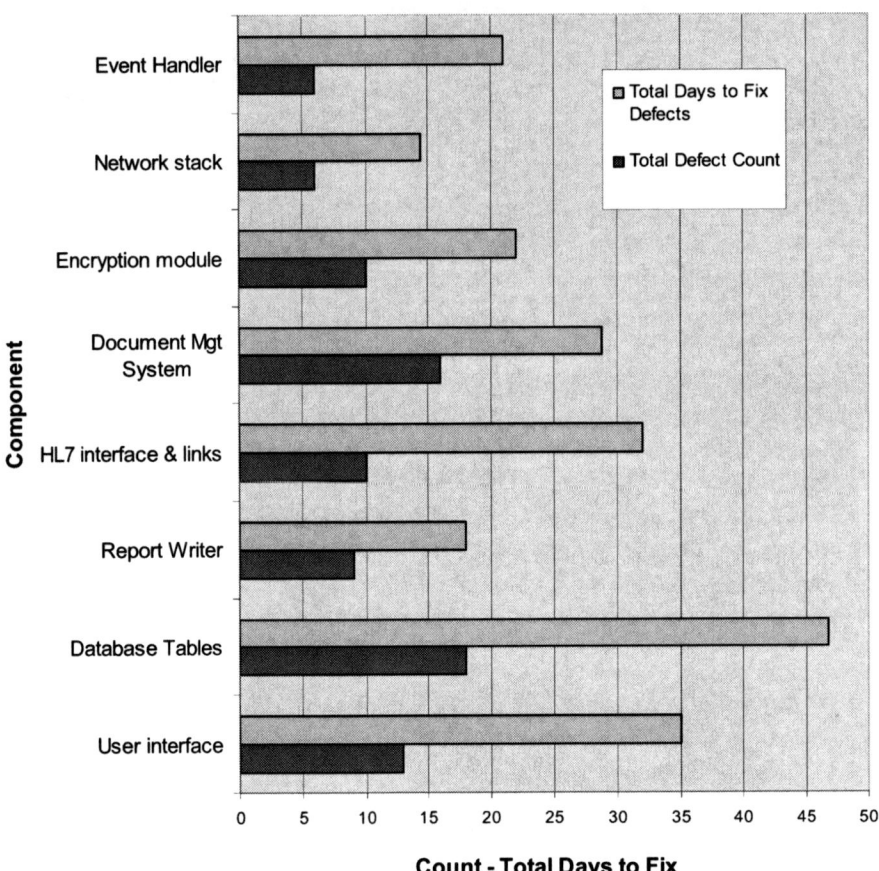

Fig 11.5 – Defect & Costing Dashboard for a Particular IT Application

In a study of 13 programs at North Carolina State University, Mladen Vouk and colleagues found a strong correlation between software reliability and M1 and M2 metrics, but smaller correlation between reliability and M3. Higher M4 ratios are a sign that the program is becoming too brittle as a result of excessive code changes. A mathematical model that computes the confidence levels in quality of software is shown in Appendix D.

IT Metrics Example: Microsoft MSN Business Unit

Microsoft MSN line of business maintains a global but distributed support team for MSN. As part of it continuous improvement initiative, it gathers data from its customer support centers located in five continents.

Each center keeps track of several metrics such as:

- The Number of calls per day, per region

- Average minutes spent on resolving a customer issue, per day and per region
- Average minutes customer was on hold by time of day
- Number of calls per hour
- Number of trouble tickets received in each category of: Software, Network, Security, Updates, and Documentation

Keeping these metrics allows Microsoft to focus its attention on areas that cause the most customer trouble tickets and to adequately staff support for each product line.

Other application-specific metrics have been proposed. For example, an e-commerce web portal can be measured in terms of:

- Number of user visits per hour
- No of clicks per user visit
- Number of minutes spent per page by each user
- Number of clicks per minute
- Number of times users visited the page before making their first purchase
- Number clicks per items added to in-basket (for purchase)
- What other items were purchased
- Number of clicks per page

Another approach for discovering pertinent metrics is the Goal-Question-Measurement (GQM) tool which was discussed in prior chapters. GQM is a goal-oriented method for identifying metrics and creating a measurement plan. Basically, GQM begins with stating the "Goal", then asking "Questions" about factors that affect the goal and finally determine which measurements are needed. To illustrate, let's consider a case study that measures effectiveness of Intranet and internet portals for a company.

Case Study: A Firm's Intranet vs. Internet Effectiveness

The goal of internet for a major online merchandizing firm is to reach a broad audience and generate repeat visits boosting sales and consumer awareness about the company's solutions. In contrast, Intranets are developed to fulfill a different purpose. They are designed to facilitate internal business objectives, inform knowledge workers, organize corporate knowledge and promote cross functional collaboration. The measures of effectiveness between the two systems vary because of difference in questions. For the internet platform, the questions might include: What is important to customers? What are customer's decision influencers? How do we engage customers in our products? How do we become the customer's portal of choice? How do we inspire confidence in customers on our products and services? How do we get customers to ...

> ... come back to the portal? For the intranet platform, the questions might include: What are the critical business requirements that must be met internally? How do we create value for our customers? What are the business drivers for return on investment? What information is most vital for us to achieve our business objectives?
>
> Using GQM and based on this line of questions, the company was able to define and measure analytical data about the effectiveness of its intranet and internet presence. The data served as feedback indicating which features were more desirable to its customers. Overtime, the firm was able to gain a more competitive web position in the market.

In their paper, "Intranet Models and Metrics", professors Grant Jacoby and Luqi, state that there are three types of metrics: *Hard*, *Soft* and *Derived*. Authors write: "Efficiency measures are typically quantifiable or hard metrics. Effectiveness measures are typically qualitative factors (soft and derived metrics)."

Measurements that apply to internet platform and their type include:

- Time to first purchase (or time to locate) [Hard metric]
- Number of abandons [Hard metric]
- Number of clicks to find an item [Hard metric]
- Number of errors per session [Hard metric]
- Ratio of new user registrations to all visits per day [Hard metric]
- Ratio of purchased dollars to total clicks [Hard metric]
- Ratio of purchased dollars per visit [Hard metric]
- Top 10 downloads, or top 10 items purchased [Hard metric]
- Top 10 searches [Hard metric]
- Ratio of customer surveys completed over all visits per day [Hard metric]
- Usefulness of portal based on customer feedback [Soft & derived metric]
- Ease of use ranking by customers [Soft & derived metric]

Similarly measurements that apply to intranet platform include:

- Average frequency of visits per employee [Hard metric]
- Number of searches per site visit [Hard metric]
- Top 10 decision support searches [Hard metric]
- Top 10 content or document downloaded or reviewed [Hard metric]
- Ratio of suggestion box entries to all site visits [Hard metric]

- Relevance of the information to the employee's search [Soft & derived metric]
- Relevance of the information to the corporate business objectives [Soft & derived metric]

Of these metrics, the last two are "soft" and "derived" metrics. Hard metrics are measurements obtained by direct observation. Derived metrics are the kind of measurement captured when users enter their feedback in form of suggestions or ranking of relevance. Soft and derived metrics are just as useful since they can be converted to hard metrics for dashboard display or for strategic and tactical analysis.

Finally, let's review 'Quality in use' metrics, namely the user's perspective of a product's quality. Quality in use represents the customer's view of the IT solution, rather than the quality metrics of the solution itself. Quality in use is a combination of internal and external quality characteristics, mainly usability, functionality, reliability and efficiency for the end user.

The table in Figure 11.6 gives a definition of the four quality-in-use characteristics. Metrics developed to measure these four characteristics provide clues to the quality-in-use aspect of an IT solution.

Similarly, measurements of system usage have four dimensions: Automation level, Extent, Frequency and Thoroughness. They are defined as follows.[61]

- Automation level, the proportion of business process encoded by the information system; Automation level describes the degree that a process has been automated by using an information system.

- Extent, the proportion of the functions used by the business process; Extent of use is the ratio of number of function points used to the total function points available.

- Frequency, the rate at which system functions are used by participants in the process; Frequency of use is the ratio of number of times a function was used to the total number of times the function could have been used.

- Thoroughness, the level of use of information or functionality provided by the system. Thoroughness of use is the ratio of depth of using a function to possible depths of using the function where appropriate.

To ensure certain level of usage and quality, IT management can define lower bound or minimum targets for these metrics.

---

[61] "The Measurement of Information System Use: Preliminary Considerations", Michael J. Cuellar, Ephraim, R. Mclean, Roy D. Johnson, ACM-SIGMIS-CPR, April 13-15, 2006

Characteristic	Definition
Effectiveness	The capability of the IT solution to enable users achieve their specified goals with accuracy and completeness in a specified context of use
Productivity	The capability of the IT solution to enable users achieve a higher level of output by reducing the time and resources necessary to perform a task or process in a specified context of use
Reliability	The capability of the IT solution to achieve the expected level of safety and acceptable level of risk of harm to people, property, users, environment in a specified context of use
Satisfaction	The capability of the IT solution to satisfy users and their managers in a specified context of use.

Fig 11.6 The Four "Quality-in-Use" Measurements

Summary:

- Six Sigma is fact based and data driven. It seeks to make decisions not based on opinions but based on data from critical to (quality, cost, performance, etc) variables.
- Six Sigma transforms the role of analyst to engineer. With this transformation comes engineering disciplines such as design, prototyping and measurements.
- Measurements can be hard, soft or derived. Metrics are either internal or external. We need all type of measurements that indicate critical to variables.
- Continuous measurement allows tracking process capability over the long run.
- Six Sigma tools demonstrate and aid in improving operational accuracy and product quality through emphasis on design and building quality into design.

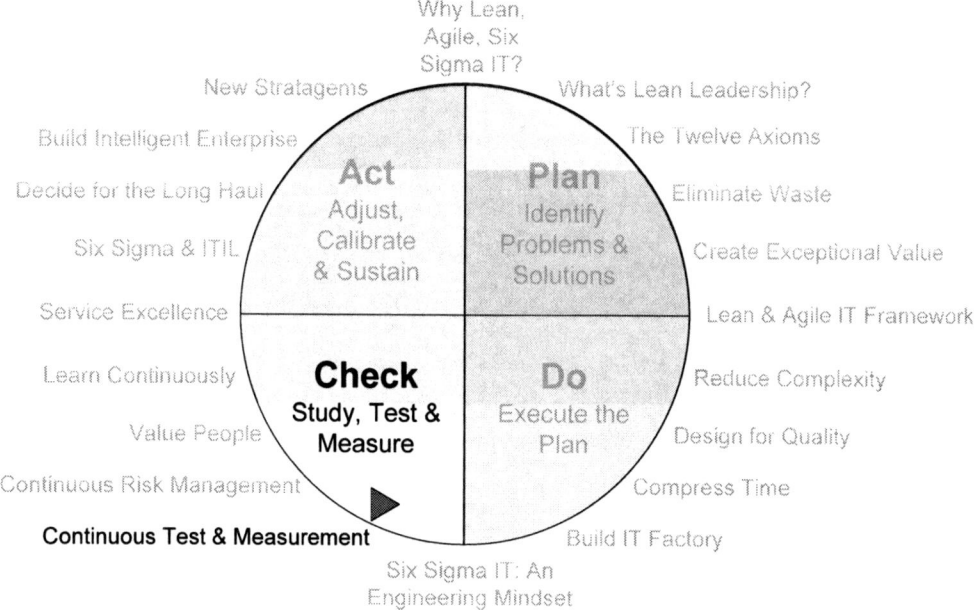

"As soon as we started programming, we found to our surprise that it wasn't as easy to get programs right as we had thought. Debugging had to be discovered. I can remember the exact instant when I realized that a large part of my life from then on was going to be spent in finding mistakes in my own programs".

Maurice Wilkes discovers debugging, 1949

Chapter 12: Continuous Testing & Measurements

In Agile IT environments where rapid application development and concurrent development principles are adopted, test planning occurs in tandem and alongside development. Often prototypes are used for early testing. Test engineers develop their test harnesses and automated testing tools in tandem with developers as developers develop or configure the application.

> **Stratagem:** Start with a testing strategy. Build the corporate IT infrastructure and resources to support testing activities. The budget invested in testing pays off if it uncovers enough errors that would have been more costly to detect and fix later.

There are two views to testing: One is the developer-perspective testing. The other is user-perspective testing. We want to ensure that both perspectives are fully utilized. Often in a Lean IT environment, we want super-users to participate in development and also in testing. This allows super-users to test from user perspective, but also it gives them the deep application knowledge which they will use for training the other users. In his seminal book, "The Art of Software Testing", Glen Myers recommends having a strategy and adequate infrastructure for testing.

His advice is to define the purpose of testing in advance. He writes, "One should start with the assumption that the program contains errors and then test the program to find as many of the errors as possible." Finding errors early also accelerates the development cycle and allows early, higher quality product introductions.

Testing Fundamentals – Testing is a destructive process. A successful test case is one that finds errors. We must begin with the assumption that the program does contain errors. An effective test program should be written in such a way to detect them. It's not recommended that programmers write their own test programs. The best practice is to have individuals other than programmers test the application. Test engineers have the responsibility to develop the test plan, the test cases and the test tools if necessary. Super users are often a great resource to exercise the test scripts.

A test case must include a definition of the expected output for a given set of inputs. In addition to testing for valid and normal conditions, test cases must exercise invalid data, unexpected situations, unreasonable cases, boundary conditions. Results of test cases must be inspected thoroughly. When we run test cases, we are looking for defects and also side effects. Often an application may run perfectly under test cases producing the correct outputs, but cause undesirable side-effects. Testers should watch for these abnormal behaviors as well.

A test case must include a concrete set of steps from start to completion. It must list the expected results or desired outcome. The concrete steps in a test case are helpful to show how an error can be reproduced. An error is an internal state of a program that is invalid. A failure is a program that deviates from specification. Faults are causes that allow errors to occur.

A fault can be a design fault, a software bug or hardware fault. I always stress that testing is not debugging; testing attempts to find failures. Debugging attempts to find the error states that are tracked down to faults to be removed. Testing is performed at multiple layers. At the lowest level, testing is performed on individual programs. This is called *unit testing*. Unit testing can be "*white-box*" or "*black-box*" oriented. When we know the internal structure or can look inside the application, we can perform white-box testing.

When we cannot see the code inside the program we are performing black box testing. Testing most IT applications purchased from vendors tend to be black-box testing. This places IT managers at a huge disadvantage. Without the ability to see the inside, they must report bugs to the vendor "over the wall" and wait to hear back from the vendor about debugging. Often as IT managers, we spend enormous efforts to isolate the fault and help the vendor reproduce it.

This activity can be fraught with confusion, frustrations and perilous delays to the project schedule. In order to minimize this challenge, it serves IT managers to encourage these principles:

A) Maintain an ongoing issues list for each application.
B) Document all defects and provide exact steps to reproduce the faults for the vendor
C) Ask the vendor to commit to a fix date for each defect

D) As mentioned already, always ask for the vendor's "Release Notes" documentation. You can find the existing defects listed in the document, so you won't have to find them again.

Integrated testing is an example of the higher order testing. This involves integrated tests of multiple application components together. During integrated testing, we can remove the stubs with actual components. A more complete testing called *"End-to-End" testing* can occur after integrated testing. End to end testing must exercise the new system through the entire firm's value stream.

An end-to-end testing considers all facets of application testing including user experience, security, disaster recovery, stress testing, load testing, interfaces to other applications and the workflow itself. A good test plan also includes testing the steps for release, namely the "go-live" plan. These tests are often called the mock go-live tests or simulated go-live activities.

Stress testing attempts to find faults when the application is stressed by either high transaction rates, high volume of data, repetitions or high number of concurrent users. *HALT* and *HASS* are two widely used methods for accelerated reliability testing. Highly Accelerated Life Testing (HALT) seeks to test the product in a "live" environment (similar to a mock go-live or simulated go-live) with the intent to break the system and identify the weakest parts of the system.

The weakest parts are fixed or re-designed. Another round of testing resumes and the cycle continues until the desired level of robustness is reached. HALT tests involve a group of users with the intent to subject the application to normal as well as abnormal data inputs and workflow patterns. Highly Accelerated Stress Screening (HASS) is mostly applied to production lines. It seeks to screen 100% of system components during a stress test before product is shipped to customers. During HASS testing, the goal is to test all features of the application in a "simulated live" environment. Each round of testing could take one to 5 days.

When a defect is fixed, the application is either patched or upgraded. In either case, the test team is required to re-run the entire battery of test cases all over again. This is called regression testing because it attempts to find defects after fixes have been applied. It is a quality assurance step to verify that the patch has indeed fixed the defect. A few years ago I encouraged my staff to use automated test tools. Known as "robo-testers", these programs generate test loads by simply learning the keystrokes of testers during their initial tests.

This was a HALT and HASS approach. The automated test tools would run during the night and in the morning we could see what the automated test tools had done to the application by examining the test logs, error patterns and system logs. We would fix our solution and repeat the test cycle by end of the day.

Longevity testing is a method to find meantime between failures. Basically, several instances of the application or the system are started until a crash is observed. The duration of uptime is recorded, and the test is repeated again. After a certain period of time, we can determine the average uptime or the Mean Time Between Failures (MTBF).

Verification and Validation - The final stages of quality control are verification and validation. Verification testing is performed to verify that an application works correctly. This implies that we test for all input/output combinations and permutations using while box and black box testing methods. Our aim is to ensure that the application does not fail and it performs without errors, in particular ensuring that it does not produce critical, or life-safety errors. Validation seeks to ensure that the functionality meets the intended user functional specification. It considers validity of application function in the workflow and work environment it was intended for.

RAISE The Bar on Testing - RAISE testing is a common approach to testing applications for Reliability, Availability, Installability, Serviceability, and Ease of use. A RAISE test environment attempts to simulate a customer-like environment as much as possible. Test cases are written to measure the IT solution against these five criteria. Dashboards can provide executive management a summary view of the application quality by reporting measurements on these five metrics. A form of non-execution testing is inspection and walkthroughs. It's advisable to perform design reviews, code inspections and walkthroughs with developers periodically and as development moves from one stage to another stage, say from design to code.

The ideal test plan has a complete coverage of the entire application. In white box testing, the test plan must exercise all loops, conditions and paths of the code. In black-box testing we must test for "all" permutations of input and usage conditions. This is not always possible due to limited time and vast number of test case permutations. For example, in black-box testing, we might still miss infinite loops or portions of the code that are unreachable under any input.

IEEE Standards - There are several testing standards and guidelines available. I've found the IEEE standards to be among the best and most practical guidelines. The Institute of Electrical and Electronics Engineers (IEEE) maintains a wide range of standards including software development and testing. The IEEE829 is a standard and framework for managing software testing process. It defines the testing stages and communication standards between those stages. The seven test stages defined by the standard are:

1. **Test plan:** Describes the overall strategy, scope, approach, resources and schedule of testing activities. It identifies which items will be tested and how. It describes the human resources and test environment that are required for conducting the tests.

2. **Test Design:** This is the test specification that describes testing approach, test cases, test procedure, and criteria for test item pass/fail.

3. **Test Cases:** These are individual test scenarios including data input and conditions for individual tests. Test cases define the expected result, pass/fail criteria and a method for reproducing a test failure.

4. **Test Procedures:** Are instructions for running tests, including how to operate the system and execute the test cases.

5. **Test Logs:** Test logs are used to record the test results for each test case. They include all cases that passed and failed, including description of failures and steps to reproduce them.

6. **Incident Reports:** Are descriptions of any defects, failures or anomalies that occur during testing which require further investigation.

7. **Test Summary Report:** The test summary report is a summary of test results indicating the number of defects measured from test cases for the application by module or by functional area.

Testing Maturity Model - Some experts have proposed a maturity model for testing similar to the Capability Maturity model (CMM), developed originally at Carnegie Mellon Software Engineering Institute. CMM scores the capability maturity of each organization into five levels, where level five is the highest level of maturity. We can evaluate an organization's testing capability using a Testing Maturity Model (TMM).

The maturity levels described below are based on a TMM perspective documented by Brian Heys[62]. The goal of TMM is to enhance the testing process capability and maturity. Organizations which aim for highest quality standards should aim for the highest maturity level.

Level 1. Initial: This level represents an organization with no maturity goals and no formal process, structured or documented testing processes. Test plans are developed in an ad-hoc manner and testing itself is seen as debugging activity.

Level 2. Defined: At this maturity level the organization has developed standards for testing strategy, test plans, test reports and basic testing techniques and methods.

Level 3. Integrated: This maturity level means that the testing process is integrated into the entire development and implementation lifecycle. There are standards for testing, reporting, monitoring and test techniques. Test plans are designed to maximize coverage and quality.

Level 4. Managed and Measured: Level four represents the maturity level where testing process includes measurements and review of test results from a quality assurance perspective. At this level, metrics regarding testing productivity, code coverage and quality measurements are considered. Measurements are analyzed to provide a quality index and confidence level in the quality of the application.

Level 5. Optimization: Level five is achieved when data from testing process is used to prevent future defects and feedback testing form can be used to improve the development process.

Agile Testing - Agile testing methods encourage three principles:

1. A hands-on approach for all project participants including users testing the application.

2. Encourages testing immediately as soon as a component becomes available for testing.

---

[62] See www.brianheys.com, 2007. Access date: July 2008.

3. Integrated test plans must attempt to identify the 20% of the application that cause 80% of the defects. This approach helps test coverage to find the most defects as early as possible in the development and implementation cycle. This 20% of the application must be tested more than the remainder of the application.

Since Agile development relies less on strategic planning and more on user involvement, agile testing similarly relies on user involvement throughout testing process. This requires that we train users on at least the basic testing techniques. While it's preferable that test plans be developed from user requirements, from use cases and functional requirement definitions, in Agile testing, we may ask users to help create test cases by verbally describing their workflows.

From such narratives, we can develop story boards or workflow diagrams to guide our test cases. Again in Agile testing, users, developers and testers are a collaborative team to produce quality products. Testing occurs by all team members, and from the very early stages of the development cycle, not just towards the end of the project.

Common Test Metrics - Test metrics are key indicators of quality and maintenance cost. The Software Engineering Institute (SEI) has a set of core metrics that can be measured and charted in a dashboard for almost any IT solution. Most metrics begin with measuring size, effort, defect, time and complexity. Typically, the source line of code (SLOC) is a measure of size. But increasingly *Function Points* are being used as a metric for size of IT solutions.

A function point is defined as an end-user business function, like a data query or printing a page. Complexity is measured by various techniques such as cyclomatic complexity, an index based on how many loops and decision paths are involved in the application. These metrics are outside the scope of this book. Tracking metrics in an IT organization builds a baseline for quality from which we can begin continuous improvement.

There are hundreds of metrics possible, but a few are crucial. Here are some of the fundamental metrics:

- **Quality of IT Solution or Defect Density:** The ratio of number of severity-1 and serverity-2 defects divided by the number of function points. A similar metric is commonly used to measure the ratio of number of defects divided by the source lines of code (SLOC). Severity-1 defects are typically defined as defects that cause application crash or critical errors. Severity-2 errors are those defects that partially disable an application but a workaround exists to keep the solution operational.

- **Testing Effectiveness:** The ratio of number of defects discovered during testing divided by the sum of all defects discovered before and after release.

- **User Satisfaction Index:** The ratio of number of user trouble tickets generated within the first 3 months of the release divided by the number of users.

- **User Win Index:** The ratio of number of features released divided by the total user-valued features requested.

- **Mean Time to Failure (MTTF):** The average time lapsed between discovery of major defects before release and after release.

- **Quality Convergence:** The number of defects discovered plotted over time. An IT solution is converging towards expected quality if the number of defects decreases over time, and time elapsed between discovering defects increases. The same metric can apply to the number of patch releases and time latency between patches. In other words, a product is converging towards stability as the frequency of patches decrease, namely the time interval between patches increases.

- **Ease of Use index:** The ratio of number of hours required to train users divided by the number of features released.

- **Cost of Fix per defect:** The ratio of total cost of fixes divided by the total number of defects in each phase of development.

- **Test Coverage index:** The ratio of quantity of features fully tested divided by the total number of features delivered.

- **User Productivity metric:** The average number of clicks required for a user to complete a function point. A variation of these metric measures the average number of web pages a user must navigate to complete a business function.

Other Testing Methods: Conformance testing is an activity to determine whether a software product meets the requirements of a particular specification or standard. These standards are in most cases set by consortiums, regulatory or standardization committees such as IEEE, Food and Drug Administration (FDA), Federal Aviation Administration (FAA) and similar entities.

Interoperability testing, sometimes referred to as intersystem testing, in an activity to assess whether a software product will exchange and share information (interoperate) with other products. Interoperability testing is used to determine whether the proper pieces of information are correctly passed between systems. This is one of the most critical types of testing in IT and one that defines a successful IT organization.

Compatibility testing is a similar activity with the goal of finding if a new system or software is compatible with an existing architecture or technology platform. Both require writing a set of test cases and test scenarios to determine the degree of compatibility or interoperability between applications and systems. I recall an application vendor who sold its software to an academic institution but forgot to mention its software is incompatible with Apple workstations.

The IT department neglected to perform interoperability tests on the Apple platform and as a result it caused a major division in its information system architecture. Successful systems integration relies heavily on interoperability and compatibility testing.

Performance testing determines the performance of an IT solution with respect to specified metrics. The target metrics are usually standards established internally by the firm or by the SLAs.

For example, one firm specified a maximum response time of three seconds for all user functions. Performance testing measures how well the software system executes according to its required response times, throughput, CPU usage, and other quantified features.

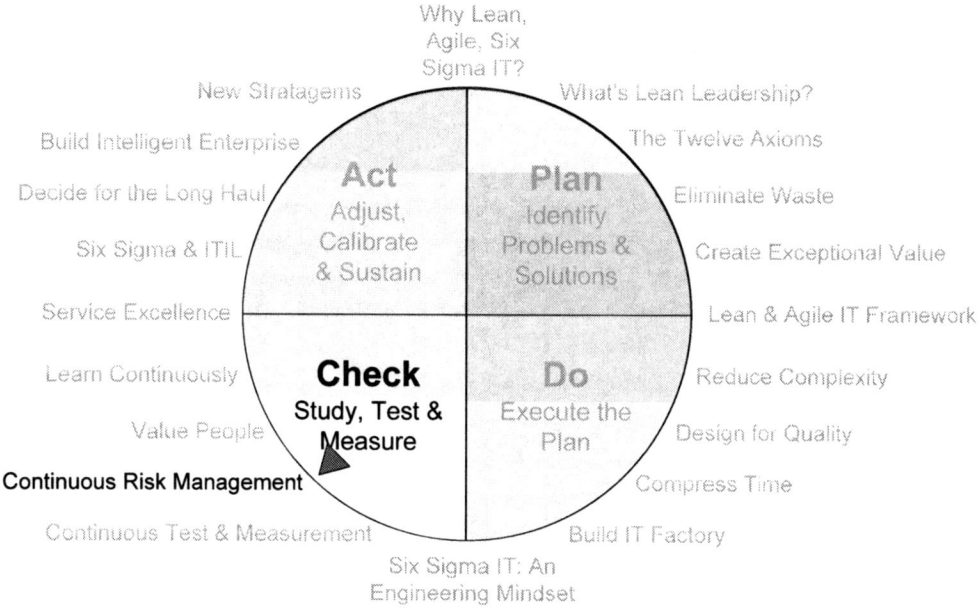

"The pessimist sees difficulty in every opportunity. The optimist sees the opportunity in every difficulty."

Winston Churchill

Chapter 13. Continuous Risk Management

The sociological norms and prevalent philosophy in information technology tend to encourage "positive-problem solving". As a result most of us view risks as challenges to overcome during the IT projects as they occur, not before.

This is a precarious tendency since it leads to underestimating the risks ahead. Unfortunately, risk mitigation planning, predicting risks in advance (or even simulating risks and their impact which I advocate) before starting the project tend to be perceived as negative thoughts and are typically ignored or suppressed.

Classical risk management divides risk into two classes of *"recognizable risks"* and *"unmanaged assumptions"*. Recognizable risks are those that can be identified during planning and engagement contracting activities. For the most part, they are highly visible and immediately apparent to everyone (or at least someone) involved with the project.

Typical examples include new technology, financial resource constraints, staff resource limitations, changes to business process, etc. Historically, mitigation strategies have often been put in place for these kinds of risks.

Unmanaged assumptions consist of false assumptions and unexpected events, simply "surprises" that arise through course of the project. Deming's PDCA cycle is inherently a risk mitigation tool. When applied to continuous risk management, in the PLAN stage, we want to understand risk, its origins and what mitigation plans can be devised. In the DO stage, we implement the risk mitigation and better yet those risk avoidance stratagems.

The CHECK stage determines the status of projects and risks to determine which risks are about to occur or have impacted the project. Finally, the ACT stage determines steps to remedy the risk.

In February 1999, NASA's Continuous Risk Management methodology was presented at the Applied Software Measurement - Software Management Conference, in San Jose, California. The methodology consists of five steps:

1. Identify risks
2. Analyze risk
3. Plan
4. Track
5. Control

In the Analyze phase, the intent is to better understand the risk by qualifying the expected *impact*, *probability*, and *timeframe* of a risk. This involves establishing values for:

Impact: the loss or negative affect on the project should the risk occur

Probability: the likelihood the risk will occur

Timeframe: the period when you must take action in order to mitigate the risk

NASA's five steps track the Deming cycle closely. The table in Figure 13.1 demonstrates sample values that might be used to evaluate a risk's attributes. Timeframe refers to when action must be taken.

Predefining risk categories provides a way to classify risks for inclusion in the organizational knowledge base.

There following nine risk categories are common considerations:

1. Scope/change management risk.
2. Operational risk.
3. Financial risk.
4. Project management risk.
5. Strategic risk.
6. Technology risk.
7. Process maturity risk.
8. Standardization risk.
9. Failed assumptions.

Attribute	Probability Value	Value Description
Probability	Very Likely (H)	High chance of this risk occurring, thus becoming a problem > 70%
	Probable (M)	Risk like this may turn into a problem once in a while {30% < x < 70%}
	Improbable (L)	Not much chance this will become a problem {0% < x < 30%}
Impact	Catastrophic (H)	Loss of system; unrecoverable failure of system operations; major damage to system; schedule slip causing launch date to be missed; cost overrun greater than 50% of budget
	Critical (M)	Minor system damage to system with recoverable operational capacity; cost overrun exceeding 10% (but less than 50% of planned cost
	Marginal (L)	Minor system damage to project; recoverable loss of operational capacity; internal schedule slip that does not impact launch date cost overrun less than 10% of planned cost
Timeframe	Near-term (N)	Within 30 days
	Mid-term (M)	1 to 4 months from now
	Far-term (F)	more than 4 months from now

Fig 13.1 – Categorization of Risk by Probability, Timeframe & Impact

PLAN Phase

Barry Boehm is a pioneer in software risk management, developing his risk management methodology in conjunction with his risk driven spiral development model. Boehm has identified a list of top ten causes of development failures as:

1. Personnel shortfalls
2. Unrealistic schedules and budgets
3. Developing the wrong functions and properties
4. Developing the wrong user interfaces
5. Gold plating (feature creep)
6. Continuing stream of requirements changes

7. Shortfalls in externally finished components
8. Shortfalls in externally performed tasks
9. Real-time performance shortfalls
10. Straining computer science capabilities

In traditional risk assessment methods, the definitions for Risk probability are given as:

- **High Risk probability:** Without mitigation and monitoring, the project deliverable/milestone completion will interrupt the project's critical path.
- **Medium Risk probability:** Without mitigation and monitoring, project deliverable/milestone completion will enter the project critical path.
- **Low Risk probability:** No project deliverable/milestone is at risk unless delays become excessive; therefore, it should be documented and monitored.

Traditional Risk assessment uses risk probability in categorical terms, either as High, Medium, Low or ranking of 1-5 (1 being the least probable). These probability categories are somewhat crude estimations. They provide rule of thumb estimates for impact of risk which could be good enough for most situations. But, these categories ignore the compounding effects of risks which can be identified using project simulation programs.

Internal and External Risks: In his research notes on "Risk Management", Dr S. Beauchemin offers a quantitative approach to risk classification. He offers the following as sources of risk:

"External risks are those that have their sources outside the organization sponsoring the project". Some examples include:

- Competitive disadvantage
- Fluctuations of markets
- External sponsorship
- Client support
- Market base and niche

"Internal risks are those that have their source within the organization including the project". Some examples include:

- Availability of expertise
- Technological factors
- Budget approval
- Project visibility
- Procurement availability

Beauchemin's internal risks echo Barry Bohm's risk factors. However there are additional external influential risk factors for Lean IT managers to consider such as:

- Outsourcing expertise
- Availability of off-the-shelf components
- Inter-operability & integrability of system deliverables
- Customer requirement changes

In his book, "Assessment and Control of Software Risks", Capers Jones[63] identifies the key factors for success and failures of software and information technology projects. The table in Figure 13.2 summarizes his findings. His research found that MIS projects fail for multiple reasons, the majority due to poor execution and lack of process maturity.

Studies of project failures hint that many IT managers do not fully grasp the nature of risks and are not well equipped with tools to measure and prepare risk mitigation plans.

No.	Risk Factor	Root Cause	% of MIS Projects Failing
1	"Creeping" requirements	Lack of well-defined user requirements & control	80%
2	Excessive "schedule pressure"	Inadequate scoping of project and process	65%
3	Low Quality	Poor design, inadequate testing, lack of processes	60%
4	Cost Overruns	Lack of design, inadequate testing, low skill set	55%
5	Inadequate Configuration Management	Lack of version control & rigorous process for integration	50%

Fig. 13.2 – Top 5 Risk Factors Causing MIS Project Failures

IT managers face two categories of risk. One is the operational risks which are better understood in terms of vulnerabilities. These vulnerabilities include system failures, network downtimes and security attacks. The second form of risk is portfolio risk. This is better explained by understanding the risks associated with project management, since most structured activities involving IT involve some form of projects. In Figure 13.2, of the top five risk factors identified by Capers Jones, the risk factors 1-2 can be addressed by Six Sigma DMADV approach. Risk factors 3-5 can be best handled by Six Sigma DMAIC process.

---

[63] "Assessment and Control of Software Risks", Capers Jones, Yourdon Press, 1994.

I repeatedly mention to my staff (to the point of being told I'm preaching) that IT projects are inherently risky endeavors. This is due to the fact that most IT projects have been structured as non-repeatable activities by their managers. Such projects are planned as unique and new set of activities. It's true that IT projects usher new technologies to the organization, but the process to do so need not be re-invented every time.

The other source of risk comes from the multi-faceted aspect of projects since we must coordinate, control and satisfy a wide range of entities, such as: stakeholders, technology, regulatory and change management issues, to name a few. These facets add to the uncertainty of decisions and unforeseen events. As uncertainty and complexity of projects rise, so do the risk levels, but only faster. This is partly due to the compounding effect of risks, where impact of one risk causes other risks to become more probable. To be effective, IT managers must deal with both dimensions of uncertainty and complexity inherent in risk management.

The goal of risk assessment is to identify vulnerabilities and provide guidance in prioritizing corrective action. There are *portfolio vulnerabilities* and *operational vulnerabilities*. Portfolio risks are vulnerabilities that deal with projects that deploy a solution and introduce change. Dealing with operational vulnerabilities includes addressing business continuity and disaster recovery planning. Certain risks such as security vulnerabilities or environmental disasters are evaluated in hierarchical layers based on their impact and scope. The layered approach as we saw before comes in handy for business continuity analysis and risk mitigation.

Risk management objectives are to identify, address, and eliminate IT risk items before they become threats to success or major sources of rework. In general, good project managers are also good risk managers. It makes good business sense for projects to incorporate risk management as part of project planning. Simulation models can compute the impact & linkage between risk and assumptions. In fact when IT managers simulate their project they can identify real risk factors and their compounding effect on the project. Simulation programs can help measure risk factors, risk triggers (risk events, warning signs, namely the risk triggering circumstances), measure potential losses, and identify the high impact risks and effect of risk mitigation. Once risks and their underlying factors are better understood by simulation, more effective risk mitigation plans can be developed and implemented. By the end of this phase, we want to know as many sources of risk as possible and a mitigation plan and contingency plan for each. Mitigation plans attempt to reduce the likelihood of risk and its impact. Contingency plans determine an action plan if and when the risk occurs. We identify sources of risk through challenging assumptions.

DO Phase

There are a number of definitions and uses for the term risk, but there is no universally accepted definition. What all definitions have in common is agreement that risk has two characteristics:

Uncertainty: An event may or may not happen.

Loss: An event has unwanted consequences or losses.

The aim for a risk statement is that it be clear, concise, and sufficiently informative that the risk is easily understood. Risk statements in standard format must contain two parts, the condition and the consequence. The condition-consequence format provides a complete picture of the risk, which is critical during mitigation planning. It is read as follows:

"Given the <condition> there is a probability that <consequence> will occur."

The condition component focuses on what is currently causing concern; it must be something that is true or widely perceived to be true. "Condition" is linked to origins of risk and provides clues, information that we use to mitigate the risk. "Consequence" focuses on the intermediate and long-term impact of risk. Understanding the depth and breadth of the impact is useful to determine how much time, resources, and effort should be allocated to the mitigation effort. A well-formed risk statement usually has only one condition, but may have more than one consequence.

The NASA Goddard Space Flight Center (GSFC) Software Assurance Technology Center (SATC) teaches a risk management process based on a course developed in collaboration with the Software Engineering Institute (SEI) at Carnegie Mellon University. This risk management process has been taught to projects at all NASA centers and is being successfully implemented on many projects.

NASA has adopted a "continuous risk management" paradigm which can be applied to any development process: hardware, software, systems, etc. It provides a disciplined environment for proactive decision making to:

- Continually assess what could go wrong.
- Determine which risks are important.
- Implement strategies to deal with them.
- Assure measured effectiveness of implemented strategies.

NASA's Continuous Risk Management methodology requires routinely identifying and managing risks throughout all phases of the project's life. Managing risk throughout a project's life cycle is the foundation for the application of continuous risk management. Risks are usually tracked in parallel while new risks are identified and analyzed, and the mitigation plan for one risk may yield another risk.

Operational Risk Management

Operational risks are known as vulnerabilities. All information systems have a vulnerability of one kind or another. Operational risks are either caused by a particular malfunction in information systems or predominantly due to human error. Studies have shown that as much as 70% of application downtimes are caused by human error. To avoid system malfunctions, it is recommended that we identify vulnerabilities in advance and devise secondary and tertiary backup solutions.

For example, establishing redundant network paths, database replication and server virtualization are among stratagems in this category. To avoid human error, the best practices recommend creating standard operational procedures. Among standards, the ITIL practices offer excellent guidelines that improve operational consistency. Information Technology Infrastructure Library is a set of techniques for managing IT infrastructure, operations and services. Developed in the 1980's, ITIL provides a set of guidelines for problem management, change management, configuration management and software asset management. ITIL[64] prescribes activities such as documentation, pre-definition and review of tasks, testing before applying changes and change control management in order to reduce chances of human error. Change control reviews must identify risks associated with applying change.

Portfolio Risk Management

Over time, traditional project managers learn to manage risk by shielding themselves, not eliminating the conditions that foster the risk. They've developed various patterns of behavior to fend off the impact of risk-based failures which produce expensive and wasteful approaches. These behaviors include reducing scope, cutting corners on quality and testing, adding unjustified time or money, even finger pointing as the last resort.

All of these behavior patterns are either reactive or stem from gut-feel decision making. They are neither supported by data nor by scientific methods of project management. Such tactics lead to project failures, and cause loss of credibility and confidence in the project manager[65]. These behaviors prevent learning and as a result failures tend to be repeated. The aim of a Lean IT manager should be to predict the interaction of risk factors that lead to project risk by accounting and simulating the development risks in advance.

NASA's continuous risk management principles advocate that both risk mitigation strategies and contingency plans cost time, money, and resources to develop and implement. In addition, project sponsors often don't want to spend the time and money for detailed risk mitigation planning. NASA advocates that it may be more appropriate to set an overall risk mitigation budget as a percentage of the overall projected costs, rather than detail costing individual risk mitigation plans. Industry experience suggests a 5% contingency budget for identifying and tracking known risks, and at least another 5% risk mitigation contingency budget for those risks not preplanned.

Barry Boehm offers a six step risk management process, composed of two main steps, each divided into three sub-steps:

A) Risk assessment, consisting of:
1. Identification of those risks likely to cause problems
2. Analysis to determine the loss probability and loss magnitude for each risk and to develop a compound risk
3. Prioritization to rank the identified risk items according to their compound risks

---

[64] ITIL is a registered trademark of the United Kingdom's Office of Government Commerce (OGC).
[65] "Risk management: The undiscovered dimension of project management Project Management Journal"; Sylva; Mar 2000; Paul S Royer; Vol 31, Issue 1, page 6-13.

B) Risk control, consisting of:
4. Management planning to bring the risk items under control
5. Resolution to eliminate or resolve the risk items
6. Monitoring to track the project's risk reduction progress and to apply corrective action where necessary.

Boehm discusses sample tools for use at each of these steps, ranging from checklists to cost models to cost-benefit analysis. I believe that combining all IT projects into a single portfolio actually raises the overall risk of the portfolio. That's because all projects appear to complete for the same level of management attention and risk mitigation. Instead, I believe it's better to have multiple portfolios of projects. Each portfolio must contain a category of like projects grouped together either by risk level, by complexity or by layers of IT technology food chain (such as the layers shown in the layered pyramid example in Chapter 8). Project portfolios can be divided into high risk projects, medium risk projects and low risk projects. Alternatively, if we grouped projects by their place in the IT technology food chain layers, we would create a project portfolio for all infrastructure projects, separated from the portfolio of applications projects and from the portfolio of middle-tier projects. One of my colleagues calls this multi-portfolio arrangement a flight plan for projects, as he lists the projects in each portfolio according to their priority and risk.

Risk Contingency Plans

Traditional risk contingency and mitigation plans attempted to identify all risks in advance. The Agile risk management methods avoid risk by cutting the project timelines and rapid delivery. But even before risks occur, Lean and Agile methods are great methods for risk contingency planning. The Agile project manager considers a list of potential risks and the contingency plans for each. The contingency plans (or as some call them backup plans) can be in place in advance. To illustrate, let's consider Barry Boehm's list of top 10 reasons for project failures. For each of these reasons, we must have a contingency plan in place.

There are operational risk contingency plans as well. These are the failure mode operations plans that define what must be done in the event of a system failure. There are many business continuity and disaster recovery planning guides and books available which are outside the scope of this book. Let me only mention that my IT staff has extensive plans in place for downtime and disaster recovery situations. In short, they follow a four step workflow:

1. They establish an incident commander, and two separate teams, team A and Team B.
2. Team A continues to resolve the issue often working with the solution vendor. It focuses on isolating the problem, identifying the root cause and fixing the defect to restore service levels.
3. Team B continues to identify short term workarounds to workflows and works with customers and users to enable their workflows using a workaround.

4. After service is restored, perform post-incident review and apply lessons learned to prevent the risk event from occurring again.

When we plan for risk contingency, we must consider the residual and secondary risks. A residual risk is the left-over risks after the primary risk has been removed or mitigated. The secondary risks are risks associated with the contingency plan, namely risks that affect or arise as a result of the contingency plan.

Just to illustrate what goes into risk contingency planning, here are some contingency plans as examples that one project manager was able to devise in Figure 13.3.

No.	Risk Event	Contingency Factor
1	Personnel Shortfalls	Identify outsourcing & contractor resources. Have contracts ready or in place to use external resources.
2	Unrealistic schedules	Determine the minimum early deliverables. Divide project into parallel Agile mini-projects. Outsource portions of the project if possible.
3	Wrong functions	Focus on customer valued features only. Modify wrong functions to meet customer needs rapidly.
4	Wrong User interfaces	Create rapid web-based bolt-on pages for the user.
5	Gold Plating	Identify the 20% of features that add value. Postpone the 80% that add minimal value to future releases
6	Continuous changes of requirements	Build the solution iteratively to allow for customer requirements changes. Keep flexibility by using component-based architecture.
7	Shortfalls in external finished components	Review vendor quality practices and perform incoming tests & inspections to catch early mortality components
8	Shortfalls in externally performed tasks	Select vendors that have done this particular work before successfully. Perform periodic audits of the work performed externally. Apply strict quality guidelines and acceptance criteria to the external outsourced company.
9	Performance shortfalls	Purchase additional hardware to improve performance. Apply optimizations to performance bottlenecks.
10.	Strained Computer science capability	Maintain contracts with subject matter experts, chief architects, and designers to gain support & skilled resources. Establish student internship programs with computer science departments at colleges.

Fig 13.3 – Risk Contingency Plan Example

In the Six Sigma view, every risk is a function of certain variables or conditions. The ideal risk management plan is the one that prevents risk conditions to materialize. The experienced project managers have developed an intuition to monitor and manage the variables that cause risk conditions to occur.

CHECK Phase

Being data-driven, Six Sigma IT managers seek to measure and categorize project risks using probability, impact or severity. They also recognize that variation is the enemy as the cause of many quality and risk factors. Within any organization, certain risk categories may pose higher risks for project failure. For example, some organizations may have a long history of introducing new technology and the know-how to deal with technology risks better than other firms. Organizations that have not implemented a large scale enterprise application may need to be especially careful when doing so. During the course of time the nature and severity of risks change. We need a method to measure risks by severity continuously. Risk severity corresponds to the impact of risk on the project and business. Risk severity should be rated for objective evaluation.

The traditional risk assessment techniques use a simple high-medium-low scale for risk severity defined as follows:

High Severity: Without mitigation, project objectives are in jeopardy.

Medium Severity: Without mitigation, a deliverable or milestone is at risk.

Low Severity: No deliverable/milestone is currently at risk, but an issue bears watching, and is a candidate for active mitigation.

Another risk assessment technique called Severity-Probability-Risk (SPR) is a tool that combines matrix of risk severity versus probability in a matrix to provide a ranking for project risks.. For example, let's assume that for a given project, eleven risks denoted R1, R2,..., R11 were identified. SPR method uses a table as shown in Figure 13.4 to classify each risk based on severity and probability of occurrence.

As shown in the SPR diagram risks are assigned based on their probability of occurrence and severity of impact. For example, risks R2, R8, and R10 are most critical because of their higher probability of occurrence and impact. The most critical risks are those with high severity and high probability. These risks should have a mitigation strategy developed and included in the project plan and budget. If only one factor is high, then the risk has medium criticality. For these risks we may outline a contingency strategy with a trigger and leave the planning details until the risk condition is triggered.

By aggregating the number of high risks, it is possible to classify the entire project as either high, medium or low risk. Each shade of gray represents either a high risk (dark gray), medium risk (light gray) and low risk (white cells) categories.

Obviously, the risks can change during a project's life cycle. By tracking the individual risk changes, namely the shift in risk ranking, one can calculate the direction of change. A shift into higher risk score would be an early alert that a project is getting into further trouble and needs immediate attention to avoid failure.

Risk Prioritization Matrix – Severity vs. Probability Ranking (SPR)					
Probability > Severity V	1. Low Prob.	2. Low to Med Prob.	3. Medium Prob.	4. Med to Hi Prob.	5. High Prob.
5. Very Severe	R3, R5		R2	R8	
4. Severe		R1			
3. Somewhat Severe			R6	R9	R10
2. Not Very Severe		R11			R4
1. Not Severe			R7		

Fig 13.4 – Risk Classification According to Severity & Probability

To avoid surprises that require reactive management decisions, assumptions about the project should also be documented and monitored to ensure that changing circumstances don't negate assumptions and transform them into risks. Assumptions should be managed in much the same way as risks, because, in fact, they confirm a new source of risk. Some project management practices suggest that for every assumption, a metric can be defined to test its continued accuracy. By establishing measures for assumptions and monitoring them, the project manager can proactively develop contingency plans to be triggered when change happens.

Assumption Risks

Assumptions can be identified and managed using any of the approaches discussed below:

Experience-based Assumptions. Prior project experience gives the project manager a source for risk identification and planning, but it also provides knowledge about assumptions that hold true within an organization and types of projects

Brainstorming-based. Assumptions, metrics to monitor their continued applicability, and potential mitigation strategies can be identified and examined in a brain storming session.

Converting Assumptions into Risk Factors. Convert assumptions into quantified risk factors using condition-event method. This is accomplished by linking assumptions to the project variables, capturing the probabilities associated with each assumption and calculating the impact of each false assumption. The Software Engineering Institute (SEI) has also developed a risk management guidebook for software acquisition managers, with steps very similar to Boehm's six step model mentioned earlier. Software development staff profile is composed of several components which managers can measure and assess during the risk identification period:

- Staff level, which deals with actual availability for the project. All this data is measurable and can be plotted against estimated staff requirements.

- Staff availability, which deals with whether the team member is actually available, in place and trained at the appropriate time of the development life cycle

- Historic project and company retention rates, which can help project managers predict whether their team will be intact throughout the project, or whether they should plan for turnover and build sufficient slack in their estimates

- Staff mix, which measures distribution by activity such as Quality Assurance (QA) and Configuration Management (CM), security engineering, and helps managers determine whether they have enough people for each task

- Staff experience, or personnel qualification, which deals with individual team members' proficiencies, years of experience working for the firm and IT development.

To assess risks for very large projects, IT management should call for independent internal or outside consulting firms to evaluate risks before the project gets underway. Unfortunately, much of the traditional IT wisdom has called for independent study of risks after projects are well in trouble. There are intrinsic flaws in project structures that pose fundamental risks. These intrinsic flaws include programmatic risks, schedule risks and cost risks.

Programmatic Risks: Those are risks that flow from or impose an impact on program governance and program performance. The risks for governance may be external (political, statutory, litigious, or contractual) or internal (business priorities, staff limitations, ROI constraints, and learning curves). Risks that impact program performance generally flow from issues of competence, experience, organizational culture, and skills of the management team.

Schedule Risks: At the highest level of concern, schedule risks simply imply not enough time exists to do the required job with the resources allocated, people and/or money and/or material.

Cost Risks: At the highest level, cost risks simply mean there is not enough money to do the job required in the time allocated including reserves for reasonable contingencies. These are the intrinsic flaws in the program. The causes of such risks can be estimating errors, low ball bids, business decisions, lack of understanding of requirements and political expediency.

A management technique to mitigate cost risks is to focus on all elements of the program that are new and to insure that management reserves are at least adequate compared to the costs of the new elements.

Technical Risk: The technical risks are performance risks associated with the end items. From the perspective of the buying organization the concern is that the system will not perform as required. From the perspective of the performing organization the concern is that the system will not meet its specifications (and hence not be purchased and/or not meet customer satisfaction goals). There is a gap between the two risk views, which in itself can lead to dysfunctional risk mitigation plans between application vendors and the IT management.

Supportability Risk: The supportability risk is that an otherwise acceptable system will cost too much to operate and maintain over its life cycle in terms of time, personnel and material resources.

It is a fact that most systems cost more to sustain than to develop, and this fact is not new. The goal of Lean IT is to build systems for supportability and maintainability in order to lower the total cost of ownership.

Development Risks: The development effort always entails some measure of risk because it introduces a new activity to the performing organization. The risks associated with developing a single component of a system is less than the risk associated with a major development project stretching all envelopes for all subsystems of a complex system.

Here is one advantage in using SOA (Service Oriented Architectures) in that they have smaller, component-sized risks which are easier to control and manage. Better yet, with SaaS (software as a Service) models, vendors absorb the upfront cost risks and operating risks.

Risk Metrics

To summarize risk quantification, researchers apply methods that in general use their probability of risk and exposure (either by schedule, cost or other measures). To rank risks, they calculate Exposure using the following numerical method:

Exposure = Risk probability x Risk amount

For example, let's consider the same eleven risk factors that we covered in the previous SPR diagram. The probabilities and financial impact given for each risk are shown in Figure 13.5.

Based on this approach, risk exposure for each risk is calculated for each risk event. Per this example, R2 has higher criticality than R3 and R4, even though R3 and R4 are each at extremes of probabilities and financial impact are at.

As discussed before, this approach is highly non-scalar but simple to apply. One risk may cause or amplify the impact of another risk. This is based on the principle that risks have compounding effect on each other in a non-linear way.

Risk	Probability	Financial impact	Risk Exposure
R1	40%	$450,000	$180,000
R2	60%	$650,000	$390,000
...	...	...	...
R8	80%	$600,000	$480,000
R9	75%	$400,000	$300,000
R10	80%	$400,000	$320,000
R11	40%	$250,000	$100,000

Fig 13.5 – Risk Exposure Calculation Example

ACT Phase

At this phase of continuous risk management, we must assess the current situation and what actions and adjustments to the project plan are required. In a Scrum project management method, the Scrum master and the team determines the course of action for the next iteration of their sprint or project milestone. With input from customers and users, they formulate new risk mitigation and contingency plans. The risk exposure assessment presented in Figure 13.5 can be used periodically to assess the new risk exposures and hence re-prioritize the risks.

In order to visualize the effects of our decisions on projects, simulation is a powerful tool to consider all possible combinations and permutations of future events. Using simulation, we can identify the impact of risks and false assumptions. For example, we can analyze the impact of losing a project team member or a poorly developed product quality by a supplier.

Simulation tools today are so powerful that they allow you to visually analyze the impact on service levels, costs and workload by changing input variables such as skill level, staff level, equipment, defects and similar factors.

Summary

- Continuously assess risks by identifying their impact and probability.
- Report risks to upper management immediately.
- Having a portfolio of projects does not necessarily distribute individual project risks across multiple projects.

- Conduct project simulations in advance to identify compounded effects of risk on projects.
- Many risks are interrelated and have common cause but can create a chain of adverse effects.
- The first key to risk management is control of variability and variables that produce risk.
- The second key to risk management is to have risk avoidance plans, namely take steps to monitor and manage the conditions that lead to risk events.
- The third key to risk management is having risk contingency plans: flexible backup plans and workaround workflows ready to be put in place when the risk occurs.

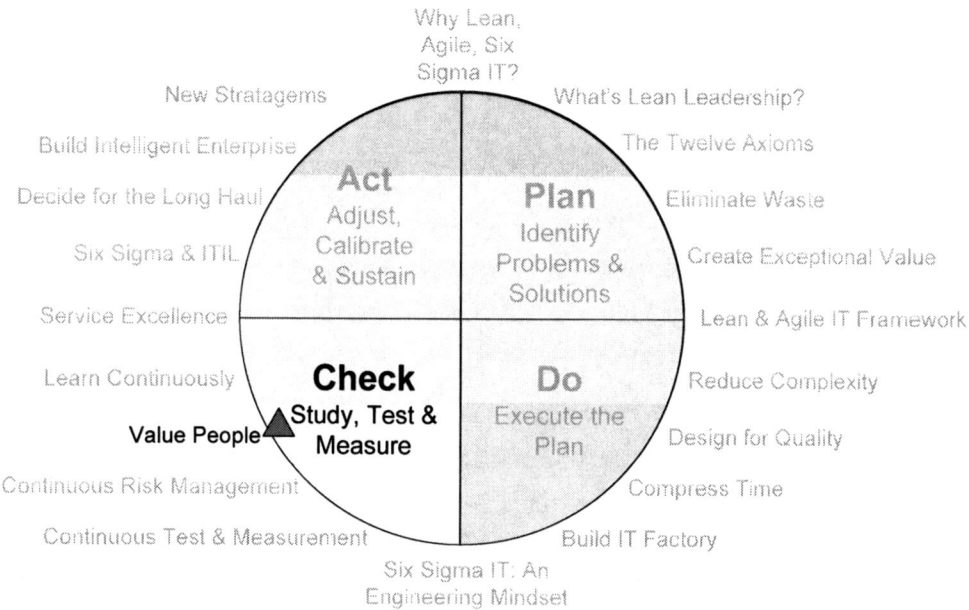

"I would rather be surrounded by smart people than have a huge budget. Smart people will get you there faster."

A former McKinsey Associate

Chapter 14: Value People

The Emergence of Knowledge worker

The world economy is now well entrenched in the information age. Leaving behind the agrarian and then the industrial age, today's employees are more educated and experienced than their predecessors. Knowledge workers, employees with high degree of education and experience are integral parts of innovation, driving business growth and competitiveness[66]. Doctors, Engineers, Lawyers, Teachers, Nurses, Financial Analysts and new specializations of almost every field are examples of knowledge workers who think for a living. Yet for these employees so far, many information technology systems fall short of ideal. They are either inundated with too much irrelevant information or famished with inadequate systems.

The Business Competitiveness Index released by the World Economic Forum was developed by Michael Porter, director of Harvard Business School's Institute for Strategy and Competitiveness. The index evaluates the health of a country's business environment. This evaluation considers factors such as health, primary education, infrastructure, market efficiency, business sophistication, innovation and technological readiness. The former McKinsey associate had a point when he stated his preference for intelligent people over huge budget. "Smart people get you to your destination", a CIO once confided in me. In his bestselling book, "Good to Great", author Jim Collins

---

[66] "Knowledge Workers, Key to Increasing Canadian Competitiveness", by Doug Cooper, Canadian Business Magazine, October 9-22, 2006, Volume 79, Issue 20

identified five factors common to the great companies that he selected in his study. One of those factors was hiring the right people. Other studies have shown a high correlation between success of startup companies and quality of staffing. These research results point to one stratagem: Hire the best people.

Business leaders recognize they play an important role in motivating, training and retention of best knowledge worker talent. The goal of management is to create the perfect orchestration of work performed by knowledge workers such that it produces intelligent business results. When it comes to managing knowledge workers, managers must:

- Empower knowledge workers to define their processes, metrics and measurements of success. They must determine the efficiency, quality, effectiveness and productivity methods for their teams.
- Develop approaches that make it possible for the knowledge workers to easily develop and capture innovative thoughts and to promote those thoughts in the firm.
- Provide knowledge workers with the frames of information and decision making context so they operate with the autonomy they need.
- Think of the corporation as a collection of knowledge workers, each operating as a micro-corporation that collectively form the large enterprise. Each individual knowledge worker can be a corporate unit responsible for profit-loss and achieving competitive success.

According to surveys, knowledge workers use technology for three to four hours per day in the following ways:

- Email: 45% - A basic tool for communication and collaboration
- Telephone and voice mail : 19%
- Other: 36% - Organize information, decide which information is most important and organize it; use lists and seek help when they need it; enter data or analyze information, create reports.

Information technology managers must seek to enhance experience and relevance of appropriate information to knowledge workers. Consider an electronic medical record application. The classic approach for most applications is to allow physicians to search online for a patient by name and find the patient status. This seemingly straight forward task becomes surmountable as physicians must stay aware of tens of patient cases every day. It would be too time consuming for a physician to check every patient's folder one at a time, to determine which patient requires immediate attention.

On the other hand consider a similar application, but one that's designed to display an alert page as soon as a physician logs in. The display shows which patients should be attended to immediately, based on previously defined business logic in that practice. Similarly, consider a publish and subscribe model. Physicians can subscribe to certain information, such as critical results about their patients. The application publishes such information to its subscribers as alerts and updates become available regardless of type of end devices. The users (Physicians in this example) in essence are able to tailor the business logic about alerts to their personal preference and practice requirements. Business logic is the set of practice, process and protocol rules that define how work should be performed by all levels and roles of the organization. It belongs to the province of workflow and process definition and software design. The secret recipe for successful IT organizations lies in clearly defining business logic for value steams in modular, component based manner. The elements of business logic depend on details of mental frames for the organization. In other words, how value streams are perceived and placed into operation. The mental frames define our perception of reality and the business formula for each value stream. By mental frame, we create a mental picture of business logic and workflow. Creating common mental pictures among knowledge workers leads to coordination, harmony and enterprise wide high performance.

Agile Organizational Structures

Lean IT managers must promote small, high performance teams. They can create larger organizational structures by connecting chains of smaller groups. The smallest teams are often "Teams-of-Two", two individuals are assigned as a team to a particular work. Teams-of-Two, I call them T2 for short, create strong bonds for communication, sharing knowledge, continuity of service and project advancement. As shown in Figure 14.1, each individual belongs to multiple interconnected teams thus forming a continuous chain. This organizational structure has a great amount of resilience, self-healing and load-sharing inherently built-in. In situations when business continuity is key or when individuals are absent, the organization can continue to function and heal itself as the chain of employees reconnects itself. The result is that support and services continue without interruption, namely "the ball does not get dropped."

In every "Team-of-Two", each IT staff is a back-up to another individual, so their projects overlap and they can assist each other when necessary. Teams-of-Two is an Agile organizational model that creates a flexible and resilient ring. The goal of a Lean organization is to think and behave as a single intelligent organism; to thrive and take advantage of business opportunities when they arise; to survive and adapt when faced with adverse events; ultimately to achieve great results.

Agile IT organizations form small interconnected teams. Among such organizational models, leaders are using frameworks such as: *"Teams of Two"*, *"Quality Circles"*, *"Responsibility Assignment Matrix"*, and *"Responsibility Interface Matrix"*. These small, virtual teams are able to adjust and respond to business challenges rapidly. Some effective IT organizations have implemented the best practices based on Microsoft Operating Framework (MOF), ITIL and ISO20000 standards. The ISO20000 is an IT service delivery and management standard completed in 2005 by the British Standards Institute (BSI). The ISO standard is a framework for managing service improvement projects, benchmarking best practices, alignment of IT services to firm's strategy and improved perception and proactive approach to IT issues. Again, all these organizational frameworks are based on virtual teams where IT staff takes on multiple roles, layered and interconnected to each other. These Agile organizational structures are cross functional and overlay on one another. They all co-exist and interconnect at the same time.

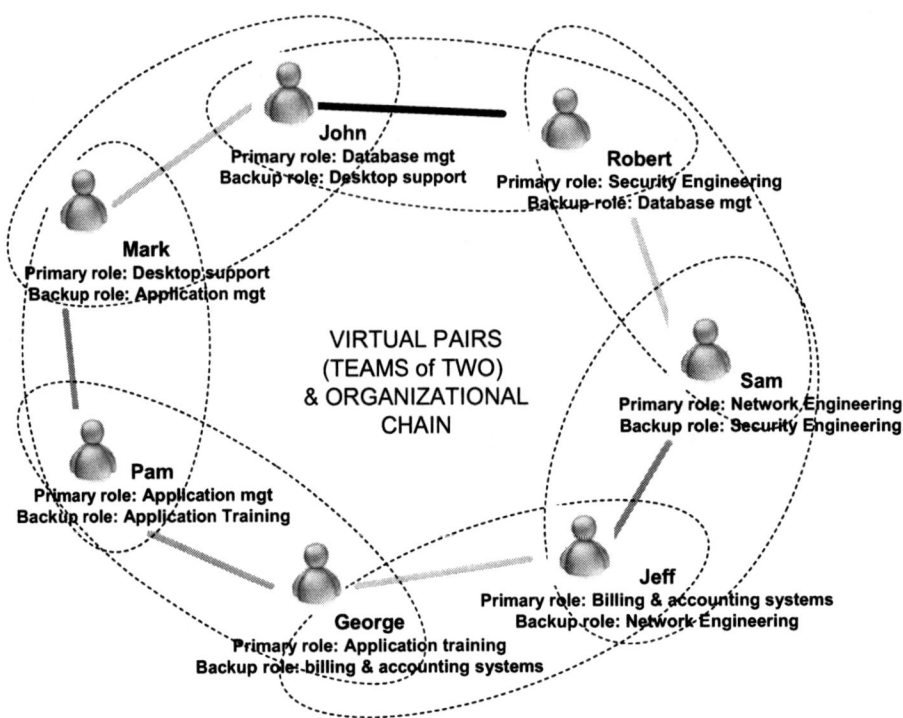

Fig 14.1 – Teams of Two Creates a Virtual Single Chain Organization

While almost every firm has a mission, vision and objective statement, rarely the staff's performance goals in IT organizations are aligned with the corporate objectives. At Indiana State University, a set of objectives called SMART were written to facilitate mapping IT activities to the University's mission as well as individual performance goals. SMART has simply set the standards for Specific, Measurable, Aggressive but Attainable, Rewarding and Time-bound frame of context for conducting activities in pursuit of University's objectives[67]. The success of this standard is due to linking the individual's activities and performance to corporate-wide objectives and metrics, deadlines for achieving objectives, and measurements.

Resource Mapping

With Lean IT, work leveling and resource leveling[68], two buzz words often cited by traditional IT managers to justify hiring more people or explain their longer than usual project timelines, take on a different meaning. Lean IT managers apply resource leveling in two dimensions: They recognize what resources are required as well as the complexity associated with different tasks and projects Some rank the complexity of work, for example on a scale of 1 to 10 (10 being most complex). They strive to build a mixed team of entry level and highly specialized "black belt" experts

---

[67] "Tying Benchmarks and Metrics to Evaluations and Organizational Performance: The role of Facilitating Activities", Susan Owen and Kenneth Janz, ACM-SIGUCCS, Nov 6-9, 2005
[68] "Heijunka" in Toyota Way: 14 Management Principles From the World's Greatest Manufacturer", Jeffrey Liker, McGraw Hill, 2004

with diverse scope and depth of expertise. This way they can match staff to the complexity of tasks as well as the resource demands of the project. They maintain a balanced mix of senior level IT professionals (who can handle level 5-10 complexity and junior IT staff who can handle 1-5 level successfully).

Another goal of Lean IT should be to create a single, cohesive intelligent system out of the divisions and departments in the organization. This is based on a well developed systems theory that looks at organizations as organisms. The interactions of a firm's various business units and departments must be coordinated and orchestrated to align with each other and the overall corporate objectives[69]. This demands a certain level of thinking in and among those units as cybernetic leadership. A corporation that can achieve this level of coordinated thinking is an intelligent organization.

The intelligent organizations are known for their organizational memory, ability to learn and retain knowledge, adaptability, problem solving, goal seeking, response to situations, and demands of the enterprise in a collectively intelligent way. In these organizations, by using information systems and intelligent workflows managers are able to create "*intellectual bonding*" between employees. Employee interactions are basically internal transactions. These transactions include exchange of ideas, knowledge, experience and learning. In information-based companies, higher value transactions between employees ultimately yield higher value for the company. Other principles of Agile IT Management promote incorporating flexibility into application and infrastructure architecture, and building IT solutions with maintainability in mind. Our goal is to create workflow harmony between IT staff and their work. Among IT design criteria, Lean and Agile IT managers emphasize maintainability and modularity to make future modifications easier.

Cases of Agile & Lean Success

Hygeia Corp. in Miami Lakes, Florida is a health service intermediary, providing medical cost containment solutions including claim arbitration services, out of network and foreign travel benefit plans. The company deployed a connectivity tool kit to enable on line claims services. The company saw online claims grow from zero to 40 percent in one year. The client portal allows customers to work with their data directly, thus reducing operating costs.

Mapping Tasks to Skills

The theory of constraints and Lean thinking teach us how to identify bottlenecks and remove them. They encourage us to even out the workload and create single flow of deliverables. During one of my consulting engagements, I had the opportunity to compile all of the IT tasks that an organization performed. Simply I interviewed the staff and gathered a list of their tasks. Then I assigned a "complexity level" to each task, indicating the level of skill and experience required to complete

---

[69] "Images of Organization", G. Morgan, Sage Publications, 1997

each task. For each task, I asked if there was a written procedure or defined process. Less than 50% of those tasks had any well defined processes or documentation.

Task	Complexity (1-10)	Process Defined & Documented?
System and data backup	2	Yes
Applications training	3	No
Security design	9	No
Network switch configuration	7	Yes
Configure workstations and laptops	4	No
Application testing	6	Yes
Change control and reviews	6	Yes
Interface development	9	No
Remote application monitoring	6	No
Benchmarking & Performance Improvement	7	No
Web application development	8	No

Fig 14.2 – Sample inventory of IT tasks and their complexity ranking

Not far into the study, I identified certain tasks that the staff generally struggled to complete. These were the relatively more complex and specialized tasks which the IT staff were not equipped and experienced to handle in that firm. Although it sounds basic, ironically the exercise was a huge success with the IT executives. It gave the IT managers a clear idea of what their staff is doing and which areas needed skill improvements. Overall, there were about 300 tasks ranging from simpler procedures like routine data backups to more complex such as creating custom decision support queries, interface development and security engineering. The table in Figure 14.2 is a small sample of the longer task list.

Once you have identified and catalogued all IT tasks, then look to document a process for each. This is the inventory of IT tasks at your organization. The next step is to perform a skills assessment of the IT staff. Skills assessment would rank the skill and experience of each individual on a scale of 1 to 5 (Five being the highest skill level). A ranking similar to the table in Figure 14.3 can be used to evaluate the overall skill set of the IT organization.

This assessment is not to be confused or used for employee evaluations. It merely highlights where in the IT organization skills are lacking and must be improved. Improvement can come either by training or by hiring new talent. We want to maintain a flexible mix of talent and expertise. Such flexibility can be achieved by hiring the subject matter experts either as employees or contractors.

Capability	Competency Level
Can design & develop the application or solution	5
Can fix the defect or remedy the problem	4
Can troubleshoot & identify root cause of problem	3
Can train others in the system & its components	2
Can use the tool or application as a super user	1

Fig 14.3 – IT Skill Levels

An IT staff at level-5 is the most skilled individual in that field. During my career in IT and development management, I require a staff with minimum skill level of 3-5 for all skill areas. It's surprising how many IT managers are content with staff at skill level-3. It's not surprising that such organizations have difficulty fixing their IT problems. When IT solutions take longer than expected to complete, many of the causes can be traced to inadequate skill level.

The point of this exercise is that we can ask: A) Which areas of IT do we need to hire technically stronger individuals, and B) Which tasks are complex and should be assigned to the more skilled professionals. As IT managers, we strive to maintain a balance of resources with capabilities ranging from level 3 to level 5. If an organization hires too many individuals at say level 4 but not enough at level 3 and level 5, it causes unnecessary inefficiencies and imbalance. The subsequent benefit of this exercise is that it eventually removes uneven technical workload. Thus streamlined operations and continuous flow of innovation become possible. So, we are not done by just having streamlined the workload but we must also level out the complexity by matching tasks to the right resources.

Stretch Goals

Recognizing people leads to significant boost of commitment to performance. On the other hand barriers such as inadequate tools or bureaucratic delays are a significant source of frustration for people to perform their tasks. The barriers to high performance are lack of recognition, lack of tools and unclear sense of purpose. Throughout the daily challenges, the IT staff needs to be recognized for their accomplishments. They need to be reminded of the purpose and importance of their work. Knowing the purpose, they why behind their work re-inforces the sense of commitment and accomplishment. Finally, IT managers must ensure that they sufficiently equip their staff with needed tools for their job.

Applied to Information Technology Management, Lean thinking urges us to establish a system of continuous improvement and value creation. Building this system is supported by forming matrix organizational structures. This is a departure from traditional hierarchical or functional organization structures. In a matrix organization, each IT manager wears multiple hats. Each hat carries a particular responsibility associated with different facets of Lean thinking, Agile and Six Sigma.

In a matrix organization, aside from being responsible for managing their staff, each manager is also be responsible for: "customer satisfaction" of a department or a value stream; maintaining a technical center of excellence; facilitating or performing key role in customers' continuous improvement initiatives; and other quality driven programs in the firm. Likewise, the IT staff has vertical and horizontal responsibilities.

You might think of this as overloading a manager, and that's intentional. In fact, that's the inherent principle of stretch- and results-oriented management in Lean thinking. Lean organizations set stretch goals and metrics for their work force. Stretch metrics are key to learning and improvement goals. They work by establishing targets on a monthly or quarterly basis and measuring management effectiveness towards achieving those metrics.

Summary

- Hire the best people and trust that they get they'll get the work done.
- Hire the subject matter experts for various disciplines in IT. Seek input and opinion from your people. Respect their opinions.
- Remind people of purpose, meaning and importance of their work. Recognize and reward performance and results, not just hard work.
- Set stretch goals. Define stretch goals clearly through planning.
- Give people tools, training and opportunities to excel. Coach & develop your people by continuous feedback.
- Set a career path for all individuals. Define clear lines of responsibility and accountability for their work.

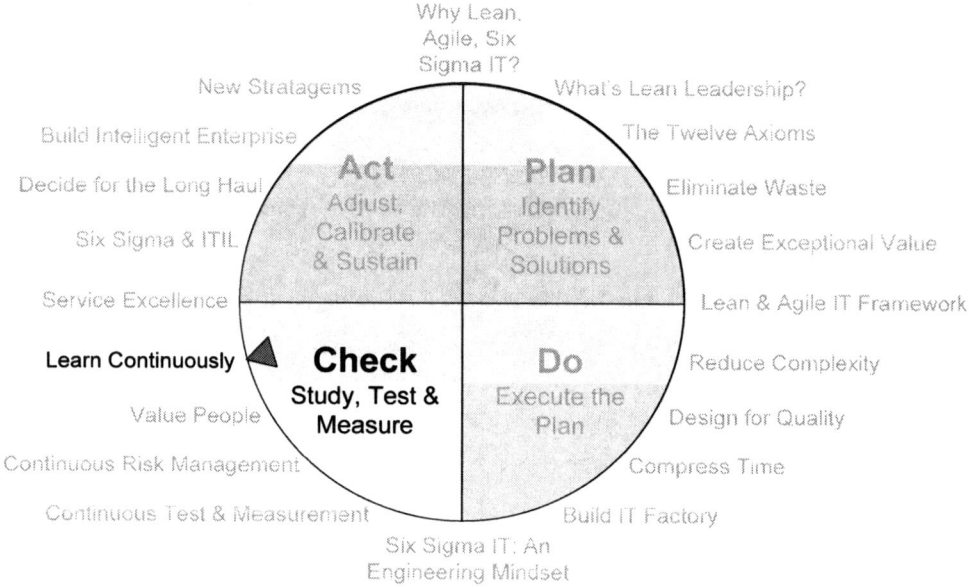

"Companies can learn how to resolve the learning dilemma. What it takes is to make the ways managers and employees reason about their behavior a focus of organizational learning and continuous improvement programs. Teaching people how to reason about their behavior in new and more effective ways breaks down the defenses that block learning."[70]

Chris Argyris

Chapter 15: Continuous Learning

Noise is the enemy of knowledge. Without accurate facts and information employees are left with ambiguity, incomplete picture of problems and deprived of the opportunity to learn. Learning based on noise is miss-information that leads to repeated failures. If you have implemented the Lean, Agile and Six Sigma axioms up to this point, then you have created a leading edge learning environment for your staff. The combination of quality and fact-based culture creates the natural feedback loops that increase learning. This is how it works: Listening to the voice of the customer and understanding customer's business is a learning opportunity; Performing Kaizen events and root cause analysis add to organizational knowledge that accumulate over time to deliver customer value; Focus on Six Sigma design and design reviews encourage critical thinking to solve technical and business problems. Furthermore, design activities enhance learning.

Feedback obtained from design reviews, workflow analysis and optimizations offer additional opportunities for learning. Finally, testing and measurements provide additional sources of knowledge. Together, Lean, Agile and Six Sigma principles inherently promote knowledge accumulation both by every individual and at organizational level. Our understanding about information, information seeking behavior has increased since the advent of PCs and the World Wide Web. Edward

---

[70] "Teaching Smart People How to Learn", Chris Argyris, Harvard Business Review, May-June 1991

Deming stated: "Learning is not compulsory. Neither is survival". In his book, "Looking for Information, A Survey of Research on Information Seeking, Needs and Behavior", author Donald Case writes that[71] "Information seeking is a dynamic process. It's interpretation depends on context. Information needs may arise quickly and dissipate as the need for other information rises." The nature of our questions may change during various points in a search. When a piece of information becomes available, added knowledge leads to yet another inquiry and problem to be answered. The accumulated information brings knowledge and understanding.

Effective knowledge creation works when information is created within the right context with the intent for another employee to use. Finally, people tend to seek information in a least effort basis. They'll use the applications that are information rich. Many such channels consist of the online social networks. Thus applications must be highly intuitive and personalizable for users to depend on for information. In addition, much of information gathering is about creativity, how people use information to solve problems and make decisions. For example, the way Google organizes results of searches is a valuable means to finding information. Google search website is regarded as the second most popular application on the world wide web, second to email. In 2002, two researchers, DeLone and Mclean proposed an "IS Success Model" based on several dimensions of Information Systems. In their paper published in 2003 entitled, "Measuring E-Commerce Effectiveness: A Conceptual Model", the authors offer a number of metrics for evaluating IT effectiveness. Among them, system usage, information value and user satisfaction were ranked highest. User satisfaction is regarded as a service indicator of success. It can be measured using periodic surveys of users. A survey typically includes questions on the three dimensions of product quality, knowledge of personnel and service quality. IT managers can plot the responses on a time series graph, like a Six Sigma Control Chart to track if the trend is up or down for each dimension over time. Lean IT managers determine which core competencies are needed in the supply-side of IT organization to meet the demand-side of IT (the firm's service and project requests). As a step to improve IT staff's knowledge and expertise in the core areas, they establish IT centers of excellence focused on those core areas.

In 2003, another research study called "The Invitation to Innovate" examined the user behavior toward participating in design learning. This study and similar research have shown that 45% of innovation comes from outside of the firm, mostly from customers. The parallel is true about IT, in that many IT customers are innovating and leading the way to advance IT. In some cases the customers demand IT organization to catch up and support those innovations. One stratagem is to use these customers as resource (the Supra-user concept). Generally, user innovation in most corporations have been underestimated and under appreciated by IT management. This has curbed the opportunity for IT to learn from its customers and to innovate collaboratively. Some of the best examples of cross learning and innovation are in the computer game industry (which promotes the idea of systemically empowering its customers to create), Wikipedia and Google. A number of game manufacturers offer a development toolkit to their customers so they can innovate and create variations of

---

[71] "Looking for Information. A Survey of Research on Information Seeking, Needs, and Behavior", Donald O. Case, Elsevier Ltd, Oxford, UK. 2007

their favorite games. Several companies have offered products and systems to create collaborative knowledgebase environments. Microsoft Sharepoint, Groove and Talisma's Knowledgebase offer the platforms to capture, distribute, orchestrate and develop knowledge content. Talisma has conducted a study which shows its Knowledgebase product has actually reduced email volume by 80% and call volume by 50% while increasing search accuracy of knowledge by up to 90%.

Learning and Applying Knowledge

Experience and data are the basis of knowledge when retained in the correct context. In a white paper entitled "Purpose-driven Storage", authors encourage considering a life cycle view of information[72]. The focus is on "what is the purpose of each data at different points in the life cycle?" Namely, the lifecycle of information matches its purpose. This principle includes considerations for how data is managed, its performance, longevity, access and retention. Data is to be classified by its purpose. Some classifications include: Critical, Vital, Sensitive and Required. Other classifications categorize data into realtime, business intelligence, knowledge and archive depending on the access and use of the data. A study performed at a medical center revealed that more than 75% of access to patient imaging data occurred within the first 2 weeks of their visit to the medical center. Ninety percent of access to patient records occurred within 2 years of the patient's last visit. A study done at University of California in Berkeley concluded that the probability that a user will need to re-access an email message falls to less than 50 percent after three days, 25 percent after two weeks and less than five percent after 60 days[73]. Knowledge workers are most interested in the present real time information so they can apply it to create new knowledge.

> **Cases in Enterprise Learning & Innovation**
>
> Clarian Health Partners in Indianapolis implemented a physician order entry system and intelligent alerting system that notifies doctors when they deviate from industry-defined best practices. Centralized data repository and automated algorithms were developed to respond to new donor transplant law. It created a Department of Business Innovations to serve as internal consultants to the rest of the company. Products, such as one by Nuance Corporation called Decision Support, score the appropriateness of the physicians' orders to lab or Radiology. Using the rule-based system, the application evaluates the appropriateness of the physician order against medical conditions and necessity by providing a score to the physician. Overtime, physicians learn which radiology exams are more suitable for a given medical condition and avoid ordering unnecessary exams. One hospital was able to substantially reduce medical costs and repeated radiation of patients by using this application.

---

[72] "Storage De-Mystified: Purpose-Driven Storage Management Solutions for Mainframes", Computer Associates, June 2003

[73] "Purpose-driven Storage", White paper by Storage Technology Corp, Louisville, CO, 2004.

Beyond Value: IT Ladder of Purpose

I often ask users and IT mangers "what is the purpose of IT in their organization". The answers vary quite a bit. In institutions where the value of IT is less palpable, the answers typically reference PCs and names of applications. For example, I hear the role of IT is to manage the document imaging, or general ledger, MRP, electronic medical record or electronic banking applications depending on the industry that the firm belongs to. In firms where the value of IT is widely recognized, respondents give descriptions like: "The purpose of IT is to support our mission", or "IT is the machinery that runs the business" or as another manager put it, "IT is the backbone of our company".

Let's face it, in some institutions replacing paper has unfortunately become the primary purpose for information systems. If IT's purpose stopped there, that would be grossly unfortunate and a big waste of opportunity. Not surprisingly, only few IT managers ponder about the strategic intent or higher order purpose of IT for their institution. In fact a minority of IT organizations are truly capable of deploying IT solutions that achieve drastically improved benefits. In many institutions, IT applications have become mere replacements for pad and paper. Often forms, documents, notes, work orders and reports are first written on paper, later scanned into an application, later printed again.

In some institutions, users print, then scan and then re-print similar pieces of information multiple times throughout the value stream. The immediate observation from such sites is that electronic applications are not integrated to deliver a single-flow process across various functional units. The question that comes to mind is: "What was the initial purpose for launching these applications?" What workflow design led to these disjointed, islands of information that are not integrated across the value stream and workflow continuum? Again, such questions bring us to the primary question of purpose. What is the purpose of IT in your organization?

The goal of this exercise is gaining insight and focused direction for learning and acquiring organizational knowledge.

Purpose-Driven Management and Pursuit of Meaning

In the late 1930's, a psychologist by the name of Viktor Frankl wrote a manuscript called "Man's Search for Meaning", which later became known as the Third School of Viennese Psychiatry. Like many Jews in Europe, he was incarcerated in Nazi concentration camps during WWII. While captive in Auschwitz, he saw many of his compatriots perish; some, from brutal conditions and others from disease, hunger or illness. To Dr. Frankl, the only item of value was his manuscript which he hoped to publish someday. In every moment of captivity, his attention was focused on preserving the manuscript.

During captivity, many of his friends gave up hope and perished. But despite the low odds of survival, Dr. Frankl lived to publish his manuscript. The desire to preserve the manuscript gave him the meaning and purpose to live. Dr. Frankl is the father of Logo-therapy, which focuses on the meaning of human existence as well as man's search for such ...

... a meaning. He chose Logo from the Greek word Logos which denotes meaning. Dr. Frankl writes: "By declaring that man is responsible and must actualize the potential meaning of his life, I wish to stress that the true meaning of life is to be discovered in the world rather than within man or his own psyche, as though it were a closed system".

Purpose driven leaders know how to take a challenge and convert it in to opportunity. There are many styles of leadership out there, but the purpose driven leaders ask "what drives you?" They are team oriented, always have a plan, do their homework and come prepared. They understand the underlying purpose of IT and have formed a ladder of purpose to climb.

An example of such Ladder of Purpose is developed for a healthcare is shown on the following page. As we climb up the ladder of purpose, we discover more powerful paradigms that go beyond application features, function and benefits. They cut across the entire enterprise, delivering more powerful transformations of the corporate value streams.

With taking each step up, higher levels of IT power are realized. Notice the rising steps of purpose and corresponding information technology adaptation in the diagram; starting from replacing paper, then to enhance personal productivity, foster communication, workflow orchestration, then on to foster collaboration, decision support and finally computer aided medicine.

At each step, the benefits that can be achieved are also listed. At the lowest step, paperless and digital workflows reduce waste and save employee time. At the highest step, better diagnosis accuracy, timely patient treatment and error prevention are achievable benefits. Each organization is likely to identify a different ladder of purpose unique to its mission and strategy.

> **Stratagem:** Develop the IT ladder of purpose for your organization. Identify the steps and a roadmap to reach the highest step.

With the traditional IT approach, CIO might be concerned with the nuts and bolts of technology, projects and customer demands. She might ask questions like "What storage options are available for our data?" In contrast, using the Ladder of Purpose as a guide, the CIO would ask "What have we done to improve communication? Or "what is needed to increase personal productivity of our users?" or "What can IT do to prevent medical errors?"

As another example of higher IT purpose, a large firm commissioned its CIO to coalesce its many IT divisions into a unified, coordinated intelligent organization. Intelligent organizations are known for their adaptability, organizational memory, learning and retaining knowledge, problem solving, being goal-driven, responsive to market or competitive situations collectively and intelligently. To be Lean and Agile, most of the organizational structures that we have created are virtual, role-based and flexible.

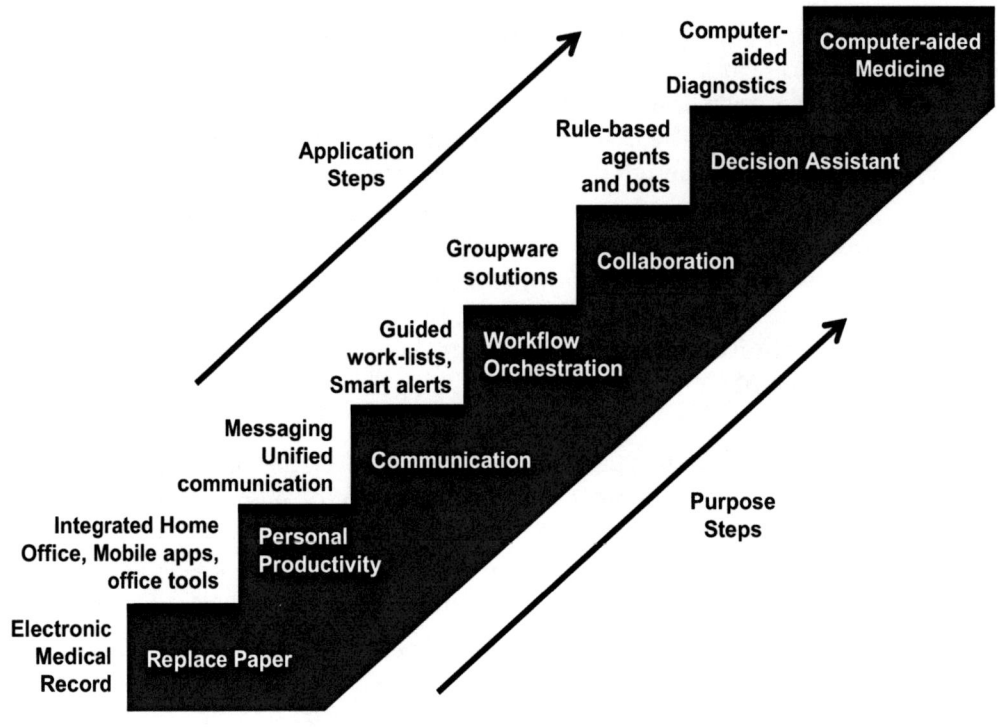

Fig 15.1 – Ladder of IT purpose

Summary: Knowledge as purpose

- Learn about customer workflows and vendor products better than anyone.
- Maintain a knowledge base of technology and products that you manage.
- Perform root cause analysis to find the causes of defects. Learn and apply new knowledge to prevent defects.
- Identify which core competencies are needed for IT success.
- Emphasize deep knowledge and expertise in core competency areas.
- Develop the IT Ladder of Purpose for your organization. Promote and socialize the highest purpose of IT in your organization.
- Establish IT Centers of Excellence to focus on the enhancing expertise and knowledge level of the IT staff in the needed core capabilities.

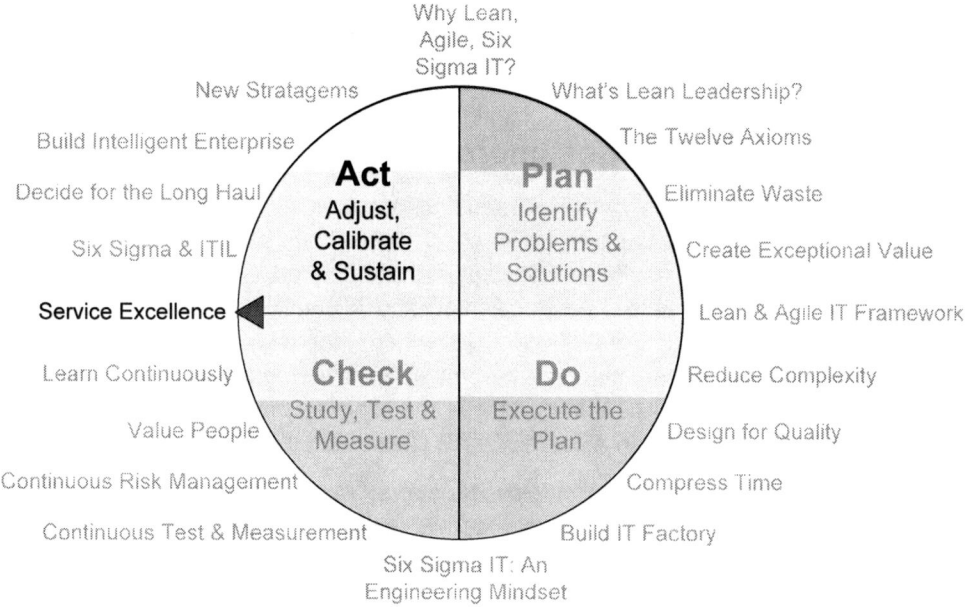

"Be a yardstick of quality. Some people aren't used to an environment where excellence is expected."

Steve Jobs

Chapter 16. Service Excellence

Service Delivery

The hallmark of a Lean IT organization is the high marks it receives for service. Lean IT organizations are passionate about customer satisfaction. They strive to continuously gauge customer satisfaction levels, listen to suggestions, immediately address issues and focus on service excellence. To achieve service excellence, service delivery must follow systemic and repeatable processes. Like every other IT activity, service delivery encompasses processes. Service levels can be measured, calibrated and improved as customer preferences for service change over time.

> **Stratagem:** Know what services your customers prefer and expect from your IT staff. Determine what are the influence factors that shape your customer's opinion about service? What are the customer's basic, performance and unspoken requirements?

The Toyota Production System advocates visibility of work and workers' accomplishments. In view of customer satisfaction, it should be easy to link the customer experience with the IT staff who delivers that service. Visibility has other palpable benefits.

When staff accomplishments are visible, they are more likely to take pride in their work and more likely to feel accountable. The challenge for the IT manager is to clearly assign roles and domains of responsibility to each IT staff. Clear lines of responsibility for the IT staff will make a marked improvement in customer satisfaction. This is supported by the notion that people are motivated by recognition on one hand and pride in their work on the other.

From Surveys to Service Improvement

Based on periodic customer satisfaction surveys, IT managers are able to compute an IT satisfaction index for each of the various areas of service and track them over time. Survey results can be captured and ranked in a Kaizen table as shown in Figure 16.1. For example, at a large international bank, user surveys showed that they expect faster reply from IT services when they call for help. Users ranked 'intermittent system downtimes' as the most annoying aspect of IT. The ranking measured two factors: A) how important is the topic to the user and, B) how the IT organization is doing, both on a scale of 1-10 (Ten being the highest).

The table in Figure 16.1 shows the survey results tabulated by the IT service manager. The Kaizen table reveals some important information about what is happening with this IT organization's services and what the customers are asking for.

We're able to determine which services need to be improved by comparing the Kaizen score. Kaizen score shows which service factors need the biggest and most immediate improvements. To obtain the Kaizen score, we survey the customers to rank the importance of service factors between 1 to 10 (10 is the highest). We then ask customers to rate how well IT is meeting their expectations in each of those service factors using a score between 1 to 10.

Column A lists 9 areas of service delivery that customers are concerned about. The customer can add other service factors if they are not listed on the survey. Column B shows how a particular IT service is rated. Column C shows the ranked importance of service factors. Column D shows the gap, or service deficiency between perfection (a perfect score of 10) and the rating by the customer. The deficiency value in Column D is computed by subtracting the rating, in column C from the perfect score of 10. As the survey results are tabulated we find that service factors one and two are most critical (they have the highest priority scores of 40 and 28). Customers in this survey value application support and application uptime the most (since they are rated 8 out of 10 points). The next most important service factors are network uptime and decision support reports (rated at 7 out of 10 points).

Given this survey result, which service factor needs the most attention? The answer is in column E. The value in column E is computed by multiplying relative importance (column D) by the deficiency, or gap value (column C). The result is a Kaizen priority score. Looking at this particular survey result, the service factors with highest Kaizen scores are prime candidates for immediate improvement. As the table indicates, focusing on areas 1, and 2, and 4 will have the biggest payback.

After this survey, specific Kaizen events were conducted to address the specific service problems. The Kaizen meetings prioritized and changed the service focus to what customers valued. It also resulted in some practical metrics.

Customer Survey Results* - Continuous Service Improvement Model:					
1) Which IT Services are important to you?					
2) How are we doing on each service factor?					
No.	(A) Service Factors	(B) Customer Satisfaction Level	(C) Importance to Customer	(D) Gap (current vs. Perfect)	(E) Kaizen Priority Score**
1	Response time from Service Desk	5	8	5	40 ←
2	Speed to resolve a service request	6	7	4	28 ←
3	Application uptime	8	10	2	20
4	Network uptime	7	9	3	27 ←
5	Decision Support Reports	7	3	3	9
6	Application support	8	6	2	12
7	Microsoft Office/desktop support	6	5	4	20
8	General service requests	6	4	4	16
9	New feature releases	6	2	4	8

* On a Scale of 1-10 (10 is high).

** The service factors with higher Kaizen scores need improvement

Fig 16.1 – An Example of Customer Satisfaction Rating Using Kaizen Score Table

Some of the metrics and indices included: overall customer satisfaction index, service desk effectiveness, application availability, overall application response time, desktop support efficiency, and training satisfaction. For example, an index to measure the Help Desk effectiveness as a function of response-time and speed-to-resolve relative to SLA for a service request can be computed as:

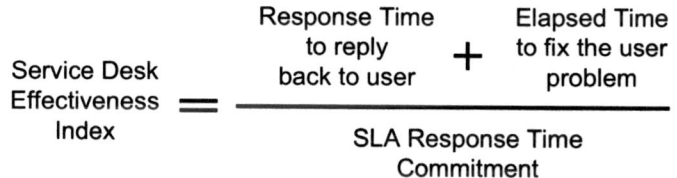

Over time such indices can be used for trending. In large IT organizations, quality emphasis on certain service areas will undoubtedly require a team approach. To focus on service excellence, first the core functions and capabilities that support the organization's workflows must be identified. Working on non-value adding tasks is a distraction and a cost to quality. They're costly because they waste resources which could be working on customer valued work. Focusing on tasks that serve the customer can directly be linked to higher perceived value and customer satisfaction.

IT Circles of Excellence (ICE)

Lean IT managers identify the core capabilities needed in their organization and plan to enhance those capabilities through a variety of methods. Some Lean IT managers have recruited outside consultants to transfer knowledge to their staff. Other Lean IT organizations have created Information Technology Quality Circles, and IT

Circles of Excellence (ICE) as one Lean organization calls them. Each ICE team focuses on a specific core capability.

The mission of ICE is to focus and encourage developing best practices and deep learning in a specific technology or technical area of expertise. Membership in an ICE team is voluntary and the members strive to become gurus or subject matter experts in different areas. The ICE members are encouraged to "dive deep & specialize" into a particular area of technical expertise that supports a core IT capability. The ICE members have a common goal: to enhance their knowledge and skills to the level of becoming black belt experts in their area of focus. The particular areas of focus are chosen based on their linkage to organization's strategy and IT needs.

For example, one large medical center assessed the technical expertise of its IT organization and identified core competencies and capability areas that were needed to improve. When they completed their internal skill assessment, it became clear that while skill levels were adequate for the current time, the IT staff were weak in the areas demanded by the upcoming IT initiatives. The IT organization formed new ICE centers of excellence to improve the weaker knowledge areas. To bolster their core competency areas, IT management formed the following ICE centers:

- SOA Application architectures
- Process re-engineering
- Integration & interface development
- Security engineering

By the time this book is going to print, their list might have changed or added other areas. That's to be expected from a Lean and Agile IT organization. But the methodology and principles behind it remain the same as listed in a 4-step plan below:

1. Identify expertise areas needed to meet current and future demand. Future demands are based on business strategies, stratagems, initiatives and technology needs. These are the essential core competencies required.
2. Conduct skills assessment. Rate the IT staff's skill levels in the required core and non-care capability areas including technical, analytical, business and management.
3. Perform gap analysis to identify which skill areas are deficient which require deep knowledge and expertise
4. Create centers of emphasis (through centers of excellence or quality circles) for each deficient area

In each IT Circle of Excellence, one or several individuals commit to deep learning of their focus area. Their goal is to enhance their know-how to level-5, the highest level. Some organizations have coined titles for these subject matter experts such as "advisers", "gurus" and "black belts". Whatever the title, the role of these highly skilled IT professionals is to provide the organization with high expertise.

> **IT Circles of Excellence – A Success Story**
>
> Anthem Blue Cross Blue Shields is a $16.8 billion healthcare network company with 20,000 employees. The company created IT centers of excellence for key technologies, including e-business, contact centers and document management solutions. Anthem was able to build a new service model for 72,000 customer accounts in less than 90 days. The key to its IT success was rapid development processes and focus on centers of excellence.

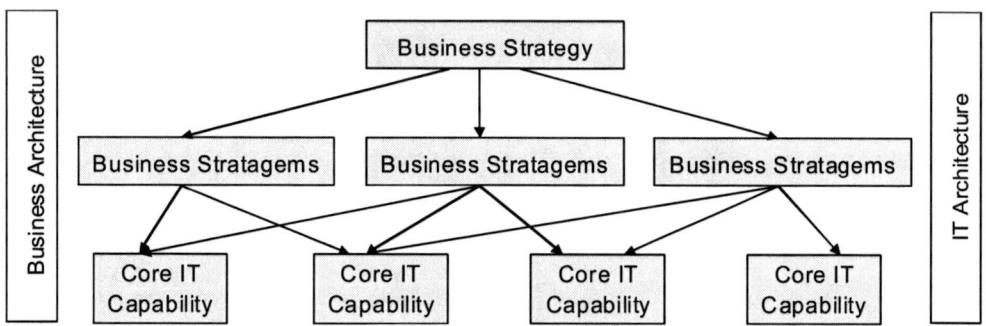

Fig 16.2 – Linking Business Strategy to Core IT Capability Required By the Firm

Agile Service Portfolio: Gold, Silver or Bronze?

Service levels are typically balanced by the organization's expectations from IT and willingness to invest in Information technology. The goal of Lean IT is to deliver the maximum benefits for an IT investment. However, details of exactly what will be provided are needed to be established with C-level executives in advance. Some organizations are content with minimum investment. But, others want full services and are willing to pay for it. In a recent study, IT managers generally perceived three levels of service offering to their customer executives. These three levels start from Bronze (basic support) to Silver (comprehensive support) and to Gold (premium support). The next two diagrams in Fig. 16.3 illustrate taxonomy of IT services consisting of 12 distinct IT service disciplines. The diagrams show the levels of service in a service portfolio from basic to premium for each of the 12 areas. The 12 areas in the service portfolio are: Server Management, Network Management, Security Management, Storage Management, Applications Management, Technology Management and Quality Assurance, Interface and integration, Desktop support, Standards, Business Intelligence, Program management and Professional Services. You can add or remove other service areas for your firm's service portfolio.

What is included in each level of service varies across the industry and is negotiable between IT management and customer executive management or the IT governance body. Lean IT managers negotiate the service levels and specific services included in each level. The executive customers appreciate having the option to choose which services they want and the costs to deliver those services. Consequently, they are more likely to budget for those levels of services accordingly. Another advantage of creating a service portfolio is to use it as a tool to explain what IT accomplishes and what the customer can expect for each level of investment in IT.

Service Gaps – Service Levels vs. Customer Expectations (1)

	Server Management	Network Management	Security Management	Storage Management	Applications Management	Technology Management Quality Assurance
Gold Service Level	Virtualization		Security architecture		Useability factors	
	Capacity Planning	Traffic optimization	Spam control Virus control	Central, enterprise storage	Enhancement requests	Design for Six Sigma
	Performance tuning	Traffic monitoring	DMZ management	Central backup	Performance tuning	Test reports
Silver Service Level	Repairs	Switch & router updates	Device security management	Capacity planning	Data Design	Test lab
	Remote Monitoring	Wireless Upgrades	Intrusion detection & prevention	Monitoring	Application testing	Development lab & environment
	Patching	Network design		Upgrades		
				Repairs	Application Customization	
Bronze Service Level	Disaster Recovery	Wireless support	Alert response	Disaster recovery	Training	Testing services
	Power & Cooling; Facility Planning	Switch & router configurations	Security policy	Business Continuity	Performance monitoring	Design reviews
			Security design	Backups	Upgrades	Code walkthrough
	Upgrades	Aggregation & device cabling	Firewall configurations	Tape management	Patches	Program inspections

Fig 16.3 – Service Portfolio (part I)

Service Gaps – Service Levels vs. Customer Expectations (2)

	Interface Integration	Desktop Support	Standards Methods & Tools	Business Intelligence	Program Office	Professional Services
Gold Service Level	Technology integration	Office software support				Customized services
	Interface monitoring		Software tools	Real time reports	Outsourcing management	Consulting services
Silver Service Level	Interface design	Laptops, Handhelds	Policy, procedures, & communication	Custom reports	Vendor management	Product & technology evaluations
		Email & Calendar Support	Integration standards	Forecasting models	Project management tools	Technology management Consulting
	Interface development	Printers		Scenario analysis	Purchasing	
Bronze Service Level	Systems integration	Replacements	Technology Acquisition	Monthly business reports	Contract management	Advanced application training
	Integrated testing	Repairs	Testing & QA standards	Weekly business reports	Project management	Help desk / Service desk
	Dataflow design	Patches				
		Troubleshoot	Architecture & design standards	Quarterly business reports	Project portfolio management	General application services

Fig 16.3 – Service Portfolio (part II)

User Satisfaction Drivers

How does customer satisfaction happen? Lean IT managers have found some simple recipes that pay off. At the top of the list are two simple directions: listen to the customer's wants and become a virtual member of their organization. Being fast and responsive to customer requests are key drivers of customer satisfaction. The Lean IT organization strives to exceed customer's expectations. In the eyes of Six Sigma, in order to reach "perfection", IT staff anticipates customer's needs and eliminate the sources of bugs or problems that cause issues for users, thereby eradicating the root causes that produce user trouble tickets. Less trouble tickets man less fire fighting and more resources available to work in the customer valued projects.

Through conducting Kaizen events we can gather a great deal of insight from users about their preferences and satisfaction drivers. The fishbone analysis (Dr. Ishikawa's method) and Kano's model are handy tools to determine the satisfaction drivers and dissatisfiers. We've looked at similar techniques in previous chapters to determine customer value drivers.

To give customer satisfaction the highest attention it deserves, some CIOs regard themselves as the customer advocate, ultimately responsible for customer satisfaction. Similarly in some Lean organizations, aside from their functional duties, IT managers assume customer advocate responsibility. They maintain ongoing business relationship with their key customers, typically the company's division managers. Similarly, the IT value stream managers accept the responsibility for the overall user satisfaction for the value stream.

> **Stratagem:** Win customers' loyalty through customer satisfaction. Assign each IT manager to be responsible for satisfaction of a division manager, or a strategic value stream in your organization.

User satisfaction is the result of meeting and exceeding user expectations. At one large firm, aside from many venues for users to send requests by e-forms, email or phone, the IT team created an "IT Concierge Board". The concierge board was simply a portal where users could send their service requests, suggestions, wishes and wants from IT, freely. The IT staff regularly compiled these requests into a Service Request tracking database, then assigned a team member to each request and reviewed their progress regularly with the user.

If you ask CIOs about their Service Level Agreements (SLA) with customers, the answer reveals a lot about the maturity and sophistication of the IT organization. Some organizations do not have an SLA. The majority have a tiered SLA that defines the response time corresponding to the urgency and criticality of the problem. Those with best SLA performance have a tier with 30 minutes resolution time for critical tickets.

The next tiers target 2 hours for urgent tickets, and 4 hours for most other tickets. Some of the best response times are claimed by Motorola. Motorola's IT organizations have an average trouble ticket resolution time of 2 hours for all Help Desk tickets.

Six Sigma IT highlights two fine points about SLAs: First, that committing to an N-minute response time, means committing to a N/2 minute target response time. This is due to the bell curve effect. In order to achieve the SLA commitment, more than 99.9999% of incidents have to be within N minutes. As a result the bell curve median would have to be N/2 minutes. For example, let's consider Motorola's 2-hour problem resolution time. In order for Motorola IT group to meet a 2-hour resolution time consistently, the target resolution time for the service team must be 1-hour. This is simply illustrated using the standard bell curve.

The second point is that for users in mission critical and emergent situations a 2-hour SLA would seem like eternity. A real example of an emergent trouble ticket is when a physician urgently needs to resolve an IT issue in the midst of a surgical procedure or treating a patient. This illustrates a crisis even for a single user when a mission critical application fails. While SLA's are a necessary contract between customer and IT organization, they are insufficient for these situations. Hence, the other rule of service excellence is access: give customers with emergent problems quick access to get IT help when users find themselves in such crisis situations.

In many conventional IT organizations, SLAs are often used as alibis to defend IT's poor performance. In Lean IT organizations, SLAs are just the starting point, the minimum performance expectation. They're additional tools for continuous service improvement, as IT staff strives to exceed service targets. The internal performance targets on SLAs must be 2 times better than the specified targets in the contract.

Customer Relationship Management

Most IT organizations recognize the significant role of "super users", the more knowledgeable individuals who can train and aid other users with computer applications. Their role is essential to support IT initiatives and new application releases. Super users strengthen IT's value proposition and relationship with end users. But there is another group of users who are key to user community satisfaction. These are the luminary and visionary users. They often have novel ideas about applications of Information Technology in the workplace. It's not uncommon for these users to demand new computer applications and stretch the conventional boundaries of IT.

Sometimes, such users develop applications for their personal or departmental use. I've named these users the "Supra-Users". Supra-users often track the latest technologies and trends in their line of work. They share best practices, experience and ideas with their counterparts in other companies. They are the likely leaders in their field. At workplace, supra-users are found among early technology adopters, visionary users and managers. Supra-users are an asset to the Lean IT organization. Their satisfaction with IT management is imperative, their opinions consequential. Their input and support guides the IT organization towards solutions which inevitably produce higher customer satisfaction levels.

Stratagem: Identify supra-users in your organization. Have regular meetings and focus group studies with them. Become engaged in their work. Include them in IT planning and problem solving.

Lean IT managers engage the IT staff in the enterprise work activity in such a way that IT becomes a seamless, ubiquitous piece of everyone's work; the lines simply blur between business and information systems. In order to stay focused, the IT staff is encouraged to concentrate on just three types of activities for their customers: Service delivery, Innovation, and Consulting. The IT staff is discouraged from engaging in non-value adding activities. Non-core and non-value adding functions are to be eliminated or outsourced to other organizations[74].

We've discussed customer service and innovation so far. But what does internal consulting role for IT staff mean? This is one of the most overlooked benefits of IT. The IT staff provides consulting to internal customers in a variety of ways. Consulting might be in the form of technology evaluations, technical advice, training, decision support and analytics. As consultants, Information Technology staff brings a myriad of tools and solutions to solve their customers' problems. In instances where internal consulting resources are not available, the IT staff engages with outside consultants to help with specific customer needs, but maintain supervision of the contractor's deliverables. Agile IT organizations, keep a portfolio of such contractors and pre-arranged contracts so they can quickly acquire their skills when needed.

These 3 activities reinforce each other in compounding ways. Many of the innovative products and services that one particular Lean IT team developed were simply as a result of their routine, daily work to serve users. The willingness to accept and resolve a wide range of service requests resulted in gaining new knowledge, thus made a stronger, more capable team. When users ask for advice regarding a new technology or request an application to streamline their work, that's an opportunity for the IT staff to learn and acquire new knowledge. The IT team responds by researching new technologies (consulting role), or creating a software tool (innovating role). Taking on these tasks helps the IT staff accumulate more skill, knowledge, and in turn become more effective over the long haul.

The salient point about Lean IT management is its long term view of how IT improves through serving its customer. It is that many of the value-adding services and applications which users enjoy in such enterprises are as a result of routine customer service, not through large-scale, expensive, monolithic IT projects.

Lean and Agile IT teams are opportunistic in the sense that they reuse their solutions or re-factor legacy components to benefit and enable the entire enterprise to generate value. Once they complete a service request for a user, if that solution has potential to help the entire organization, they craft their solution into a service from which the entire firm can benefit. For example, when a Lean IT organization created a telemedicine solution for the cardiology department, it offered instances of the same solution to other clinical departments such as radiology, surgery and oncology clinics. They were essentially transforming results of individual service requests into enterprise wide solutions at very low implementation and operational costs. The reverse is also value-generating: in order to deliver the maximum benefit to users, a Lean IT organization takes a generic application and applies personalization and customization configurations to adapt the application to individual workflows. An example for this

---

[74] "Smart-Sourcing for Competitive Advantage", Peter Ghavami and Paul Jackson, Sourcing Magazine, November 1996.

approach is that a Lean IT group developed a bolt-on application that allowed department managers to create custom reports for their departments.

The telling characteristics of Lean IT management are exactly that: IT managers work side-by-side with their clients (user community), often attending their planning meetings or joining other managers as a team member on their projects; The IT services are woven seamlessly into the fabric of the organization; IT managers anticipate the needs of the organization and users; and have prepared components of solutions in advance.

Customer Service: IT as a Utility

In the early late 1970's, IBM promoted a utility model for Information Systems. It envisioned information systems to be as dependable and indispensable as a utility, such as water or electricity. In the late 1980's the move towards open standards made client-server architectures possible. In the 1990's a new frame of thinking began to spread in the industry. With the advent of the internet and web applications, Service Oriented Architectures (SOA) and Software as a Service (SaaS) started to gain popularity as new IT models.

No matter how IT organizations offer services, through new applications, by re-factoring legacy applications, or through Application Service Provider (ASP), what users ultimately care about is service, not the brand or type of technology. They simply want ubiquitous, seamless services. Surveys show that, users care about which IT services are available and for quality of those services. As discussed earlier, transforming applications into services represents the most value for the least cost because they directly affect user satisfaction.

> **Stratagem:** In pursuit of IT perfection must we stress adherence to standards and process consistency. Processes are to be respected and upheld by the IT staff as a creed.

> **Stratagem:** Every IT work must have a written process. Document, catalogue and number your processes. Do not confuse processes with policies. Policies are about the institution. Processes are about how and what people are supposed to do.

Service Excellence

Our quest for service excellence follows a few simple rules. One of those rules is to anticipate customer's needs and prepare to respond in advance. Anticipating customer's needs are possible when we learn their business and partner to meet their objectives. Timely and clear communication by service staff is imperative. Simple, short notifications are critical to informing and intellectual bonding in a Lean IT organization. Notifications are major elements of change management, team building and control. I've adopted a simple communication paradigm that has proven effective for my staff.

My staff follows a three step technique whenever they plan to change a system or work on a task:

1. Tell what you intend to do (Inform peers, users and stakeholders of your intent)
2. Do it (perform the task)
3. Tell what you did (provide a report of what was done. Notify interested parties)

This simple communication rule notifies the service team members, customers and other stakeholders of what is going to happen and what was accomplished. It helps me be aware what they are working on. If they are working on a non-value adding task, I can intervene and adjust their work plan.

Successful service organizations offer a wide spectrum of services. On one end of the spectrum they offer the necessary tools for self-service. On the other end of the spectrum, they offer full services for which they can charge a premium. The options are available to customers. The customer has the option to choose and pay accordingly for their choice of services.

Stratagem: Offer service options to your customers. Let the customer choose which level of services they want. Offer tiered pricing for your services accordingly.

Summary

- Your internal service level targets must be 2X better than the SLA terms signed in the contract
- Catalog services that the organization offers. Measure customer satisfaction on each area of the service portfolio.
- Perform Kaizen score of service factors for your organization. Improve specific service factors through Plan-Do-Check-Act process.

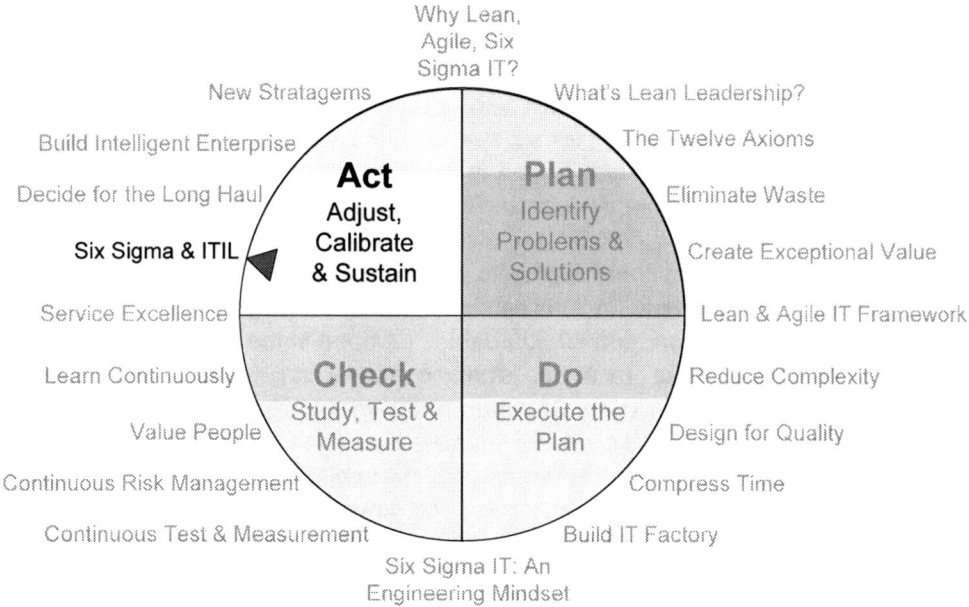

"We have to grasp not only the 'know-how' but also 'know-why', if we want to master the Toyota Production System."

Shigeo Shingo

"The quality of a leader is reflected in the standards they set for themselves.."

Ray Kroc

Chapter 17: Six Sigma IT and ITIL

Six Sigma offers a structured problem solving methodology. It is ideal for getting quality results and improving repetitive processes. Six Sigma was introduced in the 1980's by engineers at Motorola. The notion behind Six Sigma is that there is a cost to poor quality, because poor quality causes lost market share, sales and profitability. The primary goal of Six Sigma is to improve customer satisfaction by reducing defects and undesirable side effects caused by a product or process.

On the other hand, ITIL (IT Information Library) offers a comprehensive, consistent and coherent set of best practices for IT Service Management processes. It promotes quality approach to achieving business effectiveness and efficiency in the use of information systems. The authors of IT Infrastructure Library have tried to introduce the "engineering" approach, practices and thinking to the IT world. IT service providers are continually asked to deliver and support IT services that are appropriate to the business requirements and objectives of the organization. This must be done while maintaining high quality, timeliness and reducing costs.

In many ways, Six Sigma and ITIL complement each other. Six Sigma embraces high precision, small deviation and tight tolerances. ITIL provides the framework that can help achieve Six Sigma in IT management.

Return to Six Sigma IT Management

Six Sigma simply means a measure of quality that strives for near perfection. Six Sigma is a data driven approach and methodology for eliminating defects. A Six Sigma process implies reaching for six standard deviations between the mean and the nearest specification limit. Each Sigma is a statistical term that measures how far a given process deviates from perfection. Statistically, Six sigma means the number of errors cannot exceed 3.4 defects per million. Three sigma quality is 99.73% defect free. But, by going from three sigma to six sigma quality, there is a major quality improvement. For example, in a three sigma world, there would be 54,000 incorrect drug prescriptions per year and 40,500 babies dropped in the delivery room each year in the United States. But, in a Six Sigma quality world, there would be only one incorrect drug prescription every 25 years and three newborn babies dropped every century[75]. The central idea behind Six Sigma is that if you can measure the number of defects in a process, then you can figure out how to eliminate them systematically and get as close to "zero defects" as possible. The stretch for even higher quality rates is entering the industry as well. The FAA safety regulations are even more stringent. The FAA safety goal is to limit the three-year rolling average fatal accident rate to 0.010 fatal accidents per 100,000 departures. That is equivalent to less than one accident per 10 million flights. Similarly, in the late 1990s, as the director of development for a broadband company, I was tasked to develop a video streaming product with a target quality rate of less than 1 video defect over 24 hour continuous movie broadcast. That goal translated into developing a video streaming system at a quality rate of less than 1 defect in 2.5 million image transfers. The goal of the FAA is to cut the rate of fatalities per 100 million persons on board in half by FY2025. The following two cases studies illustrate the importance of Six Sigma IT management[76].

Case Study: How IT Can Prevent Operational Defects

Mechanical problems can be catastrophically bad news at 30,000 feet. The need to automate and maintain extensive information databases for aviation safety and security are increasing. Take the aviation industry for example: A number of aircraft crashes that have been attributed to faulty parts, some were bogus or improperly installed during maintenance. The National Transportation Safety Board database may show some accidents due to "unapproved parts". Tracking parts and their history is only possible by a national parts database. An investigation by Business Week revealed that "bogus" parts including fake, used parts sold as new have found their way into inventory of many commercial airliners in the country. Not even Air Force One is exempt. In the late 1990s, fire extinguishers intended for the President's plane were found to be falsely certified by a repair station. The station pled guilty to making false statements to the FAA. The challenge for quality and safety become bigger as we consider the number of parts. A Boeing 747 has roughly ...

---

[75] "Lean Sigma and Simulation, So What's The Correlation? V2", David M. Ferrin, Martin J. Miller, David Muthler, Proceedings of the 2005 Winter Simulation Conference, pg 2011-2016

[76] The following cases studies are from "Dow Chemical Design for Six Sigma Rail Delivery Project", Patti Buss, Nathan Ivey, Proceedings of the 2001 Winter Simulation Conference, page 1248

.... 6 million parts. By the time it's 10 years old, many of those parts have been replaced five times or more. Airlines depend on a network of approximately 5,000 dealers to keep spares in stock, but the parts are not tracked and the dealers are unregulated. So why doesn't the FAA simply require that all parts be tracked? The response is that it is prohibitively expensive for airlines to trace every part back to an approved manufacturer. Instead, the FAA is working on an accreditation program for certifying the 5,000 dealers. The FAA reports that 26 million parts are installed on airplanes every year in the U.S. The cost of keeping a plane grounded for repairs is somewhere between $20,000 to $100,000 per day. At this cost, and for higher safety, it makes business sense to create a cohesive information system to track parts, maintenance history, flight history and quality inspection reports online. Design for Six Sigma (DFSS) is an ideal design methodology to develop such an information system.

A Six Sigma defect is regarded as anything outside of the customer specifications. When IT misses a customer expectation, or any application downtime, network outage, late delivery of application releases it has introduced a defect. Again, a defect is failing to deliver what the customer wants. Related to Defects are attributes that are most important to the customer. These attributes are regarded Critical-to Quality or CTQ. The IT organization must be aware of these attributes for each application, service or product. Six Sigma IT organizations must strive to offer "Stable Operations". This implies that IT management should build and operate IT environments that are consistent, predictable and minimize process variation. Another definition for process variation is "what customer sees and feels" about a product or service.

Case Study: How Dow Chemical Applied DFSS and Saved $$

When Dow Chemical needed to find a solution for a new rail system to handle increased demand in a line of products, they conducted a Six Sigma project. They utilized Design for Six Sigma (DFSS) method combined with discrete event simulation to verify their solution. They chose the DMEDI (Define, Measure, Explore, Develop and Implement) process. Without the Six Sigma process, the plan was to build additional storage at the cost of $3.2M. After the Six Sigma process, Dow was able to meet the forecasted rail demand through re-engineering work processes with a much smaller capital investment1. As a result, Dow Chemical was able to avoid the costly construction of additional storage facilities.

Another aspect of Six Sigma IT is improving Process Capability, or Cp, which we discussed in the previous chapter. Process capability indicates what the IT processes can deliver consistently to its customers that are within customer's expectations. A typical DMEDI (Define, Measure, Explore, Develop and Implement) project would start with a Champion, a Black belt and a project team. At the end of each phase, the team reviews its findings with the Champion, so there is stage gating.

Stage gating is a quality and control step at the end of each phase to ensure that the findings and deliverables are on target before proceeding with the next phase.

In a DFSS project the team would start with Define phase with the goal of completing three deliverables:

- Define the opportunity
- Determine the scope
- Develop project plans

At the Measure phase, the team identifies the Critical Customer Requirements (CCRs). During this phase, critical-to (CTx) variables are identified. The team also documents the metrics, thresholds and target measurements for CCRs. During the Explore phase, the team identifies a number of options and solutions. The potential impact of each solution on CCRs and CTx variables are captured in a matrix for comparison. Typically, CCRs are sorted by their weights and the solutions get a cumulative score for their ability in form, fit and function to satisfy the CCRs. Analytical tools such as simulation can be used to forecast the output of each potential solution[77]. Once the best solution is identified, the team proceeds with Develop phase. At the Develop phase, the team drafts a low level design, also known as a detailed design. This design is reviewed and any potential issues associated with its side effects or short comings are highlighted for revising the design. Once the team is certain that it has a workable design, it reviews the design with the Champion and the Black belt. Implement phase defines the roles and responsibilities for the team members. It defines training and process re-engineering steps for the customer. Each of these phases can be managed using Scrum project management technique.

QFD and GQM: Tools for Service Quality

Quality Function Deployment (QFD) and Goal-Question-Measurement (GQM) are proven tools for service quality improvement. QFD begins with the voice of the customer. From the customer's input, (The Y in the Six Sigma transfer function), we proceed to identify the causes (X's). Root causes are found through root cause analysis or Kaizen events. The team continues the root cause analysis until they reach a metric that can be measured for each cause. We write the customer input or requirement in a box, and the subcomponents or causes in the subsequent boxes, and so on. These steps form a CTQ Tree. As an example, let's apply this technique to an aspect of IT operations. We'll consider the IT help desk, or service desk operations. The customer's requirement is "timely resolution of trouble ticket". The question is what affects the customer's request. The answer points to two causes: average calls received per hour and average time to fix. You'll note that we can use the GQM method to develop a CTQ Tree.

Figure 17.1 shows the tree for this CTQ. The results of performing periodic measurements indicate which areas of service delivery need to be improved. The improvements come in form of workflow redesign.

---

[77] "DEA as Simulation Post Processing Tool", Timothy R. Andersen, Peter Ghavami, et. al., INFORMS Conference, Seattle, 1998.

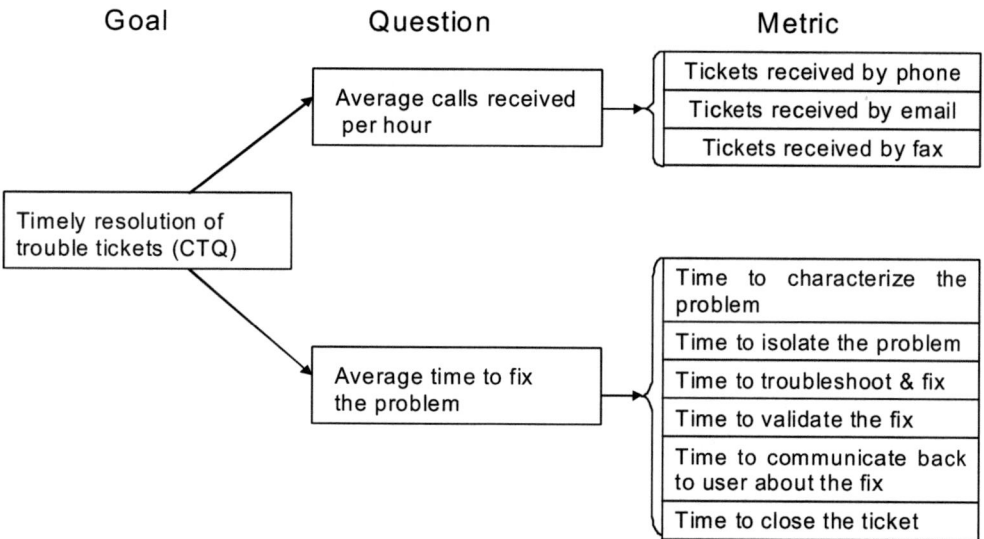

Fig 17.1 – Goal-Question-Metric (GQM) Example

Failure Modes and Effect Analysis (FMEA)

A failure modes and effect analysis (FMEA) is a tool to define the potential failures of a process or system, its potential impact on the customer and how to deal with the problem. FMEA is a tool to predict and eliminate potential failures and also to be prepared to respond in case a failure occurs. FMEA was used by NASA in the 1960's during the Apollo missions. But, the roots of FMEA are in scientific problem solving techniques. When we consider the Y=f(X) transfer function, FMEA is a tool to eliminate X's that cause the undesirable Y's.

FMEA in IT can be applied to failures associated with systems, design, process, implementations, and service, as follows:

Systems FMEA: is used to analyze systems such as network infrastructure, servers, applications and their subsystems. These studies focus on potential failure modes related to the functions of a system caused by a design characteristic. They identify potential points of failure in each subsystem and interaction between subsystems.

Design FMEA: is used for study of failures before a product is released to production. It includes validation of IT solutions before going live. It works by intentionally inducing failures during testing to identify weak design parameters.

Process FMEA: is used to identify issues associated with IT processes. These are studies of operational failures. They might include procedures that IT staff use for troubleshooting, change management, server management, database management, tape backups and business continuity.

Implementation FMEA: considers potential failures with implementations and particularly new product introductions. It considers potential failures during upgrades, training, lack of application fit and disruption of business activities due to potential failures during an application or IT solution roll out.

Service FMEA: also known as SFMEA, evaluates failures in IT service functions. Using the generic steps of FMEA we identify potential points of failure in providing services, their impact, detection methods and recommended actions to resolve service issues.

A generic FMEA analysis follows the following steps. These steps are adapted to IT work activities:

1. List process steps and functions.
2. List potential failure modes for each step of the process. The failure modes are the answer to the question: "What could go wrong?" The answer is the Y's of the process.
3. List potential effects of failure. This is the result or impact of an IT failure on customers.
4. Identify severity of each effect. Severity is a rating from 1 to 10. Severity classifications and ratings usually range from none(score of 1), very minor(2), minor(3), very low(4), low(5), and moderate(6), to high(7), very high(8), dangerous with warning(9), and dangerous without warning(10).
5. Define potential causes of each failure. The causes are the X's.
6. Assign probability of occurrence to each cause. Occurrence is either a probability from 0% to 100%, or rating scale from 1 to 10.
7. List current process controls to prevent or detect failure modes.
8. Assign detection level to failure modes. This rating defines the difficulty level of detecting a failure. In other words, how difficult is the detection of the failure? For easily discoverable defects place a 1; for defects that are most difficult and obscure to discover, place a 10.
9. Calculate the failure risk priority ranking by multiplying severity by occurrence probability by detection rate.
10. Specify recommended actions.

The table in Figure 17.3 illustrates the FMEA analysis tool for a WiFi infrastructure. The first column is the item number. The second column is the process step, followed by failure modes, potential failure effects, severity, potential causes of failure, probability of occurrence, process controls, detectability and ranking of the failure modes. This table was used by an IT project team for a wireless access point (AP) implementation in a large enterprise. The goal of this FMEA exercise was to determine if it was sufficiently "good enough" to just install the AP hardware equipment, or whether additional software tools were needed to remotely monitor and manage the access points. The table demonstrated that the severity, impact and probability of failures were high enough that it would be wise to install the additional tools for active monitoring of the WiFi access points. In addition, using a remote monitoring tool would give IT the control and detection ability which would result in mistake-proofing[78] the wireless implementation. Experts believe that any failure risk priority ranking of 150 or higher is an indicator of a failure that needs to be resolved. A

---

[78] In Japanese texts, error proofing or mistake-proofing is called poka-yoke

risk priority ranking of 300 or higher signals a critical potential failure that needs immediate attention. A severity rating of over 500 usually starts into mission critical or safety-related defects. A high risk priority ranking with a high "ease of detection" rating implies our inability to capture potential defects during internal testing before releasing the IT solution into production.

Simulation

Simulation is a powerful tool to serve IT and strategic management. Simulation programs can help in two ways: First, they can determine the impact of a decision by analyzing future scenarios quickly before management implements the decision. Second, it can analyze the impact of process changes and provide results on metrics of interest. The key to a successful simulation model is the initial build and calibration to mimic the actual real world situation. There are a number of graphical simulation programs on the market that can handle dynamic simulation problems and probability based scenarios. Simulation models come in three general varieties: *Discrete event*, *Continuous flow* and *Hybrid*.

Discrete event models have discrete time steps where in each time interval certain activities take place. In these models, discrete entities change the state of the model as events occur. For example, parts being assembled, customers calling, and orders arriving are examples of events. In Discrete event models, each individual item can be tracked. Items can flow in either first in-first out, or last in-first out order. Generally, this type of simulation model is ideal for manufacturing, service industries, business process redesign, strategic decisions and systems engineering.

FMEA Matrix for WiFi Access Point Infrastructure

No.	Process Step	Potential Failure Modes	Potential failure effect	Severity Rate	Potential Causes of Failure	Probability of Occurrence	Current Process Controls	Difficulty of Detecting Failure	Risk Priority Ranking
	Function	(Y's)	Impact	(1 - 10)	(X's)	(1 - 10)	Controls	(1 - 10)	1- 1000)
1	Install Access Point	Wrong Config.	Signal loss	10	Wrong config	4	None	8	320
2	Configure Access Point	Wrong Config.	Security violation	10	Wrong config	4	None	9	360
3	Maintain	Hardware Failure	Signal loss	10	Hardware Failure	1	None	2	20

Fig 17.3 - FMEA Model for WiFi Downtime Analysis

Continuous flow simulations consider the flow of materials from one source to another using constant and sequential time steps. Simulating flow of water or heat transfer between objects or fluids are good examples. Flows are first in-first out. These models are ideal for study of biological systems, chemicals, bulk processes and systems dynamics modeling.

Hybrid models are a combination of discrete event and continuous flow models. Simulation can give management a low cost tool to visualize the effect of their decisions. Similarly, simulation models can give management the ability to select the best alternative among many decision options.

ITIL: A Best Practices Approach

IT Infrastructure Library (ITIL) practices are based on CMMI framework. CMMI was designed to assist an organization with aligning the application of the ITIL model with its business objectives. ITIL was developed in the late 1980s and since then has become the world wide de facto standard in service management. ITIL prescribes both tactical and operational level practices. Tactical processes center on the relationships between the IT organization and their Customers. At the operational level, the Service Support processes and Service Delivery policies are set up with agreements, such as service level agreements (SLA), and monitoring of how well those targets are met.

A parallel standard for IT service management (ITSM) grew out of BS-15000 standard, now known as the ISO-20000. This standard consists of 10 sections: Scope, Terms and definitions, Requirements for management system, Planning and implementing service management, Planning and implementing new or changed services, Service delivery process, Resolution process, Release process and Control processes.

On both the tactical and operational levels, ITIL has a close relationship with the ISO-20000 and other quality systems such as: The ISO9000, CMMI, Malcolm Baldridge award, project management systems such as PRINCE-2 (Projects in Controlled Environment -2) and PMI (Project Management Institute). ITIL views problems, *incidents* and *errors* differently.

To ITIL, an *incident* is "any event that is not part of the standard operation of a service and which causes or may cause an interruption to or reduction in the quality of that service." A *problem* is an underlying but unknown cause of one or more incident. An *error* is a problem for which the root cause has been identified. Incidents and problems are to be logged separately.

ITIL' s components overlap each other and are often compared to pieces of puzzle. At a high level these components are concerned with:

1. Delivering IT Services
2. Managing Applications
3. Supporting IT Services
4. Managing the Infrastructure
5. The Business Perspective

Figure 17.4 illustrates the components of ITIL best practices in a cognitive map. Let's review each component in more detail.

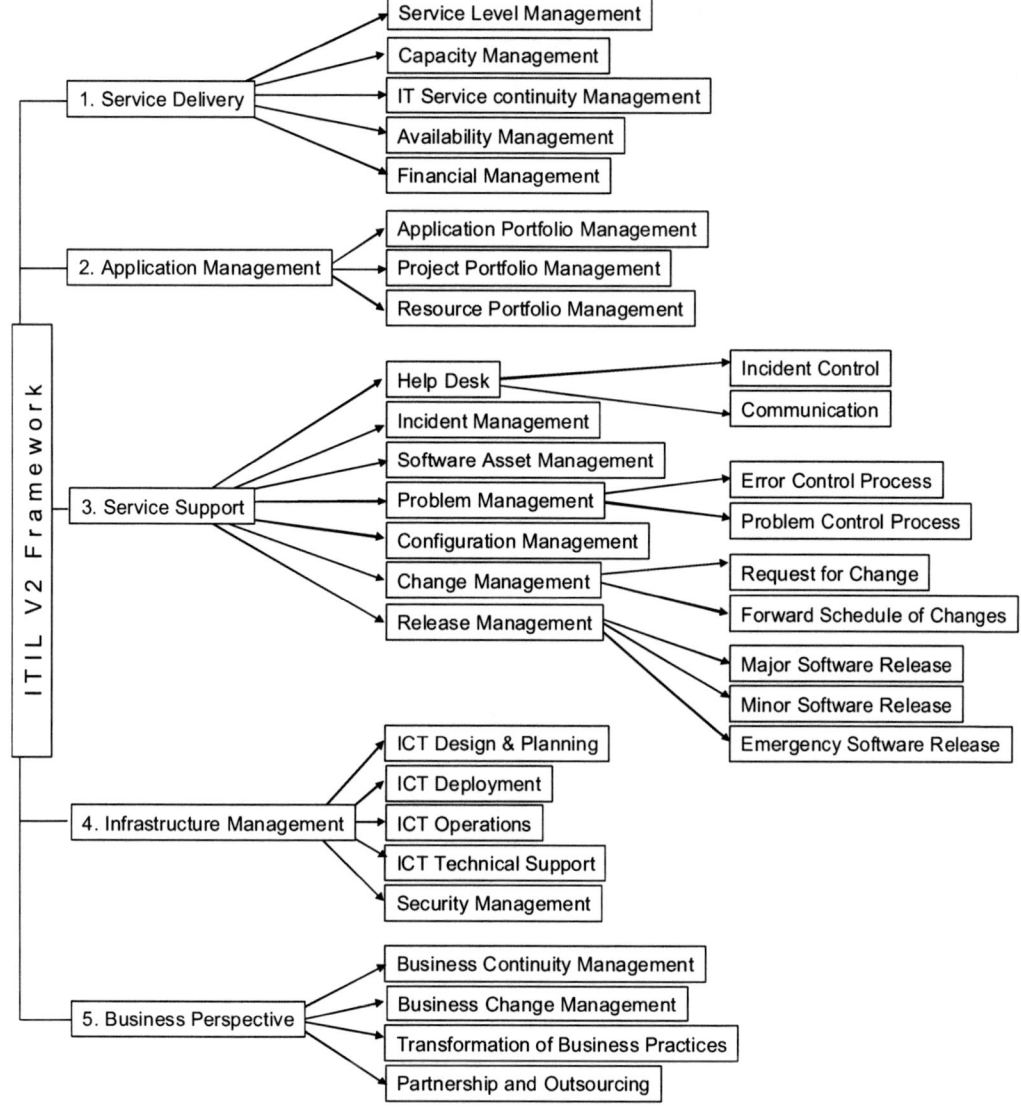

Fig 17.4 – A Cognitive Map of ITIL Best Practices

1. IT Service Delivery: considers what services are expected from IT for the business to provide adequate support, and meet its value proposition to its business customers. Service Delivery deals with best practices in the following areas:

- *Capacity management:* Capacity planning, capacity forecasting and provisioning of network bandwidth, server capacity, storage and transaction volume planning

- *Availability Management:* Managing systems for high availability, reduce downtimes and unscheduled system failures

- *Service Level Management:* Understand and set targets for Service Level Agreements (SLAs). Implement systems that meet customer's expectations for availability, support, troubleshooting and performance. The key elements of this process are: reliability engineering, maintainability, serviceability, and security consisting of confidentiality, integrity and access controls.

- *IT Service Continuity Management:* Devise plans for service during downtimes and workarounds as necessary for continuity of business.
- *Financial Management:* Involves contract management, purchasing and procurement, budgets and accounting.

2. Application Management: covers the software development lifecycle from cradle to sunset, expanding on the topics covered under Software Lifecycle Support and Testing of IT Service. Throughout this book, I've emphasized controlled processes for application implementations. Controlled processes start with a well defined set of requirements, specifications, followed by high level and low-level design, then implementation, detailed testing and release planning. Each stage requires an "engineered" approach to document and review the product as it evolves through these stages.

3. Support Services: ensures that users have access to IT services to support their business functions. It's broken down to:

1) *Service Desk:* Creating an operational support group to provide service and support. In one instance, I've implemented a concierge desk to provide a wide range of services. Service Desk is the user's prime interface to IT. It's not a process, but considered by ITIL to be an essential function.

2) *Incident Management:* Best practices for handling incidents and to protect service continuity. When an incident occurs, this process works to quickly restore normal service. A triage conference call is used for all stake holders and IT personnel involved to communicate and resolve the incident. An Incident Manager (or Commander as I call it) is identified who stays with the progress of events until the incident is resolved. A post mortem after each incident provides root cause of the incident and steps to prevent it from occurring again.

3) *Problem Management:* A problem is an incident which has a known root cause. Managing problems requires a proposal to make appropriate changes to systems or workflow as preventative measure.

4) *Configuration Management:* Procedures for proper configuration of systems and maintaining the system configurations. Its goal is to maintain and control all version of existing configuration items. These include the Definitive Software Library (DSL) and Definitive Hardware Library (DHL) for any product or system in production. Configuration of applications and systems should be stored in a Configuration Management Database (CMDB). Good practices require updating CMDB, or any "as-build" documents to keep configuration documentation current. Configuration Management consists of 5 main processes:

    a. *Planning:* Creating a rolling 3-6 month schedule or time horizon for upcoming configuration changes, upgrades and releases

- b. *Identification:* Naming all configuration items (usually known by their application or system name), owners, relationships and interdependencies between configuration items
- c. *Control:* Ensuring that only authorized changes are applied. This is accomplished through submitting a "request for change" to a Change Review Committee that meets regularly to review and approve such requests."
- d. *Status Accounting:* This refers to ability to track all prior changes through records kept by IT staff
- e. *Verification and Audit:* conducting reviews of configuration records and verifying that they are correct

5) *Change Management:* Requires meeting with the change control group and presenting the impact of change, test results, fall-back plans, the appropriate date and time for change and downtime procedures during the change. You may require analysis of "as-is" versus "to-be" to identify what exactly is being modified, require diagrams and documents that specify the change in more detail. All configurations and upgrades require documented Method of Procedure (MOP) plans that are previewed and approved by the Customer, vendor and IT personnel.

6) *Release Management:* A release is defined as a set of approved changes to the IT environment. It ensures that only compatible, licensed and appropriately planned applications are put into production. It includes processes for test result reviews, performing pre-release operational readiness, release plan, training, triage of issues, and transition from implementation to operational support. A release can simply be a fix to remedy a known error in response to a problem/incident.

4. Infrastructure Management: based on information and communication technology (ICT) infrastructure management, it covers:

1) *Network Service Management:* including services based on fiber, copper and WiFi infrastructure and their components such as routers, switches and access points

2) *Operations Management:* Guidelines for operations of systems, such as remote monitoring, setting proper thresholds for alarms, remote access and resolution of issues. It outlines backup plans, frequency of backup and routine preventative maintenance of servers, operating system patches and updates.

3) *Management of Local Processors:* Identifies the system operators and application managers for local or departmental systems. Creates a common protocol for tape backup management, etc.

4) *Computer Installation and Acceptance:* Outlines process for facilities planning, and server placement process including datacenter space, power, cooling and networking requirements. A server placement document must be completed before installing servers. Acceptance criteria

are defined as 30-day un-interrupted service without any Severity-1 error and any Severity-2 error which the vendor has agreed to a specific fix date.

5) *Systems Management:* Documents the systems integration, security, data integrity and access lists, domains and data messaging procedures.

5. *Business Perspective:* Under the Business Perspective, ITIL covers a wide range of issues concerning how IT becomes an integral part of overall business and meeting business requirements, with high quality. The issues include:

1) Business Continuity Management, Disaster-model operations and disaster recovery
2) Change Management, change control and configuration management
3) Vendor management, partnerships and outsourcing
4) Transforming business practice through radical change

Summary

- Six Sigma and ITIL are congruent and reinforce one another. Apply Design for Six Sigma and Quality Function Deployment to reduce overall cost of maintenance and cost of ownership. Implement ITIL to cultivate best practices in IT operations management.
- Develop internal ITIL methods to achieve a consistent operational and service delivery system.
- Assign one manager to the overall integrity of ITIL procedures in your IT organization.
- Continuously seek and learn best practices from other IT professionals and organizations. Compare your best practices against the industry best practices. Adjust your processes and workflows to meet the best practice objectives.

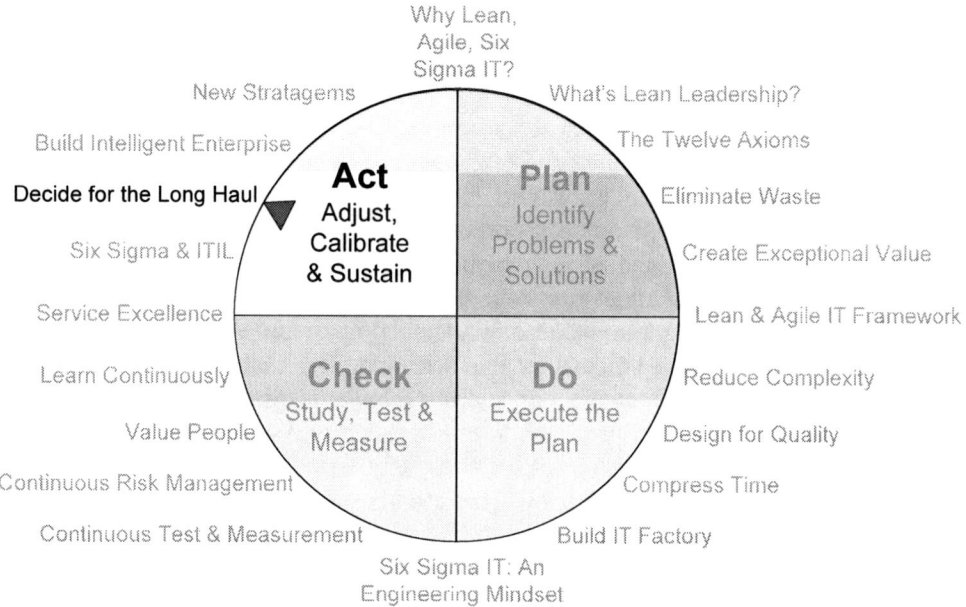

"Even a correct decision is wrong when it was taken too late."

Lee Iacocca

Chapter 18. Decide for the Long Haul

Lean, Agile and Six Sigma IT decision makers take a long term view of decision time horizon. They follow rational decision making processes supported by facts and data. The term decision analysis was first coined n 1964 by Ronald A. Howard, a professor at Stanford University. Since then he has made major contributions to this discipline including much of the practice and applications of decision analysis. In this chapter we'll discuss the essential methods for decision analysis for IT managers. Among rational decision making techniques, Lean IT managers have successfully applied other methods from Theory of Constraints (TOC), Linear programming, Fuzzy Logic and Decisions under uncertainty. Since our goal is to consider a long time horizon in our decisions, it's important to consider the uncertainties of the future in our decision analysis.

Considering the Six Sigma transfer function $Y = f(X)$, we are interested in making decisions about X's to achieve a desired outcome 'Y'. In another perspective, decisions that we make are about direction and control; whether to control a process, a project, a group or to direct them. The X's of a decision might include, cost, schedule, quality, performance, competitive advantage, strategic value, resources, morale, customer satisfaction to name a few. The X's can consist of tactical and strategic as well as hard and soft variables.

Decisions carry both rewards and risks. *Payoff* is the possible outcome and reward of a decision. Each Individual's tolerance towards risk varies. Some leaders are risk takers and others are risk averse. When we adjust the payoff by associated risks, we have identified the *Utility* for each decision. In other words, utility is the sum of risk-adjusted benefits. Making rash decisions without adequate facts and analysis can be dangerous and costly. Lean IT managers postpone decision making until as many facts are known, but not until it's too late. Decisions have to be made in uncertain conditions and that's a constant challenge for IT leadership.

A rational decision maker would choose the decision with highest utility. But the decision maker has the challenge of identifying all benefits, including those that are intangible which should be translated into tangible values. For example, if an IT manager is deciding to outsource a portion of her project, the benefits include faster delivery of the product and slightly higher quality software. The cash outlays are higher. The IT manager must translate the intangible benefits of quality and faster delivery into savings and then make a financial comparison. We'll review a case study that explains the decision process for this scenario. The Utility value is a combination of profit, loss and risk. Because our tolerance towards risk varies, the risk-adjusted payoffs present different utility values to the decision maker. The utility value depends on the perception of the decision maker and attitude towards risk. Most people have a decreasing marginal utility for money. This means that the more money you have the less another increment of money is important to you. If you have less money, you are unlikely to take big gambles. Thus utility curve U is concave and increasing as shown in Figure 18.4.

Similarly a company that has a large cash position is likely to be a risk-taker when making decisions. In contrast, a company that has suffered losses is likely to be a risk avoider, or risk averse. IT leadership are likely to follow the same attitudes towards risk. This is justifiable unless the executive management are intentional in making changes to the picture of utility function. For certain IT initiatives which could bring substantial profits or market share, this would be a conceivable executive gamble. A vast number of IT organizations suffer from late decisions too. Late decisions are wrong because they have lost their value for control and guidance, or missed the opportunity to capture the payoff. Traditional IT organizations often become rigid and stagnant because they suffer from "paralysis by analysis". Simply these organizations either don't know how to make rational decisions, or they're too slow to complete the rational decision making process, or they cannot defend their decision to upper management. All these stem from lack of practice and knowledge about decision making process.

When we apply the decision theory principles to IT decisions, we must consider the future possible scenarios and payoffs from our decisions. We are either certain about facts if they have occurred but often we are uncertain about some facts, in particular those that are in the future time horizon. Certainty about future results means that parameters which influence the outcome such as cost, schedule, requirements, performance and technology have known values. Uncertainty means that our knowledge about future value of these parameters is unknown. Many decision makers seeking to maximize short term gains inadvertently increase the long term risks of their decision.

The worst decisions are those that limit the flexibility and availability of future decision alternatives. The Lean IT managers avoid making short term decisions that adversely seal the fate of their projects in the long run.

Pyramid of Priority

One of the management tools that can assist with making Lean decisions is to understand the global, enterprise-wide decision priorities of the organization. When faced with multiple objectives and decision alternatives, which IT decision is optimal? The pyramid is a way to keep in focus the ranking of objectives. The most important objectives are at the pinnacle while the less important objectives are at the lower layers of the pyramid. For an IT decision to be valid, its decisions must comply with these priorities starting at the top of the pyramid

Different industries have different pyramids of priority. One factory placed labor safety first, quality second and productivity at lower levels. Another company regarded data security as the highest objective, followed by customer satisfaction, innovation and efficiency at the lower tiers. An example of the pyramid from a healthcare organization is shown in the next diagram. At the top of the pyramid, 'Patient Safety' trumps all other priorities any decision or technical work which impacts 'Patient Safety' receives the most attention and highest priority. Similarly, an IT decision must be gauged with its impact on patient safety as the number one priority. Below that, 'Compliance', meaning regulatory or legal policies, and 'Patient Care' take precedence over 'Practice Efficiency'.

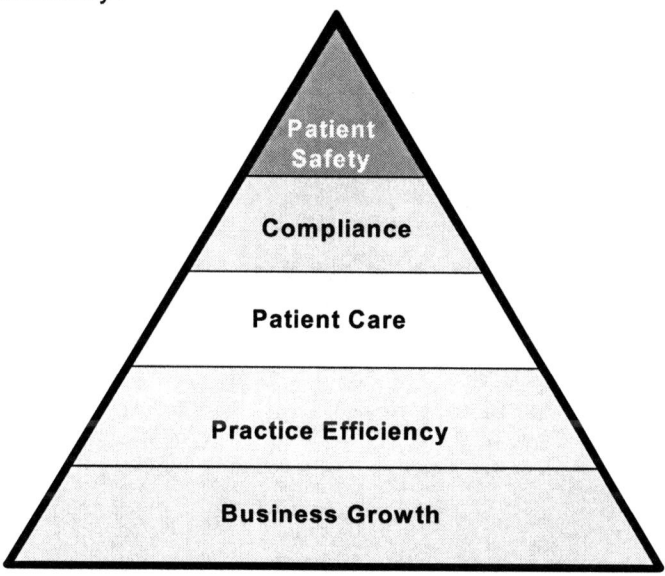

Fig 18.1 – Pyramid of Priority Example

We can use the pyramid of priority to apply objective criteria in our decision making in Information Technology Management. Two questions should be answered for each priority. How does my decision affect the criteria on the pyramid? And, is my decision consistent with the ranking of the pyramid? In other words, does your decision improve the organization's ability to achieve its highest priority objectives? Conversely, a decision that satisfies the lower ranking objectives should not sacrifice or hinder the firm's ability to achieve the higher rank objective.

The difficulty with optimizing decisions and processes across large enterprise is that each layer has its plane of decision criteria and objective. One has to superimpose these layers to get a clear picture of how these goals are competing or collaborating with one another. Inefficiencies and frictions that lead to waste occur when these goals are in discord. Sorting out conflicting decisions is a dilemma facing most executives who seek organizational coordination and efficiency. In the next chapter, I'll discuss how IT can overcome this dilemma, to create a harmonized, productive intelligent organization.

In a survey of most innovative IT organizations conducted by the CIO Magazine, the respondents were asked to note which business drivers are the force behind new IT initiatives. The response was summarized in a report called "CIO 100 – Innovation for Growth" in 2006[79]. The next diagram (Figure 18.2) is an adaptation from the report. It shows that collectively among the most innovative IT organizations, increasing efficiency and productivity rank as the most frequent driver for new initiatives, followed by competitive advantage, customer satisfaction and business innovation. In fact these drivers of IT initiatives were cited 2X to 3X more frequently than some other drives such as improve supply chain or regulatory compliance. This ranking illustrates the priority of decision making by CIOs. Creating a pyramid of priority for your organization is a great exercise because through the process the C-executives explicitly define their decision priorities for IT initiatives.

Decisions for the Long Haul

In previous pages, we reviewed Lean, Agile and Six Sigma IT principles which guide the organization towards eliminating waste and flawless execution. These principles teach us rules about "how to do it right". The next few pages discuss "what is the right thing to do". They evaluate how some tough IT decisions can be made despite an uncertain future.

CIOs are frequently asked to explain the value of IT and to justify IT investments. C-executives commonly ask questions such as: "What are we getting for our investment in IT? How does our IT organization compare to the competition? Are we as efficient as we can be? Where do we need to improve?" The Lean IT organization is both the value engine and cost reduction force of the organization. It is the logistics source and workflow driver. Finally, it's the strategy enabler. The better the IT decisions gets, the better the financial results will be.

In order to perform rational decisions analysis, we must consider the following seven steps:

1. Identify the structure of the problem or decision, including the variables affecting the outcome of the decision.
2. Develop a list of decision alternatives from which to choose.
3. Identify a set of future conditions that have a bearing on the results of each decision.
4. Determine the payoff for each alternative under each future condition.
5. Estimate the probability of each future condition.

---

[79] "CIO 100 – Innovation For Growth", The CIO Magazine, Cxo Media Inc. 2006

6. Determine your organization's tolerance towards risk. Calculate risk-adjusted utility of each decision alternative.

7. Evaluate the alternatives using an optimum decision criterion, either to minimize regret or maximize utility.

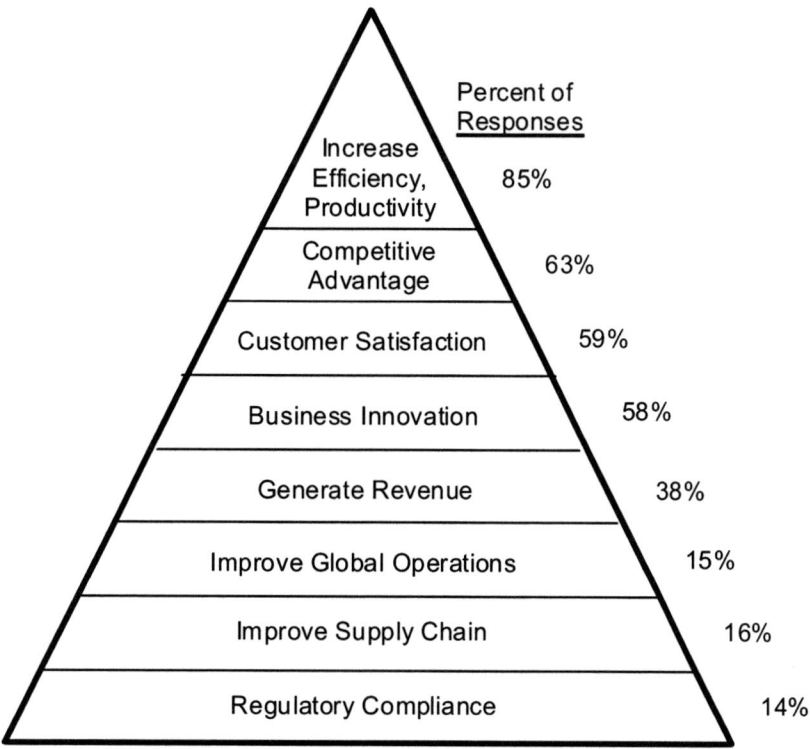

Source: CIO 100. Respondents chose all that applied.

Fig 18.2 – Pyramid of Priority From an Industry-wide Survey of CIOs. Ranking of Important IT Objectives For the Firm

I will illustrate these steps in more detail by an example. Let's assume that we want to build a new datacenter for the IT organization. We have to decide between three options: building a small datacenter, a medium datacenter or a large datacenter. The future about the company growth is uncertain. If the company grows fast by acquiring another firm, the future demand for datacenter space will be high. Otherwise, the company will experience a slow or moderate growth in the next 5 years. The time horizon for this decision is 5 years.

This example was a decision scenario during one of my consulting engagements at a large manufacturing company. The cost to build a data center varied by size ranging from $20M for a small center, $30M for the medium sized, and $40M for the large data center. The dilemma facing the IT management was that if they built a small datacenter, in the event of rapid growth, they'd have to lease external data center space.

But if the company built a large datacenter, in the event of slow growth, they could sublease only a portion to recoup their investment. The table below is a payoff table created as an example of an IT decision analysis.

Datacenter Decision	Possible Future Demand	Possible Future Demand	Possible Future Demand
Decision Alternatives	Low Growth	Moderate Growth	High Growth
Small Data Center	$10M	$10M	$10M
Medium Data Center	$7	$12	$12
Large Data Center	($4)	$2	$16

Fig 18.3 – Payoff Table for Data Center Decision Analysis

The table shows the expected payoffs for each alternative for various possible future states. The payoff shown in each cell is the result of considering the net monetary outcome. It considers total expenses for construction and operating costs compared to the expense of using outside datacenter services. The future demand for datacenter space can be low, moderate or high. In this example, we assume that all three future states have equal probabilities. Later we'll examine the same decision scenario using probability-based approach.

The payoffs are shown in the body of the table. For example, if the future demand is moderate and we decide to build a medium datacenter, the payoff will be $12 million. But if we decide to build a large datacenter and the future demand turns out to be low, we will incur a loss of $4 million. Every decision has a return (pay off) and a regret (loss). The goal of a Lean decision maker is to minimize waste. Here waste is synonymous with a decision's risks of failure and regret. When considering making decisions under uncertainty, there are four possible decision criteria available: Maximin, Maximax, Laplace and Minimax Regret. These criteria can be defined as follows:

Maximin: This is essentially a pessimist's approach to decisions. This decision criteria selects the maximum of minimum payoffs. The IT manager determines the worst possible payoff for each alternative, and then chooses the "best among the worst" payoffs. Hence, it establishes a guaranteed minimum. Let's look at the payoff table once again. The worst payoffs across each row for each alternative are as follows:

Small Data Center:	$10 million
Medium Data Center	$7
Large Data Center	- $4

Since $10 million is the best among the lowest payoffs, the pessimistic IT manager chooses to build the small data center.

Maximax: This decision criteria selects the maximum of the highest payoffs. The IT manager first determines the best payoffs, and then chooses the alternative that delivers the highest payoff. This approach is overly optimistic and does not take into account any payoff other than the best.

Again we consult the payoff table in Figure 18.3. The best payoffs across each row are:

Small Datacenter:	$10 million
Medium Datacenter	$12
Large Datacenter	$16

Since $16 million is the best overall payoff, IT manager chooses to build the large Datacenter. This is a "go for it" strategy which builds a lot of enthusiasm based on the psychology of "positive economics" or plain wishful thinking. But the overly optimistic approach could give way to disappointing surprises for all stake-holders as the future events pose "unexpected" risks. This decision criterion is not suitable for everyone. It might be more suited to cash-rich companies or firms on the fast growth track.

Laplace: This criterion considers the average payoff for each alternative. The IT manager assumes that all future states have equal probability. The IT manager computes the average payoff for each alternative, and chooses the alternative with best average.

For Laplace criterion, we sum the row values, and then we divide the total by the number of future states. (here are the 3 states).

	Row total	Row Average
Small Data Center:	$30 million	$10 million
Medium Data Center	$31	$10.33
Large Data Center	$14	$4.67

Since the medium data center has the highest average, the IT manager chooses to build the medium data center.

Minimax Regret: This decision criterion determines the maximum losses and then selects the options with minimum loss or lowest regret. The regret for each alternative is computed as the difference between a given payoff and the best payoff in the same column. The IT manager then selects the alternative with lowest difference.

Figure 18.4 shows how we can determine the opportunity losses namely the decision regrets. This is accomplished by subtracting every payoff in each column from the largest positive payoff in that column.

Again we consult the payoff table in Figure 18.3. For example, in the first column, we subtract $10M, $7M and -$4M from $10M to get the values for the first column: $0M, $3M and $14M respectively. We repeat this process for other columns accordingly.

In the second column the largest payoff is $12M. To find regrets for the second column we subtract $10M, $12M and $2M from $12M. The result is shown in the Minimax Regret table shown in Figure 18.4.

Decision Alternatives	Regrets Low Growth	Regrets Moderate Growth	Regrets High Growth	Regrets Worst Regret
Small Datacenter	$0	$2	$6	$6
Medium Datacenter	$3	$0	$4	$4
Large Datacenter	$14	$10	$0	$14

Fig 18.4 – Minimax Regret Computation Table

The next step is to determine the worst regret for each alternative using the Minimax algorithm. The maximum (or worst) regret for the first alternative (Small Datacenter) is $6M, for the second alternative (Medium Datacenter) the worst regret is $4M and for the third alternative (Large Datacenter) the worst regret is $14M. To minimize decision regret, the IT manager chooses the Minimax of worst regrets, thus selects the Medium Datacenter alternative which has a regret of $4 million. This is the best decision for a risk neutral company. In other words, the IT manager chooses a decision alternative that carries the lowest regret in the worst possible case.

Decision Trees: Decision trees are easy to construct and are rather intuitive tools for analyzing decisions. Figure 18.5 shows a decision tree for the data center decision scenario. Constructing a decision tree starts with the decision alternatives on the far left side of the page.

The scenarios are added as branches of the tree for each decision alternative. Here they are: Low demand, Moderate demand and High demand. If we know an approximation or estimated probability of those future scenarios, the probability can be written next to each branch. In this case, we are told about the executive's predictions about the growth of the company.

Depending on the company growth rate, the demand will be either 20% for low growth, 50% for moderate growth or 30% for high growth. The next step is to write the payoffs and regrets for each branch. If the probability of future scenarios is known, we can multiply the payoff by their probability and compute a probability-adjusted payoff. The next decision tree illustrates the graph for this decision analysis.

Long Haul Decisions Using Probability

While our knowledge about the future is never perfect, we can at least have some ideas about the future states in terms of probability of those states. If we were able to assign a probability to future states, we can use the *Expected Monetary Value* criteria (EMV) in our decisions.

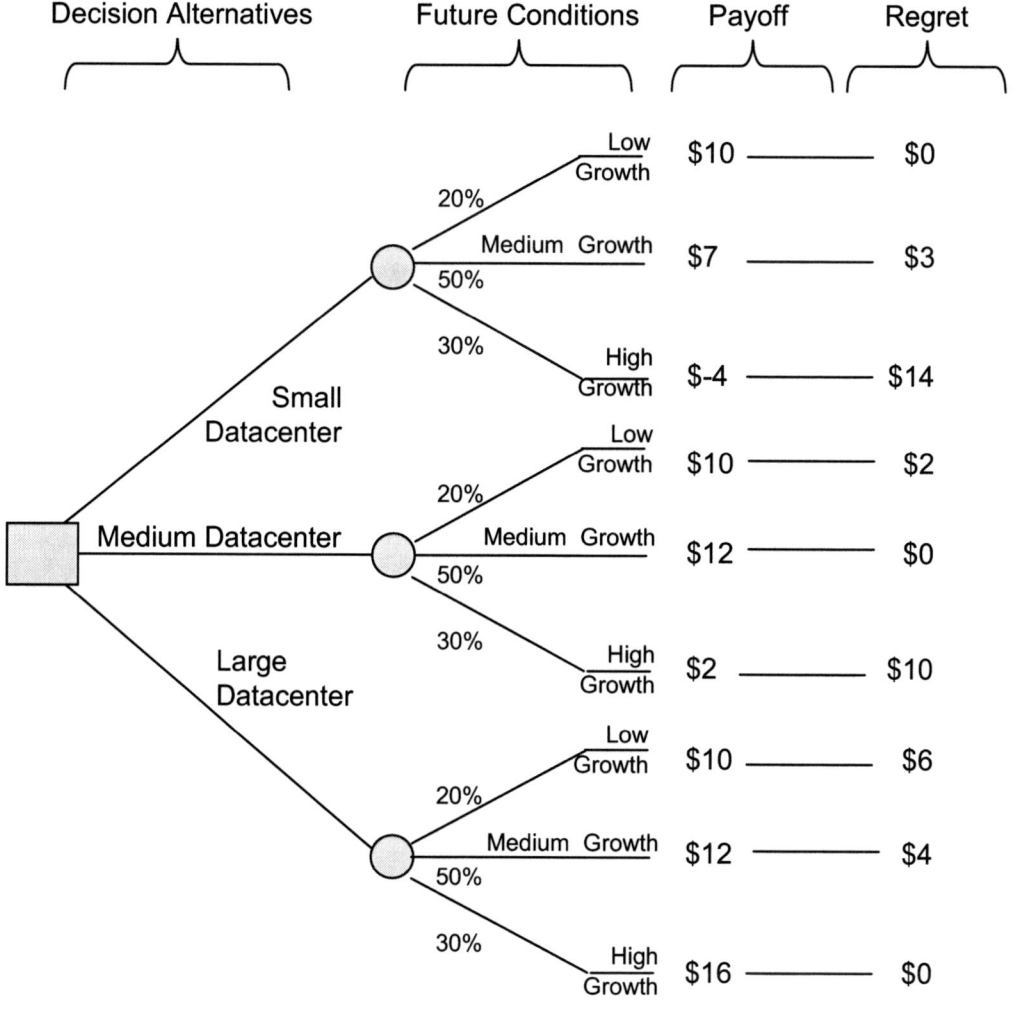

Fig 18.5 – Decision Tree for Datacenter Investment Selection

For example, let's suppose that the firm's executives disclosed their forecast for future growth as follows: "We expect the probability of low growth to be 20%, probability of medium growth to be 50% and probability of high growth to be 30%." Then the IT manager can calculate the expected monetary value (EMV) for each alternative as follows:

EMV (Small data center) = .3 ($10) + .50 ($10) + .30 ($10) = $10

EMV (Med-size data center) = .3 ($7) + .50 ($12) + .30 ($12) = $10.5

EMV (Large data center) = .3 (-$4) + .50 ($2) + .30 ($16) = $3

The IT manager based on the above calculation chooses the med-size datacenter alternative since it has the highest expected monetary value. But, we should also analyze our decision on the basis of regret. The regret table for the same probabilities would provide the *Expected Monetary Regret* (EMR) which looks like the following.

EMR (Small data center) = .3 ($0) + .50 ($2) + .30 ($6) = $2.8

EMR (Med-size data center) = .3 ($3) + .50 ($0) + .30 ($4) = $2.1

EMR (Large data center) = .3 ($14) + .50 ($10) + .30 ($0) = $9.2

Once again, building the medium datacenter has the lowest regret as well. These decisions are selected if the decision maker is risk neutral. The risk taker or risk-averse decision maker would use a different utility function for their decision.

Typically, companies that are on the fast growth track can handle and might welcome a risk taking posture as part of their quest for achieving higher return on investment. Other decision makers might be risk-averse, in particular those companies who are concerned with their profitability or economic slowdown.

Case Study: **To Outsource or Not?**

In this case study, we will apply the concepts reviewed already namely the utility theory and decisions under uncertainty. The IT manager is debating whether to develop in-house (Decision A) or to outsource the project to an outside firm (Decision B). The costs, benefits and risks associated with outsource versus in-house development are as follows:

Alternatives	Cost	Benefits	Net Cost	Risk Profile
Decision A: In-House Development	$24M	- Internal knowledge creation. Value:$3M	$21M	Risk: Key personnel may leave the project. Probability: 50% Risk Impact: ($2M)
Decision B: Outsource to an outside Firm	$32M	- Personnel savings: $2M - Higher quality: $5M - Faster delivery: $6M	$19M	Risk: Outsource firm becomes insolvent. Probability: 10% Risk Impact: ($12M)

Fig 18.6 – Translating Cost, Benefit, Risk & Intangibles into Monetary Value For Decision Analysis

The project manager has translated intangibles such as higher quality and faster market delivery into monetary value as shown in Figure 18.6. For each decision alternative, a risk has been identified as follows: If the manager decides to develop in-house there is 50% chance of losing key personnel during the project. The impact of this risk is a loss of $2M. If the manager decides to outsource there is a 10% chance that the outsource firm becomes insolvent. In that event, the impact on the project is a loss of $12M. Given this scenario, we can construct the decision tree and compute the expected monetary value from each decision. Figure 18.7 shows the decision tree for this case study. Given the probabilities for the future states, we can compute expected monetary cost for each decision:

- *Expected Monetary Cost of Decision A = .50 * ($23M) + .50* ($21M)*

Which equals to: $22M. This is the risk adjusted expected cost of decision A.

- *Expected Monetary Cost of Decision B= .90 * ($19M) + .10* ($31M)*

Which equals to: $20.2M. This is the risk adjusted expected cost of decision B.

Given the results of expected monetary costs, outsourcing to an outside firm is the more economical decision.

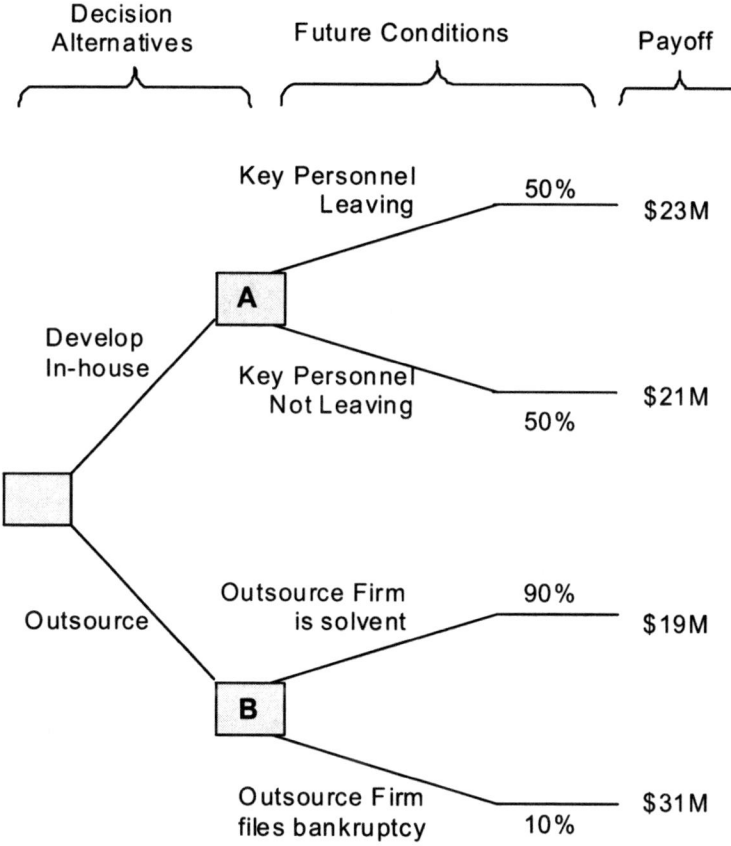

Fig 18.7 – Decision Tree for Outsourcing Decision

In conclusion, it's wise to choose the decision alternatives which minimize regret, not just those that maximize payoff. Weigh your decisions against risks that are associated with each. Determine if your organization can handle the risks and is willing to absorb the impact of risks before making your decision final. The experienced IT manager has developed an intuitive sense for measuring risk. But even the experienced managers will benefit from decision analysis since they can explain and defend their decisions by communicating the calculated risks and regrets for all decision alternatives. In a nutshell, if your organization is a risk taker and can handle the impact of risk and regret, then you should make your selection based on the highest payoff (maximax) from the list of choices. If you are risk averse, your decisions will be based on the Maximin approach.

In most instances Lean IT managers consider the utility of their decisions and select the option that carries a low regret and a high utility according to their corporate situation. If you are seeking to make a balanced decision, that means you are neutral to risk (neither risk averse, nor risk taker) then you should consider maximizing utility of your decision by considering the expected monetary value (EMV) as well as the lower expected monetary regret (EMR).

Summary

- Make management decisions with a long time horizon in mind.
- Make agility a decision factor. Avoid over reliance on strategic plans. Strategic planning is costly and often obsolete as soon as it's completed. The strategic planning approach has shown a high degree of failure because it limits organization's agility and decision making flexibility in the long run.
- Consider the following factors when making decisions:
    - Technology forecasts for software, hardware, tools and methods. Technology turns every 18 months.
    - Business trends, operational and regulatory changes ahead.
    - Return on investment over short term and long term.
    - Determine regret associated with each decision alternative.
    - Consider what will be your customer's needs now, in 18 months and in 5 years.
- Keep decision options open for as long as possible. Do not adopt decisions that narrow your future decision options or become dead-end. Decisions that lock your organization into a dead-end are highly costly to reverse.
- Defer commitment to decisions or actions until they are absolutely necessary, or until all necessary facts are known.
- Avoid analysis paralysis. If analysis gets stuck, apply 5S technique ("5S" technique was presented in earlier chapters).
- All decisions are reversible.

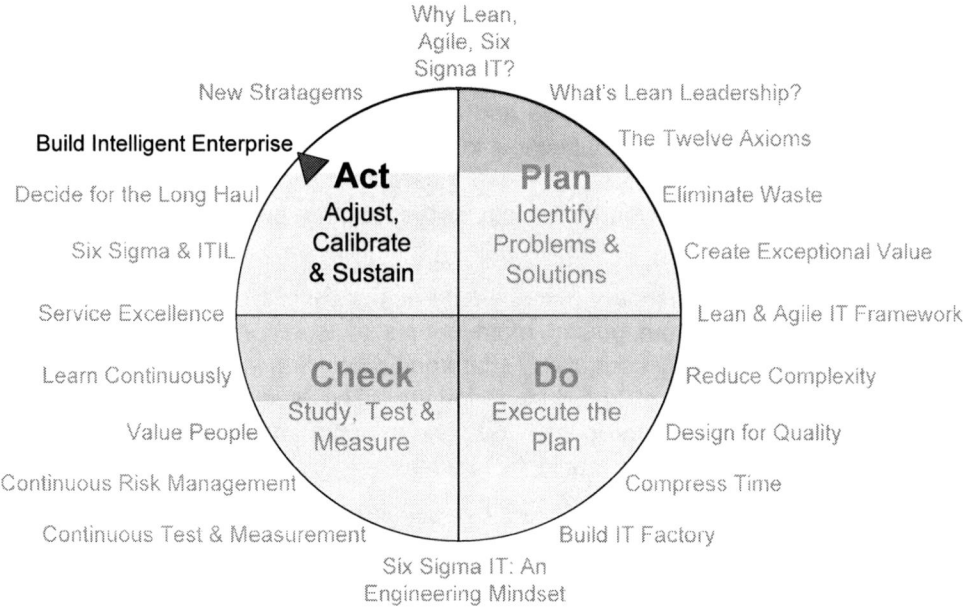

"We not only need complex, organic views of organizations, but we would benefit from not being put off by either the complexity or its mysteries."

J. Ralls and K. Webb

"The context in which people work is of vital importance. That means articulating a concise and relevant purpose which defines the shared tasks on all staff."

Robert Heller

Chapter 19. Build Intelligent Organizations

James Womack once stated: "How is it that perfectly rational people, behaving rationally produce such irrational results?" The amount of human energy that is wasted due to discordant and dysfunctional organizations is staggering. In the pursuit of perfection, the whole must be bigger and more intelligent than the sum of its parts.

Definitions for intelligent organizations vary depending on purpose and perspective. But generally, an intelligent organization consists of a team or groups of individuals who collectively do their best to pursue a common goal and achieve it with minimum cost, attrition and waste. In the context of Six Sigma, an intelligent organization can be defined as a group of individuals who despite internal or external noise, environmental variation and unexpected challenges, work together to produce outputs within specified target limits.

Another definition might characterize such organizations as a group of employees who are self organized, goal seeking and versatile. Intelligent organizations are self managed. They either adapt to or change the environmental, internal and external challenges that crop up. By nature they are good problem solvers. So, what does IT have to do with this chapter? Quite a lot. Information and communication technologies provide the platform, framework and medium to create and maintain an intelligent organization.

Modern management wisdom points out that the key to corporate competitiveness is people. It's a well known fact that people are a firm's most valuable asset. Derivatives of people asset are the intellectual property assets, inventions and innovations, but also workflows and processes that have been tried and tested by your organization. If you subscribe to the asset theory of information, then you must consider IT investments that make information and knowledge available at all levels of the firm. Information technology is the fuel that powers the firm's people, its intellectual engine.

According to legendary management author Peter Drucker, "economic growth can no longer come from putting more people to work or from greater economic demand. It can come only from a very sharp and continuing increase in the productivity of knowledge work and of knowledge workers." The level of people's cooperation, knowledge and ability to appropriately respond to opportunities and challenges will set the organization ahead of the rest in the industry.

During the industrial age, a firm's prosperity was measured in terms of material output and efficiency. Management's goals were simply to increase efficiency and reduce cost. In the present information age, we are measured by our intellectual productivity, how well we innovate and produce new goods that obsolete the previous ones. Intellectual productivity is the underlying measurement of the intelligent organization[80].

Peter Drucker on self management

Peter Drucker was a proponent of self management. He believed the professionals and knowledge workers, given the necessary tools and means to perform their work needed minimal supervision and management. "Working together as a team is like performing in an opera with a script and a conductor", he observed. All players serve each other in a performance. He also believed that "The Corporation that plays together, stays together".

In an interview in 2000, Peter Drucker commented on how corporations should abandon the old successful means for new ones that innovate. "A company should build a process that systematically looks at every product, every service, every process, every policy, every market with the question, "If we weren't doing this already, knowing what we now know, would we start it, would we go into it?" states Drucker. "If the answer is no", he adds, then they must ask, "What do we do? Not, let's make another study!"

Peter Drucker once stated that: "If you don't abandon [the old ways], you can't innovate." The ever increase in complexity is moving the enterprise towards unknowns where repetitive circumstances become less common and the ability to innovate new solutions becomes an undocumented job description for people. In his book, "The Ingenuity Gap", author Thomas Homer-Dixon explains how the magnitude and

---

[80] The next case study is from Peter Drucker, In an interview Telecast by Public Broadcasting Corporation, January 2000

complexity of challenges that face humanity today are far beyond the ingenuity available to solve them.

Traditional top-down intelligence must give way to bottom-up intelligence where people who are at the front lines of work make the appropriate decisions, in real time. What role can information technologies play? With proper management, information systems will create the intelligence needed to bridge the ingenuity gap.

The stark difference between Toyota Production System and traditional manufacturing systems was that the quality and productivity decisions were made by individuals on the assembly line, not by a QA manager, or worse yet in the corporate boardroom. How could a giant company like Toyota survive when individuals could bring the assembly line to a halt with a single button? We've seen that not only Toyota has survived, it has indeed thrived.

Although the Toyota Production System was based on relatively low-tech approaches such as kanbans, Andan and JIT, nevertheless it was highly information based. Information was to be visible, facts to be collected, and feedback valued. The workers understood production "messages" inherent in the "flow of goods", and knew what was expected of them at each stage of production[81].

Case Study: Lessons learned

How do well-funded organizations fail to perform? The alternative to intelligent organizations can have devastating consequences. When random shootings began in Washington, D.C. area in October 2004, more than 67,000 tips poured into the FBI's computerized database called Rapid Start.

But the volume overwhelmed FBI's information systems1. Rapid Response was set up because the agency's previous system was unable to share information among agents in different offices. Worse yet, the system was to blame for losing more than four thousand documents pertaining to the trial of Timothy McVeigh who blew up the FBI building in Oklahoma City in 1995, killing 168 people.

Shortly after 9/11, FBI began a project to overhaul its information technology. Three years later, then FBI director Robert Mueller announced that restructuring the bureau's information technology would take nearly two years. In 2005, the FBI was criticized when it disclosed plans to scrap a key element of the upgrade and delay the project another four years.

When the Slammer virus broke out of nowhere to contaminate hundreds of thousands of computer systems, the FBI took thirteen hours to publicly acknowledge the threat. By that time private antivirus companies had already issued alerts. A White House official explained, "FBI experts were at home and it was hard for the right personnel to respond"...

---

[81] The details of the following case studies are adapted from "Revolutionary Wealth" by Alvin and Heidi Toffler, Published by Alfred A. Knopf, Borzoi Books a subsidiary of Random House, Inc.

> ... Some believe that the FBI experts' computers were already infected with the virus and thus could not be reached. This pales in comparison to the information systems of the U.S. Immigration and Naturalization Service, which issued student visas to two dead terrorists who six months earlier had crashed into the World Trade Center. These examples illustrate irrational and obtuse organizational behaviors due to disjointed information systems that are out of tune with the organization's mission and workflows. It also demonstrates a lack of cooperation and willingness to share information between various agencies. The devastation of Hurricane Katrina in 2005 and the breakdown of the emergency response system and confusion between local, state and federal agencies to deliver help is another example of failed organizations. The hurricane response was a low point in information sharing, group coordination and organizations working in synchronicity. It clearly demonstrated a lack of coordinated decision making process because information was not commonly shared on the same frame of reference. Some claim that Katrina was more of a human made disaster than a natural disaster where thousands died and hundreds of thousands were forced to relocate.

Bureaucracies thrive on confusion and misinformation. Intentionally they attempt to cause dysfunction and mismatch of information such that the individual decision makers are left with ambiguous and incomplete picture of their situation, leading them to make the collectively imperceptive decisions. For example, before 9/11 neither the FBI, nor the CIA were communicating and coordinating their information and decision processes collaboratively and from a common frame of thinking. The differences between traditional, bureaucratic organizations and Lean organization are quite lucid. How can we tell the difference? The table on the next page describes some of the attributes for both types of organizations. In his seminal article entitled "Managing Complexity—The Path Toward Intelligent Organizations", professor Markus Schwaninger presents a framework for the design of intelligent organizations that links three organizational cybernetic models. The Models are: *Systemic Control*, the *Viable System Model*, and the *Team Syntegrity model*. Basically, Professor Schwaninger believes that a systemic approach to control of activities and integrated team approach are the basis for *organizational cybernetics*. His proposition is that a combined use of these models, guided by the integrative conceptual framework, enables a more effective response to complex situations than merely pragmatic approaches to "integrative management."

Organizational cybernetics rests on a basic framework in whichever organization is described to be composed of four functional layers: process, coordination, adaption and self-organization. One goal of organizational cybernetics is to minimize the difference between the overall purpose (or strategy) of the organization and each function it plays. Cybernetics was defined by the mathematician Norbert Wiener in 1947 as a discipline to study communication and control in living organisms and machine. Cybernetics principles are founded on communication theory and feedback loops. Organizational cybernetics has made major contributions to new forms of governance.

Attributes	Bureaucratic Organizations	Lean & Agile Organizations
Workflow	<ul><li>Ad-hoc;</li><li>Processes are not documented;</li><li>People are confused about the best practices;</li><li>The bully's way wins;</li><li>There are high degrees of variation in production</li></ul>	<ul><li>Process driven;</li><li>Processes are documented</li><li>People are trained on consistent methods;</li><li>Work is consistent;</li><li>Results are predictable;</li></ul>
Decisions	<ul><li>Are reactive in response to unexpected outcomes</li><li>Are for damage control;</li><li>The facts are either so obvious or are forcing the decision;</li><li>Are made by top management</li><li>Are delayed to preserve the status quo</li></ul>	<ul><li>Are proactive in pursuit of common goals</li><li>Are made in anticipation and to meet the future demands;</li><li>Are based on facts, information & analysis;</li><li>Analysis considers simulation of possible scenarios</li><li>Are made by workers</li></ul>
Authority	<ul><li>Authority is centralized</li><li>Employees are powerless</li><li>Employees wait for decisions to be issued</li></ul>	<ul><li>Authority is shared by employees</li><li>Authority is distributed by responsibility & accountability</li><li>Employees are empowered</li></ul>
Culture	<ul><li>Can not function without policies</li><li>Finger pointing is common</li><li>The means are more important than results</li></ul>	<ul><li>Promotes business architecture</li><li>Promotes PDCA</li><li>Accountability and results are expected</li></ul>
Organizational Form	<ul><li>Organized as departments and divisions</li><li>Low trust relationship between departments</li><li>Departments are silos</li></ul>	<ul><li>Team oriented</li><li>Teams are cross functional</li><li>High trust relationship between employees</li><li>Teams collaborate as partnerships</li></ul>

Fig 19.1 – A Comparison of Bureaucratic versus Lean & Agile Organizations

Principles of Intelligent Organization

Creating an Intelligent organization is founded on four principles. All four are enabled by Lean, Agile and Six Sigma Information Technology implementation. It provides that individuals work in such a way that the entire organization collectively exhibits intelligent behavior. The four principles are:

- **Organizational harmony and congruence.** Signs of harmony are evident in how staff works together, not against each other. It is evident when individual goals are congruent with the overall corporate objectives. The work performed by employees occurs in orchestration across functional boundaries. There is less rift, dispute and friction between employees. The workforce harmony is made possible by uniform, clear communication, process definition, workflow orchestration and consistent decision support. All are enabled by targeted information technology applications.

- **Transform workplace from analog to digital.** This is accomplished by systemically eradicating analog forms of data and communication. Eliminating paper forms and printed material in favor of paperless processes are good starting steps. Converting all forms of analog data into digital form requires mass storage and long term data strategies. Creating a digital work environment allows easy access to data and increases worker efficiency.

- **Adaptability, feedback and responsiveness:** This principle allows organizations to respond properly to threats as well as to opportunities. Feedback loops provide control and work based on taking constant measurements. Adaptability is a sign of natural intelligence. The organization which can adapt to new situations, sets targets and achieves them is an intelligent organism: a collection of employees identify threats who can adapt to new situations, set targets and achieve them as collection of individuals.

- **Transforming working staff from ad hoc work habits to disciplined knowledge workers:** Discipline comes from process definition and documentation.

Despite their seemingly routine work, intelligent organizations and their employees function and behave in alignment to reach a common optimization objective. They are goal seeking people who use feedback and real time information to adjust their work decisions[82].

The Case for Real Time Data

7-Eleven has developed a business intelligence database that collects 22 million records every day from its stores and operations worldwide. Previously, the company used traditional data gathering methods which allowed focusing on past trends. The new real time business intelligence database has caused a cultural shift as 7-Eleven can forecast future business opportunities. Real time decision support...

---

[82] The following case study is from "IT-Based Decision Tools For Item Processing Operations Management in Retail Banking", Charles J. Malmborg, in Annals of Cases in Information Technology.

> ... systems can provide huge savings. When the executives of a medium size bank in the United States decided to reduce expenses from retail operations, they considered implementing a decision support system to optimize their check processing operations1. The bank had over 1,000 retail branches spread over 16 states. Management hired a consulting firm to study and implement a decision support system to improve check processing operations.
>
> The goal of this project was to save $80 million dollars per year. The consulting team successfully delivered the system by combining real time data reporting from branches and imaging software to create updated scheduling criteria that reflected current business conditions. These projects were performed successfully and in a short amount of time.

The Rise of Intelligent Organizations

So, what's all the fuss about creating an intelligent organization? Futurists Alvin and Heidi Toffler in their recent book, "Revolutionary Wealth", talk about increased complexity in all facets of work and products we use. They site examples such as Microsoft's Windows XP software containing fifty million lines of code and Windows Vista with even more, which point to increased complexity in IT products[83].

Alvin and Heidi Toffler argue that as civilization moved from agrarian to industrial and now to a knowledge based society, it creates a larger volume of information and increased levels of complexity. They write: "Yet another measure of skyrocketing complexity is the increase in sub and sub-sub-specialties in many fields. Half a century ago, before the shift to a knowledge economy began, the health-care profession was divided into about ten specializations. Today there are more than 220 categories of medical professionals. In the 1970s they had to stay abreast of approximately one hundred randomized, controlled clinical research trials a year. Today the annual number is ten thousand."

As the number of interacting components of systems and functional features increase, complexity increases by the same power. The result of increased complexity is confusion and a tendency to lose sight of uniformity, standardization and intended purpose for applications. Information Technology architects face growing complexity in every layer of data, application, networks and information hierarchy while conflicting goals and priorities add to their challenge to create a cohesive enterprise information architecture.

Two other forces that engorge this challenge are simultaneous trends of convergence and divergence. As an example of convergence, consider cell phones. Increasingly cell phones offer rich functionality, from taking digital pictures, emails, text messaging, online shopping, calendars, contact management and hopefully making phone calls. As the other force, we are accelerating towards the biggest divergence of technology ever. Many applications and information technology products do not

---

[83] "Revolutionary Wealth", Alvin and Heidi Toffler, Knopf, Borzoi Books, a division of Random House Inc.

interface with each other. Consider how you interact with your automobile GPS guidance system, smart phone, onboard computer in your car, Tivo system, microwave, game box, laptop and other gadgets. Each device requires a different password, a different method of interaction, and perhaps none are similar when it comes to programming its clock. Amidst the dynamic and ever changing business demands on information technology, we must create a stable, but flexible IT platform to meet those challenges.

Second Order Thinking

Intelligent organizations promote thinking from the bottom up. In his book, "Emergence: The Connected Lives of Ants, Brains, Cities and Software", author Steven Johnson describes how ants despite their limited brains and intelligence are able to function in an orchestrated manner building such feats as their colonies and storing supplies for all winter. In such organizations, the individual actors are highly loyal to the process and mission. Each individual is aware and supportive of their coworkers. As a result their actions are in concert with one another. Workflow-driven applications that cross multiple functional areas promise to create organizational harmony and feedback.

Web technologies are creating communities of users and netizens connecting thousands of people by creating information portals and common themes. For example, consider the world record for simultaneous webcast viewers for one video stream event at 100,000 hits, which was set by Pope Benedict XVI's first mass. Web portals which used to post expert opinions, now seek user feedback and post ratings instead[84].

> **On Personal Software Process**
>
> **Watts S. Humphrey, has been a research scientist at Carnegie Mellon University's Software Engineering Institute. In 2005, he received the National Medal of Technology for his work in improving intellectual productivity in computer programming. Humphrey, a retired IBM executive believes that the industrial changes of the 19th and 20th centuries were driven by time-motion studies. The studies helped companies find the most cost-effective ways for workers to build products. "Our approach, sort of the dream we've followed, is to use those principles in intellectual work," he stated in an interview. "Finding ways to improve intellectual productivity is easy compared to the task of getting programmers to adopt new work methods", adds Humphrey, "You can't tell people how to think. They're going to think the way they think." In the institute's Personal Software Process, participants keep track of their work habits while they write computer programs. Then, as they try different techniques, the data shows them that they're writing more code with fewer errors and taking less time to do it", adds Humphrey. A CIO at Microsoft...**

---

[84] The next case study is from "President honors CMU fellow for scientific achievement", Brian Bowling, Pittsburgh Tribune-Review, March 15, 2005.

> ... is reported to have said: "IT must also accelerate and increase the intellectual productivity, which is our most valuable resource, our people." He believes that there are three IT principles that can exponentially increase intellectual productivity at Microsoft. These principles are tightly integrated systems, reliability and flexibility of IT tools that allow change.

Feedback is important to creating adaptive systems. Encouraging what's known as second order thinking throughout the organization is likely to produce the desired bottom-up intelligence. A thermostat is a good example that describes second order thinking. If you set the thermostat to 70 degrees, it has a feedback mechanism that keeps the temperature in the room at that level.

It basically monitors and controls the operation of the heating unit. That's first order intelligence. But, if the thermostat asks: "Why is the temperature set to 70 degrees?" that's second order intelligence. A similar concept occurs with intelligent organizations. Information technologies provide up to date feedback about current state and forecasts about future conditions. These are provided in the form of personalized dashboards (dashlets), alerts, and personalized, automated decision support reports. Decision support systems guide the knowledge worker when required.

Information Technology provides frames of reference for decision making and intelligence. Through a revolutionary psychology work in 1955 by Gregory Bateson, observing monkeys playing with each other in a zoo, we know that while animals cannot directly communicate nevertheless they seem to "understand" each other. Bateson proposed the concept of psychological frame that resolves ambiguity of what is "inside", what is "outside" like a picture frame. Monkeys do not negotiate an agreement to play but their social life has taught them the frame "play". Humans have enormous levels and number of frames. Frames are meta communicative and allow norms for interaction and work.

The notion of frames has a high place in artificial intelligence. Noam Chomsky has published a number of papers and books on this subject, providing frames as communication structures for semantics and meaning. When we consider the 5S, 6M or Six Sigma methods, they are indeed frames of thought and business operation. Creating an intelligent organization through Information Systems requires that we build and support the right frames in the organization. Let's consider the pyramid of priority and corresponding planes of optimization.

The diagram in Figure 19.2 attempts to illustrate that in each layer of priority, employees make decisions in alignment with the optimization objectives of that plane. For example, in the "Patient Safety" plane, the organization attempts to minimize patient safety incidents.

In the "Practice Efficiency" mental frame, the employees attempt to accelerate patient recovery and reduce patient length of stay in the hospital. These two optimization goals are almost congruent as long as they do not squeeze the length of stay to the point that negatively affects patient care. All lower level optimization goals should subordinate to the higher levels of the pyramid.

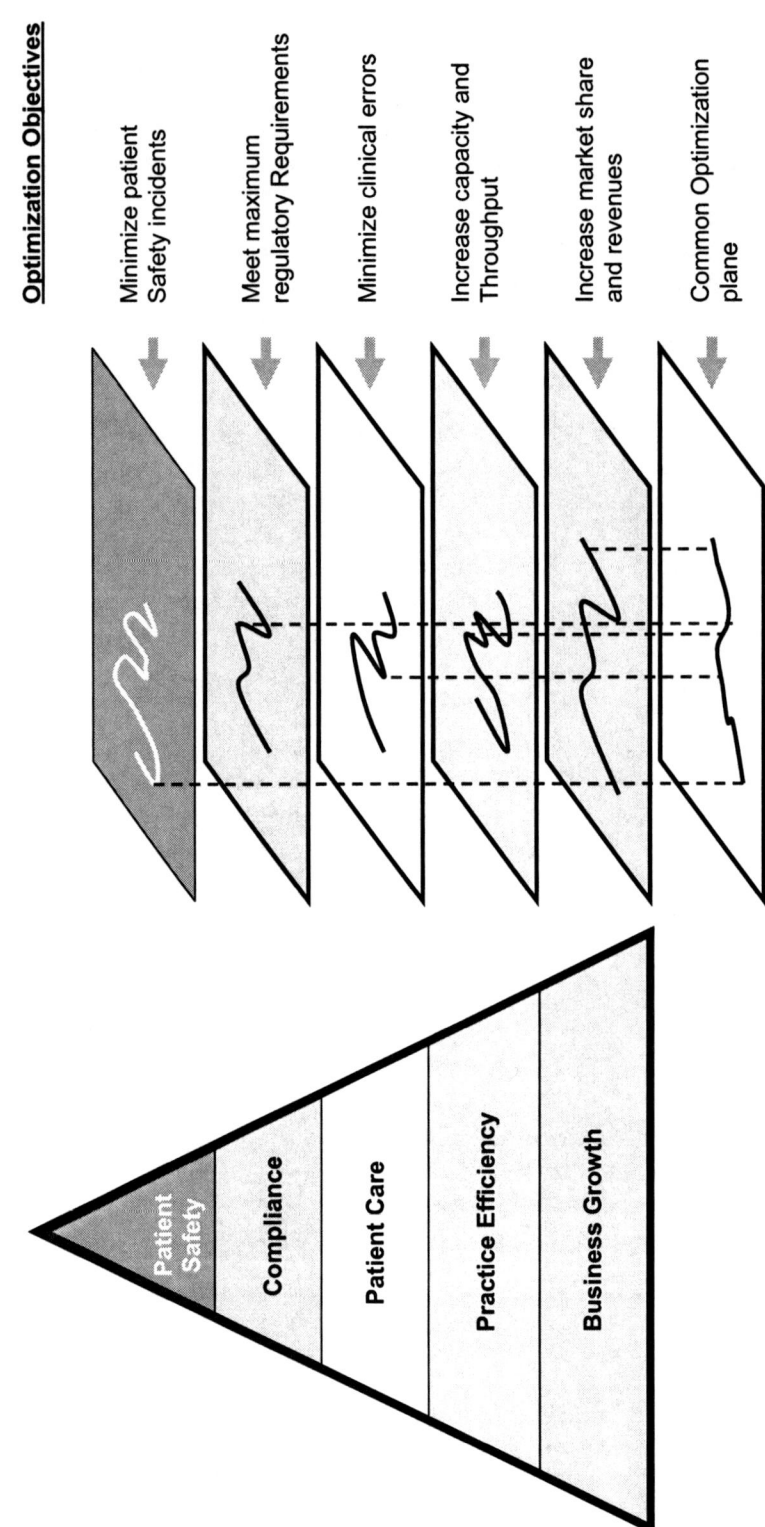

Fig 19.2 – Pyramid of Priority as Blueprint for Global Optimization of the Enterprise

If we map these optimization points on a single plane, by overlaying all planes, we collect a number of minimum and maximum points. Is it possible for information systems to bring all these optimization objectives into a single frame? If so, how? One possible answer is to use influence diagrams (see Six Sigma IT Methods and Standard Chapter). Influence diagrams attempt to answer questions like: "What factors influence and contribute to achieving a particular optimization point? This is a difficult challenge because the optimization planes are non-linear, some are disjointed and some are interconnected. Following the Six Sigma transfer function, we are seeking to find the correct weights for the X's in each plane. Using influence diagrams we try to bring some normative scale to the cause and effect factors. Influence diagrams can point out the weight (or importance) associated to each X's. This approach can lead to using *Optimized Score Cards*, and for decision testing ultimately simulation provides the globally optimal answers.

In Figure 19.2, I've super-imposed the five layers of the priority for illustration. On each layer the employees attempt to optimize for that level of priority. The plane on the right side shows a hypothetical optimization graph. On each plane, a set of mental frames attempt to optimize for that layer. In intelligent organizations, the lower level mental frames must be subordinated to the higher level priority. The far bottom plane shows what the optimization graph could look like from combining the graphs from the upper levels. The optimizations at the upper levels take precedence (and should have higher weights) over the optimization goals at the lower levels. But, what is the appropriate combination of weights and how do we maintain correct course towards organizational goals and objectives? Not a balanced score card, but an optimized score card can be an answer.

Influence diagrams (or causal diagrams), point us to primary causal factors that guide the employees towards achieving the optimization goal. Looking at the Common Optimization Plan shown on the diagram, clearly meeting all these objectives can be conflicting and confusing to employees. Clarity and harmony of work in an intelligent enterprise is possible by identifying and harmonizing the primary causal factors. Goal seeking nature of such organizations assures achievement while preserving energy and resources.

Information Technology can enable all four principles to transform a less than optimal organization to an intelligent organization. Influence diagrams can be created to show which variables ('X's) influence the optimization goals at each level. A brain storming session with company executives can bring all optimization objectives into a clear and coherent set of information technology framework using influence diagrams. The brain storming session should include managers from all functions of the organization representing the priority levels of the organization.

Using Simulation to Optimize inventory management

A laboratory performs procedures which use a variety of devices, some are perishable and must be used before their end of life date. Once devices are used, they must be disposed of. The lab manger carries close to $3M in device inventory, and would like to reduce it in half. There are about 100 different models of devices. Every day the lab uses as many as 10-20 devices. The cost of each device ranges from $500 to $2000. The structural variation in this system is that the majority of lab tests are done Mon-Thurs. About two-thirds of the lab tests are scheduled a few days in advance. Only one-third of tests are scheduled on the same day. Can IT help? The answer is "yes".

After simulating the various usage patterns, the lab was able to reduce its inventory level by $1M. Traditional problem solving approaches worked with static and deterministic data sets. However, in the more complex, high-mix, multi-procedure environments (such as the example presented in the laboratory case study) static data analysis is inadequate. IT can help in at least three ways: A) Adjust inventory to usage patterns from historical data, B) Identify optimal inventory level by optimization using Linear Programming, C) Perform simulations based on forecasted or scheduled procedures.

Analyzing historical usage patterns in option A, using data mining techniques will discover the structural randomness and trends about specific device usage. The lab manager can gradually adjust purchasing volumes to reduce inventory levels, but there is no guarantee that the inventory level is optimal going forward. Option B utilizes Linear Programming, a problem solving technique commonly used in Operations Research. This is a powerful tool for solving deterministic problems such as finding the shortest path problems in transportation or finding the most profitable mix of products to produce from a given set of resources. This approach is based on constraints.

We wish to find the optimum inventory level for each device type while keeping the total inventory cost within budget. A linear programming model can be solved to determine a minimum stock level for devices and a total inventory cost not to exceed $2M. For example, there must be at least "N" number of devices in stock and the total inventory cost not to exceed $2M. While this is an improvement over the previous option, it is still deterministic and does not consider random patterns.

In option C, simulation can provide a distribution curve of device usage. The distribution curve determines the probability that a certain quantity will be consumed. Given the probability distribution, we can say with some confidence how much inventory to stock. Simulation takes into account prior usage patterns as well as the forecast of procedures and structural variation. Simulation allows the pull system to become a predictive system, thereby reducing the wait time and inventory levels. Before changing workflows, we can simulate the results by modeling a micro world of the environment.

Simulation allows performing "what-if" analysis to help managers make informed decisions. We can run the same simulation model with sensitivity analysis to determine which variables are critical to the output variations.

Extend is a simulation model program that has been successfully used to model various business scenarios. It was used by a group of students at Ohio State University in 2002 to correctly predict the winner of the 2001 World Series baseball games[85]. Using Extend simulation tool, another researcher, J.J. Curry was able to simulate the results of converting a manufacturing resource planning (MRP) based push process to a demand-driven pull process in a single plant operation factory

---

[85] "OSU Students Predict World Series Outcome Using Simulation from Imagine That!", Press Release, Imagine That!, September 10, 2002

floor[86]. The simulation program allowed plant managers to visually see and measure how processes perform overtime, including materials, information and financial flows, and how probabilistic variables impacted them.

Matrix Organizations – RIM & RAM

Hierarchical organizational charts neither have no place nor value in a Lean organization. They only convey lack of empowerment for individuals in the lower echelons. They protract a culture that confines thinking to the top management. Two models for Matrix organization are presented in this section. The goal of the matrix organization is to create intentional overlap of roles and responsibilities for individuals. The models are also designed to clarify the responsibilities.

The first model is *Responsibility Assignment Matrix (RAM)*. It not only shows who is accountable for what, but also shows who should be contacted for their expertise. In the RAM model, specific domains of work are listed as rows (in the example, the rows are application domains). The roles are listed as columns. The name of individuals (initials are shown in the example) are placed where the roles and responsibilities meet.

The diagram is an example from a small IT department. Each row and each column represent the formation of two separate virtual teams. The initials represent employee names that are responsible for each cell in the table, as well as their virtual team formation.

> **Cases of Success from Matrix Organizations**
>
> The Vanguard Group, headquartered in Valley Forge, Pennsylvania employs about 10,000 people. As an Agile company, forming virtual and cross functional teams to achieve strategic initiatives are common in the company culture. During peak customer calls a cross functional team of employees, IT staffers and even the CEO answer customer calls. The team is referred to as a "Swiss Army". The IT department uses Java and XML to allow custom applications to run in multiple operating environments without changing code, thus reducing IT maintenance costs.
>
> General Motors Corporation is a complex organization with many functional divisions and strategies. The company implemented a unique matrix of process information officers and business process officers. By combining these management points, GM was able to gain tremendous improvement in its IT operations. The company was able to achieve cost flexibility by using outsourced IT resources for almost 95 percent of its information technology needs. The management matrix supervised the outsourced IT staff.

---

[86] "A Lean Analysis Methodology Using Simulation", J.J. Curry, Society of Manufacturing Engineers, 2007

Responsibility Assignment Matrix (RAM)

Functional Area > Application Area ∨	Systems Support	Network Engineering	Security	Backups	Business Intelligence	Application Maintenance	Customer Support	Desktop Support	Interface Development
Surgery Application	CP	CP	CP	CP	JM	ME	ME	MS	ME
Radiology Info System V9	ZA	CP	ZA	CP	JM	ZA, JM	ZA, MS	MS	ME
Radiology Info System V10	CP	CP	CP	CP	ZA, MM, JM	ZA, MM, JM	ZA, MM, JM	MS	ZA, ME
Research Application	MM	MM	MM	MM	MM	MM	MM	---	ME
PACS Application	GC, CP	CP	CP	GC, JF	GC, JF	GC, JF, DL	GC, JF, DL	GC, JF, DL	GC, ME
Voice Recognition	CP	CP	CP	CP	MM	MM, JM, ZA	MM, JM, ZA	MS	ME
EKG Application	CP	CP	CP	CP	JM	JM, BA, CP	JM, BA, CP	CLE	ME
Echo Application	CP	CP	CP	CP	CP	CP, BA	CP, BA	CLE	ME
Cath Application	CP	CP	CP	CP	JM, MM	CP, BA	CP, BA	CLE	ME
Endoscopy Application	BA	BA	BA	CP	BA	BA	BA, CP	CLE	ME
Anesthesia Application	CP	CP	CP	CP	JM	ME	ME	BA	ME
TeleConsulst Application	CP	CP	CP	CP	ME	ME	ME	ME	ME
Application Factory	ME, CP, BA	ME, CP, BA	ME, CP, BA	ME, CP, BA	ME, CP, BA	ME, CP, BA	ME, CP, BA	ME, CP, BA	ME

Fig 19.3 – Responsibility Assignment Matrix Example

The other model is the *Responsibility Interface Matrix (RIM)*. In this organization chart, the name of individuals are listed as rows and field of work as columns. Each cell in the matrix describes the role and responsibility of the individual with respect to the domain, in an action verb. The initials imply what the individual is expected to perform. For example, the letter 'P' means 'Purchases'. 'A' is for 'Approves'. 'S' means 'Supports', and so on. The example below is from a paperless manufacturing company who designs and manufactures robotics in the United States. Can you tell who is the VP of manufacturing or the CEO by looking at this matrix? It's hard to tell, but you can clearly point out who is performing those roles.

Responsibility Interface Matrix (RIM)								
Names - Domains	Design	Supplies	Mfg. Eng.	Sales Proposal	Staffing	Testing	Inventory Mgt	Shipping
John Holmes	I, A	I	A	C, A	---	D	---	---
April Milam	P	---	I, A	---	---	I, C	---	---
Sam Johnson	A	D	P	I, A	A	I, C	I	I
Paul Maneli	P, A	A, I	A, I, C	A, I, C	A, I	I, C	I	A
Maury Smith	---	---	---	I, C	P	---	---	---
Adam Benson	---	---	C	---	---	P	---	S, R
Greg Harrison	---	R, I	I, C	---	---	---	P, I	P, I
Norma Belany	P	---	D	P, D	I	---	---	---
James Lancaster	---	---	---	---	---	P, A	A, I, C	I, C
John Schefield	P	---	P	---	---	P	---	---
Peter Schwartz	---	P, I	---	---	---	I, C	I, C	S, R
Glen Morrison	D	---	I, C	---	P	I, C	I	---

Approves	A
Performs	P
Inspects/Reviews	I
Sends	S
Receives	R
Develops	D
Comments	C

Fig 19.4 – Responsibility Interface Matrix Example

Intellectual Productivity

Peter Drucker, who is recognized as the father of modern management coined the famous term "knowledge worker" and is believed to have introduced the knowledge economy, essentially challenging Karl Marx's economic thesis. Peter Drucker believed that the ideal team does not have one leader, but all team members serve each other.

Peter Drucker writes: "The new challenge facing the post-capitalist society is the productivity of knowledge workers and service workers. To improve the productivity of knowledge workers will in fact require drastic changes in the structure of the organizations of post-capitalist society and in the structure of society itself. Forty years ago people doing knowledge work and service work were still less than one-third of the workforce. Now such people account for three-quarters if not four-fifths of the workforce in all developed countries – and their share is still going up. Their productivity, rather than the productivity of the people who make and move things, is the productivity of a developed economy... and that's abysmally low. " Clifford A. Lynch is the executive director of the Coalition for Networked Information (CNI) and a leading analyst for technology trends in education, libraries, publishing and cultural arenas.

The goal of CNI is to transform networked information technology for the advancement of scholarly communication and the enrichment of intellectual productivity. Clifford Lynch believes that as the world moves towards digital information objects, we are likely to see a great deal of cyber infrastructure leading to digital economy, digital asset management and other digital forms of knowledge which present new tools and challenges[87]. In an interview, Lynch stated "We're going to be facing an enormous amount of observational data, of experimental data, of data that represents the results of various kinds of simulations. Software is, in itself, going to become an important component of scholarship and scholarly communication, and frankly, I don't think we're well-equipped to manage this—at many different levels. Those who are starting to think about this issue talk about a new breed of support people called *data scientists*. But it's not at all clear where we're going to find these people, how we're going to train them, what they need to know, or where they fit in our organizations."

The points raised by Lynch force us to rethink the information technology staff roles and organizational structure. Increasingly information technology applications are falling behind users expectations in this area. For the organization to act intelligently, decision support is no longer sufficient. It requires decision simulation, real time what-if analysis and scenario testing. Workflow changes can occur more rapidly than before. Overall workflow orchestration across the enterprise is needed. Applications featuring real time data acquisition and continuous optimization that can guide management to make best possible decisions are required.

Intelligent Enterprise

A more powerful use of information systems is to manage the organization as a real time enterprise. Today's decision support systems are used as a reflection of the past events to enable executive decisions. Businesses rarely take advantage of detecting events and information in real time to run their business more effectively. The way Federated Retail Stores – a synonym for an actual national retail chain- and power utility corporations manage information are good examples for real time information systems. T

he cash registers in Federated Retail Store report the volume of sales by item to the headquarters every 5 minutes. The headquarters is able to detect which items are selling fast and which items are slow to sell. Armed with this information, Federated Retail Stores announces daily sales on items that are not selling fast enough. Likewise, the power utility company is aware of power consumption in its grid in real time and adjusts purchase or sales of power to energy wholesalers. Information systems can be harnessed to inform status of business at any given moment and provide management with an operational management model that can respond

---

[87] "Educause Review", March/April 2006, pages 40-46

quickly. Moreover, many of such real time events if not detected early can lead to escalated, unpredictable and undesirable consequences. Real time information systems can help prevent bigger issues.

But the Federated Retail Stores and the power utilities use information systems in even more effective ways. Both enterprises use simulation models to forecast the future possible events. Both enterprises use the weather models and economic forecasts to predict demand. If a cold winter is predicted, consumers will need more coats and more power to heat their homes. If the interest rates rise, consumers are likely to spend less on luxury items. Such rules of thumb can feed into the real time simulator to make an adaptable decision making process available to the enterprise executives. Information systems can be used to approximate the future in real time, based on previously built models that mimic the organization's business patterns. These approximations give executives the insight into better decisions and strategies.

> **The Case of a Failed Consortium**
>
> A consortium of eight of the largest Savings and Loan firms began a project to update their information and data processing systems. To start the project, they needed a large datacenter. Each firm contributed its share of people who understood their bank for converting their systems into the new common datacenter.
>
> The system consisted of two applications: one for loan processing and another for deposit-withdrawals. The project emphasized security, but security was designed as an external system. After years of delay, the consortium leaders decided to buy a package rather than build from scratch. After a search for software, the decision was made. However, each piece of software for loan, deposit and security would come from different vendors.
>
> The problems continued as the IT people discovered that the loan software did not have the exact functions that an S&L needed. Worse, yet, one of the consortium members decided to keep its savings package rather than use the new system. Furthermore, a middleware was needed to connect the loan and deposit packages. The bank employees were not involved in the design process. They were not consulted on many project decisions either. Soon the troubles for IT management became worse as auditors discovered the cost of operations for the new datacenter was about $500,000 per month! Soon four out of eight banks pulled out of the project. This meant that the remaining four banks had to pay more to carry the project.
>
> Management had sunk so much money in this project that it would lose face if it agreed that the project would not deliver the intended results. Another blow came when it was announced that the datacenter was not operationally ready. The online security system did not function as intended and it was hard to maintain. The stress tests failed decisively. However, the system was finally introduced to the first bank. The release went well, but the users were unhappy because they had to contend ...

... with two different user interfaces to perform their work. The poor performance issues were traced to the security system which was located at a remote datacenter. The transactions were sent each time to the security system and tellers had to wait for permission over long distance network. Sometimes when a response did not arrive in time, tellers repeated their transaction. This caused duplication of transactions and as a result the bank would not balance at end of the day. The issues lingered for almost 3 more years, but by that time the bank leadership had enough. One of the consortium banks purchased the interests of the other three. The president of the remaining bank hired an accounting firm to conduct a search for the new ideal in-house system. But that effort failed as well, and the bank decided to live with the problematic datacenter. But soon, the bank who operated the datacenter became insolvent and was purchased by a larger bank which repossessed the datacenter. Eventually all remaining four banks were repossessed or purchased costing many jobs.

The auditor summed up the case as: "It is significant that not one but four organizations buried themselves in this project. While I feel Management was always informed of difficulties, political considerations prevented any thought of withdrawal from the project..." One moral of this case study is that the eight institutions were not operating from the same mental frame and business compass. Each had a different view of what the new data center was intended to be. Lack of cooperation from one or two institutions made huge marks towards failure of this consortium. Although seemingly the project failed, it was the consortium that failed. Lack of cooperation is a sign of lack of organizational intelligence.

Balanced Scorecard

Balanced Score Card was developed in 1993 by Robert S. Kaplan and David P. Norton through several journal articles. The roots of balanced score card go back to management by objective principles which were publicized by the same authors in the early 1990s. The purpose of balanced score card is to provide a performance planning and measurement framework using financial and non-financial measurements on execution metrics of the company's vision, objectives and strategies. Balanced score card focuses management on strategic issues and implementation strategy. The latest methods work by selecting measurements based on a set of strategic objectives plotted on a strategic linkage model or a strategy map. Managers define strategic objectives and link them to a set of measurements similar to a causal or influence diagram. To create a Balance Scorecard, we consider performance measure in four dimensions: Financial perspective, Customer perspective, Internal process perspective, Learning and Growth perspective:

1. **Financial Perspective:** Meet corporate financial initiatives and improve internal IT financial performance.

2. **Customer Perspective:** To Partner with our customers by providing the technology and services to enable their success

3. **Internal Process Perspective:** Develop and maintain an information systems environment which meets customers' strategic and operational needs.

4. **Innovation and Learning:** To foster an environment where we attract and retain employees, encourage creativity, and support adoption of relevant new technology.

Balanced score card has been useful in linking budgets with strategy, making strategies operational and alignment of the organization with strategy. Our modification to the Balanced Scorecard overcomes the criticism that it does not necessarily optimize the performance of the organization nor give a prescription for which decisions are necessary to produce an optimal outcome. The modified version which I've called the Optimized Scorecard is more in line with Hoshin Kanri and more suitable for Agile and Lean organizations.

Optimized Scorecard

The Optimized Scorecard for IT lists a number of objectives that support the corporate strategy. For each objective, metrics, target performance, initiatives and business case are defined. In the objective and business case segment, we identify the priority and how we intend to optimize for that objective. Figure 19.5 shows a framework for Optimized Scorecard. The weights applied to each objective define the level of focus that management wants the staff to exercise on its corresponding initiatives.

Perspective: **Financial**
Goal: **Meet corporate financial initiatives and improve internal IT financial performance.**

Objectives	Measures	Targets	Initiatives	Business Case
Manage Operating Expense within budget Priority: Low Weight: 20%	Budget shortfall from forecast Frequency: Quarterly. Owner: Mary	Target: 100% within budget	- Budget planning - Periodic budget reviews	IMPROVE FINANCIAL CONTROLS
Improve accounts receivable accuracy Priority: High Weight: 70%	Reduction of customer payment denials Frequency: Monthly. Owner: Nancy	Target: 100% reduction in customer payment denials	- Improve Help Desk support tools - Train more users on applications	IMPROVE REVENUES

Perspective: **Customer**
Goal: **To Partner with our customers by providing the technology and services to enable their success.**

Objectives	Measures	Targets	Initiatives	Business Case
Increase Application support level Priority: Low Weight: 20%	1. Rating from internal and external customers Frequency: Quarterly. Owner: John	Target: 99% satisfaction	- Improve Help Desk support tools - Train more users on applications	IMPROVE QUALITY: To improve the quality of our customer service.

Perspective: **Internal Processes - Operations**
Goal: **Develop and maintain an information systems environment which meets customers' strategic and operational needs.**

Objectives	Measures	Targets	Initiatives	Business Case
Improve internal testing processes Priority: Medium Weight: 60%	Days reduced from project cycle Frequency: Weekly. Owner: Adam	Target: 200% reduction in testing cycle	- Improve testing processes & organization's tools - Train more testers on consistent internal processes	IMPROVE QUALITY: To improve the quality of our products. IMPROVE TIME TO MARKET: Reduce project schedules

Perspective: **Innovation & Learning**
Goal: **To foster an environment where we attract and retain employees, encourage creativity, and support adoption of relevant new technology.**

Objectives	Measures	Targets	Initiatives	Business Case
Attract & retain high quality staff Priority: Medium Weight: 60%	1. New employees hired in target skill areas 2. Number of internal courses completed Frequency: Quarterly. Owner: James	1. Target: 100% positions filled 2. Target: 75 courses completed	- Human resources workshops - On-site training courses	IMPROVE KNOWLEDGE LEVEL: Increase skills and staff knowledge

Fig 19.5 – Balance Score Card Dash Board

Hoshin Kanri

Hoshin Kanri is a powerful management tool for planning breakthrough or quantum leap objectives. The Hoshin method provides the mechanism for linking short term projects and activities to mid-term plans and ultimately to long-term, breakthrough plans.

I close this chapter by discussing Hoshin Kanri because of its keen ability to align the enterprise, employees and management to the corporate objectives over a long sustainable time span and to produce spectacular results.

While Kaizen is the method of choice for continuous improvement at incremental steps, Hoshin is the tool for long range planning and execution for all levels of organization, the executive, the mid-level management and the staff.

Hoshin consists of tiered and layerd management systems. As a tool for governance and steering, it embraces four management systems:

1. Long range planning to define go-forward strategy and long term direction of the organization
2. Daily management to focus on local operational activities and projects
3. Cross-functional management to direct and control horizontal processes across local operations, departments and divisions
4. Strategy management to execute and manage change

Hoshin planning is a management methodology that offers many advantages to Lean, Agile and Six Sigma organizations. For example, it maintains both long term and short term, agility and focus. It helps align the organization with external and environmental changes such as competitive, economic and regulatory changes. Hoshin identifies challenges and gaps between the ideal future and the present situation. It also mobilizes the entire organization to close the gaps.

Hoshin is different from strategic planning in many ways. Similar to Six Sigma methods, it listens to the voice of the customer, not just the market or profitability. Hoshin is a system of continuous management that transcends calendar-based objectives. It drives the methods and means of strategy execution, not just the results. Since Hoshin recommends frequent reviews and checks through the entire echelon of the organization, it is strategically agile by design.

Hoshin method starts with a Study-Act followed by a full Deming cycle of Plan-Do-Check-Act (PDCA), also known as the Plan-Do-Study-Act cycle. The initial Study-Act steps identify the reality of the current situation and identify strategic gaps between the current situation and the future customer needs. The Act step narrows down the strategic choices into a few vital breakthroughs needed to bridge the gaps. The Plan step identifies the mid-term objectives necessary to achieve the breakthroughs. Employees are invited to participate in the planning process and develop ideas and projects that help close the gaps.

There are annual Hoshin meetings designed to review and monitor the progress towards achieving the long range plans. The Do-Check steps identify the methods and measurements at all levels of the organization and help manage the execution of plans. At the regular Hoshin meetings, employees can make adjustments and correction to short term plans if necessary. The short term plans are translated into Daily Management activities by employees.

Hoshin planning creates alignment across all echelons of the company, across daily activities, weekly, monthly, quarterly and annual plans. To practice Hoshin in IT organizations, we can review the SA-PDSA cycle more closely. The next diagram (Figure 19.6) illustrates the Hoshin process. Once again, the Hoshin method begins with the Study-Act steps:

Study: This step answers questions such as:

- What is the current situation?
- What business are we in?
- Who will be our customers in 5 or 10 years?
- What do our customers want in 5 or 10 years?
- What are our core competencies?
- What is our primary purpose as an organization?

Act: The goal of this step is to identify a compelling vision of the company of the future, its products and services. The result of this step is a map that connects the current situation to an idealized future for the company. It works from an ideal future and works backwards to the current situation. In other words, the planning process works backwards.

This step considers questions, data and facts that can describe the vision of the future, such as:

- What are the trends and forecasts in the market, industry, customer life styles, and work habits?
- In what direction the external factors such as regulation, economic forces, competition, and technology are headed?
- What purpose and benefit could we fulfill for our customers in 5 or 10 years?
- What products or services should we offer to be the vendor of choice to our customers?
- What should our internal structure and organization be to deliver those products or services?
- What will our information systems look like to enable those organizational structures, products and services?

When this step is completed, a strategic vision of the company, its organization, structure, products, services along with its information systems are presented.

Plan: This step identifies a vital few breakthrough objectives for the company to pursue. The advantage of Hoshin is in its ability to align employees with the corporate vision and breakthrough objectives. Employees are encouraged to participate in selection and ranking of breakthrough objectives.

The goal of this step is to rank the objectives based on their impact on a set of attributes that make the strategic vision possible. Any objectives that are incremental are removed from the list and added under Kaizen continuous improvement projects. Management must select only a few, preferably only one or two breakthrough objectives.

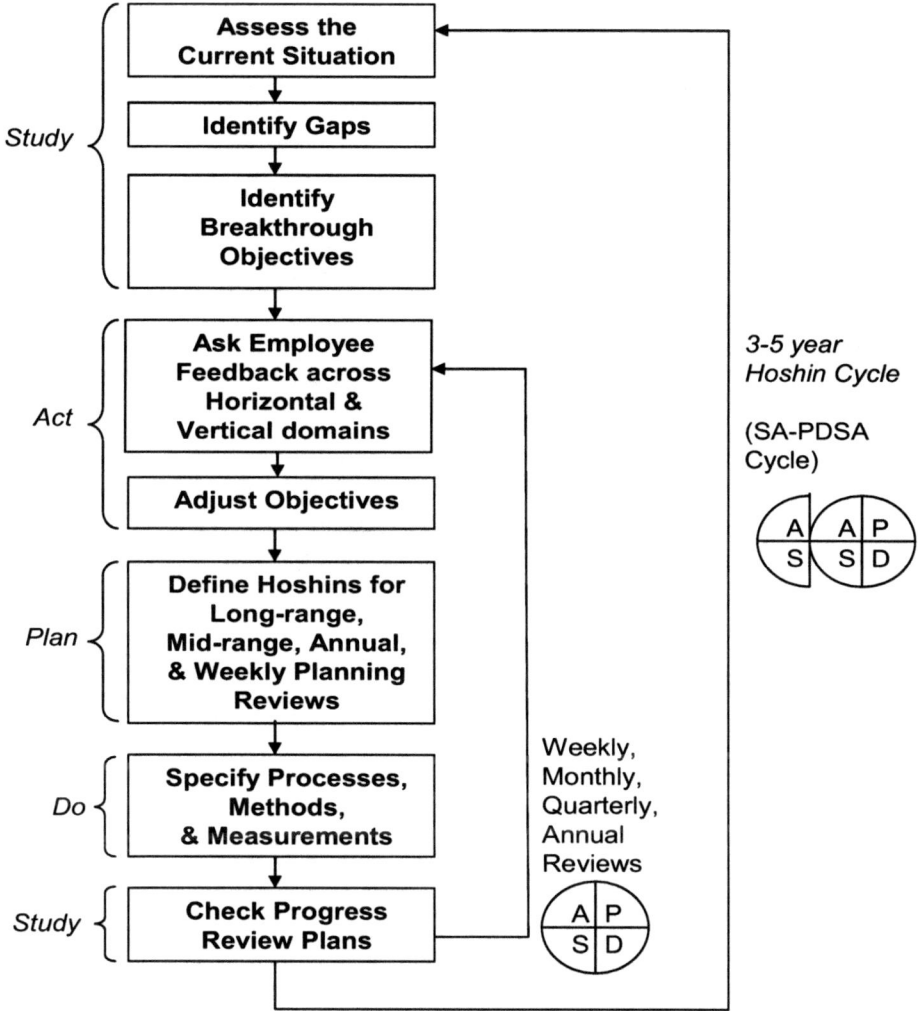

Fig 19.6 – Hoshin Planning Process

Once the final breakthrough objective(s) are defined, the planning team proceeds with the following activities:

Mid-range planning – The goal of mid-range planning is to define where the organization should spend its resources, focus and attention on gaps that must be closed within three to five years. Mid range plans identify areas that need to be

309

improved and define plans to achieve those performance improvements. Performance measures are defined for each breakthrough objective and its supportive mid-range plan.

Annual planning – The goal of annual planning is to define where management must intervene to correct a process or adjust the project course during annual and periodic reviews. The purpose of annual Hoshin plans is to develop concentrated short term plans and policies that drive towards mid-term breakthrough objectives.

Do: Galvanizing the entire organization to work towards achieving annual and mid-range plans is possible through three management principles:

1. Ask employees to participate in the drafting the plan
2. Specify the means, methods and processes, not just the end result.
3. Seek early indicators that measure alignment and linkage to the plan both horizontally and vertically

Companies create a simple matrix by listing the breakthrough objectives, mid-range plans, annual Hoshins and specific projects that align the company in the direction of its strategic vision. The matrix lists specific metrics and measurements at each tier of planning. The Hoshin matrix is adopted by all employees and is a daily reminder of what tasks and measures are important.

Check: This step is intended to align and control the daily activity and operations to the plan. Daily management is concerned with issues and problem resolution, fixing process and training staff to control and align activities. Root-cause analysis is a key tool for identifying and fixing the operational and process problems. As part of the process and planning control, managers strive to eliminate variation in their operations and daily tasks.

Act: The Hoshin method like the Deming cycle is an iterative process. In this step of the process, managers seek customer and employee feedback. Periodic reviews are conducted at monthly, quarterly and annual intervals. Reviews are intended to find immediate root-cause of effects. Feedback is the result of reducing the delays between cause and effect.

Correcting issues and resolving problems in the prior step, lead to opportunities for learning and organizational knowledge that guide the company towards achieving its breakthrough objectives. Hoshin review evaluates results longitudinally and lattitudinally: at the executive level, the review audits results in order to evaluate and improve the planning process and identify issues for the next round of planning cycle.

At the quarterly interval, the review identifies barriers and issues to making progress. It integrates company-wide efforts and escalates findings and facts upward to executive management. In the monthly reviews, employees identify obstacles, corrective action and lessons learned.

Every Hoshin Review produces a report to highlight three things:

A) what policies and plans have been successful,

B) what are the red flags that need management attention,

C) what lessons have been learned.

Note that the Hoshin planning process contains two feedback loops that facilitate double loop learning and second order thinking in the organization.

Hoshin Kanri X-Matrix

In many industries, a tool called X-Matrix is used to capture the entire Hoshin kanri development plan on one page. The X-Matrix consists of four quadrants. Starting in the bottom quadrant, we list the long range Hoshin plans that are three to five year breakthroughs. Then we move to the left quadrant to list the annual initiatives and objectives.

To show how the long range plans and annual objectives are related, we place an "X" where they are linked. The third quadrant is at the top and it shows the areas of process improvement and Kaizen.

Finally in the fourth quadrant we list the metrics associated to the process improvement initiatives. To complete the loop, we place "X" marks when a metric and a long range Hoshin breakthrough are related.

The X-Matrix in Figure 19.7 shows an example applied to an IT initiative at a firm. The firm's long range plans were to create IT governance to increase IT effectiveness, converge the desktop and collaborative applications, consolidate databases across the enterprise, and strengthen the IT infrastructure as shown in the first quadrant of Figure 19.7.

Using the X-Matrix the CIO is able to communicate the entire long range and short term plans in a summary form and report on the progress of those initiative using the metrics and the Green, Yellow and Red status letters.

The X-Matrix is a powerful to bring the entire IT initiatives and priorities into a single view for easier governance and measurement.

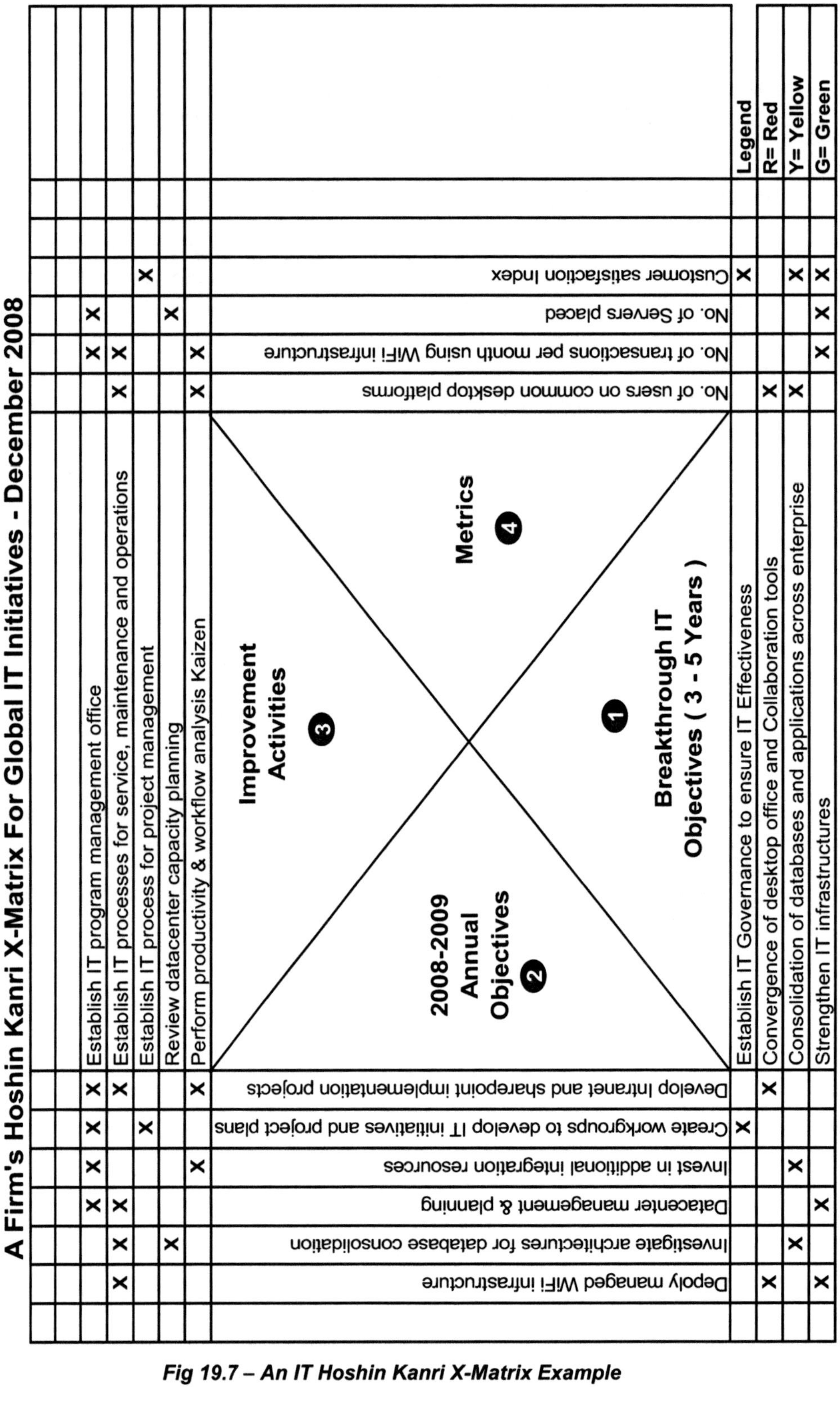

Fig 19.7 – An IT Hoshin Kanri X-Matrix Example

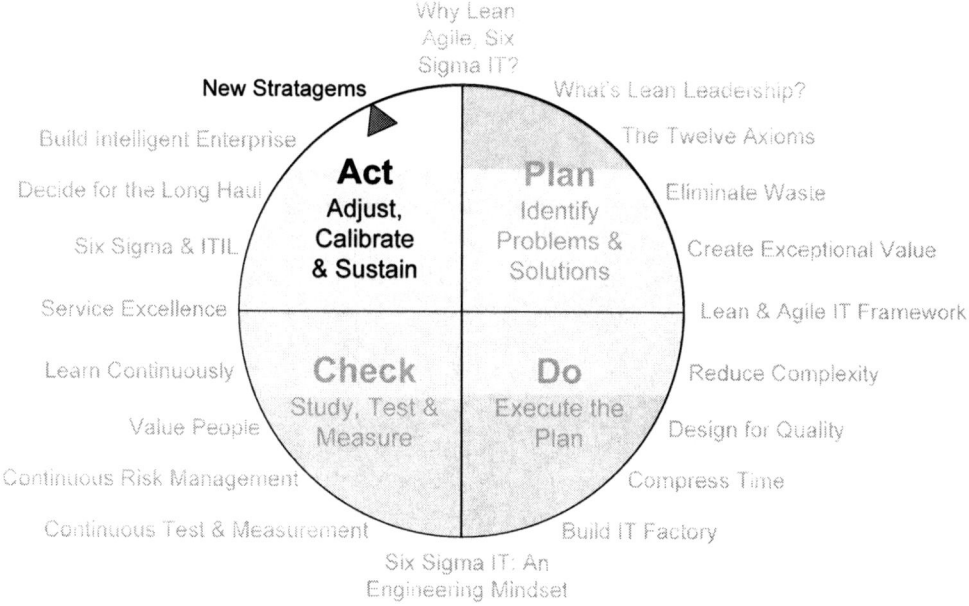

"It is not enough to do your best: you must know what to do, and THEN do your best."

W. Edwards Deming

Chapter 20: New Stratagems for a New Era

The summary of all stratagems in this book and the essence of Lean, Agile and Six Sigma IT management are distilled in this chapter written as IT maxims There is one timely and timeless stratagem: No matter what the information technology situation might be, to remain competitive, we must re-invent new stratagems. Business and competitive pressures change at all times. Information technologies change every eighteen months. That implies that we must re-think our stratagems and recreate new ones at least every eighteen months.

To recap the book, I wish to summarize the stratagems from different perspectives. First, let's review the twelve irrefutable axioms of Lean, Agile and Six Sigma IT management as follows:

1. **Eliminate Waste:** Identify sources of waste and eliminate them. Perform Kaizen events to remove non value adding tasks.

2. **Deliver exceptional value:** Identify customers' value drivers and focus on delivering value beyond customers' expectation.

3. **Reduce Complexity:** Manage risk by reducing complexity and interdependencies. Apply 5S methods to reduce IT complexity

4. **Design for Quality:** Develop processes for every IT task. Establish a high expectation for quality. Perform high-level and low-level designs followed by design reviews to ensure quality

5. **Compress Time:** Apply Lean and Agile methods to deliver IT solutions faster by reducing Cycle Time.
6. **Build IT Factory:** Practice continuous innovation. Create consistent processes and component-based development to deliver solutions at regular intervals.
7. **Continuously Test & Measure:** Develop a culture of testing, gathering facts and measurement data about processes, applications and services.
8. **Continuously Manage Risk:** Continuously identify risks and mitigate them. Prepare risk response plans in advance.
9. **Value People:** Respect your people. Keep them accountable and trust them with the responsibility to make decisions.
10. **Learn Continuously:** Implement IT projects with intent to create new knowledge and apply it to other projects. Learn from your customers about their business and listen to the voice of the customer.
11. **Decide for the Long Haul:** Maintain a long time horizon for IT decisions. Defer decisions to the latest time possible until more facts are available.
12. **Build Intelligent Organizations:** Create intellectual bonding by providing real time, collaborative and relevant information to employees. Strive to make decisions that optimize the entire organization and workflows.

Next let's begin with the seven fundamental stratagems:

The Ten Fundamental Stratagems:

1. Continually strive for enhancing customer service excellence.
2. Create a high-velocity, high-quality, high-precision work culture and support the culture by eliminating causes of delay and waste.
3. Accelerate implementations and streamline operations by building Information Technology factories.
4. Standardize methods, architecture and operations to create single flow of innovation.
5. Focus on learning and knowledge by creating centers of excellence.
6. Streamline the value streams first, then automate the workflows through IT.
7. Assess risk and prepare risk contingency plans.
8. Make decisions based on both upside value and downside cost (regret) of the alternatives.
9. Identify the business architecture before drafting the IT architecture.
10. Create a unified intelligent organization across all functional boundaries through adaptation of IT solutions into the company's workflows.

If I could condense the entire book into a few simple management tips, for the IT management staff, I would summarize those principles into a management system outlined as the following.

Creating a Lean & Agile Management System for IT Staff

1. Have staff keep a task list. Review tasks with them.
2. Tasks must have a due date and deadline. Staff must understand that deadlines are important to meet
3. Assign tasks to individuals so that lines of responsibility and accountability are clear
4. Have staff work on deliverables that add value. Do not work on tasks that do not add value
5. Do not focus on gold plating tasks. Focus on what is needed.
6. Help staff take on larger projects and see the path to completions. This is done by taking a large project and breaking it down into smaller deliverables.
7. Help staff develop time management skills. Help them find the sequential tasks and parallel tasks.
8. Explain to staff the importance of the work they are doing to the overall mission of the organization
9. Remember you are a role model. Maintain positive, can-do attitude.
10. Encourage "eager" approach to implementations. Avoid the "lazy" approach.
11. Start with well-defined customer requirements, then design.
12. Emphasize testing as much as you can.
13. Plan each release with an engineer's precision.
14. Start with the 20% of the project that delivers 80% of customer requirements
15. Help your staff visualize their projects from start to finish. Run a mental walkthrough of the project with your staff to identify the hurdles early.

The Toyota Precepts

Finally, for the last words, I'll close with the Toyota Precepts. In 1930s, Sakichi Toyoda the founder of Toyota Industries, and his colleagues developed a set of five guiding principles that came to be known as the "Toyoda precepts". The higher purpose of management and holistic approach are rooted in these percepts. The five precepts are:

1. Be contributive to the development and welfare of the country by working together, regardless of position, in faithfully fulfilling your duties.
2. Be ahead of the times through endless creativity, inquisitiveness and pursuit of improvement.
3. Be practical and avoid frivolity.
4. Be kind and generous; strive to create a warm, homelike atmosphere.
5. Be reverent, and show gratitude for things great and small in thought and deed.

Appendix A – IT Laws

A survey of general axioms and laws of Information Management are presented in this section for reference. The general axioms of information management can be grouped into several domains including Networks, Systems, Project Management, Quality, and Development. These axioms are not universally applicable to every situation but are results of observations and patterns discovered in the industry.

Networks:

Metcalf's Law: *The value of a network expands by the square of the number of users.*

Gilder's Law: *Communication bandwidth doubles every 6 months.*

Law of Cable Compatibility: *If you choose a cable and a connector at random, the probability that they are compatible is equal to zero. (Murphy's Law).*

Law of Noise: *Noise bursts occur so as to cause the most, and/or most serious, errors in data communications, regardless of the actual amount of noise present.*

Amdahl's Law of Networks: *The slowest device in the network will determine the maximum speed of the network.*

Nacchio's Law: *The number of ports and price per port of an IP gateway (analog voice to digital IP) improves by two orders of magnitude every 18 months.*

Shannon's Law: *The maximum attainable data transfer speed for a given channel is a function of the channel bandwidth and signal to noise ratio.*

Project Management:

Murphy's Law: *Anything that can go wrong, will – at the worst possible moment.*

Murphy's Law (original): *If there are two or more ways to do something, and one of those ways can result in a catastrophe, then someone will do it.*

Law of Expectation: *Consumer expectations always outpace advances in hardware technology.*

Amara's Law: *We tend to overestimate the effect of a technology in the short run and underestimate the effect in the long run.*

Systems

Amdahl's Law of Systems: *The overall system speed is governed by the slowest component.*

Law of Inconvenient Malfunction: *A device will fail at the least opportune possible moment. (Murphy's Law).*

Conway's Law: *Organizations which design systems are constrained to produce systems which are copies of the communication structures of these organizations.*

Goldratt's Law of Convergence: *The more complex a system is to describe, the easier it is to manage.*

Goldratt's Law of Constraints: Every organization has at least one constraint active in any given point in time.

Goldratt's Law of Consistency: If two interpretations of the same phenomenon are in conflict, one or possibly both must be wrong

Goldratt's Law of Respect: Even when people do things that seem stupid they have a reason for that.

Parkinson's Law of Information: Data expands to fill the space available.

Gilders Law: Total bandwidth doubles every nine months.

Neilsen's Law: Internet connection bandwidth grows by 50 percenter per year.

Philipson's Law: The number of computer users grows tenfold each decade.

Wirless Law: Mobile bandwidth grows fourfold every four years.

Malthuse's Law of Information: Despite the exponential growth of information, our use of information grows linearly at best. New Information content is doubling every year.

Gresham's Law of Information: Bad information crowds out good information (Low quality info on the internet causes problems for providers of high-quality information).

Fitt's Law: Movement time to move an object is a function of distance from the object and its size.

Zipf's Law of Information Theory: People use words that attribute meaning to their documents in the frequency of their relative importance to the document.

Reiser's Law of Information Economics: The expressive power of an information system is proportional not to the number of objects that get implemented for it, but instead is proportional to the number of possible effective interactions between objects in it.

Finagle's Law of information: The information you have is not the information you want; The information you want is not the information you need; The information you need is not going to be available.

Wirth's Law: Software slows down faster than hardware speeds up.

Development

Moore's Law: Computer technology advances such that the number of switches that may be placed on a computer microchip doubles every eighteen months.

Moore's Law corollary: Every 18 months microchip technology becomes twice faster at the same cost, or half the cost at the same density.

Brook's Law: Adding manpower to a late software project makes it later.

Law of Debugging: The difficulty of debugging software is directly proportional to the number of people who will ultimately use it.

Law of Software Compatibility: If two programs are chosen at random, the probability that they are compatible is equal to zero.

Law of the Titanic: Bug-free software isn't.

Gilb's Law: *Anything you need to quantify can be measured in some way that is superior to not measuring it at all.*

Hofstadter's Law: *It always take longer than you expect, even if you take Hofstadter's Law into account.*

Brooks' Law: *Adding manpower to a late software project makes it later.*

Lubarsky's Law of Cybernetic Entomology: *There's always one more bug.*

Sturgeon's Law: *Ninety percent of everything is crud.*

Ninety-Ninety Rule: *The first 90% of the code accounts for the first 90% of the development time. The remaining 10% of the code accounts for the other 90% of the development time.*

Hartree's Law: *The time from now until the completion of the project tends to become constant.*

First Law of Software Evolution: Continuing Change - *An application program that is used must be continually adapted else it becomes progressively less satisfactory.*

Second Law of Software Evolution: Increasing Complexity - *As a program is evolved its complexity increases unless work is done to maintain or reduce it.*

Third Law of Software Evolution: Self Regulation - *The program evolution process is self regulating with close to normal distribution of measures of product and process attributes.*

Fourth Law of Software Evolution: Conservation of Organizational Stability (invariant work rate) - *The average effective global activity rate on an evolving system is invariant over the product life time.*

Fifth Law of Software Evolution: Conservation of Familiarity - *During the active life of an evolving program, the content of successive releases is statistically invariant.*

Sixth Law of Software Evolution: Continuing Growth - *Functional content of a program must be continually increased to maintain user satisfaction over its lifetime.*

Seventh Law of Software Evolution: Declining Quality – *Application programs will be perceived as of declining quality unless rigorously maintained and adapted to a changing operational environment.*

Eighth Law of Software Evolution: Feedback System - *Application Programming Processes constitute Multi-loop, Multi-level Feedback systems and must be treated as such to be successfully modified or improved.*

Postel's Law of data exchange: *Be liberal in what you accept, and conservative in what you send.*

Quality

Hamming's quote: *You cannot have a science without measurement.*

Andrejs Dunkel's quote: *It is easy to lie with statistics. It is hard to tell the truth without statistics.*

Myers' Law: *The number of defects identified before software release will be equal to the number of defects found after software release.*

Appendix B – Process and Project Templates

In this appendix, three examples are included to illustrate Lean, Agile and Six Sigma tools put in IT practice:

Document 1: Project Specification and Charter.

This document is an outline of the project specification document that defines what will be delivered. It covers a brief overview of functional specification, theory of operation, release plan and only a high level list of project milestones. The document acts as a contract between the IT staff and the customer.

Notice that the document specifies the deliverables, technology components, roles and responsibilities for the IT staff and the vendor. This is intended to be a living plan for the project and change accordingly. It encourages rapid prototyping as a form of low level design and Scrum project management for rapid delivery.

XYZ Application Project

Project Overview
Requirements, Specification, Design, Implementation,
Test & Release

Sponsors	
Project Manager:	
Creation Date:	
System Owner	
System Operator	

Revision History	Date	Change
Version 1.0		Initial Draft

Review & Sign-off:

Stake Holder #1	Stake Holder #2
Stake Holder #3	Application Manager
Project Manager	Application Specialist #1
Scrum Master	Application Specialist #2

Project Identification

Project Name
Enter project Name

Justification
Provide business and functional needs for the application. Provide priority and preliminary Return on Investment data such as breakeven point, ROI.

Executive Sponsors
List the executive Sponsors for this project.

Customer
List the customers and users of this IT solution.

Primary Participants

Name	Role
IT staff names	Roles
Vendor member names	Roles
Sponsors & stakeholders	Roles

Primary Value Streams Involved:
Define the workflow and value streams affected. Explain how the value stream will be improved as a result of this project.

Primary System(s) Involved:

List the systems and infrastructure elements that will be involved. Use the layered pyramid model to define the systems in layers.

Primary Implementation Process:
Explain the implementation process that will be used in this implementation

Interface System(s) Involved
Define the interfaces and interface systems.

Ancillary System(s) Involved
Define boundary and ancillary systems that will be involved outside of the primary IT systems.

Requirements Definition

User Requirements
Define user requirements. Define current and future needs. List the implicit expectations and assumptions.

Systems Requirements
Define the systems requirements for the solution in layers as defined by the layered pyramid model.

Operational Requirements
Define the operational needs to make the solution operational and functional.

Maintenance Requirements
Define requirements to maintain, operate and staff support of the new solution.

Deliverable Specification

Project Objectives
Explain the objectives of the project.

Scope of Effort
Define the deliverables of this project. Define what is not included in the deliverables.

Systems Overview
Define the systems specifications for each of the layers in the layered pyramid model.

Interface Overview
List the interface specifications.

Theory of operation
Define how the new solution will operate and how the internal functional system interactions function as users interact and go through their workflows. Describe how the system functionality produces the expected results as the user navigates through the system.

User Requirements Specification

Define the users requirements in form of user cases and workflow diagrams as described in the book. Explain the workflows for each value stream.

Compliance Specifications
Define the regulatory, performance, operational, security and maintainability specifications.

Design & Implementation Overview

High Level Design Overview
Describe the high level design of the system, its subcomponents and how they will be integrated. Describe the architectural fit of this design.

Detailed Design Overview
Describe the low level design by defining the sub components of the system. Describe design review process and criteria for design evaluations.

Prototype Description
Define the prototype components, features and functions.

Implementation methodology
Define how the new solution will be implemented including standards adopted for implementation.

Test Strategy
Define the test strategy, plans and staffing to carry out the tests. Define how test reviews will be conducted and rework will be planned.

Test Environment
Define the test environment and the system components.

Release Engineering

Product Packaging
Describe how each release will be packaged, and what will be included in each release. Describe the version control plans for all subcomponents.

Customer Description
Describe the customers and their ability to adopt the new solution. Describes barriers to release of products

Training Plan
Define the training strategy. Will there be train the trainers and super user designations?

Roll out Plan
Define how the new solution will be released to users including the multi-stage release plan such as technical release, business release, and functional release.

Project Definition

Communications Plan
Define the methods and frequency of communication to stakeholders, vendor, customers and sponsors.

Vendor Management Strategy:
Describe how the vendor relations and the contract will be managed.

Assumptions & Critical Success Factors
Describe the assumptions and the Critical Success Factors (CSF) for the project to be successful.

Project Constraints
Describe the project constraints and how the project manager intends to overcome the constraints.

Dependencies
Describe the dependencies on outside events, resources and decisions. Define the internal interdependencies in the project organization.

Project Management

Project Management Process
Define the Agile project management processes for this project such as Scrum, RAD or similar processes.

Budget & Cost Management
Describe the budget and cost estimations for the project. Define the project accounting framework.

Work breakdown structure:
Describe the work breakdown structure how each component will be integrated into the entire project.

Risk Management:
Describe the known risks and assumption risks. Prioritize risks based on heir probability and impact. Describe the continuous risk management plans including risk mitigation and backup plans.

Quality Management:
Define the quality metrics and criteria for incoming quality and release quality.

Issues Management:
Define how issues will be collected, prioritized and tracked through the project.

Vendor Roles & Responsibilities:
Define vendor's roles and responsibilities throughout the project. Match these responsibilities to contractual terms.

IT Roles & Responsibilities
Define IT staff roles and responsibilities.

Customer Roles & Responsibilities.
Define what customers and users will be responsible to provide.

Plan Summary/Milestones:
Describe the high level milestones and target dates to complete as shown:

Milestone	Start Date	Completion Date
Project Initiation	Enter date	Enter date
Business & Technical Requirements	Enter date	Enter date
Functional Specifications	Enter date	Enter date
High Level Design	Enter date	Enter date
Low Level Design, or prototype	Enter date	Enter date
Build & Construct Unit components	Enter date	Enter date
Unit/System/Performance Test	Enter date	Enter date
Integration & integrated tests	Enter date	Enter date
User Training	Enter date	Enter date
Technical Release	Enter date	Enter date
Business Release	Enter date	Enter date
Acceptance/Production Test	Enter date	Enter date
Post Release Evaluation	Enter date	Enter date

Deliverables and Acceptance

Customer and Project Deliverables
Define vendor's deliverables and milestones for delivery.

Acceptance Criteria
Define the negotiated acceptance criteria with vendor and IT customers.

Project Change Management

Change of Scope
Describe process for scope and risk review and approval process for change. Define procedures such as Request for Comment (RFC) in this section.

Change Management Process
Describe the process for introducing technology and workflow changes. Define version control for all system subcomponents.

Maintenance Plan
Describe the standards and plans on how the new solution will be maintained and operated. Standards such as Methods of Procedure (MOP) are to be described here.

Document 2: Method of Procedure (MOP).

This document is a change management tool. It was developed as design documentation for applying a change to an existing Information system. The document is called a MOP, -Method of Procedure, also known as Methods, Operations Procedure. This document details the steps required for applying a change. You'll notice the intense level of detail in this document as it captures every step and corresponding scripts and program commands necessary to carry out the change.

This document is reviewed by the change review committee before the change is applied. It's intended to be reviewed by the application vendor and stake holders before the change is authorized. It specifies the step by step procedures for conducting the change as well as impact, notification to all parties, duration of downtime and workaround procedures for users during the downtime.

IT Services

Method of Procedure

Last Edit Date: 2/4/2009 8:35:00 AM

Method of Procedure No: M143

Subject/Title
Update XYZ application from V9.92 to V9.93 – Wednesday August, 24, 2006 0200hrs

Engineer	Date
Name	8/5/06

MOP Category (Check one box)			
Application#5			
Application#3			
Application#2			
XYZ Application	X		

MOP Information

- All maintenance work must be done & completed before 6:00AM

- All scheduled & unscheduled maintenance work must have a MOP (Method of Procedure).

- The MOP must be pre-screened and signed off by the vendor (example: XYZ Corporation)

- The MOP must be pre-screened by Informatics and/or IT manager, change review, security review or other applicable manager for signoff 48 hours before execution.

- Notification detailing start, finish and downtime must be sent at least 72 hours in advance.

Description of Work

Update XYZ Application from V9.92 to V9.93 on Wednesday August 24, 2006 0200hrs. There will be 2 hours of downtime and a total of 6 hours to update the client PCs in the Customer Dept. XYZ Corp. will perform this update remotely.

Changes it causes on Workflow & Other Systems

XYZ Application will be unavailable for duration of backup. Other devices will not get user information from XYZ Application during this period. Application#2 data will not go to Application#3.

Impact on Users During this Work and After This Work

Downtime procedures will be followed during work. Reports will be post-scheduled in XYZ Application once XYZ Application is back up, XYZ Application exam information will be applied to Application#1 reports generated during downtime.

Prep Work

Testing has been done on XYZ test server
Testing with downstream systems for data propogation integrity has been completed with Application#4 dev. Team.

Notification to other customer and outside partners has been issued. Company#1 have been notified. They are aware of the changes required. An RDC icon will be installed on a specific Company#1 workstation for access to IT Services V9.93 client.

Side Effects

Application#5 data will not receive user info from XYZ Application/Application#2/Application#3.

Clean up Required

Post schedule XYZ Application reports, fix Application#2 reports and Appliation#5 database..

Notification List (Who should be notified?)

All customers, partner company personnel, XYZ Application users, users of Application#2 and #3.

Detailed Instructions and Procedures (Step by Step Procedure)

1.) Obtain last-minute confirmation from late night users regarding XYZ downtime
2.) Complete backup of XYZ Application system
3.) Bring XYZ Application down
4.) Hand control over to XYZ for the update
5.) IT staff will begin to update 1200 Customer computers with XYZ Application V9.93 client
6.) There are also 240 Application#5 workstations that need the client installed also
7.) The XYZ Application system will be up after 2 hours of downtime.
8.) Bring XYZ Application back up and confirm updated clients can connect

9.) IT staff will continue to update clients until finished ~ 6 hours
10.) Add XYZ V9.93 GUI client to RDC server for partner company users
11.) Verify sales team access to XYZ after upgrade
12.) IT Staff will leave after all clients are completed.

Materials, Tools needed (passwords, privilege, other staff, etc)

IT Analysts will assist with client updates. A backup tape is needed. The client software is located at http://www.xyz.org/doc/Downloads/software/XYZ Application993.exe

Vendor Signoff by: (XYZ Company)

IT Services Staff Signoff by: _____

Customer Mgr Signoff by: _____

Document 3: Information Technology Food Chain.
The Layered Cake Model

The diagram below illustrates another layered model to simplify IT design and implementations. In a technology food chain, the lower layers are developed and managed to provide services to upper layers. The layered cake model shows how the main concept (the large cake) can be stacked and replicated in multiple environments or divisions of a firm.

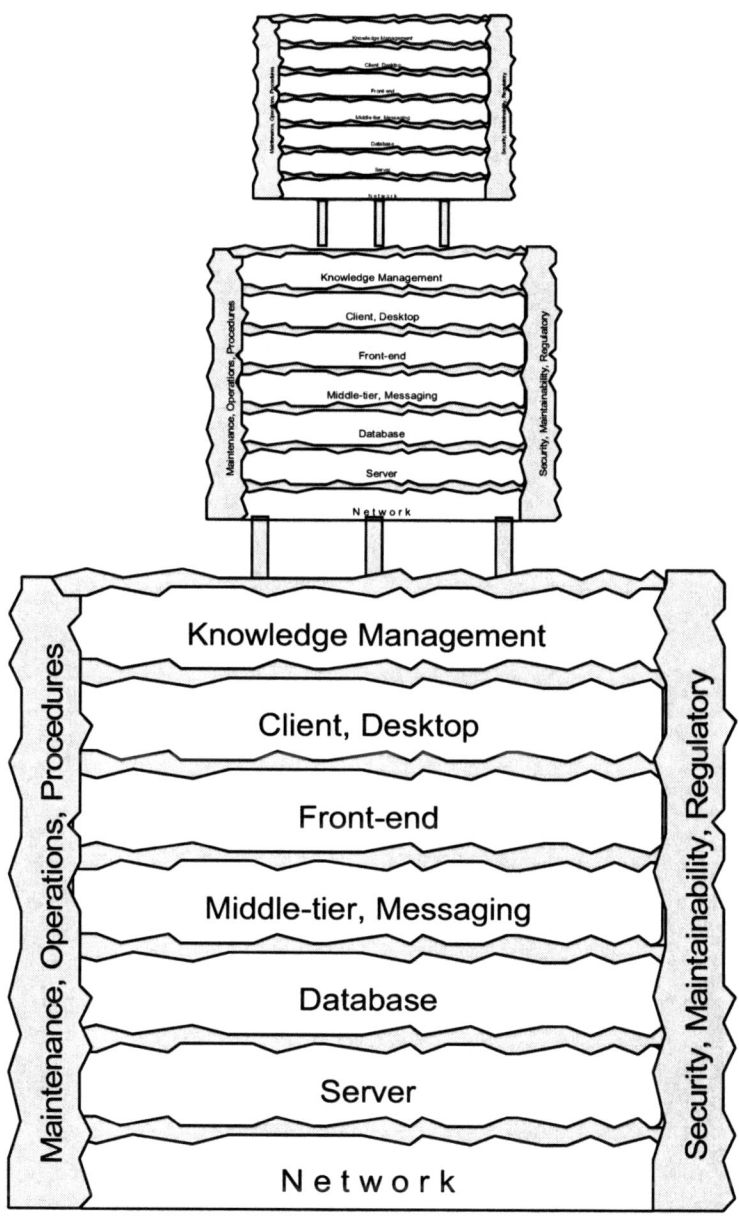

Appendix C – Sample Scrum Project Plan

SCRUM Project Plan Example

Sample Implementation Project Using SCRUM	141 days	1-Nov-06	15-May-07
Product Manager: John, Scrum Master: Bob		1-Nov-06	1-Nov-06
Team: John, Bob, Alison, Jamie		1-Nov-06	1-Nov-06
SPRINT 1	1 day	1-Nov-06	1-Nov-06
Kick-off meeting	5 days?	1-Nov-06	7-Nov-06
Resources identified	1 day	1-Nov-06	1-Nov-06
Project Teams defined	1 day	1-Nov-06	1-Nov-06
Review Quotation of Services	1 day	1-Nov-06	1-Nov-06
Contact List Established	1 day	1-Nov-06	1-Nov-06
Network and Hardware assessment	5 days	1-Nov-06	7-Nov-06
Design & define firewall rules	5 days	1-Nov-06	7-Nov-06
Review hardware specifications	1 day	1-Nov-06	1-Nov-06
Workflow defined (Verify unique exam identifier)	3.5 days	1-Nov-06	6-Nov-06
Obtain list of most used exam codes	3 days	1-Nov-06	3-Nov-06
Verify unique identifier	1 day	1-Nov-06	1-Nov-06
Verify MRN number	1 day	1-Nov-06	1-Nov-06
Obtain sample standard reporting templates from Application	2.5 days	1-Nov-06	3-Nov-06
Define standard reporting template	2 days	1-Nov-06	2-Nov-06
Obtain - Define standard reporting templates	3.5 days	1-Nov-06	6-Nov-06
Identify site configuration	0.5 days	1-Nov-06	1-Nov-06
Configuration identified - server, OS, firewall, network	3 days	1-Nov-06	3-Nov-06
Productivity expectations set (metrics: TAT, Usage, Accuracy, reliability, report errors/less associations)	2 days	1-Nov-06	2-Nov-06
Process for issue resolution defined (user issues)	1 day	1-Nov-06	1-Nov-06
Develop back-up procedures - system admin	4 days	1-Nov-06	6-Nov-06
Discuss downtime procedures	1 day	1-Nov-06	1-Nov-06
Target dates identified	1 day	1-Nov-06	1-Nov-06
Schedule weekly status calls	1 day	1-Nov-06	1-Nov-06
Request TRACK APPL link to Application -HL7	1 day?	1-Nov-06	1-Nov-06
System Setup	35.5 days	6-Nov-06	22-Dec-06
Required Customer Documentation	35.5 days	6-Nov-06	22-Dec-06
Site Readiness	1 day	6-Nov-06	7-Nov-06
TRACK APPL refresh Test system	6 days	10-Dec-06	15-Dec-06
Physician ID Listing	1 day	6-Nov-06	7-Nov-06
build TRACK APPL Test link to Application	5 days	18-Dec-06	22-Dec-06
Hardware Network Information Sheet	1 day	6-Nov-06	7-Nov-06

Logistics	2 days	6-Nov-06	8-Nov-06
Server Ordered (Using Backup Server)	1 day	7-Nov-06	8-Nov-06
Workstations Ordered & memory ordered	1 day	7-Nov-06	8-Nov-06
Date of order software shipment	1 day	6-Nov-06	7-Nov-06
Site Network preparation:	3 days	6-Nov-06	9-Nov-06
Network Drops in place	3 days	6-Nov-06	9-Nov-06
All network drops tested and verified at 100mb or greater	1 day	6-Nov-06	7-Nov-06
All network communications between all locations are setup & validated by customer	1 day	6-Nov-06	7-Nov-06
Remote access preparation:	2 days	6-Nov-06	8-Nov-06
Determine mode of remote connectivity (I.e. VPN/PCAnywhere)	2 days	6-Nov-06	8-Nov-06
Method of Remote connectivity in place	2 days	6-Nov-06	8-Nov-06
SPRINT 2	*1 day?*	*1-Nov-06*	*1-Nov-06*
Receive and install hardware/software	45 days?	8-Nov-06	9-Jan-07
Receive hardware - servers	1 day?	10-Nov-06	13-Nov-06
Install memory on PACS workstations	38 days	17-Nov-06	9-Jan-07
Rack and power up the servers	3 days	6-Dec-06	8-Dec-06
Remote connectivity information supplied to Application	1 day	8-Nov-06	9-Nov-06
Configuration of Application Server:	40 days?	10-Dec-06	1-Feb-07
Installation of Operating System - Server	7 days	10-Dec-06	18-Dec-06
Windows OS loaded and validated	5 days	10-Dec-06	14-Dec-06
Installation and configuration of SQL database	2 days	15-Dec-06	18-Dec-06
Installation and configuration of Application Server software	4 days	19-Dec-06	22-Dec-06
Server placement, SIT review & security certification	7 days	18-Jan-07	26-Jan-07
Port numbers determined (Direct or via interface Engine)	4 days?	29-Jan-07	1-Feb-07
IP number provided to Comm - VPN	3 days	29-Jan-07	31-Jan-07
Interface Information Provided	1 day?	1-Feb-07	1-Feb-07
Interface	37 days?	2-Feb-07	26-Mar-07
Configure custom link from TRACK APPL to Application	2 days	2-Feb-07	5-Feb-07
Interface tested (Refer to HL-7 document)	4 days	6-Feb-07	9-Feb-07
Test Application-2 inbound (via HL7 engine) interface	20 days	2-Feb-07	1-Mar-07
Test Application-2 outbound (via HL7 engine) interface	20 days	2-Feb-07	1-Mar-07
Interface validated and accepted	1 day	12-Feb-07	12-Feb-07
Sample Site to sign Interface Acceptance document	30 days	13-Feb-07	26-Mar-07

SPRINT 3	1 day?	2-Feb-07	2-Feb-07
Disaster Recovery - backup plan	7 days?	13-Feb-07	21-Feb-07
Disaster Recovery - backup planning	1 day?	13-Feb-07	13-Feb-07
Purchase Disaster Recovery equipment (recorders, etc)	1 day?	14-Feb-07	14-Feb-07
Disaster Mode workflow definition	2 days	15-Feb-07	16-Feb-07
Disaster Mode Test	3 days	19-Feb-07	21-Feb-07
Configuration of Pilot workstations & Testing	77 days?	29-Jan-07	15-May-07
Installation of operating system - WS	26 days	29-Jan-07	5-Mar-07
Windows OS loaded and validated - XP for PACS /Barco W/S	10 days	29-Jan-07	9-Feb-07
Install Test workstation in the Lab & prelim Testing	3 days	29-Jan-07	31-Jan-07
Perform simulated test (from Lab)	10 days	1-Feb-07	14-Feb-07
Application on site for installation	1 day	12-Feb-07	12-Feb-07
Train the Informatics team	2 days	13-Feb-07	14-Feb-07
Test remote user (home access) workflow	3 days	15-Feb-07	19-Feb-07
Point Application Station SQL database to Live RIS	2 days	20-Feb-07	21-Feb-07
Training Materials	2 days	15-Feb-07	16-Feb-07
Train the pilot doctors	10 days	20-Feb-07	5-Mar-07
Deploy the first pilot workstation - Mammo area	1 day	15-Feb-07	15-Feb-07
Deploy second pilot workstation - MSK	1 day	16-Feb-07	16-Feb-07
Training	13 days?	15-Feb-07	5-Mar-07
Sysadmin Training	5 days	15-Feb-07	21-Feb-07
Workflow modification - finalization	3 days	19-Feb-07	21-Feb-07
Data management review	3 days	15-Feb-07	19-Feb-07
Converstion to Production Use	11 days	19-Feb-07	5-Mar-07
Productive use monitoring	10 days	19-Feb-07	2-Mar-07
System monitoring and validation	10 days	19-Feb-07	2-Mar-07
Sample Site to sign Applications Acceptance document	1 day	5-Mar-07	5-Mar-07
SPRINT 4	1 day?	15-Feb-07	15-Feb-07
Deployment	23 days	19-Feb-07	21-Mar-07
workstations upgraded	1 day	20-Feb-07	20-Feb-07
Zone 1 Workstations Deployed	5 days	19-Feb-07	23-Feb-07
Zone 2 Workstations deployed	5 days	26-Feb-07	2-Mar-07
Zone 3 Workstations deployed	3 days	5-Mar-07	7-Mar-07
Zone 4 Workstations deployed	3 days	8-Mar-07	12-Mar-07
Zone 5 Workstations deployed	2 days	13-Mar-07	14-Mar-07
Workstations tested at final locations	3 days	15-Mar-07	19-Mar-07
Deactivate OLD APPL links	2 days	20-Mar-07	21-Mar-07
Transition to Application Support	51 days	6-Mar-07	15-May-07
Sample Site to sign Final Acceptance of System	1 day	1-May-07	1-May-07
Review all support procedures and protocols	1 day	6-Mar-07	6-Mar-07
Decision to Retire OLD APPL servers	10 days	2-May-07	15-May-07

Appendix D - Quality Indicators & Confidence

Research has shown that given these metrics, one can develop mathematical models of confidence in the quality of the program using probability. Thayer[88], Vouk[89] and colleagues have provided ample analytical tools for this purpose. Among such models, one states that if we have N test cases that do not fail, we can compute an upper confidence bound on the actual system failure rate Θ that implies this rate is below some level Θ with probability $(1 - \alpha)$.

The value Θ is a lower confidence bound on the failure rate of our application. The mathematical representation of this model is:

$$1 - (1 - \Theta)^N \le \alpha$$

We can use this mathematical model as indicator of reliability. Let's assume LL is the Lower Limit, μ is the mean of the metric and R is the metric name. Then we can write:

$$LL = \mu - 1.96 * (\text{Std Dev of R})/\text{Sqrt}(N)$$

Here the value 1.96 is the t-table value at 95% confidence interval. If the sample size is greater than 30, then we can reference the normal table to find the appropriate value for the desired confidence interval.

The result of this equation is the value of Lower Limit, LL. If the value of R is less than LL, then confidence in reliability is far less. If the value of R is more than the mean μ, then we can expect higher reliability from our software. You can use color coding to show confidence in reliability. For example, the following color coding has been used in the literature:

RED: $R < LL$

ORANGE: $LL \le R \le \mu$,

GREEN: $R > \mu$

---

[88] "Software Reliability", R. Thayer, M. Lipow and E. Nelson, Amsterdam: North Holland, 1978

[89] "Software Reliability Field Data Analysis", M.A. Vouk and W. Jones in "Handbook of Software Reliability Engineering", M. Lyu, Editor, McGraw Hill, 1996

INDEX

5

5 S · 122, 125

A

A3 · 152
A3 Method · 73
A-Frame Model · 187
Agile Manifesto · 166
Agile Method · 168
Agile Methods · 164
Amazon.com · 100
Andon · 144

B

Balanced Score Card · 304
Blackbox Testing · 214
Boehm, Barry · 223
Bohem, Barry · 228
Business Architecture · 39
Business Metrics · 195
Business Process Redesign (BPR) · 40
Business Stratagem · 45

C

Capability Maturity Model · 26
Causal Diagrams · 24
Causal Models · 76
CIO-CEO Relationship · 36
CIO-CFO Relationship · 36
COCOMO Model · 159
Cognitive Maps · 80
Communication Matrix · 148, 151
Compressing Time · 54, 85, 175, 176
Constraint · 63
Continuous Improvement · 29
Continuous Innovation · 29
Continuous Risk Management · 221
  ACT · 235
  Assumption Risk · 232
  Check · 231
  Contingency Plans · 229
  DO · 226
  PLAN · 223
  Risk Prioritization Matrix · 231
Continuous Testing · 213
Control Chart · 192, 198

Critical Customer Requirements (CCR) · 54, 152, 192, 266
Critical to Profitability · 196
Critical to Quality · 195
  Example · 266
Critical-to · 192

D

Decision Making
  Laplace · 281
  Maximax · 281
  Maximin · 280
  Regret · 278, 280, 282
Decision Tree · 282, 285
Defects Per Million Opportunity · 194
Deming · 50
  Deming Cycle · 50
Design
  For Quality · 54
  Kano Model · 141
  Layered Pyramid Model · 139
  Quality Function Deployment (QFD) · 142
  Use case · 71
Design for Six Sigma (DFSS) · 127, 134, 140
DMADV · 200
DMAIC · 200
DMDIVR · 201
Druker, Peter · 288
DSDM · 169

E

Extreme Programming · 174

F

Feature Driven Development · 90
Feature Driven Development (FDD) · 133
Fishbone Diagram · 74, 78, 126
FMEA
  Design · 267
  Failure Mode Effect Analysis · 267
  Implementation · 267
  NASA · 267
  Process · 267
  Service · 267
  System · 267
Ford Motor Company · 38
Forrester Research · 164

G

Gartner Group · 36
Genchi Genbutsu · 100
Goldratt, Eliyahu · 62
Google · 99, 103
GQM Method · 47
GQM Model · 47, 209, 266

H

HALT Tests · 215
HASS Tests · 215
Hoshin Kanri · 30, 33, 307, 311

I

IEEE Standards · 216
I-Frame Model · 185, 187
Information & Communication Technology (ICT) · 273
Information Flow Diagrams · 151
Intellectual Productivity · 301
Intelligent Enterprise · 302
Intelligent Organizations
    Definition · 287
Ishikawa · 75
Ishikawa Method · 74
Ishikawa QC Tools · 203
ISO Standards · 173, 205, 239, 270
IT
    Effectiveness · 105
IT Complexity
    5 S · 121, 131
IT Factories · 177, 178, 181
IT Future Liability · 44
IT Governance · 37, 39, 41
IT Inventory · 44
IT Metrics · 208, 210
IT Skill Mapping · 242
IT Stratagem · 45
IT Tecnical Debt · 45
IT Throughput · 42
Iterative Model · 167
ITIL · 270, 272

J

JAD · 171
J-Curve · 8

K

Kaizen · 7, 15, 29
Kaizen events · 70, 71
Kano Model · 141
Kano, Noriaki · 142
KPMG · 25

L

Lean · 51
    Definition · 21
    Design & Architecture · 134
    Eager Approach · 175, 176
    IT Framework · 32
    IT Leadership · 35
    Why? · 22
Lean CIO · 36, 39
Lean Management · 171
Lean, Agile and Six Sigma Axioms · 28
Lean, Agile, Six Sigma Comparison · 23
Long Tail · 123

M

Matrix Organizations · 299
Maturity Model
    CMMI · 25
    Testing · 217
Microsoft Operating Framework (MOF) · 239
MTBF · 75
Muda, Mura, Muri · 64, 69

N

Netflix · 100
New Economics of IT · 42
Nike · 84
Normal Distribution · 194

O

Ohno, Taiichi · 83
Oracle · 103

P

Pareto · 122
PDCA Cycle · 133
PDCA Gap Analysis · 147

PDCA Requirements Analysis · 145
PDSA · 308
PMBOK · 173
Process Capability · 196, 197
Production Planning · 180
Project Management Institute · 173
Pull system · 50
Pyramid of Priority · 277

Q

Quality Dashboard · 206
Quality Function Deployment (QFD) · 85, 152, 266

R

RAD · 30, 171, 173
RAISE Tests · 216
Resource Mapping · 240
Responsibility Interface Matrix · 301
Return on Investment (ROI) · 8, 42
Return On Investment (ROI) · 55, 85
Risk Assessment
    Deming · 222
    NASA · 222
Risk Management
    NASA · 227
    PDCA · 223
    Portfolio Risk · 228
    Recognizable Risks · 221
    Risk Factors · 225
    Uncertainty · 226
    Unmanaged Assumptions · 221
Risk Metrics · 234
Root Cause Analysis · 24

S

Schwaber, Ken · 174
Scrum · 171, 173
Second Order Thinking · 294
Segmentation · 130
Service Level Agreement (SLA) · 199
Service Loss Hierarchy · 129
Service Oriented Architecture (SOA) · 135, 136
Service Oriented Modeling Framework · 137
Service Oriented Modeling Process · 138
Shigeo Shingo
    Method · 66, 67
Simulation · 130, 269, 295
    Project Simulation · 159
Six Sigma · 194

IT Framework · 33
Six Sigma IT Metrics · 203
Six Sigma Organization · 200
Six Sigma Transfer Function · 154, 192
SMART · 240
Smart Sourcing · 130
Software As A Service (SaaS) · 138
Spiral Model · 168
Stratagem, definition · 10
Stress Testing · 215
Stretch Goals · 243
Succession · 131
Sutherland, Jeff · 173
Synergy · 129
Systems Thinking · 62

T

Takt Time · 67
Test
    Use cases · 54
Test Measurements · 207
Test Metrics · 218, 219
T-Frame Model · 186, 187
Theory of Constraints · 62, 275
Time Compression · 175
Toyoda, Kiishiro · 83
Toyoda, Sakichi · 83
Toyota Production System · 50, 83, 144

U

Unified Modeling Language (UML) · 71, 112, 142
User Satisfaction · 119

V

Value
    Conjoint Analysis · 93
    Measured Value · 95
Value chain · 84, 85, 86
Value Creation · 84
Value Equation · 85
value stream · 49
Value stream · 49, 84, 86, 89
Value Stream · 36
Value Stream Mapping (VSM) · 65
Variation · 192, 193
Virtual Teams
    IT Workcells · 87
    Teams of Two · 239
Voice of the Customer · 53
Voice Of the Customer (VOC) · 142

W

Whitebox Testing · 214
Workflow
    Practice · 110
    Process · 110
    Protocol · 110
Workflow Automation Categories · 147

X

X-Matrix · 311

Z

Zachmann Model · 102, 183

About the Author

Peter Ghavami holds a masters degree in *Engineering Management* from Portland State University. He is currently the **Director of Informatics** at *University of Washington Medicine - Harborview Medical Center*. His research interests *include IT Strategy, Project Simulation & Modeling, Lean & Six Sigma Software Development Process, Artificial Life, and Optimizations Research*. Peter has more than **20 years of experience** in software and product development and managing projects and development teams.

His career began as a *software engineer* with a supercomputer manufacturer in the 1980's and later as product development manager at several high-tech companies where he was instrumental in their successful initial public offering. Prior to his current position, he held leadership roles as *VP of Engineering, Director of Engineering and Systems Integration Manager for several software and information systems companies* including *IBM Corp, HCorp and RadiSys Corp*.

He has written numerous articles on *software quality, software development process simulation and intelligent networks*. He has practiced *Kaizen* since 1992. He specializes in rapid technology implementations and has established a proven track record in successful turnaround of many major software and telecommunications projects.

He has been a *management consultant* to several high-tech companies and professor at several universities. He has experience *teaching* on subjects such as *object oriented programming, software engineering methodologies and Information technology management*.

He blogs at ***www.ITManagementResearch.com***.

CPSIA information can be obtained at www.ICGtesting.com
Printed in the USA
245053LV00011B/24/P